FROM ADJUSTMENT TO DEVELOPMENT IN AFRICA

Also by Giovanni Andrea Cornia

ADJUSTMENT WITH A HUMAN FACE: Protecting the Vulnerable and Protecting Growth, Volume 1 (*edited with Richard Jolly and Frances Stewart*)
ADJUSTMENT WITH A HUMAN FACE: Ten Country Case-Studies, Volume 2 (*edited with Richard Jolly and Frances Stewart*)
AFRICA'S RECOVERY IN THE 1990s: From Stagnation and Adjustment to Human Development (*edited with Rolph van der Hoeven and Thandika Mkandawire*)
CHILDREN AND THE TRANSITION TO THE MARKET ECONOMY: Safety Nets and Social Policies in Central and Eastern Europe (*edited with Sándor Sipos*)
THE IMPACT OF WORLD RECESSION ON CHILDREN: A Study Prepared for UNICEF (*edited with Richard Jolly*)

Also by Gerald K. Helleiner

INTERNATIONAL ECONOMIC DISORDER: Essays in North–South Relations
PEASANT AGRICULTURE, GOVERNMENT AND ECONOMIC GROWTH IN NIGERIA
THE NEW GLOBAL ECONOMY AND THE DEVELOPING COUNTRIES
AFRICA AND THE INTERNATIONAL MONETARY FUND (*editor*)
AGRICULTURAL PLANNING IN EAST AFRICA (*editor*)
A WORLD DIVIDED: The Less Developed Countries in the International Economy (*editor*)
FOR GOOD OR EVIL: Economic Theory and North–South Negotiations (*editor*)
TRADE POLICY AND INDUSTRIALIZATION IN TURBULENT TIMES (*editor*)
TRADE POLICY, INDUSTRIALIZATION AND DEVELOPMENT: New Perspectives

From Adjustment to Development in Africa

Conflict, Controversy, Convergence, Consensus?

Edited by

Giovanni Andrea Cornia

and

Gerald K. Helleiner

M

St. Martin's Press

First published in Great Britain 1994 by
THE MACMILLAN PRESS LTD
Houndmills, Basingstoke, Hampshire RG21 2XS
and London
Companies and representatives
throughout the world

The contents of this book are the responsibility of the editors and the contributors and do not necessarily reflect the policies and views of the United Nations Children's Fund (UNICEF).

A catalogue record for this book is available from the British Library.

ISBN 0–333–61361–9 hardcover
ISBN 0–333–61362–7 paperback

Printed in Great Britain by
Antony Rowe Ltd, Chippenham, Wiltshire

First published in the United States of America 1994 by
Scholarly and Reference Division,
ST. MARTIN'S PRESS, INC.,
175 Fifth Avenue,
New York, N.Y. 10010

ISBN 0–312–12135–0

Library of Congress Cataloging-in-Publication Data
From adjustment to development in Africa : conflict, controversy, convergence, consensus? / edited by Giovanni Andrea Cornia and Gerald K. Helleiner.
p. cm.
Published simultaneously in Great Britain by The Macmillan Press Ltd.
Includes bibliographical references and index.
ISBN 0–312–12135–0
1. Structural adjustment (Economic policy)—Africa, Sub-Saharan.
2. Africa, Sub-Saharan—Economic conditions. I. Cornia, Giovanni Andrea. II. Helleiner, Gerald K. III. Series.
HC800.F76 1994
338.967—dc20 93–48286
CIP

Contents

List of Tables

List of Figures

Foreword

For UNICEF, as for the United Nations as a whole, Africa is a continent requiring international priority for development. No other region of the world has experienced such severe setbacks over the decade of the 1980s and no other region of the world has so many economic and social indicators for so many countries which remain so poor. Africa is the only region of the world where the number of children dying each year is projected to increase over the 1990s.

Nearly ten years ago, UNICEF launched a call for 'adjustment with a human face'. This was an urgent plea for a sharper focus on the poor and vulnerable in the making of adjustment policy, both in analysis and action. The two editors of this volume, Giovanni Andrea Cornia and Gerry Helleiner, played major roles at that time in helping UNICEF formulate this policy. Critically important to UNICEF's own efforts were support from and interaction with countries and groups within Africa – and notably with the Economic Commission for Africa, which produced AAF-SAP, the African Alternative Framework to Structural Adjustment Programmes. Through dialogue, debate and country experimentation and action, the focus and emphasis of adjustment was considerably broadened. As in all matters of adjustment, the Bank and the IMF played a central and important part in this shift: first, in acknowledging the need for changes; second, in identifying many of the points where changes of policy and action were required; and thirdly, in adapting their policy and lending instruments to the increasingly difficult situation.

By the second half of the 1980s, it had become clear to all that longer time horizons were needed. The World Bank issued its Long-Term Perspective Study; the United Nations developed NADAF, the New Agenda for African Development. Both of these documents recognised the need for more rapid economic growth in Africa. The Bank study noted that 5.5 per cent growth per annum was the minimum if the number of Africans living in poverty was not to increase further. NADAF set a target of 6 per cent economic growth per annum and, in addition, called for structural changes in agriculture, industry, employment and the informal sector. NADAF also identified essential changes in international policy and support in the areas of debt relief, commodity prices and international aid.

Goals for human development were also set in other fora. The World Summit for Children, held in 1990, agreed to major goals for reducing child and maternal mortality over the 1990s, for halving malnutrition, for making access to education and to water and sanitation universal. Two years later, African and donor governments, in the 'Consensus of Dakar', agreed on a framework of actions to support the implementation of these goals at country level. These included priorities for restructuring national budgets and aid expenditures to support these goals as well as new measures of debt relief. At the same time, considerable debate on the most effective policy for adjustment and development has taken place in almost every single country in Africa, a debate which has involved growing sections of society.

In spite of these major efforts and clear commitments and in spite of Africa's urgent needs, performance still falls far short of goals. And while there have undoubtedly been moves to greater consensus, there has also been greater questioning among almost all parties, both about existing priorities, approaches and programmes and about the next steps. This questioning covers both national and international policy and actions.

Rigorous, frank and open debate is now needed on these issues in many quarters and among many partners. UNICEF is pleased to have contributed to this process through the meeting held at the UNICEF International Child Development Centre in Florence in November 1992. The intense discussion and debate at the meeting form the basis of the chapters in this volume. It was especially pleasing and appropriate that the meeting was co-hosted by CODESRIA and EADI, the two major networks of social science research in Africa and Europe. These organisations helped to bring together a wide range of researchers and analysts.

African development is far from being the only challenge on the development agenda for the 1990s. But Africa is without doubt the continent where the crisis of development is most obvious. African development cries out for rethinking and for new action. UNICEF hopes that the views and debate recorded in this volume will help the process of rethinking and renewal of national and international action required for long-run recovery and sustained human development in Africa.

RICHARD JOLLY
Deputy Executive Director
Programmes, UNICEF

Acknowledgements

This book was made possible by the ideas, support and contributions of many people and organisations. A particular thanks is extended first of all to the organisers and participants of the seminar 'Adjustment and Development in Sub-Saharan Africa: Is the Current Approach Satisfactory? Is There Another Way', held at the UNICEF International Child Development Centre in Florence, Italy, in November 1992. The participants, drawn from academic institutions in the North and South, international organisations and UNICEF, took part in frank, sometimes heated, always constructive and stimulating, discussions. Many of their contributions have been incorporated into this book.

The strong support, continuing interest and involvement in development and adjustment issues of the senior management in UNICEF as well as among colleagues in New York, Florence and in the country offices, particularly in Nairobi and Abidjan, is very much appreciated. Their support, encouragement and assistance has played an important part in helping this book come to light. Warm thanks are also due to colleagues in other organisations, particularly EADI and CODRESRIA who co-sponsored the 1992 seminar and who work with unflagging commitment on African development issues, and the African Development Bank, Food and Agriculture Organization, International Labour Organisation, International Monetary Fund and the World Bank for contributing their valuable time and efforts to this undertaking and for providing documentation.

Sincere thanks are also due to the people involved in the production of this book. Cinzia Iusco-Bruschi provided competent secretarial assistance throughout, and the ICDC library staff swiftly tracked down necessary documentation. A special thanks goes to Anny Bremner, who edited the text and prepared it for publication. Her competence, patience and hard work certainly made our task much easier.

None of the people or organisations mentioned is responsible for the views expressed in this book or for any errors that may have remained.

GIOVANNI ANDREA CORNIA
GERALD K. HELLEINER

Notes on the Contributors

Giovanni Andrea Cornia is the Director of the Economic and Social Research Programme at the International Child Development Centre of UNICEF in Florence. He has worked at the UNICEF Headquarters, with UNCTAD, the UN Economic Commission for Europe and the Economic Studies Centre of FIAT, and has also held visiting professorships at the Universities of Florence and Pavia. He has co-authored and co-edited five books and many articles in the field of land reform, savings, public economics, human resource development and macroeconomic stabilisation in developing countries.

Befekadu Degefe is Director of the Beaman Center for Economic Studies in Addis Ababa. He was Professor of Economics and Head of the Economics Studies Unit at the University of Addis Ababa from 1969 to 1993. He has also worked as a consultant for UNECA and as regional adviser and country economist for the World Bank. He has written widely on development issues, including works on economic integration, human capacity building and debt.

Lionel Demery currently works in the Education and Social Policy Department of the World Bank. He spent eight years with the International Labour Organisation and has held posts in the University of Wales, Overseas Development Institute (London) and the University of Warwick. He has published extensively in the field of adjustment and income distribution, and he has co-edited a major volume on the subject, *Understanding the Social Effects of Policy Reform*, recently published by the World Bank.

Sébastien Dessus is a Principal Research Assistant for the OECD Development Centre, where his main area of research is agricultural trade liberalisation and the political feasibility of adjustment. He has published papers on export performance and adjustment, and on the consequences of trade liberalisation.

Riccardo Faini is Professor of Economics at the University of Brescia, Italy. He has taught at the Universities of Essex and Venezia and at the Bologna Center of Johns Hopkins University. He has also acted as a consultant for the World Bank, the OECD Development Centre, UNIDO and UNCTAD. He has published widely in the fields of regional development, investment and adjustment in developing countries, and is most recently the author of *Fiscal Issues in Adjustment in Developing Countries*, published by Macmillan.

Gerald K. Helleiner is Professor of Economics at the University of Toronto. He is also Research Coordinator of the IMF/World Bank 'Group of Twenty-four' and Director of a research project on trade and industrialisation for the World Institute for Development Economics Research (WIDER), as well as being a member of various academic advisory committees and editorial boards. Among his many published works, his most recent book is entitled *The New Global Economy and the Developing Countries.*

Jean-Dominique Lafay is Professor of Economics at the University of Paris I (Panthéon-Sorbonne). He has published extensively in the areas of public choice, bureaucracy, politico-economic modelling and adjustment.

Thandika Mkandawire is the Director of CODESRIA in Dakar, Senegal, an international organisation coordinating research in Africa. He obtained a doctorate in economics in Sweden. He has published widely on development issues and is the author of various books on political and development issues in Africa. He is also a member of a large number of academic advisory committees.

Paul Mosley is Professor of Economics at the University of Reading, England. He has held academic appointments at the Universities of Bath and Manchester, and advisory posts in the Kenya Treasury and the UK Overseas Development Administration. His major interests are in macroeconomics, agricultural development and international finance, and he has written extensively in these fields. His publications include *The Settler Economies: Kenya and Zimbabwe 1900–1963*, *Overseas Aid: Its Defence and Reform*, and he is co-author of *Aid and Power*.

Christian Morrisson is Head of Research Programme at the OECD Development Centre. He has published many books and articles on income distribution, adjustment, agriculture and education in developing countries.

O.O. Ojo is Research Coordinator with the African Development Bank in Abidjan. Former Professor of Economics at the Obafemi Awolowo University, Ile-Ife, Nigeria, he has published widely in the fields of development, international and monetary economics.

Temitope W. Oshikoya is a senior economist with the African Development Bank. He has also served as economic consultant to the World Bank. Among his most recent publications is *The Nigerian Economy: A Macroeconometric and Input-Output Model.*

T. Ademola Oyejide is Professor of Economics and Director of the Trade Policy Research and Training Programme at the University of Ibadan, Nigeria. He has been a member of the United Nations Committee for Development Planning, and has consulted for the World Bank. He has also been on the Advisory Committee of the African Economic Research Consortium, for whom he is currently directing a research project on regional integration and trade liberalisation.

Alessandro Pio lectures in Development Economics and Macroeconomics at the Università Bocconi in Milan, Italy, where he is also involved in research activities with the Institute of Latin American Studies. He is the author of various publications on the relationship between social and economic development, foreign direct investment and general economic development issues.

Mufutau I. Raheem is a Lecturer in Economics at the University of Ibadan, Nigeria. He is currently undertaking research on external debt management with the support of the African Economic Research Consortium and is also a visiting scholar at the World Bank.

David E. Sahn is an Associate Professor of Economics at Cornell University, and Director of the Cornell University Food and Nutrition Policy Program. Formerly, he was a Research Fellow at the International Food Policy Research Institute and has consulted for numerous international organisations, including the World Bank, FAO, World Food Programme, World Food Council and UNICEF. He has published extensively on economic development and poverty alleviation.

Frances Stewart is Director of Queen Elizabeth House and a Fellow of Sommerville College, Oxford. She worked at UNICEF as a Special Adviser on Adjustment. She is a development economist and has published widely on technology and development, basic needs, adjustment issues and fiscal policy. Among the best-known books that she has authored or co-authored are *Technology and Underdevelopment*, *Adjustment with a Human Face* and *Alternative Development Strategies in Sub-Saharan Africa*.

Vito Tanzi is Director of the Fiscal Affairs Department of the International Monetary Fund. He is also President of the International Institute of Public Finance. His main fields of concern include public finance, particularly in developing countries, and macroeconomic and monetary theory. He has published many books and articles in these areas.

Samuel Wangwe is Senior Research Fellow at the United Nations University, Institute for New Technologies in Maastricht, where he is coordinating a project on new technologies and export orientation in Africa. He has taken leave from his post of Professor of Economics at the University of Dar es Salaam. He has published several books and many articles in the field of economic development, particularly on issues relating to industrial development and technology.

List of Abbreviations

AEC	African Economic Community
CFA	Communauté Financière Africaine
CGIAR	Consultative Group on International Agricultural Research
DFI	Direct Foreign Investment
ECA	Economic Commission for Africa
EFF	Extended Fund Facility
ESAF	Enhanced Structural Adjustment Facility
GDP	Gross Domestic Product
GNP	Gross National Product
HYV	High Yielding Variety
IBRD	International Bank for Reconstruction and Development
IDA	International Development Association
ILO	International Labour Organisation
IMF	International Monetary Fund
ISI	Import Substituting Industrialisation
LDC	Less Developed Country
LIC	Low-income Country
LPA	Lagos Plan of Action
MIC	Middle-income Country
NAR	National Agricultural Research Centre
NIC	Newly Industrialising Country
OAU	Organization of African Unity
OECD	Organisation for Economic Co-operation and Development
PFP	Policy Framework Paper
PTA	Preferential Trade Area
RAL	Review of Adjustment Lending
SAF	Structural Adjustment Facility
SAL	Structural Adjustment Loan
SAP	Structural Adjustment Programme
SDR	Special Drawing Rights
SECAL	Sectoral Adjustment Loan
SPA	Social Program of Assistance
SSA	Sub-Saharan Africa
TNC	Transnational Corporation
UNCTAD	United Nations Conference on Trade and Development
UNDP	United Nations Development Programme

Introduction

Giovanni Andrea Cornia and Gerald K. Helleiner

The last decade has been characterised by an intense and, at times, acrimonious debate about the nature of the policies to be introduced in response to the large macroeconomic shocks affecting most developing countries since the early 1980s. Because of the underdevelopment and fragility of its economy and greater vulnerability to changes in the external environment, nowhere has such debate been as fierce and controversial, and as crucially relevant for economic performance, as in sub-Saharan Africa. And nowhere has the very survival of an ever-increasing part of the population depended so much on the success of policy reform.

The debate has basically involved three schools of thought. In order to remedy Africa's economic problems, the monetarists and neoliberals broadly advocated first and foremost a Draconian stabilisation of macroeconomic imbalances, to be followed by 'laissez-faire' policies entailing an equally rapid price and trade liberalisation together with a drastic reduction of state interference in the economy. At the opposite end of the spectrum, dependency theorists defended the validity of inward-oriented solutions, particularly in industry, favoured state interventions to correct the 'market failures' typical of countries with underdeveloped and distorted structures, and generally considered the monetarist approach to stabilisation unnecessarily deflationary and the risks connected to deficit financing exaggerated or unfounded. The structuralists, finally, favoured macroeconomic balance but emphasised the limits of the monetarist approach, particularly when dealing with structural problems, and the output and welfare costs associated with orthodox stabilisation. In their view, greater priority was to be placed on agriculture, human development and state intervention to ensure access to resources by small producers, i.e. policies entailing some redistribution in assets and opportunities. More gradualist and selective trade policy reform, with particular attention to regional integration, were also called for.

These three theoretical positions evolved considerably during the 1980s and are continuing to evolve in the 1990s. Each of the three schools of thought has conceded some ground, and in some areas, but certainly not in all, the consensus is certainly greater nowadays than in the early 1980s. Policy approaches actually undertaken or, in principle, agreed upon have also changed. Preference for short-term demand management and a basic version of structural adjustment have slowly been replaced – at least on theoretical ground, much less so in the 'real world' – by agreement on a broader and longer-term approach to development encompassing economic, political and social objectives as well as a clear concern for short-term macroeconomic balance. The sectoral emphasis has also shifted, with agriculture, human development and non-traditional exports receiving greater priority than earlier on. Only the process of policy formulation – still largely dominated by the international financial institutions – seems to have remained immune to change.

Many factors explain this evolution of theory, policy and praxis. In the first place, the continued stagnation of SSA's economy throughout the 1980s forced a profound reassessment of the validity of the theoretical underpinnings, time-frame, policy instruments and degree of financial support of the dominant adjustment approach. Secondly, the end of the Cold War and the changing political conditions in some of the major Western nations have influenced the political rules of the game as well as the policy and foreign aid climate and motivations both in Africa and in the donor community. And, finally, the wave of social science research that began in the early 1980s and the heated and often trenchant debate of the last ten years have led to a better understanding of the complexity and multifaceted nature of the African crisis, a crisis whose solution will require – by everybody's admission – more time, continued external support and considerable transformation in the African economies.

We feel that this debate has not been carried out in vain and that it should be continued. While power and self-interest considerations as well as preconceived views and cultural biases often prevent the adoption of the best solutions, an open, rigorous and frank confrontation of opposing views, as well as continued validation of the efficacy of the proposed solutions – i.e. the most essential elements of the scientific process – can in the medium and long term overcome some or many of these obstacles.

It was in this spirit that the International Child Development Centre, the research branch of UNICEF based in Florence, organised at the end of 1992 a major seminar on 'African Adjustment and Development: Is the Present Approach Satisfactory? Is There Another Way?'

The organisation of the seminar reflected UNICEF's longstanding commitment to policy dialogue, to a better understanding of the factors affecting the well-being of children and other vulnerable groups, and to the search for socially and economically viable solutions.

The seminar was held under the auspices of the Council for the Development of Economic and Social Research in Africa (CODESRIA) and the European Association of Development Institutes (EADI), two of the main social science networks in Africa and Europe, and brought together a large number of economists and other social scientists from some of the main African and Western universities and research centres, from the World Bank, the IMF, several UN organisations, and from regional institutions including the European Community, the African Development Bank and the Development Centre of the OECD. The participants subscribed to a variety of doctrinal and institutional traditions and many of them had been active in the policy debate of the last ten years in different capacities. For each of the research topics discussed at the seminar, two or more papers emphasising different aspects of the issue and generally offering contrasting views were presented and discussed in a lively and open atmosphere.

This book includes many of the papers presented at the seminar as well as some papers subsequently commissioned to give the volume greater completeness and balance. We should like to emphasise that the views expressed in this book represent the personal opinions of the authors and should not necessarily be attributed to the institutions to which they are, or have been, affiliated.

The book is organised as follows. Part I presents different theoretical perspectives on the rationale, justification, evolution and limitations of structural adjustment and of the shift towards longer-term policies and instruments that have occurred or are, in the view of their proponents, necessary. This section is preceded by an overview which summarises the main evolution of the debate, the considerable convergence of viewpoints reached in a some areas, the persistence of disagreement in several crucial areas and the limited understanding of a few phenomena which require further research and experimentation. Part II deals with a generally neglected theme, i.e. the political sustainability of the economic reforms and, in particular, with the political economy of privatisation. Part III presents different perspectives on the constraints to agricultural development and on the thorny issue of the impact of changes in household incomes and public expenditure on human welfare, and child welfare in particular. Finally, Part IV discusses the external constraints to and policies for the recovery and long-term development of SSA, though several, often opposing, statements in this regard can be found also in Part I.

We wish to conclude this introduction by noting that the book is deliberately open-ended and does not offer final recommendations on the policies to follow. Though we obviously have our views about the best way ahead, we wish instead to restate our belief in the benefits of a rigorous, open and frank debate in terms of reaching greater convergence among conflicting paradigms as well as in terms of more humane and efficient policies. This has not always happened in the past, nor will it necessarily occur in the future; but gains are indeed possible and reachable. We thus hope that this book will contribute, albeit modestly, to the formulation and implementation of more appropriate policies which will give a more concrete foundation to the hopes and aspirations of the African people and, in particular, to the poorest and most deprived of them, an improvement in whose survival and living conditions is, in the end, the sole criterion for judging the success of future theories, paradigms and policies.

Part I

Changing Approaches to Adjustment and Development

1 From Adjustment to Development in Sub-Saharan Africa: Consensus and Continuing Conflict

Gerald K. Helleiner*

I FROM ADJUSTMENT TO DEVELOPMENT

It is time to call a formal end to the decade of 'structural adjustment' in sub-Saharan Africa. The intense and continuing debates over its meaning, its instruments and its efficacy no longer serve any useful purpose now that all at last agree that there are no economic 'quick fixes' for Africa and that appropriate change will take much longer than originally thought. The objective of African development that is both equitable and sustainable - in political, social, economic and environmental terms - is now virtually universally accepted among African governments, international institutions, aid donors and non-governmental organisations, in Africa and elsewhere. Whilst there is understandable impatience, particularly in Africa, over the pace of projected change and, in particular, that of poverty alleviation, there is also now broad understanding that development in Africa will take a long time. The weak initial conditions, continuing internal constraints, and unfavourable external environment make for fairly bleak medium-term prospects, even in the most optimistic scenarios. Overblown expectations of the effects of policy reforms (both those emanating from political independence and, in the 1980s, those described as 'structural adjustment') and the dimensions and effects of external assistance in their support have now been reviewed and are recognised as

* I am grateful to Giovanni Andrea Cornia, Richard Jolly, John Loxley, Paul Mosley, Benno Ndulu and Frances Stewart for useful comments on an earlier draft of this chapter. I alone am responsible for the current version.

the counterproductive influences that they were. After the 'lost decade' of the 1980s (most would assign a longer period to these years of setback), Africans and those concerned with Africa are both sadder and wiser.

Analysts in the World Bank now argue that a core group of about 15 countries, making up almost half of Africa's population, has in recent years both avoided civil strife and undertaken major policy reform – not all with Bank support – and is, on balance, performing somewhat better than other sub-Saharan African countries (see Chapter 2 of this volume; Husain, 1993; World Bank, 1994). There is little quarrel elsewhere with this general assessment, although different samples and different methodologies, even within the Bank, have generated much less optimistic results (Elbadawi, 1992; Elbadawi et al., 1992). There is universal disappointment that the record of these 'successes' is still so modest, and that the list of good performers is not much longer (franc zone countries, for example, are conspicuously absent). A great many studies have documented the continuing weak economic performance of sub-Saharan African countries, including those undertaking adjustment programmes, both in absolute terms and relative to other developing countries (see for instance Elbadawi et al., 1992; World Bank, 1992b; Mosley and Weeks, 1993).

In retrospect, the 1980s can be seen as a period of setback in African economic history, not unlike the difficult 1930s; with the important difference that in the 1980s many analysts and policy makers, particularly those in international financial institutions, ascribed Africa's problems more to internal policy errors than to exogenous influences. External shocks at the beginning of the decade were generally assumed at the time to be shorter and less severe in their consequences than they eventually proved to be. Short-term stabilisation policies, based on demand restraint, were therefore pursued for too long in circumstances where longer-term, supply-side policies were required (extensive discussion on this issue is to be found in Chapter 5). Moreover, once longer-term 'adjustment' policies were introduced, whatever else may be said about them, they failed, as all now agree, to meet original expectations and the evident needs.

Believing as they did that domestic policy errors were at the root of Africa's dismal economic performance in the 1980s, the international financial institutions' policy makers expected more from domestic policy reforms – the quicker and more comprehensive the better – than, under existing constraints, was at all reasonable. The very terminology of 'structural adjustment' seemed to imply a one-off change following which all would be 'normal' (and conducive to development) again. This terminology was also severely debased by its increasing utilisation to denote whatever policy package a government receiving a World Bank 'structural adjustment loan' was either being asked to undertake or actually did. While there was considerable commonality in these SAL programmes there was also intercountry variation, both as to what was asked and what was actually done.

Ambiguity and theoretical confusion regarding what 'structural adjustment' really was – other than a rationalisation for the provision of medium-term, quick-disbursing policy-based programme finance – began to result in its use as a synonym for good economic management, at least as assessed by the World Bank, much like the word 'planning' was used in the policy literature of the 1960s. With the emphasis shifting from demand restraint (i.e. stabilisation) to supply expansion, particularly of tradables (i.e. adjustment), the time horizon gradually lengthening, and the steady addition of new dimensions to the discussion, including equity in income distribution, environmental sustainability, participatory political forms and improved governance, it became more and more difficult to distinguish the debates about 'adjustment' from the much older ones about 'development'. It is therefore undoubtedly appropriate to return now to 'development', many would say 'human development' and/or 'sustainable development', as the central theme of economic policy debate in sub-Saharan Africa.

II CONSENSUS AND CONFLICT: GENERAL THEMES

Over the 1980s there gradually emerged a broad consensus among international financial institutions, United Nations agencies (including the Economic Commission for Africa and UNICEF), aid donors and African technocrats and politicians about major elements of Africa's development requirements. This is an important achievement, the product of some fierce debates, tough experience, considerable learning and increased humility all round. Its main elements are reviewed below. Acknowledgement of, indeed respect for, the emergence of this consensus must not be permitted, however, to blind us to the important continuing disagreements and consequent problems. These are of three major types:

1. disagreements as to the appropriateness and efficacy of the *process* through which adjustment/development programmes are designed, and thus their perceived 'ownership';

2. remaining matters of substantive policy disagreement, both in terms of *overall presumptions* as to the 'correct' policy and in terms of the *details of individual country programmes* (including their pace and sequencing);
3. disagreements as to the degree to which rhetoric accords, or even, in some instances, should accord, with reality.

It is also important to record that there continues to exist a more radical tradition in African social science which rejects existing political and economic structures both within Africa and at the global level. Those who have worked in this tradition, though probably less influential now than they once were, have not hesitated to engage in recent debates over structural adjustment and development in Africa (see for instance Onimode, 1989). Development debate in sub-Saharan Africa is nowhere near 'the end of its history'!

III CONFLICT OVER PROCESS

Most economists and policy makers, wherever they work, traditionally debate policy rather than issues of the decision-making process. In sub-Saharan Africa today, however, as in the final days of colonialism, the *manner* in which key economic (and other) policy decisions are made has acquired a degree of importance that is at least as great as that of their content. In part, this is because of the very strength of the consensus described above. When many of the principal issues and objectives are already agreed upon, and the remaining issues are recognised as less important or subject to legitimate debate or both, the salience of the decision-making process naturally increases. Increased pressures, both from internal forces and from external donors, for more transparent, participatory and democratic forms of governance in Africa have also contributed to this redirection of emphasis; so too has the increasing realisation by the IMF, World Bank and other powerful external interests, however limited their response still may be at a practical level, that local 'ownership' of economic policy is the surest basis for effective and sustained reform.

There are two levels at which disagreement and concern remain quite deep. Both are more extensively discussed, though not always in the same way, by Mkandawire in Chapter 8. First, there typically remains a deep gulf of distrust and/or misunderstanding between African non-governmental organisations – business organisations, labour unions, farmers' associations, churches, charitable bodies, and so on; indeed, the populace at large – and the organisations of the state. Fed by frequent abuses of office, rampant corruption, and erratic and inefficient provision of services, even in the 'best' of African states, public attitudes toward government are typically adversarial rather than supportive of its development programmes. In the difficult 1980s, when social and economic hardship increased and governmental performance typically deteriorated, the gulf usually deepened. Governments were blamed for the disastrous economic experiences of the 1980s, though the fault was by no means theirs alone or, in many cases, even primarily. To some degree, such 'problems' are universal and inescapable, particularly in low-income countries with very weak administrative capacities. In some respects, however, it may be possible, and many would say it will be necessary, to improve considerably on current governmental performance.

The key governmental decisions regarding economic stabilisation and some of those described as 'structural adjustment' can be made by a relatively small number of senior technocrats and politicians, backed, where necessary, by external technical advice. Currency devaluation, across-the-board budget cuts, major redirections of government spending, abolition of governmental controls and the like were typically undertaken in such a highly centralised, technocratic and non-participatory manner in sub-Saharan Africa in the 1980s. Even within the government, decisions were typically taken at the highest levels of finance ministries, central banks and presidential offices, without consultations with operational ministries, other government bodies or, for that matter, the intermediate-level technical staff of the central economic decision-making institutions themselves. Middle-level staff members of the IMF and the World Bank were more likely to know the pros and cons of the policy alternatives under consideration in individual African countries than the nationals of those countries, even most of those ostensibly responsible and/or concerned within the relevant government institutions. While such decision-making procedures may have been appropriate, or even necessary, for this kind of decision at the time, they cannot be employed for longer-run and more complex policy changes involving, for example, tax reform, privatisations, institutional change, infrastructure development, and the development and implementation of strategies for agriculture, industry, education and health. In these instances, there are far more policy actors and all must be 'brought in on' the decision-making as well as the eventual implementation of agreed policies if they are to have any prospect of 'success'.

Increased transparency and increased participation obviously relate to non-governmental actors, not simply those within the government's own system. Local 'ownership' of development programmes requires public debate and a degree of public understanding (though obviously not universal agreement) of objectives, constraints and the rationale for chosen policy instruments. Democratic and transparent processes always risk creating openings for irresponsible populist movements; and consultations with interest groups, for instance, via Ghana's Private Sector Advisory Group, risk the government's 'capture' by special interests. External donors frequently argue that their own pressure is necessary to overcome the influence of local vested interests that would otherwise frustrate needed reforms. There can be little doubt that more democratic processes will generate modifications to technocratically determined 'optimal' policies. Yet, without them, there can only be continued popular disaffection with government and its programmes, and the potential for periodic explosions. Whatever governments and technocrats may lose in the sphere of 'efficiency' they almost certainly win back in perceptions of equity and participation, and in policy stability and credibility. The engineering of appropriate means of local participation and consultation, both inside and outside government, so as to develop both broader and deeper local ownership of development programmes, remains a major challenge in Africa.

The second area of disagreement and concern over decision-making processes relates to the role of foreigners, and particularly the IMF and World Bank, in the development and implementation of African programmes. Sub-Saharan African countries are unusually heavily aid-dependent. This places them in a uniquely vulnerable position *vis-à-vis* donor pressures. During the 1980s, Africa's severe economic problems resulted in an increased dependence upon external programme finance and the policy advice/conditions that accompanied it, first from the IMF and later from the World Bank and Bank-organised donor consortia. As has been seen, much of this external advice/conditionality has, in its essentials, been uncontroversial, at least among technocrats; and IMF/Bank approaches have evolved considerably, in a 'favourable' (i.e. African-friendly) direction, during the past decade. As has also been seen (more detail appears below), however, elements of disagreement are bound to remain. Resentment over external pressures abounds even among the technocrats ostensibly 'allied' with the IMF and World Bank in IMF- and Bank-supported African countries. More important, even when there is basic agreement, the economic policy programmes are widely perceived as 'made in Washington' and, generally speaking, that is what they have been. Moreover, within Washington, the shorter-term stabilisation perspectives of the IMF continue to exercise a degree of influence over African programmes that is inconsistent with, and inappropriate for, the longer-run perspectives that all now ostensibly recognise as necessary for Africa.

Both the Development Assistance Committee of the OECD, in its statement of 'principles for effective aid', and the World Bank, in a variety of studies and statements, acknowledge the overarching importance of national 'ownership' of development programmes, however great may be the external inputs to it. This importance derives not only from its inherent appropriateness, but also from its efficacy. There are early limits to that which can be achieved by external leverage. Programmes that are locally owned, at least by the technocrats and leaders that have to implement them, have proven far more likely to be sustained and to eventually work:

> Developing countries themselves are responsible for determining and implementing their programmes and policies. This principle applies with particular force to programme assistance, which is often related to important policy reform measures and has broad-based impacts on the economy. In particular, developing countries must 'own' their own structural adjustment programmes. This implies that the basis for coordinated international action must be the policy and programme statements and actions of the developing country itself, which must also, to the largest extent possible, be in charge of international aid coordination arrangements (OECD, 1992).

This aspiration remains a long way from realisation, in the views of a great many African policy makers and much larger numbers of Africans who are further from the centres of power. Mission after mission from outside Africa prepares studies and offers advice. What begins as research studies and recommendations, frequently read by only a few of the overworked local technocrats, is rapidly transformed into the input for so-called 'policy dialogue' and thence to new conditions for external assistance. The policies upon which (usually unsolicited) advice is offered span the entire range of possibilities. The use of local consultants in such efforts has frequently been only *pro forma* and perfunctory. No one doubts that they are normally 'driven' by the external inputs. In many instances, foreign 'experts' also dominate the key 'line' policy positions in national governments. 'Technical assistance' to sub-Saharan Africa has many valuable aspects to it; but it has long been recognised as a major aid 'disaster area' which, far from building local capacity, has often worked to stifle and frustrate its development. The most comprehensive assessment of technical assistance to Africa yet undertaken, released by the UNDP in 1993, is devastating in its conclusions; and includes evidence that the performance record is particularly weak in technical cooperation related to structural adjustment and institutional development (UNDP, 1993a). Foreign donors both 'drive' and 'own' technical cooperation in Africa. It is a costly, inefficient and increasingly 'unsettling' device for overcoming domestic budget constraints and government employment freezes (ibid.). This degree of external intrusion into domestic policy formation and the concomitant failure to develop appropriate local research and decision-making capacity is not found, and would not be tolerated, elsewhere in the developing world.

While the problem of undue donor influence, and particularly that of the IMF and World Bank, is formally recognised, there are still few signs of serious change. The World Bank has announced some initiatives and has recently been remarkably forthright in its assessments:

> African development agencies failed . . . to insist on full local participation in identification and design of projects. Having failed to ensure local involvement, it is not surprising that local commitment and sense of ownership was weak.
>
> Donors also relied too heavily on foreign experts, even when qualified Africans were available. This did little to foster a receptive environment for the transfer of skills. In fact, it was often bitterly resented. Over-reliance on technical assistance also brought many difficulties. Expatriates were frequently chosen for their technical skills rather than their ability to pass on those skills. This, coupled with operational difficulties, pulled foreign consultants into operational support at the expense of capacity building.
>
> After 30 years of technical assistance, and so much money spent, Africa's weak institutions, lack of expertise, and current need for more – rather than less – assistance tell us we have failed badly in our efforts.
>
> . . . the donors have done a disservice to Africa, and many African governments have participated blindly (Jaycox, 1993a).

The World Bank now says that it is encouraging local programme ownership, 'insisting that the materials we use as the basis for . . . lending decisions be the product of Africans' (ibid.), hiring local African consultants rather than foreigners wherever possible, and attempting, through its African Capacity Building Initiative (and the African Capacity Building Foundation), to develop professional and analytical skills in public policy in Africa. These efforts are overdue, and they are probably biased in their orientations (toward orthodox Bank perspectives), but they have been welcomed in Africa.

Disagreements and concern remain about the degree to which donor practices will actually change and, in particular, about the willingness or even ability (given their own legislative and political constraints) of the IMF, World Bank and other donors to relinquish or significantly loosen their accustomed controls. The IMF and World Bank have been notably passive on proposals for reducing their own profiles in sub-Saharan Africa by encouraging greater pluralism of approaches, institutions and personnel, and such obvious measures as increased direct interchange among developing country analysts, unmediated (and unfiltered) by the IMF/Bank themselves. Are they ready, even now, to leave Africans to learn from their own mistakes? If local 'ownership' involves a programme design that differs significantly from that which these outsiders would recommend, will it receive their support?

IV ISSUES OF POLICY SUBSTANCE

(A) Consensus

Some policy issues, or at least objectives, were never in much technical dispute. The need for orderly processes of macroeconomic management in simultaneous pursuit of both external and internal balance, including full utilisation of capacity, as opposed to ad hoc and ill-considered policy measures to 'patch up' emerging macroeconomic problems, has, in principle, always been agreed. Certainly the importance of fiscal prudence, great caution in the use of seigniorage as a source of public revenue, and even greater caution with conscious resort to the inflation tax, have been broadly agreed, however frequently these precepts may, under pressure, have been breached in practice, and however much policy makers may continue to disagree on the critically important issues of the appropriate pace and 'mix' of specific policy changes (see Section (B) below). Similarly, the importance of maintaining savings and investment rates in support of sustained economic growth has never been at issue.

On a remarkable number of policy issues that previously provoked dispute there has been an emerging consensus, at least among academics, technocrats (mainly economists) and politicians in sub-Saharan Africa, the Washington financial institutions, the UN system and donor capitals. A great many lessons have been learned – on all sides – from the difficult and disappointing experiences of the past two decades in Africa. 'Alternative' approaches (see for instance UN/ECA, 1989; Loxley, 1986; Stewart et al., 1992; Cornia et al., 1992) no longer seem quite as alternative as they once were. In particular, the importance of working consciously to alleviate poverty and to protect and promote 'human' development in adjustment and development programmes, rather than allowing these matters to derive from more 'productionist' growth policies, is now agreed again, after a decade of neglect, not only in sub-Saharan Africa but in Latin America and elsewhere as well. Even the IMF, to which UNICEF first appealed on these issues in 1983 (Jolly, 1991), now purports to take a keen interest in the implications of country programmes for the welfare of the most vulnerable groups; and it apparently does so whether or not the relevant governments have requested such analysis (see Chapter 4 of this volume; see also Patel, 1992; Schadler et al., 1993). Labour-intensive, publicly funded works programmes, once discouraged in the World Bank, are now recognised as a valuable weapon in the armoury of poverty-alleviating programmes. Education, health, employment opportunities and food security are stressed in all current African development discussions. Much of the remaining controversy on the social impact of macroeconomic and adjustment policies in Africa relates to alternative interpretations of the past; see for example the conflicting views in Chapters 13 and 14. There remains much disagreement, however, as to the extent to which agreements in principle have been translated into altered policy practice (see Section V below).

Also agreed is the development strategy of building, in the first instance, primarily on agriculture, and even, where smallholders already dominate, on smallholder agriculture. Earlier African aspirations to rapid industrialisation, based upon the 'squeezing' of resources from the agricultural sector, no longer carry credibility. Nor is there any longer the same exclusive fixation, in the World Bank or elsewhere, on 'getting prices right' in order to support such agricultural development. The importance of non-price factors – notably rural infrastructure; transport, marketing and input distribution systems; and credit – is fully recognised by all, even when there remains some disagreement on appropriate policies in these areas (see Chapters 11 and 12;

and Mosley, 1993a). At the same time, there is probably increased respect for the responsiveness of Africans at all levels to market incentives, bred by the vigour and variety of parallel markets in ostensibly controlled regimes, among other factors.

There is also now widespread consensus that there is considerable underutilised potential in the small-scale and informal sectors in sub-Saharan Africa. There is still some uncertainty as to the roots of Africa's 'missing middle' (in terms of the size distribution of local industrial and other private enterprise). Many ascribe it to failures of domestic financial markets; financial sector reforms could certainly ease some of the constraints on small and medium-sized African enterprises. In any case, improved levels of education, not least basic literacy and numeracy, and the downsizing or rationalisation of the public sector suggest new potential for private and entrepreneurial efforts in a wide variety of productive activities, and the growth of small local firms to efficient medium- and large-scale ones.

Consensus has also been reached on the necessity of increasing exports and, where possible, efficient import substitution in order to respond to worsened international terms of trade and the medium-term prospect of reduced net external resource transfers. Vigorous expansion of non-traditional exports is an objective that all now share (see Chapter 17; see also Chapter 3 for a dissenting voice on this topic). 'Catching up' via productivity improvements and recapturing lost African market shares in traditional commodity markets are objectives that have sometimes elicited nervousness about potential negative terms of trade effects; but, provided appropriate care is taken and efforts at more effective market management are undertaken in cocoa, coffee and perhaps some other markets in which world price elasticities of demand are low, there is widespread agreement here as well. Renewed and more efficient efforts at regional economic cooperation now also find official favour everywhere as an appropriate response to small local markets (see Chapter 18). Inward-oriented development strategies and trade dependency theories are still discussed in some African academic circles, but they now carry little weight with policy makers addressing fundamentally weak balance of payments prospects for the foreseeable future.

All now seem also to agree on the need for rationalising public sector activities: moving government out of activities for which it is not suited, reducing the degree of attempted governmental intervention and control in local markets, providing adequate salaries and incentives for professionals in the public service, tightening audit and financial control systems, reducing military expenditures, and generally rationalising public sector expenditures. The efficiency, honesty and credibility of government can typically only be restored by fairly major reforms in the civil service, the parastatal sector, and tax and expenditure systems. These do not always involve the downsizing of government as a whole; adjustment programmes in Ghana and Uganda, for example, raised the government shares of GDP – from the severely depressed levels to which they had fallen during the depths of these countries' economic crises.

Earlier debate as to whether sub-Saharan Africa's economic crisis was primarily the product of domestic policy errors or the product of exogenous shocks and constraints has also now abated. As 'adjustment' policies were increasingly introduced – to only limited developmental effect – the importance of both the extremely hostile global economic environment and the extremely weak 'initial conditions' in sub-Saharan Africa became more evident to all (for further discussion of these issues, see Chapter 15). From these realisations also stemmed the new consensus that African development was going to take much longer than most, both African and non-Africans, had originally thought.

Earlier optimism about the prospects for private savings and investment in Africa, once policies were set right, has now dissipated. It is not entirely clear why private savings and investment have remained so low. Certainly, policy instability has not been conducive to savings or investment. Perhaps more time is required to establish the credibility and sustainability of new policies, and to restore confidence. Perhaps expansion of complementary public sector investment is first required. Oshikoya raises these and related issues in his analysis of African private investment in Chapter 7. In any case, there is a new and widely shared humility about these matters in policy circles, and a consequent shared belief in the importance of maintaining a modicum of stability and predictability in policy and in incentive structures. Clearly, simply improving incentives and policies, on a 'there, we did it' basis, has not been sufficient to increase either investment or growth.

(B) Continuing conflict

On some general issues of development policy for sub-Saharan Africa there remains significant disagreement and debate. Frequently, it stems from limited information or understanding, or both; there is also some prospect for eventual consensus. Sometimes differences are more deeply rooted in rival ideologies or views of development itself. The main such issues of continuing conflict are:

1. the appropriate role of the state in development efforts; the appropriate role for non-African expatriate private enterprise, both resident and 'truly' foreign; and the medium-term potential of African enterprise;
2. the import regime and, in particular, the appropriate approach to industrial protection;
3. the efficacy of financial liberalisation and, more generally, financial sector reforms;
4. the appropriate objectives and instruments for agricultural development;
5. the size of required external financial support; and the potential for improving, or at least stabilising, primary commodity prices and the terms of trade;
6. the role of the exchange rate.

At the national level, there is bound to be further disagreement as to the appropriate pace, timing and sequencing of development-oriented policy changes, as well as a myriad of details on distributional, participatory and other matters. These are the very stuff of domestic politics; and it is impossible to generalise about them. There is not much agreement, even among specialists, as to the likely relative political efficacy of undertaking reforms in good times as against bad. An ambitious attempt to model some of these politico-economic interactions at the country level is described in Chapter 9. The appropriate degree of country specificity of development programmes has itself been a matter of debate: the IMF and World Bank have frequently been accused of failing sufficiently to take account of local circumstances.

1 Role of the state

Disagreement over the appropriate role of the state in sub-Saharan African development lies behind many of the disagreements over policies. If the state is seen as fragile, incompetent or corrupt, as it frequently is in sub-Saharan Africa, there is an obvious rationale for 'offloading' many of its responsibilities to the private sector, however weak it may also be. The problem is that those with the greatest private capacity to respond to market incentives are frequently foreign firms and/or ethnic minorities. Giving them 'full rein' can create problems of a different kind. Moreover, particularly in small and/or poorly integrated markets, private monopolies can emerge, with consequences no less serious than those in public ones.

According to the World Bank's own assessments of the adjustment programmes it has supported in sub-Saharan Africa in the 1980s, the efforts in the sphere of privatisation are among those that have been the most disappointing (others on this list include fiscal and civil service reform, and financial sector reform). Privatisation, fiscal reform and civil service reform are all not only politically sensitive, in that powerful interests are affected by them, but, if they are to be successful in achieving social objectives, they are also technically quite complex. It is therefore not surprising that progress should be slow or that mistakes were frequent. Particularly in the case of privatisation, there has continued to be intense technical and political debate over such issues as: the appropriate range of governmental activities to be addressed in this way; the best means of ensuring an equitable and efficient transfer process; the potential of the indigenous private sector to respond to the new opportunities; the appropriate role for foreign and ethnic minority businesses; and the risk of eventual market malfunction via market concentration, continued inappropriate governmental interventions, or otherwise. These and other issues surrounding the issue of privatisation in Africa are extensively discussed in Chapter 10.

It is impossible to generalise about the relative importance of 'government failures' and other 'political' or market 'failures' in so many different African circumstances. The potential for 'reforming' government is much greater in some countries at some times than in others; so is the potential of the indigenous private sector. It can certainly be fairly stated that the World Bank, external donors and, more generally, external interests have been much less sensitive to indigenous African aspirations, or even a perceived need, for an indigenous developmental state than they have been to shortfalls in actual African government performance. They have also underestimated the consequences of cuts in public expenditures for indigenous supply responses in both the agricultural and industrial sectors. Africans typically see the foreign orientation toward market solutions as ideologically biased, self-serving and insensitive to, or ignorant of, local social and political realities. As research accumulates on the importance of the state in recent East Asian development successes, some of it undertaken within the World Bank, and with a shift in the ideological climate in the West, the strength of donor commitments to crude market solutions to African economic problems may be abating. But the 'softness' of the typical African state is bound to remain for some time; so will disagreements, ideological and pragmatic, as to what African governments can or should do.

2 *The import regime and industrial protection*

While there is now widespread agreement that quantitative restrictions upon imported goods and services, typically imposed to defend the external balance of payments, have been socially very costly in sub-Saharan Africa – creating delays, inefficiencies and rent for those with influence and power – there is still active debate as to what should eventually replace them, and the pace at which changes should be made. The orthodox answer is a uniform low tariff, with the possibility of alterations in the uniform rate in response to temporary disturbances, on the lines of the Chilean model. This use of the tariff, according to proponents, recognises the typical African government's degree of reliance upon import duties for revenue, but minimises the costs of misallocations of domestic resources and rent-seeking typical of more structured tariff systems. Most agree that changes in the import regime should be introduced in stages, although some advocate a rapid transition for maximum overall effect.

On the other hand, there is no theoretical case – either on revenue or on allocative grounds – for a totally uniform tariff. Moreover, there is still enough concern in Africa with the survival and development of an efficient manufacturing sector in extremely difficult circumstances that a degree of industrial protection is often believed justifiable on 'infant industry' or 'infant economy' grounds or both. Overenthusiastic liberalisation is therefore seen as setting back the 'tender young shoots' of local industry prior to their full maturation, in at least some instances. Reduced complexity can be attained by drastically reducing the number of tariff rates (say, to three to five) and eliminating or scaling back exemptions.

Industrial development hinges, in any case, upon local capabilities and appropriate supporting institutions no less than incentives; and, in sub-Saharan Africa, these have typically been lacking. Those who seek to promote industry in Africa increasingly agree on a multi-pronged approach, simultaneously offering reasonable (and time-bound) incentives for both import substitution and exporting; building response capacities in the local population and local firms (both large and small) via education, training, and so on; and developing supportive institutions, in such areas as technology acquisition, R&D and finance. Where agriculture is so dominant and labour so abundant, these efforts can be expected to centre on industrial activities that are linked to agriculture (or, in some cases, mining) and/or are intensive in the use of labour; many of these may be small- and medium-scale and many may be located in rural areas.

Those advocating a more 'neutral' tariff and incentive structure usually see the industrial sector as so bloated and inefficient that it requires the fairly radical cutbacks and restructuring that import liberalisation can bring; and the sooner the better. In response to the intense debate in this sphere, and the very limited record of its 'success' with import liberalisation in Africa, the World Bank appears recently to have scaled back its import liberalisation demands. However, the fundamental disagreement remains.

3 Financial sector liberalisation and reform

Financial liberalisation and financial sector reforms have been important elements in the adjustment programmes of sub-Saharan African countries. Banks and other major financial institutions, frequently government-owned, were often driven into technical insolvency in the 1980s by weaknesses in the real economy, or by mismanagement and inappropriate political interventions. Interest rates were also usually negative in real terms, operations were inefficient, and margins were high. There was therefore little public confidence in the formal financial system, and few incentives for depositors or investors to use it. At the same time, some potentially highly productive segments of the economy could not gain sufficient access to credit, notably small- and medium-scale enterprise and smallholder agriculture. The financial sector was not playing an effective role in mobilising savings or allocating them efficiently for investment; and, without major structural reforms and policy changes, had little prospect of ever doing so. There remains significant controversy, however, over the best means of reforming a financial sector in distress and, in particular, the efficacy of the recommended 'market solution' of liberalisation of financial markets and interest rate increases.

Increases in real interest rates can choke off productive investments, cripple enterprises that are essentially healthy, and increase the cost of servicing the public debt. When markets are allowed to determine the level of interest rates, particularly when there is limited confidence in the economy and the financial system, these rates may be considerably higher than is socially desirable. Where, as in sub-Saharan Africa, there is only a handful of banks or other financial institutions and the financial markets are inherently very 'thin', it is unrealistic to anticipate the usual virtues of competitive markets. More direct institutional and policy interventions by government are likely to be necessary in financial sector reform programmes; and they may be costly in terms of both finance (for instance, when taking over the non-performing assets of distressed financial institutions) and scarce skilled manpower. Deregulation and privatisation in the financial sector also require increased attention to prudential regulation and supervision; so that when these instruments of reform are deployed, their costs may be greater than they at first appear. Thus it should not be surprising that primarily 'market-driven' solutions to African financial sector difficulties are so frequently viewed with scepticism (for elaboration of some of these issues in an African context, see Caskey, 1992).

4 *Instruments and objectives for agricultural development*

Although there is now widespread agreement on the centrality of agriculture in the strategy for longer-run African development, controversy remains over important elements of an agricultural strategy. In some parts of Africa, land ownership is relatively concentrated; agricultural development, and governmental policies to encourage it, have quite different distributional and developmental implications from those in areas or countries where smallholders are dominant (see Chapter 11). Expansion of smallholder agriculture, especially through the provision of infrastructure and encouragement of technical change, stimulates more broadly based rural development and, in the view of most economic analysts, more efficient use of agricultural inputs. That being so, the objective should be smallholder agricultural and related rural development rather than agricultural development *per se*. In many cases, this would imply significant land reform; yet land reform of the appropriate type is rarely part of explicit development strategy. In part, the relative insignificance of land reform on the strategy agenda in such cases is the result of domestic political pressures and the reluctance of external agencies to be drawn into domestic political issues. In part, however, it reflects a continuing (mistaken) belief, in technocratic circles, in the efficiency of large farms and the limited capacity of the peasantry.

There is also continuing debate over the relative importance to be assigned to food production as against exports in agricultural development efforts. Whereas the structure of relative prices, until recently, usually worked against exports, government encouragements usually favoured them – in such spheres as research and extension, input supplies, credit and supportive infrastructure. Many therefore favour a disproportionate 'push' in domestic food production (see Mellor et al., 1987, for a detailed and professional exposition of this argument). Others, however, particularly in the IMF and World Bank, have explicitly or implicitly continued to encourage agricultural exporting above all other exporting.

The appropriate deployment of the instruments of government policy in pursuit of agricultural and rural development is also frequently a matter for continuing controversy. In view of the enormous importance of agriculture in the typical sub-Saharan African economy, controversies over the efficacy of privatisation are particularly salient in the spheres of agricultural marketing, agricultural input supply and agricultural credit; in these spheres, government is bound to maintain continued keen interest, and its policies may have a major bearing, for good or ill, on 'market' outcomes. Controversy also continues on the developmental efficacy of agricultural input subsidies and special provisions (including interest subsidies) for rural credit. Mosley highlights these disagreements in Chapter 12 (see also Mosley 1993a).

5 *Aid requirements*

Implicit or explicit in much of the debate about sub-Saharan Africa's economic future is disagreement about the extent of official development assistance that the region requires or 'should' receive. To a significant degree, the size of the requirements depends upon the extent and time horizon of development aspirations. If one is prepared to project stagnant per capita income over the next decade, as the World Bank and other aid donors now do, the aid requirements are obviously much lower than they would be if more rapid growth was a required primary objective. But there are also such considerations as the 'absorptive capacity' for more aid, the desirable degree of dependence upon aid, and equity among aid recipients, on each of which there is a range of opinions that need to be factored into such discussions. The majority African view, though it is not unanimous, is obviously that more aid should be provided for Africa. Such aid could also, in their view, be provided in much more useful forms. This case is argued strongly in Chapter 15.

There is by now close to unanimous professional agreement on the absolute need, if there are to be even modest growth prospects, for more debt relief for most low-income sub-Saharan African countries (see Chapter 15). The problem is no longer one of technical disagreement but, rather, the tepid political support for it in the creditor countries and the glacial pace of change in the Paris Club.

Equally, programme assistance is universally understood to be much easier to absorb than project aid. The relative importance of programme assistance rose greatly in Africa in the 1980s under the banner of 'structural adjustment'. It was popular with aid donors since it seemed to provide them, or at least the World Bank on their behalf, a seat at the highest policy-making tables. Its popularity with African governments stemmed from its flexibility of use and speed of disbursement. When the broad elements of macroeconomic and development policy are 'on track', programme assistance is undoubtedly more useful than aid on which there are more constraints. Thus, the majority of Africans press for relatively more debt relief and more programme and sectoral assistance, and less procurement tying, project aid and technical assistance. To abandon the term 'structural adjustment', as suggested above, is therefore *not* to imply the cessation or even the diminution of programme assistance to sub-Saharan African countries promoting their own development. The provision of more appropriate aid could significantly increase its effectiveness, which is shown, in many studies (for instance Killick, 1991a) to be distressingly limited.

Aid could also be provided, in the recipients' view, in such a manner as to enhance the stability – and thereby longer-term credibility of development programmes – via longer-term commitments and compensatory/contingency provisions to offset unforeseen exogenous shocks. Some also continue, against much experience, to rest hope in international agreements to stabilise, or even support, selected primary commodity prices of interest to low-income countries.

6 The exchange rate

The role of the exchange rate in macroeconomic management has stimulated professional controversy everywhere. The IMF has itself been ambivalent on the issue – sometimes emphasising the need for nominal currency devaluation to effect a real devaluation, thus creating incentives that could restore external balance; at other times, emphasising the role of the exchange rate as a nominal anchor against inflation. In sub-Saharan Africa, where hyperinflation and three-digit inflation rates have been rare, both the IMF and the World Bank have generally emphasised the former in order to provide appropriate supply-side incentives, to permit the easing and simplification of import and exchange control systems, and sometimes to maintain fiscal revenues that are highly dependent on trade taxes.

In the 1970s and early 1980s, most sub-Saharan African governments were reluctant to undertake major currency devaluations either because of the mistaken view that their balance of payments difficulties were temporary or because of their limited experience with and/or suspicion of the exchange rate as an appropriate development policy tool. Most, however, now recognise the desirability of maintaining an appropriate, reasonably stable and unified real exchange rate, and employ a variety of institutional devices to this end: auctions, foreign exchange bureaux, inter-bank markets, 'crawling pegs', periodic nominal devaluations, and so on. Some non-governmental bodies and non-economists still bemoan the official loss of value of the national currency, but the need for new exchange rate regimes in these countries, particularly those that previously saw the triumph of black markets, seems broadly understood.

Controversy and deep disagreement on this point continued much longer in the franc zone where, despite significant deterioration in the terms of trade, considerable real currency appreciation and consequent resort to very austere fiscal measures (sometimes accompanied by fiscal substitutes for devaluation – import duties and export subsidies), the nominal exchange rate remained fixed until early 1994. Franc zone countries long enjoyed lower inflation rates than other African countries and benefited, with the support of the French government, from continued convertibility of their currency, the CFA franc, with the French franc. For a long time, neither the franc zone governments nor the French government appeared persuaded, despite intense pressure from the IMF, the World Bank and others, that the latter benefits were worth risking for the uncertain prospects offered by currency devaluation. Yet the Francophones, even before the 50 per cent CFA franc devaluation in January 1994, were generally regarded as deviant from the majority/consensus view that in current sub-Saharan African circumstances there is little merit in 'permanently' fixed exchange rates. Certainly, even the devalued franc zone could not continue to function in its current mode without the backing of France.

These controversies are thoroughly analysed in Chapter 16, which presents African evidence to the effect that both the undesirable inflationary effects and the favourable balance of payments effects of real devaluation may have been exaggerated; in the five cases studied, both effects are fairly small.

V RHETORIC AND REALITY

To what degree has such consensus as has been achieved been converted into practice? Particularly in the sphere of human development and poverty alleviation, there is still widespread concern about the enormous gap between rhetoric and practice. Vigorous disagreement remains on the *means* of implementing such consensus as has been established in such spheres as the appropriateness of user fees, the narrowness of income-targeting, and the use of selective production or input subsidies.

In the African context, the very low levels of education, health and other social indicators, lend greater urgency to the need for implementing measures and developing strategies for addressing poverty directly. The World Bank's intensive efforts to improve African data on living standards and poverty are admirable (their importance is explained in Chapter 14); but they obviously have no direct impact upon poverty. Nor can they shed light on distributional changes that had already occurred. Many, including the World Bank, and Sahn in Chapter 13 of this volume, continue to argue, as does the IMF (see Chapter 4; and Schadler et al., 1993), that in the absence of adjustment policies, Africa's poverty would have been worse. That may, in many cases, be true; but this argument evades the question as to whether better design of its programmes might have generated much more favourable results; and, even more importantly, whether, even now, development programmes are 'building in' the social, employment-creating and distributional dimensions to the degree that they could and, by apparent consensus, should, rather than just adding on 'safety nets'.

A recent review of World Bank practice concludes:

> ... despite what is written in WDR 1990 and the implementation reports, the actions would seem to be based on the assumption that economic growth – any type and pattern of growth – is good for social development and poverty reduction.... [The] Bank is not only timid when it comes to the crucial question of the pattern of growth, but equally modest in taking into its care the victims of wrong patterns of development.... The actual strategy of the Bank, as opposed to its declared intentions, seems to be: economic growth,

> plus basic education, plus health and population equals improved quality of life and less poverty. This is exactly equivalent to the strategies followed in the 1960s and early 1970s. They work if you live long enough to benefit from them! (Emmerij, 1993.)

Where there are doubts on this score, it is not always clear whether the problems arise because those who mouth the rhetoric do not really believe it or because they are unable, for political reasons or because of limited knowledge as to how to go about it, to deliver. Usually, it is probably a bit of all of these.

Similar gaps between rhetoric and practice are frequently found in development discussions at the global, regional and national levels. Whether, given the particular circumstances of time and place, 'enough' is being done to promote sustainable and equitable development, either within Africa or abroad, will always be a matter of political and other judgement. On such matters there will continue to be, indeed there *should* be, disagreement – with radicals and reformers calling for more. The World Bank and aid donors profess satisfaction with the (increased) aid flows achieved in the late 1980s in the Special Program of Assistance (SPA) for low-income debt-distressed African countries (Husain, 1993). The majority of non-governmental organisations and foreign specialists in African affairs today join Africans in describing the current efforts, both within Africa and elsewhere, as still grossly deficient in terms of reasonable targets for human development in sub-Saharan Africa by the turn of the century.

2 Structural Adjustment: Its Origins, Rationale and Achievements

Lionel Demery*

I INTRODUCTION

The 1980s are known as the decade of adjustment in more ways than one. There have been major adjustments in economic policy, in both the OECD and developing countries. This has been in part a reflection of changes in economic thought, with the dissolution of the 'neo-Keynesian consensus' and the emergence of the so-called 'neo-liberal' consensus. The international financial institutions themselves have similarly been obliged to make their own adjustments in addressing the problems facing the developing world. This chapter is primarily concerned with the adjustment that has taken place in economic policy in the developing countries, particularly in sub-Saharan Africa. However, given the roles of changes in both economic thought and its application in the international financial institutions, these other perspectives of 'adjustment' cannot be neglected altogether.

There has been no emerging agreement to date as to whether the adjustments in economic policy made by the developing countries have achieved their intended final objectives of macroeconomic stability, increased economic efficiency, and enhanced economic growth. Some, based on more aggregative evidence, point out that GDP per capita continued to decline in sub-Saharan African countries in the latter half of the 1980s, despite policy reforms. Others have taken the view that where the policy changes have been implemented effectively, there has been some progress. Despite the voluminous literature on these issues, there is still little evidence of an emerging consensus. Why this should continue to be the case is the main subject of this chapter.

There have also been differences of opinion on the unintended effects of these reforms on other policy objectives, such as poverty

* The author wishes to thank Ishrat Husain for his helpful comments.

reduction and protection of the environment. Critics have argued that adjustment policy reforms at best distracted governments from these more fundamental long-term policy objectives by making the short to medium term the focus of attention. But at worst, some critics consider that adjustment policies have actually aggravated poverty problems. The critique of UNICEF (Cornia et al., 1987) brought the social dimensions of policy reform to the centre-stage of the policy debate. At about the same time, the World Bank itself was becoming more concerned with restoring the balance of policy concern (Demery and Addison, 1987), and has since been more pro-active in addressing the poverty objective within the context of its lending instruments.[1] In some senses, therefore, it could be argued that there has been an emerging consensus on the adjustment/poverty question.

The same cannot be said of the adjustment/environment debate, though it is fair to say that there has been less attention paid to this aspect until recently. The main problem here has been the lack of hard evidence one way or the other. Some studies (such as Barrett, 1990, and Pimentel et al., 1991) suggest that adjustment may have adverse environmental effects. Others (Reed, 1992, among others) reach less certain conclusions.

This chapter is not meant to be an exhaustive review of the literature on structural adjustment. It is deliberately selective. Its main objective is to explore (if not explain) why a consensus on the (intended) economic achievements of adjustment has yet to be reached. The next section reviews the *origins* of structural adjustment policies. This is followed in Section III by a summary of its *rationale*. Section IV assesses the *achievements* of adjustment, highlighting the different views to be found in the literature. Section V addresses the specific issue of adjustment *financing*, assessing the extent to which this has supported adjustment policy reforms. A list of key current policy issues is put forward in Section VI, and the final section makes some brief concluding comments.

II THE ORIGINS OF STRUCTURAL ADJUSTMENT

The origins of structural adjustment can be considered from three related perspectives: the needs of the developing countries themselves; the context of the international financial institutions; and the developments in economic thought during the 1980s.

The underlying economic realities that called for a major revision in economic policy in the developing world need not be rehearsed in detail here. The oil price hike of 1979, and the consequent downturn in OECD growth rates, represented major external shocks for the developing countries. They also set the scene for the rest of the decade, in which OECD growth rates were to remain modest and the terms of trade of most developing countries (especially those relying on commodity exports) were to decline.

In addition to these adverse effects on the current account, there were also serious problems building up in the capital accounts. The combination of restrictive monetary policy and expansionary fiscal policy (especially in the USA) caused world interest rates to rise markedly, from an average of just 1.3 per cent in 1973–80 to just below 6 per cent in 1980–6 (Toye, 1993). The double-edged effect of lower export earnings and higher debt service created a debt overhang problem that was revealed to the world when Mexico suspended its debt payments in August 1982.

External factors alone cannot explain the crisis of low-income countries during the early 1980s. Even though these countries suffered terms of trade losses, this was also true of other developing countries which did not however experience the same decline in GDP and export growth. African exporters lost ground in many international markets, and the region's *share* of world agricultural commodity exports fell from 17 per cent in 1960 to just 8 per cent in 1990. These indicators suggest that domestic policy factors were also responsible for the poor economic performance. For many low-income countries, adjustment required a fundamental revision of their economic philosophy and approaches to economic management. Such changes would inevitably take time, involving a move from a predominantly interventionist paradigm, to freer markets and less government intervention. They also required institutional change, and not simply an adjustment in relative prices.

Given the combination of adverse external circumstances and inappropriate, if not irresponsible, domestic economic management, it was inevitable that the economic performance of many developing countries suffered serious setbacks during the crisis period of the early 1980s. Table 2.1 summarises the growth record of African countries compared with non-African developing countries. Real annual GDP growth was only 1 per cent on average for the 27 low-income countries currently eligible for assistance under the Special Program of Assistance (SPA) in 1980–4, while real exports declined by 2.9 per cent per year (weighted averages).[2] The memorandum item in the

Table 2.1 Real GDP and real export growth rates in sub-Saharan Africa, 1980–90 (% per annum)

	1980–4		*1985–7*		*1988–90*	
	GDP	*Export*	*GDP*	*Export*	*GDP*	*Export*
SPA countries	1.0 (1.1)	–2.9 (–1.9)	3.7 (3.1)	3.4 (1.8)	3.0 (2.9)	4.1 (4.1)
IBRD borrowers (except Nigeria)	3.8 (5.2)	6.3 (7.4)	1.7 (1.3)	2.3 (3.0)	–0.3 (2.3)	5.0 (5.0)
Nigeria	–4.7	–15.1	3.2	0.9	7.3	10.0
Sub–Saharan Africa	0.8 (1.7)	–5.1 (–0.9)	2.6 (2.7)	2.0 (2.0)	2.7 (3.1)	5.8 (3.9)
Memorandum items:						
OECD growth	1.7		3.0		3.3	
SPA terms of trade change	–1.5		–0.6		–2.4	

Source: World Bank data files.

table serves as a reminder that during this period the developing countries faced both declining terms of trade (for the SPA countries, by 1.5 per cent per annum on average) *and* low OECD growth (of just 1.7 per cent annually).

The origins of structural adjustment can also be traced from an institutional perspective. After all, the term 'structural adjustment' as it is currently understood was first coined in the context of the World Bank. It is associated with a particular lending window of the Bank: an instrument defined as quick-disbursing, exceptional balance of payments financing, based on economy-wide conditionality. Williamson (1990) and Mosley et al. (1991) suggest that the Bank engaged in this new initiative because of the limitations of project financing. This was in part because project financing could not be disbursed quickly enough at a time when developing countries were facing serious balance of payments crises. It served both the recipient countries' and the Bank's interests to find an alternative lending instrument that could restore external financial flows.

The attraction of programme lending derived from other limitations of project financing, which stemmed from government controls and policy-induced price distortions (Toye, 1993). While these distortions could be corrected in project appraisal through the use of appropriately specified shadow and border prices, if they were not corrected in practice, as Toye (1993) states, 'the whole enterprise of development by means of projects becomes attenuated'. Structural adjustment therefore represented a major change in tactic: rather than simply making corrections for price distortions in evaluating the worth of projects, the Bank sought to get prices right in the first place. For this, the recipient countries had to be convinced of the benefits of the change. And structural adjustment lending was unveiled as the instrument to encourage this.

In some respects, the changes which were taking place institutionally within the World Bank were a reflection of more deep-seated rethinking in the broader body of the political–economic literature. This involved a break-up of the neo-Keynesian consensus, and a revival of the neo-classical approach to policy-making. The view that 'good economics' was as applicable to advanced countries as to developing nations meant that the changes in economic policy in the USA, UK and Germany (so-called 'supply-side' economics or monetarism), were also relevant to the developing countries. This became the predominant view, taking over from the 'structuralist' approach which had placed emphasis on the peculiar characteristics of the developing countries and the limits of the special (developed country) case.

III RATIONALE AND CONTENT

In its newer theoretical and institutional form, structural adjustment rests on three main components: the importance of *macroeconomic stability*; the need for *prices* to reflect relative scarcities; and a reduction in the *role of the state* in directing and administering economic activity. Each of these components of structural adjustment interacts with the others, and the distinction between them should not be taken too far. According to the 'Washington consensus' (Williamson, 1990), the developing countries were generally found wanting on all three counts during the 1970s and early 1980s: they incurred unsustainable fiscal and external deficits, which in turn led to monetary indiscipline; controls and policy-induced price distortions were endemic; and governments tended to engage directly in economic activities, including production and financial intermediation. All three conditions were considered to be impediments to sustainable and equitable growth.

(A) Macroeconomic stability

A common distinction found in the literature is that between stabilisation and structural adjustment. The former is a short-run policy objective, concerned mainly with bringing aggregate demand into line with available resources (including external resources). Stabilisation policies, therefore, aim at returning the economy to an equilibrium path that was followed prior to a shock (the shock being temporary and reversible). Given its short-run perspective, stabilisation policies tend to rely more on demand management. Structural adjustment policies, on the other hand, seek to change the configuration of the equilibrium itself, encouraging efficient resource allocation and mobilisation, and thereby increased economic growth (Buiter, 1988). Such policies are particularly needed in response to permanent and irreversible shocks.

Generally, stabilisation should precede structural adjustment. Macroeconomic distortions can make it difficult, if not impossible, to achieve microeconomic policy objectives. The classic example of this is the persistence of an overvalued exchange rate (caused by macroeconomic mismanagement) and its effect on agricultural production incentives (Krueger et al., 1991). However, microeconomic distortions can also influence macroeconomic balances (such as food subsidies and their effect on the fiscal deficit). In some cases, therefore, structural changes may be required to stabilise the economy, as in the case of financial and public enterprise reforms in Eastern Europe. It is generally acknowledged that some structural adjustment policies can be destabilising (a reduction in tariff duties, for instance, which reduces government revenue), while others enhance it (such as the replacement of controls with tariffs).

The key role of the fiscal deficit has recently been highlighted. Without sound fiscal management, governments find it impossible to maintain external balance and stable prices. Moreover, the evidence suggests that unsustainable fiscal deficits are not conducive to growth. On the basis of ten country case studies, Easterly and Schmidt-Hebbel (1993) conclude that

> . . . fiscal deficits and growth are self-reinforcing: good fiscal management preserves access to foreign lending and avoids the crowding out of private investment, while growth stabilizes the budget and improves the fiscal position. The virtuous circle of growth and good fiscal management is one of the strongest arguments for a policy of low and stable fiscal deficits.

(B) Prices and scarcities

The second tenet of structural adjustment is the need for market prices to reflect relative scarcities. This applies as much to factor as to product markets, though greater attention is generally paid to the latter. Whereas the strategy under project lending was to evaluate projects using shadow prices, relying on indirect approaches (such as moral suasion) to encourage more rational economic policies, structural adjustment lending seeks to get actual prices in line with shadow prices – that is, remove the distortions.

Three main policy tools have been used to correct the price distortions in the product market. The first is an adjustment in the *nominal exchange rate*. If combined with a consistent fiscal and monetary policy, this would lead to a real exchange rate depreciation, and correct the previously distorted relative price between tradables and non-tradables (Edwards, 1989).

Secondly, structural adjustment programmes (SAP) have sought to encourage *trade liberalisation*, which involves the removal of import controls and other quantitative restrictions as well as a unification and general reduction in the structure of tariffs. The rationale for this component of the current orthodoxy has a long and deep-rooted history in economic thought. More recently, the contributions of Little et al. (1970), Corden (1974) and Balassa (1976) have reinforced the argument for trade liberalisation.[3] Similarly, the more recent endogenous growth literature has indicated that economic policy can affect growth, and that countries with more open economies tend to experience higher growth rates. The crux of the argument, as stated by Dollar (1992), 'is that outward-oriented policies, reflected in a level of the real exchange rate that encourages exports . . . fostered the development of the tradables sector in Asia, whereas inward orientation and an overvalued exchange rate encouraged growth in the non-tradable sector in Latin America and Africa'.

The third policy tool is *product-market liberalisation*. There would be little purpose in liberalising trade regimes if the incentives so created were not effectively passed on to producers. Yet, in many low-income countries, the marketing of agricultural produce has been controlled and often directly undertaken by government agencies. Given the limited opportunities on the revenue side, governments have not been able to resist the temptation to use these price-setting powers to raise revenue. In Côte d'Ivoire, for example, the Agricultural Price Stabilization Fund generated revenues amounting to as much as 15 per cent of GDP (in 1977). Marketing boards have therefore driven a wedge between world and producer prices, thus discouraging production and investment in export agriculture. In order to avoid overtaxing the rural sector, structural adjustment policies frequently reduce the role of government in crop marketing.

The philosophy of getting prices right is also applied to factor markets. Most SAPs include *financial sector* reforms. These are generally aimed at improving the functioning of the domestic financial market, removing distortions and controls, and allowing interest rates to respond freely to market forces. As with trade policy reform, the reforms of the financial sector derive from a long-standing concern in the development literature (see especially McKinnon, 1973). More recently, King and Levine (1992) have shown that financial system indicators are closely associated with economic growth. A well-functioning financial sector raises both the level and efficiency of investment in the economy, and thereby encourages growth.

The banking system in Africa remained in a precarious situation for much of the 1980s. At the root of its problems were the large fiscal deficits, the reliance of public enterprises on the domestic financial system, and an increasing portfolio of bad debt. Government interference in the credit process (often for political purposes) frequently made matters worse. Adjustment policies have sought to achieve three main financial sector objectives: reduction of financial repression by removing ceilings on interest rates; restoration of solvency to the system, often requiring bank restructuring; and improvements in bank 'infrastructure'.

The *labour market* is viewed as critical to the success of an adjustment programme. In the short run, the stabilisation objective usually depends on real wage flexibility. In the medium term, structural adjustment implies resource transfers, which in turn require labour market 'flexibility'. However, the role of the labour market has not been fully integrated into the design of SAPs, and there remains much to be done on the research agenda in this field.

(C) Revising the role of the state

The third component of structural adjustment was a fundamental revision in the role of the state in economic affairs. The background to this is well described by Toye (1991, 1993), who contrasts the pre-adjustment view of the state as independent and benevolent, with the view taken under structural adjustment. According to the latter, the state is but one of many actors involved in economic affairs, to be counted on a par with other economic institutions (firms, households, banks, and so on). As such, the state would safeguard first and foremost its own interests. In part deriving from this, economic policy and practice became urban-biased, as governments sought to reward their urban-based support (see Chapter 8 for a critique of this thesis).

The state has traditionally played a dominant role in economic affairs in Africa, being an all-pervasive allocator of resources, distributor of goods and services and controller of economic activities. Even after a period of adjustment, Ghana, for instance, still has more than 300 public enterprises (in Africa, only Tanzania has more). In Kenya, the government owns equity in about 250 commercially oriented enterprises, and the parastatal sector comprises 11 per cent of GDP. All of Burundi's cash crops and 60 per cent of its manufacturing output are directly controlled by the state. These are but a few of the many examples which could be given, illustrating how the state continues to assume a dominant role.

The task of persuading governments to reduce their direct role in economic activities has not been an easy one. Clearly, structural adjustment faced opposition from groups benefiting from the status quo and the urban bias it implied. Van de Walle (1991) provides an excellent example of these difficulties in the context of reform in countries within the CFA franc zone. As discussed below, structural adjustments requiring institutional changes of this sort have been the most difficult to implement. The evidence to date is that very little progress has been made (at least during the 1980s) in African governments redefining their roles. Such a redefinition should emphasise activities in which state intervention is both justified and effective: acting as a facilitator and catalyst in mobilising resources; ensuring a level playing-field for all actors engaged in economic activity; providing economic and social infrastructure and other public goods; and providing services to assist the poor and vulnerable.

IV ASSESSING THE ACHIEVEMENTS

This section examines the achievements of structural adjustment. Most assessments of SAPs, especially those in sub-Saharan Africa, have been pessimistic about their outcomes. Despite the considerable effort that has been invested in assessing the effects of these programmes (both within the Bank and outside), the story has not yet been properly told.

Stewart (1991a) argues that:

> ... the balance of experience in the 1980s was undoubtedly negative.... Among the adjusting countries of sub-Saharan Africa, three quarters had declining per capita incomes, over half had declining investment and accelerating inflation.... The adjustment policies did not succeed – except in a minority of cases - in restoring economic growth.

There is a danger, however, in drawing misleading conclusions from aggregative data of this kind.

By way of illustration, consider the data previously presented in Table 2.1. Taken as a whole, the SPA countries experienced an annual increase in real GDP growth from just 1 per cent in 1980–4 to 3.7 per cent in 1985–7 (when external circumstances were generally more favourable) and 3.0 per cent in 1988–90 (when the terms of trade declined markedly). This 'growth turnaround', however, is not uniform among the SPA countries. Table 2.2 suggests a disaggregation of the SPA countries based on judgements made about the intensity

Table 2.2 Economic performance of SPA countries, 1980–90

	1980–4	*1985–7*	*1988–90*
	(% per annum)		
Growth of real GDP:			
Group A	−0.6 (0.3)	4.2 (3.6)	3.9 (3.5)
Group B	2.5 (2.2)	4.1 (3.0)	2.8 (2.2)
Group C	1.8 (−1.4)	1.8 (1.7)	2.3 (2.2)
Growth of real exports:			
Group A	−6.7 (−2.1)	8.1 (3.0)	6.9 (6.0)
Group B	0.2 (−0.8)	3.2 (2.8)	2.9 (2.2)
Group C	−7.2 (−6.1)	−3.5 (−3.9)	3.4 (2.9)
Growth of real imports:			
Group A	−5.6 (−3.8)	9.2 (3.8)	4.7 (6.8)
Group B	−5.8 (−3.2)	4.6 (2.2)	2.8 (1.6)
Group C	−7.9 (−5.8)	−3.4 (−3.0)	−0.2 (−0.7)
Growth of real domestic investment:			
Group A	−4.7 (0.3)	13.1 (8.3)	6.1 (5.7)
Group B	−4.8 (0.3)	5.1 (2.1)	1.3 (−0.1)
Group C	−13.3 (0.3)	11.1 (26.7)	8.7 (4.9)

Notes:
Group A: Burkina Faso, Burundi, Gambia, Ghana, Malawi, Mali, Mozambique, Sao Tome and Principe, Tanzania and Uganda.
Group B: Benin, Equatorial Guinea, Ethiopia, Guinea, Kenya, Mauritania, Rwanda, Senegal, Sierra Leone, Togo and Zambia.
Group C: Chad, Central African Republic, Comoros, Madagascar and Niger.
Averages are weighted. Figures in parenthesis are unweighted averages.

Source: World Bank data files.

and persistence of adjustment programmes. Group A countries are those judged to have consistently implemented adjustment programmes. At the other end, Group C countries were those considered to have been seriously off-track. Group B were considered intermittent in their adjustment efforts.[4] The turnarounds in Group A growth rates (both GDP and exports) are noticeably greater than those of Groups B and C. These data are not presented as a means of proving that adjustment works, since the judgements made in grouping the countries might be considered at best arbitrary and, at worst, a *result* of the better performance of some countries. Rather, this table simply illustrates the dangers of over-generalisation based on data aggregates.

Second, the aggregate approach ignores the effects of other factors, such as initial conditions and exogenous shocks (for example, the continued terms of trade decline). Finally, it fails to consider the counterfactual case: Were actual outcomes better or worse than would have happened in the absence of the policy reforms.[5]

Rather than playing games with aggregate statistics, it is important to take these factors into account. A number of studies based on a more refined approach have recently been carried out. But again, the conclusion, though less harshly critical of structural adjustment, is nevertheless generally unfavourable. The Bank's own assessments of its structural adjustment lending have uncovered only limited success. In all, it has conducted three major reviews of adjustment lending (RAL), which are summarised and discussed in Corbo et al. (1992). After controlling for the effects of variations in initial conditions, external shocks and financing, adjusting countries experienced higher GDP and export growth than non-adjusting countries, but lower levels of investment. The growth premium appears to have been lower in sub-Saharan Africa than elsewhere. These results are similar to those obtained by Mosley et al. (1991), which were summarised by the authors as being favourable to export growth and the external account, unfavourable to investment and, on balance, neutral to national income: in short, 'disappointing'.

These judgements, though based on more rigorous statistical analyses, do not provide a robust and reliable guide to policy choice for the following reasons. First, several studies fail to make the key distinction between the effects of *financing* and those of *policy reforms*. This criticism applies particularly to the RALs, which were in actual fact assessments of the Bank's structural adjustment *loans*, and not of structural adjustment *policies* as such. This point is taken up by Mosley et al. (1991), who distinguish between the effects of policy reforms and external finance. They find that while the effect of structural adjustment on national income is neutral, this neutrality is a result of two opposing effects. First, policy reforms appear to have a positive effect on national income but this is counteracted by the negative effect of increased external financing. They surmise that the negative effect of external flows may result from countries using finance as a substitute for painful reforms. Their results, however, were only statistically significant for middle-income countries, and depended critically on the lag structure assumed. There may also be problems of multicolinearity among the regressors in the specification adopted. The 'compliance with conditionality' variable is likely to be correlated with financial flow variables. In sum, their results are not sufficiently robust, so that this remains a hypothesis to be tested further.[6]

This leads to a third problem with the studies carried out to date: they do insufficient justice to variations in the degree of policy implementation in the countries. Mosley (1992) criticised the RAL exercises, even in their most sophisticated form,[7] as paying insufficient attention to differences in policy reform. The dichotomous dummy variable, based on whether the country was an 'early intensive adjuster' or not, is simply too crude a measure of policy change. Some countries included in this group (such as Turkey) complied in large measure to loan conditionality, but others were far short of what was required in the implementation of policy reforms (such as Côte d'Ivoire: see Demery, 1993).

Unfortunately, the more thorough analysis of Mosley et al. (1991) does not deal with this problem adequately either. Their 'compliance with conditionality' variable (ranging from 0 for no SAL to 3 for 'high compliance') is also only a crude approximation of actual policy implementation. And it is defined only in terms of loan conditionality, rather than the policy changes themselves (some of which may not have been subject to SAL conditionality). Most, if not all, previous studies have therefore failed to come to grips with this issue of variations in policy design and implementation. Few, if any, for instance, distinguish between countries operating under a fixed exchange rate regime (such as those in the CFA franc zone) and those that have achieved significant changes in their real exchange rates. Such differences, however, are critical to an understanding of how structural adjustment works.

While the disaggregation of Table 2.2 does not prove anything, it is suggestive of an interaction between a persistent application of policy reforms and improved economic outcomes. Further work on assessing whether structural adjustment policies work, therefore, must formulate more refined measures of the degree of policy reform actually carried out. Without such measures, it is impossible to judge whether the poor performance of 'structural adjustment' is due to the fact that the policies have not worked, or have simply not been implemented consistently. It must be recognised, however, that the methodological problems in generating such measures are bound to be challenging.

V THE ROLE OF EXTERNAL FINANCE

Assessments of the effects of structural adjustment have therefore failed to specify correctly an appropriate empirical test which measures with some sensitivity the degree of policy reform. Similarly, previous work has been inconclusive about the role of external finance in the adjustment process. The rationale of providing quick-disbursing finance as part of an adjustment package has been the subject of some debate. The World Bank has taken the view that it is necessary to support structural adjustment through programme loans in order to ease the transition path and reduce the costs of the adjustment (see Srinivasan, 1993, for a rigorous analytical defence of this view). This smoothing of the adjustment process is particularly important when countries are subject to large permanent shocks. This was one of the central messages of UNICEF's early critique (Cornia et al., 1987). If additional time can be bought, the transition is likely to be less painful. Others view the rationale as deriving from political considerations: the need for some leverage to entice countries to undertake the reforms; or the objective of the Bank to 'gain a purchase on high policy' (Mosley et al., 1991).

As with the effects of the policy reforms themselves, there has been some debate about the benefits or otherwise of adjustment finance. On the one hand, Mosley et al. (1991) provide some tentative evidence that finance might perversely delay or discourage policy reform, and thereby harm economic performance. On the other hand, contributors such as Helleiner (1992a) have argued that finance not only improves performance, but is more important than the policy reforms themselves. In his words, 'these financial requisites are much more important to the credibility and sustainability of adjustment efforts than the uncertain outcome of such ongoing debates as those about the purported virtues of "shock" reforms as against step-by-step confidence building efforts'. While the jury is still out on this question, some recent estimates reported in Demery and Husain (1993) suggest complementary roles for finance and policy. They calculated net ODA and net transfer flows to 24 SPA countries for which data are available (see Table 2.3). Both measures are adjusted for changes in import prices (thus expressing the flows in terms of their import-purchasing power), and for terms of trade changes. There are a number of ways in which to estimate the real income transfer effect of changes in the net barter terms of trade. This they define as the difference between the import capacity of exports (X/P_m) and real exports (X/P_n).[8] Estimates of the terms of trade effect were computed, taking 1987 as the base year. Because the terms of trade declined generally through the decade, for years prior to 1987 the terms of trade effect is positive (amounting on average to US$ 643 million annually in

Table 2.3 Net ODA and external transfers adjusted for terms of trade effects, SPA countries, 1980–91

	1981–6	*1987–91*
	(US$ millions unless otherwise indicated)	
All SPA countries:	(annual averages)	
1. Net ODA flows	4990	9495
2. Net external transfers	4220	6742
3. Real GDP (1987 US$m)	49 344	57 691
4. Real net ODA (1. deflated by P_m)	5283	8910
5. Real net transfers (2. deflated by P_m)	4454	6328
6. Real imports (deflated by P_m)	10 586	11 898
7. Real exports (deflated by P_x)	6848	8296
8. Real ToT gain/loss	643	–392
9. Real ODA net of ToT gain/loss	5926	8518
10. (9) as % of real GDP	12.3%	14.8%
11. (9) as % of real imports	57.6%	71.6%
12. Real transfers net of ToT gain/loss	5097	5936
13. (12) as % of real GDP	10.3%	10.3%
14. (12) as % of real imports	48.3%	49.8%
Average annual growth rates (%):	1981–6	1987–91
15. Net ODA flows	6.4	10.3
16. Net external transfers	2.9	10.4
17. Real GDP	1.5	3.1
18. Real net ODA	8.5	6.1
19. Real net transfers	4.9	6.2
20. Real imports	–2.5	1.6
21. Real exports	–0.6	4.3
22. Real ODA net of ToT gain/loss	6.9	1.0
23. Real transfers net of ToT gain/loss	3.8	–0.7

Source: World Bank data files.

1981–6: see line 8 of Table 2.3). For years after 1987, the declining terms of trade leads to a negative effect, averaging –US$ 392 million per year in 1987–91.

Even after adjusting for the terms of trade decline, real net ODA shows a significant turnaround during the decade (see Chapter 15). This increased from an annual average of US$ 5.9 billion in constant 1987 prices to US$ 8.5 billion. The flows on average account for almost 15 per cent of GDP in 1987–91 and 72 per cent of real imports (compared with 12 per cent and 58 per cent respectively during the earlier period). There is evidence, however, that the terms of trade losses have had a more serious effect since 1988. For example, real net ODA grew by 6.1 per cent per year in 1987–91 (line 18 of Table

2.3), but only by 1 per cent after adjusting for the terms of trade losses (line 22).

Expressed in real terms, the increase in net transfers during the decade is just as impressive: they were on average US$ 6.3 billion in 1987–91, a 42 per cent increase on the annual average in 1981–6.[9] Adjusting for the terms of trade changes reduces the turnaround in real net transfers somewhat, but Table 2.3 still indicates an increase in the annual average flows of about 16 per cent between the two periods. In both periods, the increase in net ODA flows has more than compensated for the growing debt service obligations of the SPA countries, leading to high positive net transfers. However, real net transfers as a proportion of real GDP and real imports were virtually unchanged during the two periods (at about 10 per cent and 50 per cent respectively).

As with net ODA flows, the growth rate of real net transfers was significantly reduced by the terms of trade deterioration towards the end of the 1980s. Whereas real net transfers grew by 6.2 per cent in 1987–91 (line 19 of Table 2.3), they are shown to decline annually by 0.7 per cent on average after the terms of trade adjustment (line 23). Clearly, without the substantial growth in net ODA in the 1987–91 period, the financing situation of the recipient countries would have been parlous.

Table 2.3 provides some indication of the relative contributions of external finance and domestic policy reform. If we assume that the turnaround in real imports has been critical for these 24 countries,[10] it is clear that there have been two main factors instrumental in improving economic performance. The first has been the increase in net transfers to these countries, and the second is the marked increase in real exports. Demery and Husain estimate that the turnaround in exports (deflated by the import price) accounts for 58 per cent of the turnaround in real imports. In so far as the export performance of these countries is a result of policy reforms, this accounting indicates that both external finance and improved policy performance are responsible for the increase in real imports enjoyed by these countries.

VI SOME KEY ISSUES

By way of conclusion, this section seeks to review some of the key issues raised in the literature, especially those that may be considered (by policy makers and researchers alike) as unresolved.

(A) A failure of policies or of governments?

Perhaps the most important question on the research agenda is whether the disappointing outcomes of SAPs are due to the failure of the policies themselves, or of the governments to implement them. There is evidence that many governments have not been fully committed to the policy packages of loan conditionality. Given the large number of conditions accompanying many structural adjustment loans (SAL) and sectoral adjustment loans (SECAL), there is an opportunity for governments to outwit the international financial institutions by only partially implementing reforms in order to obtain the accompanying finance.

Quite apart from the terms of loan conditionality, some countries have faced serious institutional constraints which have made structural adjustment extremely difficult to achieve. The most important example in Africa is the CFA franc zone, and the difficulties many of the member countries have faced in achieving external balance through internal adjustment. In so far as adjustment has been achieved, it has been at the expense of economic growth and, to some extent, equity. The main problem faced by these countries is that their real exchange rates have appreciated along with a strengthening French franc (and German mark). Given declines in the terms of trade (which require a depreciating real exchange rate), there has been a marked tendency for the real exchange rate in many CFA countries to become overvalued. Internal adjustment has failed to achieve the necessary correction.

On the other hand, the CFA franc zone does offer exchange rate stability. Using data from the International Comparison Project, Helleiner (1992b) notes that the variability of the real exchange rate is much lower for the franc zone than for elsewhere in Africa (or in Asia for that matter). He concludes that 'provided the degree of "distortion" is not too great, one might think that the stability of incentives would count for a lot'. To what extent have the constraints imposed by the zone distorted real exchange rates in the member countries? Devarajan et al. (1993) find that the real exchange rate for Cameroon was overvalued by about 50 per cent in 1986. Using the same methodology, Berthélemy and Bourguignon (1992) estimate a real exchange rate overvaluation in Côte d'Ivoire in 1987 of the same order. These estimates suggest that the institutional constraints of the CFA franc zone have represented serious impediments to structural adjustment in many of its member countries, and limited their room for policy manoeuvre.

This raises the more general question of whether the recipient governments have the institutional capacity to implement the needed policy reforms effectively. The implementation of many government-owned programmes was often dogged by weak institutional and administrative capacities. Such governments may not have had difficulties in adjusting economic policy instruments (such as exchange rate adjustments or the removal of import controls), but found it difficult to implement reforms requiring institutional changes. Institutional weaknesses were always present to a greater degree in Africa, and it is hardly a surprise to observe that these countries have had greater difficulties than elsewhere in carrying out economic reforms (Toye, 1993). Two areas of slower progress in the reform effort in African countries are in the financial and public sectors. Both of these can only be achieved with fundamental institutional change, and governments have proved unable to implement such changes, at least within the time-frame provided under the adjustment programmes.

(B) Adjustment and sustainability

Quick-disbursing finance to support these programmes is understood to be *exceptional* balance of payments support, and not to be considered as part of the long-run capital inflows into the recipient countries. The adjustment process must, therefore, at some point be self-defeating, and adjustment lending must likewise dwindle. To what extent is there evidence of a move towards sustainability among African adjusters? The available evidence is mixed. On the one hand, agricultural and export growth has recovered remarkably and current account deficits have been reduced. On the other hand, the debt overhang and its servicing have yet to be dealt with adequately, countries of the region seem as dependent on external aid flows as they ever were, export diversification is slow, investment has dipped, and domestic resource mobilisation remains weak. These issues are discussed in turn.

1 Agricultural and export recovery

The turnaround in real export growth has been one of the most remarkable achievements of adjustment in the region. Table 2.1 reports that the decline in real exports of the SPA countries in 1980–4 was turned into average annual growth rates of 4.1 per cent in 1988–90. Moreover, for group A countries (see Table 2.2), the turnaround was even more remarkable – something of the order of 14 per cent.[11] Although real imports have also increased markedly (see Table 2.2), most adjusting countries have succeeded in reducing trade deficits as a result of this recovery in exports (and despite the worsening terms of trade). This export surge is due in the main to an increase in agricultural exports, particularly traditional exports, which has been facilitated by a recovery in agricultural production. Husain (1993) singles out Benin, Burkina Faso, Tanzania, Nigeria, Ghana, Guinea-Bissau and Kenya as achieving notable increases in agricultural output.

Other things being equal, such an increase in export volumes would be expected to take countries some way towards sustainability. Unfortunately, for most African countries things have not remained equal, and there are other factors that have militated against this enhancement of sustainability.

2 *Terms of trade declines and export concentration*

Clearly, one of the most important counteracting factors has been the previously observed decline in the net barter terms of trade of most of the adjusting countries. To reduce the vulnerability of the exporting countries to price shocks in world markets, export diversification is clearly called for (see Chapter 17). While there can be little doubt that Africa lags behind other developing regions regarding the degree of export diversification, there are emerging signs of change. Helleiner (1992b) reports the share of the top three primary products in total exports (as an imperfect indicator of diversification) for 34 African countries (26 of which are low-income countries). Although this share increased for all the countries between 1972–6 and 1977–81, it was estimated to have fallen to only 62 per cent in 1990. During the 1980s, 25 of the countries achieved reductions in export concentration so measured.

3 *Aid dependence and debt*

While the export growth rates have been sufficient to close trade balances, they have not been as successful in closing the current account gaps. This is because of the growing debt burdens that many low-income African countries now have to service. Unless better debt relief provisions are introduced, it is unlikely that many low-income countries of Africa will be able to achieve sustainable growth without continued inflows of exceptional balance of payments support.

The total debt stock of the 27 currently eligible SPA countries increased by $33 billion in 1985–91, reaching $64 billion by the end of 1991. A recent assessment (by the World Bank) of the adequacy of current debt relief provisions for these countries finds that to attain a sustainable debt situation, the SPA countries require debt relief of about $15 billion on a present value basis. This compares with the present value debt relief under current arrangements (Toronto and enhanced Toronto terms) of just $2 billion (between October 1988 and April 1993), and an additional debt reduction (on a present value basis) of $2.5 billion through cumulative ODA cancellation (during 1981–91). The shortfall in current arrangements is obvious from these numbers.

The situation, of course, varies country by country, depending on the size and composition of the debt stock. The Bank's assessment found that only six countries were not in need of debt reduction to maintain sustainability, and 11 countries require debt relief that is not available under existing institutional arrangements. The debt overhang can be considered as a major obstacle to sustainable growth for many of the affected countries, discouraging the inflow of private capital, without which it is difficult to imagine any sustained growth in the region. As Helleiner observes in Chapter 15 of this volume:

> Reducing the current external cash flow obligations and payments on debt accounts, particularly for those countries that are pursuing serious policy reforms and getting their macroeconomic fundamentals 'right', will thus most likely be the most cost-effective form of official external resource transfer to Africa in the 1990s.

4 Investment and domestic resource mobilisation

Most assessments of structural adjustment have raised the problem of the investment 'pause', this being a tendency for investment levels to fall during a period of policy reform. Even countries with persistent reform programmes have experienced flat investment levels during the transition. Comparative studies, such as Mosley et al. (1991), have found that the investment to GDP ratio falls during adjustment, though the African experience is mixed.

Structural adjustment can be expected to affect investment behaviour in four main ways (Collier, 1992). First, if adjustment involves stabilisation, a reduction in public investment will directly reduce fixed investment. However, the role of public investment in affecting the behaviour of private investors is also important. In the textbook case, public investment is viewed as 'crowding *out*' private investment. However, in the current conventional wisdom, for Africa at least, it is thought that if public investment is well directed (towards the provision of economic and social infrastructure) it will 'crowd *in*' the private investors. The cut in public investment, according to this view, has not only directly reduced domestic investment, but has indirectly discouraged private investors. The evidence on this is mixed. Easterly and Schmidt-Hebbel (1993) found that public sector investment boosted private investment in only three out of 10 case studies.

Second, in so far as there are resource switching effects of adjustment, these will raise the marginal efficiency of investment (Bevan et al., 1987), and *ceteris paribus* lead to an increase in fixed investment. Third, if structural adjustment leads to real exchange rate depreciations, the cost of imported investment goods will rise, which will lead to a switch to non-traded capital goods. The net effect on investment will depend on the responsiveness of the domestic capital-goods producing sector. Because downward adjustments in the demand for imported capital can be rapid, and because the increase in the supply of non-traded investment goods may be slow, an initial downturn in total fixed investment may occur (Collier, 1992). This effect can be avoided if the non-traded investment goods sector is highly responsive (and is itself free from undue government controls).

Finally, if structural adjustment programmes create uncertainty about the future (if economic agents, for example, consider the programme unsustainable), investment is likely to fall. The net effect of these three negative and one positive influences on investment is therefore ambiguous in theory. Most studies conclude that the negative effects tend to dominate.[12]

However, the data on which much analysis is based are extremely unreliable, so that care must be applied in interpreting them. If non-traded activities are more difficult to measure (for example, because they are produced in the informal sector), part of the observed decline in fixed investment may be due to this switch towards the non-traded component. A similar (spurious) effect arises from the inducement under protectionist trade regimes to over-invoice capital goods imports (in order to maximise command over foreign exchange). Trade liberalisation will reduce the incentive to over-invoice, and thus result in a spurious fall in estimates of investment goods imports. It is difficult (if not impossible) to measure how important these spurious effects are.[13]

Low *domestic savings* also indicate that many African adjusting countries have some way to go in achieving sustainable growth. Savings rates of around 25 per cent of GDP are needed if annual GDP growth of 6 per cent is to be achieved for any length of time. Yet, savings in the adjusting countries of Africa are only around 9 per cent of GDP, although these vary significantly by country (see Table 2.2). Low savings rates can be attributed to the persistence of public sector deficits in many countries, unsustainable macroeconomic policies, and limited development of the financial sector.

VII CONCLUDING OBSERVATIONS

This brief review of the structural adjustment debate obviously cannot do justice to the vast literature that now exists on the subject. Our main concern has been to establish why there remains a lack of consensus on how successful the adjustment efforts have been. There are probably three main reasons for this. Firstly, most programmes have had mixed effects, so that the judgement about whether they have worked depends on the relative weighting of the various results. Countries have made some headway in correcting for the major price distortions that plagued most African economies during the 1970s and early 1980s, particularly with regard to real exchange rate adjustments (excluding countries of the CFA franc zone), but reforms that require institutional changes have been slow. The response to these mixed effects depends on whether the cup is viewed as half full or half empty.

The second reason for a lack of consensus lies in the weaknesses of the assessments that have been made so far. Existing studies have not yet presented convincing evidence one way or the other about the effects of structural adjustment policies, and the main reason for this has been the failure to measure policy reform in the countries concerned. There are limits even in the most sophisticated tests so far conducted. Until a more detailed empirical inquiry is undertaken in which such measures are adopted, the impression will continue that this remains a story largely untold.

Finally, it is possible that insufficient time has elapsed for most adjusting countries to display the effects of policy change. The claims made for structural adjustment policies were undoubtedly oversold at the beginning of the endeavour. Given the historical constraints of economic performance in Africa, it must be acknowledged that the process is likely to require more time than was originally envisaged. Whether the data to hand allow sufficient time to test the effects of structural adjustment in the African setting is very much open to question.

In sum, there is much more work to be done before a definitive assessment can be made of how these policy changes have worked. There is evidence that adjusting countries have achieved a great deal in resolving the first two items on the agenda: reducing macroeconomic imbalances and removing price distortions from product markets. But the third agenda item (a revision in the role of the state) and other items that require institutional change (such as financial sector reform), have not been properly addressed. These changes involving institutional reform may best be considered as part of the process of long-term development, and as such they require time and capacity building before the results can be seen.

NOTES

1. Van der Hoeven (1991) reviews the changes that have taken place since 1987 in the design of adjustment policy, which in part have emerged from the UNICEF critique. See also Jolly (1991).
2. The message is the same with unweighted averages.
3. More recently still, Helpman and Krugman (1985) have argued that in the presence of externalities and economies of scale, free trade is unlikely to be the optimal policy strategy. Such arguments are reinforced by the East Asian experience, where governments played a key role in export-led growth. Despite this, Corbo and Fischer (1992), in their rationale for structural adjustment lending, conclude that free trade remains a good rule of thumb.
4. These judgements were made by the World Bank's country departments as part of their regular reporting to SPA. They are qualitative in nature and, as such, are open to debate.
5. Stewart (1991a) dismisses the counterfactual approach in dealing with the effects on human conditions, 'since it is actual developments which are significant'. But if alternative approaches produce less favourable welfare outcomes, this surely must be taken into account in seeking solutions to social problems.
6. The somewhat limited time period covered by the regression analysis of the study (1980–6) also limits its usefulness in assessing the effects of many adjustment programmes that began only in the mid-1980s.
7. This being the assessment based on modified control-group estimator (see Corbo and Rojas, 1992; Elbadawi, 1992). Other, less rigorous, assessments are also open to the criticism of grouping together countries with wide variations in policy reform as 'adjusting' countries (see for example, Khan, 1992; Jespersen, 1992).
8. Given the national income accounts identities (in constant prices):
   Gross domestic product: GDP $\equiv C + I + X - M$ and
   Gross domestic income: GDY $\equiv C + I + (X/P_m) + M$
   it follows that GDY $\equiv$ GDP + $[(X/P_m) - (X/P_x)]$. The term in the square bracket gives the terms of trade effect.

9. It should be emphasised that this analysis is limited to low-income African countries. Trends for the developing countries as a whole are quite different (see van der Hoeven, 1991).
10. This derives from the fact that many of these economies were seriously constrained by import shortages during the early 1980s, and that the surge in imports that has taken place has comprised mainly intermediate and capital goods (see Demery and Husain, 1993).
11. The unweighted data tell the same story, but the turnaround is less marked.
12. The evidence is far from certain, however. Table 2.2 reports a group of low-income adjusting countries in Africa raising real investment rates significantly during periods of adjustment.
13. But see Collier (1992), who suggests that this may be an important explanation for Nigeria's apparent investment decline.

3 An African Perspective on Long-term Development in Sub-Saharan Africa

Befekadu Degefe

I INTRODUCTION

For the developing countries as a whole, the 1980s have been characterised as the 'lost decade', ten years of dismal economic performance and consequential erosion of welfare (Singer, 1989; Fischer, 1991). Economic growth rates plummeted from an annual average of 6 per cent between 1965 and 1980 to 3 per cent during the 1980s (World Bank, 1992a).

For countries in sub-Saharan Africa (SSA), the downturn was even more drastic: from an annual average of 6 per cent between 1965 and 1973 to 2.5 per cent during the 1973–80 period and down to about 1 per cent during the 1980s (World Bank, 1989a; UNDP, 1993b). With population growth estimated at 2.6, 2.8 and 3.2 per cent per year during the three respective periods (World Bank, 1990c), per capita income has consistently declined during the last two decades.

These statistics – however grim – conceal the extent and intensity of the vast human suffering in sub-Saharan Africa. Given the rising inequality in the distribution of income and assets, a growing proportion of the population became vulnerable as the economic erosion gained momentum. The proportion of the poor, i.e. that part of the population subsisting on about US$1 a day, increased from 47 per cent (184 million) in 1980 to 48 per cent (216 million) in 1990 and is projected to increase to 50 per cent (304 million) by the year 2000 (World Bank, 1992a).

The 1980s can also be identified as the decade of the Structural Adjustment Programme (SAP). Practically all developing countries, particularly those in Latin America and SSA, adopted this World Bank and Fund inspired model to rejuvenate their economies. Structural Adjustment Programmes (SAP) had the declared objectives of 'improving the current account and the overall balance of payments, achieving a satisfactory rate of growth and reducing inflation' (Khan, 1990, and various World Bank documents). The attainment of these objectives required extensive and intensive institutional and policy reforms.

The simultaneity of the 'lost decade' and the 'SAP decade' transcends mere coincidence. SAPs were implemented, with differing degrees of intensity, in almost 40 countries in SSA. The results were less than satisfactory. An impartial assessment shows that the objectives of such programmes, i.e. structural adjustment within an environment of stable prices and sustainable balance of payments, were only remotely related to what actually happened. In two recent papers reviewing economic performances in SAP-implementing countries, Elbadawi and co-researchers (Elbadawi, 1992; Elbadawi et al., 1992) empirically established that non-adjusting SSA countries outperformed the adjusting SSA countries in investment, domestic savings, exports, external dependence (measured by the resource gap) as well as inflation.

The World Bank's review of performance in 29 adjusting SSA countries revealed that per capita income increased by less than 2 per cent in five countries and by more than 3 per cent in only two (World Bank, 1992a). Even if these rates of growth are deemed satisfactory, their being limited to five (or seven, of which two are oil exporters) out of 29 of the adjusting countries casts strong doubts on whether these achievements were due to or in spite of SAP-induced policies.

The current crisis in the SSA countries is the cumulative result of inappropriate domestic policies dating back to the early 1960s exacerbated by a hostile external environment. The SAP, although evangelised as a quick and effective antidote, has been shown to be inefficient and inadequate. This chapter presents a critique of the development strategy followed in SSA (Section II) and the SAP model (Section III) and outlines a more pragmatic alternative to SAP (Sections IV and V). Section VI is a succinct summary of the chapter.

II DEVELOPMENT STRATEGY: IDENTIFYING ERRORS OF THE PAST

The sources and causes of the socioeconomic crisis in sub-Saharan Africa pre-date the SAP era. Their genesis lies in the inappropriate development strategy initiated in the 1960s by the first generation of leaders and faithfully pursued thereafter. The advantage of hindsight points to two basic problems in the development strategies adopted then: the inappropriate application of the import substituting industrialisation (ISI) strategy and the related impoverishment of the rural economy to accomplish the goals of industrialisation.

The industrialisation model pursued in SSA, though caricatured as the ISI, was very different from and markedly unfaithful to the essence and processes articulated by its promoters (for example Prebisch, 1959, 1964; Hirschman, 1958). The cardinal objectives of the ISI strategy, according to its designers, were to ameliorate the balance of payment constraints, create productive employment opportunities for the surplus agricultural labour force (Lewis, 1954) and thereby bring about an orderly socioeconomic transition to modernity. The transition process was also clearly specified: beginning with the production of light consumer goods for which there was a ready domestic market, moving then to intermediate goods, and finally to capital goods. At the same time, the evolving industrial sector was to create strong forward and backward linkages with the traditional economic activities. Local infant industries would enjoy protection from external competition until they matured. The symbiotic relationship between and within the different sectors was expected to bring about an independent and dynamic economy.

Unfortunately, the industrialisation formulae implemented were, however, far removed from this blueprint. The initial stages of substituting imported light consumer goods for local production were completed, and that was as far as the process went. The manufacturing industries were accorded protection, including quantitative restrictions and high to prohibitive tariffs.

Such an industrialisation pattern rendered the SSA economies hostage to foreign exchange. Maintenance of already installed capacity and expansion of the industrial sector through new investment required a growing volume of foreign exchange. This was one of the cardinal errors of the industrialisation drive. Rather than decreasing dependence on external factors and ameliorating the balance of payments, they were worsened. Rather than creating a dynamic linkage with the rest of the economy, industry remained an enclave.

Damage to the local economy would have been bearable had the industrial sector self-financed its growing foreign exchange needs. Instead, the burden of financing capacity utilisation as well as new investment was borne by the agricultural sector. With adequate support and development, agriculture could have provided the resources required for industrialisation. On the contrary, it was not only neglected but was severely impoverished by the continual drainage of financial, human and physical resources. The pauperisation of agriculture deepened the poverty of the rural masses, producing a multiplier effect on the rest of the economy.

The educational and training systems developed in support of ISI were no less damaging to agriculture and the rural economy. Urban-biased in location, they were specifically designed to produce manpower for the small but stagnant modern sector. Even in the most agriculture-dependent economies, agricultural education and training remained minimal or non-existent. The negative consequences of this faulty development strategy grew increasingly evident and severe. Industry failed to develop, despite the many advantages it enjoyed, partly due to limited domestic demand, especially from the vast rural majority. Agricultural production, particularly per capita food production, declined, thereby increasing dependence on imports. Between 1974 and 1990, imports of cereals nearly doubled in volume (World Bank, 1992a; see also Chapters 11 and 12). As the rural sector grew more impoverished and the rate of population growth increased, environmental degradation and imbalanced urbanisation set in, with the consequent informalisation of production, trade and services.

In summary, the crisis in SSA countries resulted from the inappropriate application of the ISI strategy and the reckless exploitation of agriculture and the vast rural population. Yet, as there is no future in the production and export of primary commodities, these countries need to expand their industrial base in an efficient manner. No country has ever succeeded in transforming itself from primary commodity or service (particularly labour) exporter to exporter of manufactured goods without going through an appropriate import substitution phase.

III STRUCTURAL ADJUSTMENT PROGRAMMES: QUESTIONS OF RELEVANCE

The SAP was introduced in the early 1980s as an antidote to the growing socioeconomic crisis in sub-Saharan countries. To their credit, African policy makers entertained no illusions about the efficacy and efficiency of SAP, but adopted it under duress. At a time when developing countries in general and SSA countries in particular were desperately reaching out for external assistance, the SAP came in with bilateral, multilateral and private sources of credit mobilised behind it. External assistance and credit from the developed market economies were conditional to adopting a SAP.

While it was claimed that SAP would provide a new and effective approach to and resources for economies in distress, in effect it includes many of the components typical of the stabilisation programmes of the IMF. In its 1984 *World Development Report*, the World Bank castigated the IMF for its growth-unfriendly and anti-poor stabilisation paradigm. It noted that higher taxes and interest rates squeezed the private sector and restricted long-term growth, while the reduction or elimination of subsidies on food, education and health decreased real income, worsened the plight of the poor and damaged growth potential (Bernstein and Boughton, 1993). No better criticism can be made of the Bank's own SAP which, despite its nobler intentions of endowing developing economies with the strategies and wherewithals for sustained growth and development, adopted the Fund's policies and implemented them with greater vigour. Countries were compelled to devalue their currencies, scrap all quantitative restrictions and slash tariffs to decrease their current account deficit; raise interest rates, tighten the money supply and purge the state from active participation in the economy; to boost and rationalise investment. In addition the elimination of subsidies on food and cost-sharing in education and health was recommended as a means of decreasing government deficit and of converting the indolent poor into vigorous entrepreneurs.

Although such an approach may seem flawed to students of economic development, the SAP policy stance was nevertheless a logical conclusion of the premises from which it is sourced. Briefly the Bank/Fund reasoning begins and proceeds from the assumption that the causes of the crisis in SSA countries are of purely domestic origin and are directly proportional to the degree of deviation of these economies from laissez-faire standards. Salvation is as simple as the diagnosis: a return to the sanctum of free enterprise. The road to atonement included limiting the economic role of the state to the barest minimum and maintaining an open market both inside and out.

(A) The burden of adjustment

While the negative impact of inappropriate domestic policies cannot be denied, the SAP model unduly focuses on the domestic front as the cause of socioeconomic dislocation and crisis and fails to acknowledge the contribution of the hostile external environment. Though the decline in the volume of exports has certainly contributed to the crisis of the 1980s, numerous studies confirm and quantify the tremendous loss of the purchasing power of SSA exports due to deteriorating terms of trade and increases in real interest rates. By the early 1990s the purchasing power of SSA exportables was 34 per cent lower than in 1980 (UNCTAD, 1993). Relative to the 1970s, the 1980s interest rate and terms of trade shock was estimated at 30 per cent of the GDP of that decade. Between 1970 and 1990, the terms of trade of mineral and agricultural exporters fell by 50 and 34 per cent respectively (World Bank, 1994). While the World Bank has acknowledged the devastating impact of such exogenous shocks, it nevertheless draws the surprising conclusion that this did not really matter and that ensuing shortfalls were adequately compensated for by increased external financing (World Bank, 1994). This is indeed an unfortunate assessment and conclusion.

The deepening current account deficit due to the deterioration in the terms of trade and the steep increase in the level of real interest rates had important implications for the SSA countries. They were faced with the unpleasant dilemma of provoking sharp domestic deflation at home to adjust to the deteriorating external conditions or maintaining economic activity through counter-cyclical policies. Both of these policies were utilised, albeit at different times. In the 1970s external credit was resorted to, while the early 1980s saw greater use of expansive domestic policies.

The collapse of primary commodity prices was partly the result of the developed countries' decision not to support efforts to maintain stable prices. Until the early 1980s, the developed countries had shared the burden through strategies aimed at stabilising primary commodity prices, notably through the international commodity agreements, the EEC's Stabex and the IMF's compensatory financing facilities supplemented by unconditional (though tied) bilateral assistance. The commodity agreements lapsed in the 1980s, while IMF and bilateral assistance were tied to SAP. Left to market forces, commodity prices plunged.

While in earlier decades booms in the developed world trickled into sub-Saharan countries in the form of higher demand as well as higher or more stable prices (Schadler, 1986), in the 1980s this relationship was reversed. Indeed, the recovery and sustained growth in the developed countries during the 1980s were subsidised by the low and falling level of commodity prices, including those exported by SSA countries.

The most devastating domestic consequence of the deterioration in terms of trade and the high interest rates was the compression of imports. The value of imports declined by 4 per cent annually between 1980 and 1991 (World Bank, 1993a), while the volume was as low as 76 per cent of their 1980 levels (UNCTAD, 1993). In import-dependent economies, this consistent decline contributed to lower capacity utilisation, declining investment and poor economic performance.

(B) Purging the state

Structural adjustment required that SSA governments decrease the extent of their involvement in the economy and assign a far greater role to market forces both from within and outside. This prescription was based on the perception that extensive and intensive state intervention and increased government expenditure were inimical to economic growth. Government deficit, which 'received much of the blame for the assorted economic ills that beset developing countries in the 1980s: overindebtedness and the debt crisis, high inflation and poor investment performance and growth' (Easterly and Schmidt-Hebbel, 1993), came in for special attention (see the discussion in Chapters 2 and 10).

While SSA governments could rightly be indicted for misallocation of resources and corruption, the solution to these and other infractions lies not in ostracising the state from active participation in the economy but in imposing and inculcating conditions of transparency and accountability. Compression of the state primarily produces a compression of public investment, which contrary to the views of the proponents of the 'crowding-out' thesis, also depresses private investment. New theories have established that economic growth is a function of capital stock, broadly defined to include physical stocks of machinery, the stock of ideas and knowledge, and the stocks of infrastructure (Romer, 1986; Lucas, 1988). In the SSA environment, most, if not all, of these prerequisites to growth are sourced from and provided by the government. Where the government is forced to cut back, the sequence of expenditure reduction, as Killick (1991b) rightly observed, was and continues to be: '. . . first capital expenditure on new projects, second the maintenance of past projects, third other non-wage recurrent expenditure such as transport, current supplies of textbooks, medicines and stationery.' Such policies are not cost-efficient, but are rational for a government that seeks to preserve political stability and social tranquillity and to protect the vulnerable to the extent possible at the cost of future growth.

Free market and private investment were substituted for the visible hand of the ostracised state with the predictable poor pay-off. A common phenomenon in all SAP-implementing countries was a perceptible decline in investment relative to their own historical performance and compared to those obtaining in the non-adjusting countries (Elbadawi et al., 1992). The promised increase in supply failed to materialise following liberalisation of the economy. Supply response in industry, which was disproportionately dependent on imports, proved elusive due to depreciation of the domestic currency and high interest rates. This increased the costs of investment and full capacity utilisation, while liberalisation of foreign trade and the higher production costs decreased profitability. Not only did private sector investment decline, but existing capacity was markedly under-utilised (Ndulu, 1990a). If economies were constrained by foreign exchange shortages prior to SAP, they were equally constrained by domestic money shortages due to the credit crunch after the reform.

Similarly, the supply response in agriculture was unsatisfactory, despite the removal of what was perceived to be production and marketing impediments. Although prior to SAP governments imposed price controls, the peasants in many SSA countries continued to operate on the basis of 'real prices' obtaining in the informal markets. What liberalisation actually did was to realign formal prices to those prevailing on the parallel market (see Chapter 13). On the other hand, increases in the price of equipment and modern inputs such as high-yielding seeds, fertilisers, chemicals, and so on, which followed the withdrawal of subsidies and the retraction of easy access to credit, affected output negatively, particularly for small-scale producers. This 'getting prices right' often means higher costs of production without concomittant increase in prices.

(C) Stability before growth

According to the World Bank and the IMF, macroeconomic stability is a necessary condition for growth (Fischer, 1991; World Bank, 1991a). Though the latest generation of adjustment programmes include several supply-enhancing measures, the achievement of supply-demand balance over the short term has generally been obtained by operating mainly on the demand side. While both the principle and procedure defining the logic of reducing aggregate demand to control inflation may be correct under certain circumstances, the fundamental weakness lies in its indiscriminate application, particularly relative to the conditions obtaining in SSA countries.

Excess demand renders an economy persistently and permanently inflationary, if the economy is at full employment level. In this case, demand suppression may be the only solution to price stability. Even under such circumstances, demand-restraining policies should be balanced with supply-enhancing measures. Where, however, the economy is well inside the production possibility frontier, the solution to the excess demand problem lies more in increasing supply than in deflating demand.

Demand-suppressing policies are inappropriate for SSA countries for both humanitarian and economic reasons. In a region where 50 per cent of the population is below the poverty line (World Bank, 1992a), the average daily calorie intake is 93 per cent of the requirement (UNDP, 1993b) and the survival of a sizeable proportion of the populace is underwritten by international charity, the consequences of economic austerity to stamp out inflation courts disaster (Cornia et al., 1987, 1988). The Bank, cognisant of these unpleasant consequences has made attempts to lessen the negative effects by including a social dimension component in its SAP. But these efforts, however laudable, have been overwhelmed by SAP's stagflationary impact.

A lasting and permanent solution to the problem of poverty and inflation in the context of massive underutilisation of natural and human resources should have focused on the supply side of the equation. By adopting the operational principle of stability through growth, the Bank could have rectified the central weakness of structural adjustment.

(D) Export and foreign investment as engines of growth

During the 1980s all the components of domestic demand remained considerably depressed. Structural adjustment therefore attempted to substitute exports and foreign investment as the engines of growth and designed policy instruments and strategies to push development in these directions. The SAP-imposed high interest rates, credit crunch and devaluation are aimed at increasing the production of tradables. However, those tradables favoured are not import substitutes, but exports, since the production of the former are hampered by the SAP-induced domestic cost structure and by stiff external competition. In a way then, countries are forced into increasing exports and searching for non-debt creating external resources.

On the other hand, Bretton Woods institutions have taken major steps to foster foreign investment in SSA countries. Initiatives include sustaining the International Foreign Corporation's activities, the establishment of the Multilateral Investment Guarantee Agency (MIGA) to make developing countries safe for foreign investors, encouraging countries to create an enabling and attractive environment while reducing the value of public enterprises all slated for sale by the depreciating local currency.

How successful are these strategies likely to be? Begin with primary commodities. In sub-Saharan Africa, the structure of merchandise exports are dominated by primary commodities, accounting for more than 90 per cent. If SSA, along with other developing countries, were to succeed in increasing the quantity of these primary commodities, the results would probably be catastrophic given the low demand elasticity and protectionism in developed countries. As Maizels (1986) has poignantly observed, adopting the primary goods-based export strategy as an engine of development is undermined by the 'fallacy of composition':

> While it would be of interest to commodity exporting countries as a whole to limit or reduce their productive capacity . . . it appears to be in the interest of each country individually to increase its share of the global market. However, this route is inevitably costly and ultimately self-defeating since it adds further to downward pressure on prices (ibid.).

The World Bank is aware of this problem, as a result of which it encourages countries to develop 'non-traditional exports'. However, there is not much mileage in this strategy as it is not in principle immune to the 'fallacy of composition' problem. Barring the discovery and development of completely new products (a safe assumption for SSA), what is non-traditional for one country is likely to be a traditional export for another, and an addition to the global supply by new entrant(s) is bound to depress world prices (see Chapter 17 for discussion of these issues). In other words, SAP's success in increasing primary commodity output, whether traditional or non-traditional, undermines its vision of turning exports into an engine of growth.

Industrialisation through foreign investment is unlikely to succeed either (see Chapter 10). There is not much that would attract investment in SSA. Despite the huge population, markets for consumer goods are limited due to fragmentation (there are 52 countries) and low purchasing capacity. The idea of cheap labour being an advantage no longer holds. What attracts foreign investors is highly skilled labour of which SSA is poorly endowed. It is therefore not surprising that direct foreign investment in SSA is extremely low, amounting to less than 10 per cent of total investment, and is unevenly distributed, favouring mainly oil- and mineral-rich countries (Pfeffermann and Madarassy, 1989).

IV ALTERNATIVE DEVELOPMENT STRATEGIES AND FUTURE PROSPECTS

It is against this background that the search for an alternative strategy leading to orderly and sustainable economic and social development becomes imperative. While earlier generations of the literature were limited to exposing the shortcomings of the SAP model, suggestions for alternative approaches were indeed scanty. As the crisis deepened, however, specific critiques and proposals started to emerge. Among the most influential are the seminal UNICEF sponsored and/or published studies (for instance Cornia et al., 1987, 1988), the Lagos Plan of Action adopted by the Organization of African Unity (OAU, 1981) supplemented by the United Nations Economic Commission for Africa's Alternative Framework (AAF-SAF) (UN/ECA, 1989).

In a recent book, Cornia et al. (1992) take the issue further by proposing specific institutional and policy reform measures. Driven by growth-cum-equity objectives, this alternative situates the onus of economic recovery and dynamics on supply-enhancing small to medium-scale economic agents. The fundamentals of the suggested reform broaden the vista to include the political, social and economic paradigms, rationalising income distribution and consumption as well as enhancing opportunities and ensuring continuity by building capacity and capability through investment in education, health, research and development (Ndulu, 1992).

The OAU, ECA and UNICEF alternatives are not substitutes, but are in fact complementary, each concerned with different dimensions of the issues and at different levels of abstraction but within an identical framework. OAU's Lagos Plan of Action could be taken as the definition of the framework, while the others specify the mechanism for its operationalisation. The strategy suggested here is an alternative to structural adjustment; its aim is to supplement the various *modus operandi* put forward by different institutions and authors. It is human rather than statistics centred, based on agriculture as the leading sector with globally shared responsibilities. Macroeconomic stability is a necessary condition along with viable population growth and environmental regeneration.

(A) Development strategy

African policy makers and the donor community must be absolutely convinced of the futility and danger of an outward-looking strategy, given the region's resource and technological endowments as well as protectionism in the developed countries. Taken to its logical conclusion, this strategy translates into specialisation in the production of primary commodities.

The development strategy should instead be inward looking with the external sector (exports, imports and capital inflows) supplementing domestic efforts. Manufacturing industries should primarily target the home consumer. The state should design and implement policies to encourage efficiency including an intensive competition among domestic industries.

(B) Macroeconomic stability

The centrepiece of the SSA strategy should aim to restore and maintain macroeconomic stability. However, the path to orderly, dynamic and holistic stability lies in equating demand and supply by increasing the latter and by not suppressing the former. There is no greater incentive or more powerful engine of growth and development than excess demand in an economy with large pools of under- or un-utilised resources. This approach is not only possible, but would also be more rewarding for sub-Saharan African countries which suffer the paradox of shortages in the midst of unlimited potential. What it requires are growth-friendly policies and visionary leadership.

The benefits of targeting supply rather than demand are enormous. In addition to mitigating, if not eliminating, absolute poverty by creating and expanding productive opportunities, it is capable of consummating the aspirations and concerns of the Bretton Woods institutions including stable prices and sustainable balance of payments.

(C) The role of the state

In sub-Saharan African countries there would be no development without the active participation of the state. The attempt by the Bretton Woods institutions to minimise its role derives from their failure to appreciate the role of the state in the early stages of development and their presumption that the degree of state involvement in the currently mature market economies is the natural order. The economic history of the G7 countries as well as the East Asian Tigers (Wade, 1990) persuasively identify the state as a crucial economic input in the growth and development process. It provided not only political but also economic leadership in these countries. It was the great entrepreneur, educator, creator and supporter of private entrepreneurship. As many economists have rightly observed, in Africa, the choice is not between the public and private sectors as much as whether certain goods and services are to be produced and distributed or not.

Incalculable errors were committed in the past, both in the extent and role of the state. It was indiscriminately overextended, and imperiously bureaucratised. Rather than energising the private sector as a vital and indispensable partner, it stifled its development and marginalised its role. Instead of working through the market, the state tended to supplant it. Rather than helping the people, particularly the rural poor, it recklessly exploited them. Indictment may be made of the state in SSA countries for gross inefficiency and misallocation of resources in the past. However, this should not be stretched to the extreme of excluding it from active participation in the economic activity of these countries.

How then should the state's role be changed in sub-Saharan African countries? The answer to this all-important question was suggested most uncompromisingly by Keynes (1926): 'The important thing for government is not to do things which individuals are doing already, and to do them a little better . . . ; but to do those things which at present are not done at all.' The economic role of the state should thus focus on those activities that are necessary but beyond the capacity and vision of the private sector.

The state must support private sector investment; one means to do this is to increase its own investments since these create profitable opportunities for the former. Two fallacious justifications are often advanced for limiting state investments. The first hinges on the issue of efficiency. Efficiency results from the quality of management, not ownership. What is important therefore is to separate politics and economics, and to endow state enterprises with the freedom to manage themselves in order to achieve clearly defined objectives. It is also important here for the state to gradually divest its productive assets through sales of shares to as wide a constituency as possible, thus spreading the benefits of profitable enterprises.

The second erroneous argument is that an increase in public sector investment crowds out private sector investment. Empirical studies suggest, however, that when public sector investment declined, so too did private investment (Elbadawi, 1992; Easterly and Schmidt-Hebbel, 1993). In SSA countries, the private sector was crowded out not by public sector investment, but by irresponsible policies and regulations. These, and not public sector investment, should be the target. An integral and decisive component of the new strategy should therefore focus on the development of the private sector, particularly small-scale operators. Policy as well as institutional support must accord them access to ownership of productive assets, help them expand their horizons and increase their productivity. For instance, the state could set up strategic industries with strong backward and forward linkages, and include domestic producers through sub-contracting and other arrangements.

Infant industries need protection from external competition, but provisions must be revised. In the past, domestically produced consumer goods enjoyed the highest level of protection, while intermediate and capital goods were unfortunately favoured by low tariffs. Such an incentive structure had pervasive results. Domestic producers intent on maximising profits neglected local production of intermediate and capital goods in favour of cheap imports. Commercial policies must be amended to stimulate local production of intermediate and capital goods. In particular and in the early stages, domestically producible intermediate goods must be encouraged and protected from external competition. This policy could be extended to include capital goods at later stages.

(D) Agriculture as the leading sector

Attempts to revive the economies of sub-Saharan African countries must begin by according primacy to the agricultural sector for a number of reasons. First and foremost, it provides the only effective alternative to the trickle-down approach to eradicating mass poverty, which is still disproportionately entrenched in the rural milieu. Furthermore, increased agricultural production and productivity is the only means of raising economy-wide income and welfare levels. Secondly, industrial development is impossible without agricultural growth. While increased incomes for the vast majority provide industry with growing markets, capital goods imports are made possible and affordable with the additional foreign exchange derived from increased exports of agricultural commodities.

Realignment of the development blueprint from the urban-biased, industry-anchored model to a rural-based and agriculture-driven strategy would necessitate revision of investment patterns, industrial policies and education and training provisions, together with radical reform in rural institutions. Agricultural research, development and dissemination must be revived and intensified. While it is easy to import industrial technology, this may not be so with respect to agricultural technology. The great discoveries and insights of worldwide research may need to be adapted to local conditions and environments. Additional resources should be devoted to the expansion of rural infrastructure, health, training and educational services as well as to the diffusion of financial institutions to mobilise resources from and provide easier credit to small operators. Since the huge agricultural population borrows not to finance consumption but to purchase inputs such as improved seeds, chemicals and fertilisers, urban-based and otherwise detached financial institutions such as commercial banks and development finance institutions should link up or use extension service systems to make these vital sources of growth and societal development widely available.

A necessary and powerful component of the new strategy is the restructuring and reorienting of the education system. Existing curriculums in the majority, if not the whole, of SSA countries are patterned after those of the developed countries, and are designed to service the modern yet shallow urban economy. Education and training therefore remain irrelevant, with the paradoxical consequence that the potentially most productive class is uprooted from the rural agricultural milieu and rendered unemployed and unemployable in the urban setting. If the SSA economies are to regenerate, the education system must be revised. Universal primary education strongly laced with directly useable skills would prove more beneficial for socioeconomic transformation than the current elitist-based learning.

An increase in agricultural productivity and production serves as a stepping stone to industrial revolution, provided there is strong and two-way linkages between the two sectors. The past industrialisation strategy based on primary product export in a domestic demand-constrained environment must be reversed to exploit the growing home market. Income growth for the vast numbers of rural consumers would gradually lead to increases in the consumption and production basket for industrial goods, thereby shifting the nature of aggregate demand and bringing about structural change. If this strategy is to succeed, policies that favour and support these efforts must be adopted by SSA governments. In particular, credit and interest rate policies, commercial and competition policies as well as taxes and government expenditure must be deployed to enhance the development of the agricultural sector.

(E) Economic integration

Sub-Saharan Africa is a subregion with 52 sovereign states. Of these, 12 have populations of less than a million, 19 of less than 3 million, and 35 of less than 10 million. Only three countries have a population exceeding 30 million (World Bank, 1993a). Nor are the resource endowments uniform: 26 of these countries are non-full primary commodity exporters, nine are oil exporters, seven are service exporters (i.e. labour) and the remainder are diversified exporters (ibid.). Thirty-five SSA countries are identified as low income, and ten are in the lower middle income category (ibid.).

Not all of these countries can be a Korea, Hong Kong, Singapore or Taiwan. Given their resource and market limitations, the most viable salvation for most if not all of them lies in integrating their economies. There is already extensive, though informal, cross-border trade exchange, but to develop these ties further requires the integration of production and formalisation of trade. So far, governments have been reluctant to minimise impediments to the free movement of people, goods and capital across borders, despite the many conventions and treaties they have signed to promote economic integration. In addition to national self-reliance, economic salvation requires collective self-reliance. Integration would create not only economic benefits, but would also serve as the best instrument for resolving conflicts both within and among SSA countries.

Converting the competitive nature of the existing economic structure into a complementary one requires coordinated planning to which governments should provide unbridled support. Since economic integration is one of the objectives enshrined in the Lagos Plan of Action, SSA governments would hopefully respect their commitments and strive for its materialisation for the greater benefit of their peoples (see Chapter 18).

V SHARING THE BURDEN OF ADJUSTMENT

The effort to revive the economies of sub-Saharan African countries cannot succeed without the support of the international community. Two specific sets of assistance are identified for immediate action: the need to share the burden of development and support in controlling population growth.

(A) The need to resurrect Keynes

The Keynes plan for the post-Second World War international economic cooperation and management was among the most far-sighted proposals for the creation of orderly and balanced economic relations among nations. His vision for the new postwar international economic order included the need to share the burden of adjustment between surplus and deficit countries. According to his proposal (Befekadu, 1988; Horsefield, 1969), both surplus and deficit countries were to be penalised for accumulating a surplus or deficit of more than 25 per cent of their quota in the International Monetary Fund. Ironically, this scheme, which could have created an orderly and balanced international economic environment, was suffocated by the USA. In consequence, the burden of adjustment was transferred in its entirety to the deficit countries, with surplus countries providing assistance and support at their discretion.

A 'resurrection' of Keynes is therefore deemed necessary and beneficial if the world is not to repeat the unpleasant experience of the interwar period which saw 'the greatest collapse of commodity prices and shrinkage of world trade that the modern world has ever known' (Horsefield, 1969), a scenario that is drawing closer to reality as the disproportionate disequilibrium among trading partners grows ever wider. Whatever the international monetary arrangement, it would appear to be in the interests of the world community, and particularly the surplus countries, to support the adjustment efforts of African countries. The alternative is for these economies to fall into recession and slowed growth, which would affect their demand for imports of manufactured goods. For their own benefit, the surplus countries must relinquish the zero sum game mentality in trade.

Support could be three-pronged. First and foremost would be the drawing up of an effective international price support for primary commodities as well as trade liberalisation. It is grossly unfair to force developing countries to eliminate trade barriers without any reciprocity.

One major factor holding up the Uruguay Round is the issue of agricultural subsidy, not between the developed and developing countries (which would have been rational), but between the European Community and the USA. The world trading system should do better than this and provide equal opportunities to all countries. Second, the external debt, which has grown impossibly difficult to service, could be written off. And finally, a re-examination needs to be made of the possibility of injecting new resources for project-financing, particularly in the rehabilitation and expansion of the physical infrastructure as well as for human capacity building. In a way, such measures also constitute an investment for the developed countries, if viewed from a longer-term perspective.

Failure to support the development of SSA would, in addition to limiting imports, force developed countries to spend more on keeping out immigrants, who for lack of opportunities at home are likely to move in search of greener pastures.

(B) Population control

One of the constraints to the economic development efforts of the SSA countries is the high population growth rates and the large proportion of dependent population. The current population is estimated at 489 million, of which 46 per cent are under 15 and 5 per cent are over 60 (World Bank, 1993a). Under the most favourable scenario, the population is projected to stand at nearly three times this number by the year 2030. The population size and rate of growth are alarming, not only because it impedes economic growth, but also because of its contribution to the rapid erosion of the environment. Relieving the population pressure on the land would help the rehabilitation of the environment and would also bring about increased public and private savings, thereby making more resources available for investment.

International organisations, and particularly the United Nations specialised agencies such as UNICEF and WHO, have done an admirable job of saving lives and improving life expectancy. The campaign to reduce the rate of population growth and to improve the quality of life in SSA must be strengthened. While encouraging, the efforts of the United Nations Population Fund (UNFPA) and the Planned Parenthood Federation (PPF), among others, are clearly not sufficient to stem the surging and detrimental rate of population growth. More needs to be done if attempts to alleviate the mass poverty are to succeed.

VI CONCLUSION

This chapter has attempted to sketch an alternative approach for the long-term development of sub-Saharan Africa. Structural adjustment should and must be criticised from the point of view of its inappropriateness to correct the ills of the SSA economies. The causes of the African socioeconomic crisis are located in the inappropriate development strategy dating back to the 1960s and compounded by hostile external environment. The unsuitable industrialisation strategy impoverished agriculture, aggravated rural poverty and deepened external dependence. The deteriorating terms of trade and the decline in agricultural output and productivity exacerbated by inordinately high rates of population growth compelled these countries to borrow heavily, increasing their external debt and debt-servicing burden. Structural adjustment programmes instituted to relieve these countries of their internal and external plight worsened the situation.

The countries of sub-Saharan Africa need to revisit their economic policy drawing-boards and approach their quandary by redeploying efforts and resources to agriculture. Increasing productivity requires investment in agricultural R&D and dissemination of the findings. Expanding rural infrastructure and improving human capacity must take precedence over urban development. Industrial development should be closely linked to agriculture. Fiscal and monetary policies consistent with and appropriate to such a strategy are necessary.

A major policy stance requiring revision is the need to support local production of intermediate and capital goods. By limiting protection to consumer goods and providing easy access to the importation of intermediate and capital goods, these countries unwittingly contributed to their underdevelopment and excessive dependence on external factors. Development of these vital sources of growth must be encouraged by providing incentives, including protection from external competition.

The burden of adjustment and development must be a universal responsibility, not just a case of charity. The surplus countries must be compelled, through positive measures, perhaps in line with Keynes' vision for the postwar international economic relations, to undertake adjustment measures of their own or provide meaningful support for the deficit-prone countries. Increased initiatives need to be undertaken by the international community to strengthen local efforts to contain the explosive population growth rate.

In the final analysis, the solution to the socioeconomic crisis of the sub-Saharan African countries depends on the African people. The governments have the onus of developing and implementing policies that are supportive of the efforts of the people. The international community must augment these efforts, including for their own long-term interests.

4 The Consistency between Long-term Development Objectives and Short-term Policy Instruments in Fund Activities

Vito Tanzi*

I INTRODUCTION

The objectives of the International Monetary Fund are pursued through various activities that fall broadly under the categories of 'surveillance', financial programmes and technical assistance. In their evaluation of Fund activities, critics have often focused on financial programmes, ignoring the role that the Fund plays through its surveillance and technical assistance activities. This role has important implications however for longer-term objectives such as growth and poverty alleviation. This chapter describes these broader Fund activities, and argues that there is no conflict between the instruments that the organisation uses and longer-term development objectives, even though the Fund is, strictly speaking, not in the development business.

Until the 1980s Fund-supported programmes were aimed at macroeconomic adjustment and tended to rely mostly on the use of macro variables, such as the exchange rate, fiscal deficit, the rate of interest, total credit expansion, and so forth. Under the *modus operandi* then prevailing, the Fund left to the countries themselves the choice of the specific or *micro* policies which may have been needed to change the macro variables. The time-frame for the programmes was generally one year. In 1974 a major innovation came with the introduction of the Extended Fund Facility (EFF), which increased the duration of

* The author wishes to acknowledge the comments and assistance received from Keyoung Chu, Karim Nashashibi and Michael Mered. The views expressed in this chapter are strictly personal and are not official International Monetary Fund views.

these programmes to three years. Kenya was the first user of this new facility. Another innovation followed in 1986 with the introduction of the Structural Adjustment Facility (SAF) for low-income countries, which provided Fund lending at concessional rates. With the creation of the EFF and the SAF facilities, the Fund and its members recognised that adjustment may take more than one year and may require *structural* reforms. These innovations brought a major reformulation of Fund thinking and of its approach to economic reform.

The second half of the 1980s witnessed the following developments:

1. Growing importance and attention placed on *structural reform*: this attention involved the Fund far more deeply in many micro policy decisions than had previously been the case and increased the role and importance of technical assistance; it also placed a much greater burden on Fund staff, since the new role was very labour intensive.
2. Explicit and growing attention paid to *economic growth*: growth was given a much greater weight as an objective of Fund activities, and was mentioned with increasing frequency in Fund documents and in official Fund pronouncements.
3. Explicit attention paid to the objective of *poverty alleviation.*
4. The beginning of attention given to the *environment*, especially towards the end of the decade.

Finally, by the beginning of the 1990s, the quality of public spending and of government policy-making, in general, started to receive closer scrutiny. However, as required by the Articles of Agreement, the *fundamental* preoccupation of Fund activity remained unchanged; namely, balance of payments viability and macroeconomic stability (see Polak, 1991, for a useful review of these developments). With these changes the Fund did not wish to enter the development business, and thus become a development institution. Rather, it wanted to ensure that its activities, carried out to achieve its fundamental objectives, were consistent with those broader objectives normally referred to as economic development.

II CONCERN FOR GROWTH

The Fund has always been concerned about growth, but in earlier years it was assumed that macroeconomic stability and equilibrium in the balance of payments would automatically generate growth. In line with the prevailing academic thinking of the time, growth was assumed to be the result of capital accumulation, of the increase in the quantity and quality of the labour force, and of exogenous technological development (Solow, 1970). These were factors that could not be influenced to any great extent, except indirectly, by the policy instruments used in Fund-supported programmes. The best contribution that the Fund could make was to ensure economic stability, and stability was considered a basic condition for long-term development. Furthermore, specialisation among international institutions required that the Fund concentrate on its mandate. Other institutions could pursue more explicitly other economic objectives. For example, the World Bank, as elaborated in Chapter 2, was focusing on stimulating investment and capital formation through its project loans and activities in general.

In the 1980s two developments required that increasing and explicit attention be paid to growth, especially in connection with the Fund work in developing countries. The first was the debt crisis, which highlighted the fact that without growth the developing countries would not be able to remove the oppressive burden of heavy external debt. Only growth or debt repudiation could solve the debt crises, and the second alternative was not considered an attractive one. The Baker initiative and the Brady plan recognised this imperative. The second development was the impact of supply-side economics on the thinking of economists and policy makers. This kind of intellectual revolution brought to the fore the need to pay closer attention not only to the effects of economic policies on demand, but also their effects on the supply side[1]. Once attention came to be focused on the supply side, the view that additional policies of a structural nature could raise potential output, especially when major distortions were widespread as was often the case, came to be widely accepted.

Many economists came to accept the idea that structural changes, which by removing policy-imposed obstacles to economic activities gave a greater role to the working of the market, could make an economy more efficient and could thus raise its growth rate. In other words, public policy was increasingly viewed as a factor influencing growth directly, rather than just through its effect on capital accumulation. It was even argued in some of the literature that structural changes, which quickly raised the potential growth of the economy, might permit some relaxation in the stabilisation policies necessary in the short run. In other words, the more ambitious and successful were the structural reforms, the less restrictive the stabilisation policy needed to be (Tanzi, 1987).

As a consequence of these developments, many Fund programmes negotiated in the second half of the 1980s covered a longer time-frame than the traditional one year; emphasised structural adjustment far more than they had done in the past; and paid closer attention to those economic policies which, apart from their impact on macro-economic adjustment, could have an impact on the growth of the economy. Important among these policies were tax reform, reform of public expenditure, price reform, reforms aimed at opening the economy and reforms of the financial sector. Thus, technical assistance activity, aimed at bringing about structural reform, came to be integrated much more than in the past with the macroeconomic policies agreed in the programmes. During the 1980s, the number of countries that signed up for Fund programmes grew dramatically and the impact of the IMF on economies throughout the developing world increased sharply. In Africa, many countries negotiated Structural Adjustment Facility (SAF) and Enhanced Structural Adjustment Facility (ESAF) programmes with the Fund and related programmes with the World Bank.

As the decade progressed, the relevant concept of growth was qualified so that it was defined not just in quantitative terms, i.e. in terms of the growth of GDP per capita, but also in qualitative terms. In a way, this change paralleled to some extent the discussion that had taken place in the economic development literature on whether economic growth and economic development were one and the same thing.

III CONCERN FOR POVERTY

The first major qualitative change to the narrow economic concept of growth resulted from the increasing preoccupation with poverty. The traditional Fund attitude towards poverty could, perhaps a bit simplistically, be described as follows. The Fund had always been concerned about *absolute* poverty; in fact, it had been created to establish rules of the game, and to support countries' policies aimed at improving the welfare of member countries.[2] However, it had assumed that the responsibility for redistributing income and for reducing *relative* poverty within a country rested with the country itself and with other international institutions, predominantly the World Bank. Within the IMF it had been thought that the economic stability produced through good Fund-supported programmes would stimulate growth, which, in turn, would reduce absolute poverty. Furthermore, the conditionality guidelines under which the Fund had operated through the 1970s (see

Gold, 1979) emphasised that micro policy decisions and structural policies in general were the responsibility of the countries themselves. Therefore, the Fund was to limit its involvement with them. For example, the Fund could require a country, with which it was negotiating a financial programme, to reduce its fiscal deficit by a certain proportion of GDP; however, it was the country's responsibility to choose the particular way of carrying out this reduction (see Tanzi, 1990, for a detailed discussion of this point). Of course, the way in which the country chose to pursue the reduction could have different implications for income distribution and for growth. The conditionality guidelines, however, did not prevent the Fund from giving advice through its technical assistance *when it was asked to do so by the countries themselves*. What it could not do was to negotiate these structural policies in its programmes.

In the mid-1980s, some significant changes in attitudes began to be evident. These changes were clearly reflected in the creation of the SAF which explicitly recognised the need for *structural* reform. Two Occasional Papers written by Fund staff reflected the increased concern for poverty. These papers attempted to address a frequent criticism of Fund programmes; namely, that they tended to hurt the poor. The first of these papers (IMF, 1986) surveyed many policy instruments that in one way or another had been advocated in Fund-supported programmes and assessed the probable impact on income distribution of each of these instruments.[3] This partial analysis, while useful, was unsatisfactory in indicating whether Fund-negotiated programmes, which used different combinations of policy instruments, had a net negative impact on the poor. However, it was helpful in identifying instruments that, from the perspective of their implications for income distribution, needed close attention.

The second paper analysed in detail 10 programmes (IMF, 1988). It concluded that half of these programmes had relied on policies which, taken together, could be held to have had a negative, short-run impact on the poor, while the other half had relied on policies which helped the poor. The main conclusion drawn by this study was that some generalisations made by critics, for example, that devaluation hurts the poor, were questionable, since they were highly dependent on whether the poor were urban dwellers consuming imports, or rural people producing export crops. In other words, this study called attention to the need to identify the poor and their characteristics, and to analyse the impact of specific policies on those well-identified groups.

This second study also suffered from obvious shortcomings, two of which were particularly important. It could not establish what would have happened to the poor in the absence of the programmes. This is the classic *counterfactual problem.*[4] Furthermore, its results concerned the short term, and could not be extended to a longer period. However, as Fund staff have always maintained, without the programmes, the economic situation of many of the programme countries would have deteriorated. This would have inevitably hurt the poor, if not necessarily relative to the rest of the population, certainly in an absolute sense.[5] For example, the acceleration of inflation imposes a very regressive tax on the poor. Fund staff have also argued that even if some of the poor might suffer in the short run, a good programme would raise their standard of living over time by creating economic stability and, hopefully, by stimulating a faster rate of growth as a result of this increased stability and the structural measures associated with the programme.

This growing concern for *relative* poverty led to the conclusion that, in negotiating programmes and in giving advice generally, the Fund should make a more concerted effort to try to prevent a deterioration in the standard of living of the most vulnerable individuals *even in the short run.*[6] The package of measures contemplated in Fund-supported programmes should therefore be selected, whenever possible, so as to protect the most vulnerable. This approach required that policies regarding public expenditure and taxation, among others, be scrutinised carefully in order to reduce the reliance on policy instruments that could be damaging to the standard of living of, say, the poorest 10 or 20 per cent of the population. In particular cases, when the instruments required to improve economic efficiency and to reduce macroeconomic disequilibrium could have a negative impact on these vulnerable groups, the Fund started advocating safety nets to protect them. Fund interest and work on safety nets, especially through technical assistance, has increased significantly in recent years. This is particularly so for economies in transition. It should, however, be reiterated that the fundamental goals of Fund-supported programmes – macroeconomic equilibrium and a sustainable balance of payments – have remained unchanged. These objectives have neither been sacrificed nor compromised, but it has been recognised that their achievement must accommodate the new concerns. Thus, the Fund has retained its distinctive traditional mandate.

To help gain an understanding of the poor, particularly who they are and what their characteristics are, *poverty profiles* have been developed for various countries and information available on the poor has been sought. Much greater coordination has been developed with the World Bank, which has expanded its information base on the poor. Contacts with other institutions, including the ILO, UNICEF, UNDP and others, have been enhanced. As mentioned earlier, information on the characteristics of the poor is essential in the choice of policy instruments. Internal seminars have been held and discussions about the impact of various policy instruments on different income groups have become normal features of recent Fund work. As a consequence of these activities, Fund economists working on country programmes increasingly use such available information and have become sensitised to the effects on the poor of the policies they recommend. Explicit concern for the poor in the design of Fund programmes is now widely shared within the institution and negotiated programmes have attempted to insulate disadvantaged groups when major macroeconomic adjustment has been necessary. For example, when price liberalisation or devaluation is undertaken, subsidies may be recommended for basic staple commodities for a period of time. Still, when budgetary or exchange rate policies are not sustainable, and a programme is negotiated, the countries are advised to change them. In the process, some groups may be negatively affected in the short term, especially when safety nets are not available or cannot be implemented soon enough.

The following section discusses the growing concern on the part of the Fund with 'unproductive' spending. Although this is a general concern, and not directly or necessarily linked with the issue of poverty, it is evident that the need to reduce unnecessary spending becomes particularly acute in periods of fiscal adjustment. The reduction in this unproductive spending may help maintain programmes that benefit the poor.

IV ENVIRONMENT AND OTHER CONCERNS

More recently, Fund thinking has begun to reflect the growing universal concern for the environment.[7] However, it is not easy to make a case that Fund activities have a direct and significant impact on the environment. Criticism directed at the Fund on this score has been more limited than that on the impact on the poor, but environmental groups are very vocal and powerful. The Fund cannot, of course, redirect its activities away from its basic mandate in order to accommodate those critics who insist that it should refocus its activity toward environmental objectives. No convincing links have yet been established between Fund activities and environmental degradation. In fact, a prevalent belief on the part of those in the Fund who have studied this issue is that Fund activities (which often advocate realistic prices and the enforcement of property rights) are quite environment-friendly. Nonetheless, the possibility that there are some negative links cannot be ruled out, and the Fund has taken the criticism seriously.[8] Recently, the Executive Board of the Fund authorised an examination of these issues. They have been working to establish whether any links can be identified between the instruments recommended by the Fund in its financial programmes to promote its traditional objectives and the environment. As this work is currently limited to two individuals, the Fund's involvement with the issue of the environment is clearly much more limited at present than its involvement with poverty.

In pursuing this environmental concern, the Fund has been relying on work done by the IBRD, the OECD and other institutions. The relevant output of these institutions is summarised for Fund staff in order to increase their understanding of environmental issues. The Fund has been closely following work undertaken by the United Nations that might result in a revision of the national accounts to make them reflect environmental degradation and excessive depletion of resources. As a frequent user of these accounts, the Fund has a particular interest in this work since they might have implications for the long-term economic development of member countries.

In addition to poverty and the environment, other areas have been receiving attention in recent speeches by the Managing Director of the IMF. One of these is *'unproductive' public expenditure*. A major concern of the Managing Director is that many countries are carrying levels of public spending that are much too high in relation to their revenue capacity. These high levels result in large fiscal deficits and/or excessive taxation. Table 4.1 shows the overall fiscal deficit for sub-Saharan Africa for the 1980–90 period. These high deficits have occurred in spite of the fact that this region had the highest average level of taxation among developing countries (Tanzi, 1992). It would therefore be helpful if these countries could reduce spending *without affecting basic economic and human needs*. This could be achieved if 'unproductive' spending could be eliminated or, at least, reduced. However, there is evidence that under the conditions of fiscal stress during the 1980s, social expenditures tended to get squeezed while some unproductive expenditures maintained their shares (Nashashibi, 1993).

The discussion on unproductive spending has run into the obvious difficulty of needing to determine objectively what is unproductive. It

Table 4.1 Overall fiscal deficit excluding grants, selected sub-Saharan countries, 1980-91 (as % of GDP)

	1980	*1981*	*1982*	*1983*	*1984*	*1985*	*1986*	*1987*	*1988*	*1989*	*1990*	*1991*
Benin	−11.4	−8.2	−14.1	−17.3	−19.1	−12.7	−10.6	−11.1	−9.6	−10.6	−10.0	−7.2
Botswana[a]	−5.2	−7.5	−6.7	4.3	9.5	16.4	17.4	11.6	13.7	8.4	11.1	−2.7
Burkina Faso	−21.2	−20.1	−20.0	−23.3	−17.2	−7.2	−12.7	−14.5	−12.4	−9.9	−5.9	−7.0
Burundi	−10.6	−12.3	−12.6	−18.1	−12.1	−10.2	−8.5	−16.7	−11.7	−9.6	−13.1	−9.7
Cameroon[b]	0.4	−0.2	0.2	3.5	−0.1	−3.3	−0.4	−13.0	−6.4	−5.1	−8.5	−8.6
Central African Republic	−5.2	−5.7	−1.4	−2.3	−8.1	−13.8	−13.8	−16.4	−13.7	−11.5	−11.9	−13.4
Congo	−11.4	0.2	−14.0	−12.6	−6.2	−4.8	−8.2	−12.9	−18.6	−11.0	−4.5	−11.8
Côte d'Ivoire	−14.0	−13.1	−13.5	−11.7	−1.6	2.0	−3.0	−8.2	−14.6	−17.6	−12.9	−13.1
Gabon	4.6	7.8	8.7	−1.4	−2.0	−4.5	−12.8	−10.8	−11.6	−8.0	−4.1	−0.3
Gambia, The[b]	−9.5	−17.9	−18.3	−12.1	−13.4	−14.5	−6.9	−15.2	−16.4	−2.8	−8.2	−4.2
Ghana	−4.2	−6.5	−5.7	−2.7	−2.2	−2.7	−0.6	−0.2	−0.8	−0.8	−1.4	0.1
Kenya[b]	−7.7	−9.6	−8.8	−5.1	−5.4	−7.6	−7.1	−7.6	−5.0	−7.1	−7.4	−8.2
Madagascar	−14.9	−12.0	−7.4	−6.0	−4.1	−4.3	−4.2	−4.0	−4.0	−9.2	−5.1	−7.8
Malawi[a]	−20.3	−16.5	−10.9	−9.5	−8.4	−10.1	−13.0	−9.4	−7.2	−6.8	−6.1	−5.4
Mali	−10.8	−15.5	−9.8	−13.7	−10.0	−15.3	−12.5	−10.4	−10.5	−10.0	−8.5	−12.1
Mauritania	−11.6	−10.0	−11.6	−6.3	−4.1	−0.3	1.1	−0.1	−1.2	−6.3	−2.8	−2.6
Mauritius[b]	−10.6	−14.1	−13.4	−8.8	−6.8	−6.5	−4.8	−2.2	−1.9	−3.4	−2.6	−1.2
Mozambique	−10.9	−15.2	−9.4	−19.3	−20.7	−14.7	−18.0	−21.1	−24.9	−24.1	−29.6	−27.4
Niger[c]	−7.2	−7.3	−8.5	−8.2	−8.5	−9.4	−8.8	−9.8	−10.6	−10.5	−13.6	−9.8
Nigeria	−0.4	−8.8	−7.4	−9.5	−4.1	−2.4	−2.8	−9.0	−10.9	−5.4	−2.9	−6.0
Rwanda[b]	2.9	−7.5	−7.6	−8.3	−5.9	−6.4	−7.1	−10.3	−8.6	−7.2	−11.5	−13.4
Senegal[b]	−5.7	−12.6	−6.9	−8.1	−5.9	−4.7	−3.9	−2.7	−2.6	−4.0	−4.3	−0.8
Sierra Leone[b]	−14.1	−15.0	−14.8	−13.4	−9.7	−12.6	−13.6	−18.1	−8.0	−8.9	−11.5	−9.5

continued on page 78

Table 4.1 continued

	1980	*1981*	*1982*	*1983*	*1984*	*1985*	*1986*	*1987*	*1988*	*1989*	*1990*	*1991*
Somalia	−12.6	−7.1	−9.3	−6.7	−11.4	−14.5	−22.7	−27.7	−23.0	−49.8	−32.5	...
Tanzania[b]	−18.1	−13.2	−16.3	−10.4	−9.7	−8.2	−8.3	−8.3	−7.8	−8.3	−6.8	−3.3
Togo	−3.5	−7.4	−3.6	−7.9	−7.0	−7.1	−9.1	−9.4	−5.3	−6.2	−6.1	−5.2
Uganda[b]	−3.1	−7.9	−9.7	−4.1	−3.5	−5.7	−5.2	−4.5	−6.4	−3.8	−6.0	−8.0
Zaire	0.0	−10.5	−10.9	−6.1	−8.7	−6.8	−9.9	−11.6	−19.2	−8.5	−9.4	...
Zambia	−19.4	−13.7	−15.3	−9.6	−7.8	−14.9	−29.9	−11.3	−13.6	−9.9	−12.6	−16.7
Zimbabwe[b]	−12.6	−9.8	−7.8	−8.9	−10.5	−10.6	−10.5	−12.7	−9.4	−10.8	−8.8	−10.8
Average	−8.9	−9.9	−9.6	−8.8	−7.5	−7.2	−8.3	−9.9	−9.4	−9.3	−8.6	−8.1

Notes: [a] Fiscal year: April–March; [b] Fiscal year: July–June; [c] Fiscal year: October–September through 1988/9, calendar years from 1989.

Source: Data provided by the authorities: IMF staff estimates; Nashashibi, 1993.

is easy to theorise on this question, and it may even be easy to occasionally point to particular public expenditure – for example, the so-called 'white elephants' – that appear obviously unproductive to the observer; however, one could argue that, like beauty, unproductivity may be a characteristic which lies in the eye of the beholder. For those who benefit from the expenditure, no spending is ever unproductive. Of course, the benefit from such spending may be political or even cultural, rather than purely economic. The following public spending categories are receiving increasing attention as likely candidates for the 'unproductive' label.

First, *military spending* absorbs a large share of the countries' resources and does not increase the security of any one country when all countries increase their spending competitively. Table 4.2 provides estimates of military expenditure in sub-Saharan African countries. It shows that these countries have been allocating more than 3 per cent of their GDPs to military spending, corresponding to about 9 billion of 1990 US dollars. While it may be said that military spending represents a lower share of the developing countries' aggregate GDP than for the industrial countries and that the share has been falling, it still remains high, especially for countries in particular regions and particularly with respect to the resources of those countries. Military expenditure by sub-Saharan African countries has averaged between 11 and almost 13 per cent of central government expenditure. For some countries, such as Angola, Ethiopia, Mozambique and a few others, the level of military spending has been much higher than the average. A reduction in this spending would release resources that could be allocated to more important social or economic needs.

Second is *inefficient investment* made up of projects carried out for political reasons, or because the financing for them is more readily available from abroad, or because influential government officials have a private interest in their being carried out. World Bank Public Expenditure Reviews have often indicated that many unproductive investments have been carried out by developing countries in general and sub-Saharan countries in particular. At the same time those reviews have indicated that the economic and social infrastructure of developing countries and especially of African countries has deteriorated because of deficient operations and maintenance expenditure.

A third category of public spending receiving close attention is that of *subsidies*, when they do not satisfy the basic objectives for which they were enacted and continue to be defended, say, for raising the standard of living of the poor. Evidence indicates that in many cases

Table 4.2 Military expenditures in sub-Saharan Africa, as percentage of GDP, 1985-90

	1985	*1986*	*1987*	*1988*	*1989*	*1990*
Angola	20.3	23.1	16.0	13.1	10.6	8.3
Benin	2.0	2.1	1.9	2.1	1.8	1.7
Botswana	2.5	2.7	4.4	2.4	1.7	1.8
Burkina Faso	2.5	3.5	3.0	2.9	2.9	2.8
Burundi	3.0	3.4	2.7	2.1	2.5	2.5
Cameroon	2.2	2.1	2.1	2.1	1.3	1.6
Central African Republic	1.0	1.8	1.7	1.7	1.6	1.6
Chad	4.6	6.3	4.2	6.4	4.8	5.0
Congo	2.6	4.0	4.0	3.2	3.4	3.2
Côte d'Ivoire	1.0	1.0	1.2	1.2	1.3	1.4
Ethiopia	9.3	8.9	10.4	11.9	13.6	14.8
Gabon	2.6	4.0	4.3	4.0	3.6	3.1
Ghana	2.0	0.9	0.9	0.4	0.6	0.6
Guinea Bissau	3.0	2.8	1.6	...	...	...
Kenya	2.4	2.8	3.0	2.6	2.5	2.4
Liberia	2.3	2.2	2.4	2.3	2.4	2.2
Madagascar	2.2	2.2	1.8	1.4	1.3	1.1
Malawi	1.5	2.1	1.8	1.6	1.6	1.5
Mali	2.4	2.2	2.2	2.9	3.0	2.9
Mauritania	...	...	...	...	...	...
Mauritius	0.2	0.2	0.2	0.2	0.3	0.2
Mozambique	7.0	6.7	7.0	7.7	8.3	7.6
Niger	0.8	0.8	0.8	0.8	0.8	0.8
Nigeria	1.3	1.3	0.7	0.9	0.8	0.8
Rwanda	1.6	1.8	1.7	1.6	1.7	1.7
Senegal	2.5	2.2	2.1	2.0	1.9	1.9
Sierra Leone	0.6	0.9	0.5	0.4	0.6	0.7
Somalia	2.0	1.9	2.2	1.2	1.1	1.2
South Africa	4.1	4.2	4.5	4.6	4.7	4.3
Sudan	3.4	2.6	2.3	2.4	2.5	2.9
Swaziland	2.1	1.7	1.5	1.6	1.5	1.3
Tanzania	3.5	4.4	4.8	4.9	5.3	4.4
Togo	2.6	2.5	3.5	3.2	3.0	2.8
Uganda	3.6	2.0	2.3	1.4	0.7	0.7
Zaire	1.4	0.8	1.2	0.8	1.3	0.5
Zambia	2.4	3.7	3.2	3.2	1.4	1.7
Zimbabwe	6.2	7.0	7.4	7.4	7.0	5.8
Average	3.1	3.4	3.6	3.5	3.4	3.2

Source: Based on SIPRI military expenditure data from *SIPRI Yearbook* and GDP, exchange rate and central government expenditure data from *International Finance Statistics* and *Government Finance Statistics*; Hewitt, 1993.

the major beneficiaries of government subsidies are not the poor but the urban middle classes. The Fund has often recommended a reduction in generalised subsidies – or in subsidies given indirectly through the overvaluation of the exchange rate, the repression of financial markets, or the control of some producer prices – and their replacement with subsidies better targeted toward the objectives that supposedly justify their existence. In some cases, this change has substantially reduced spending without a significant negative effect on the poorer sectors mostly in need of the subsidies.

Another area likely to reflect some unproductive spending is *public employment*. In many countries the number of people on the government payroll far exceeds that justified by efficiency considerations. For example, several countries continue their automatic recruitment of graduates from public administration schools regardless of needs or fiscal conditions. Often, more government jobs have been bought at the cost of lower real wages for the employees. This reduces the efficiency and the quality of the government. Public employment becomes a kind of costly transfer programme. As Table 4.3 illustrates, wages and salaries continue to constitute a very high share of GDP in sub-Saharan African countries despite some minor declines since the early 1980s. This discussion of the quality of public spending is an aspect of what is called 'good governance'. Good governance extends to issues related to excessive regulations, privatisation of public enterprises, corruption, and so forth, all of which are receiving growing attention in Fund activities. In its Public Expenditure Reviews the World Bank has also been paying close attention to these questions.

V FUND-SUPPORTED PROGRAMMES AND DEVELOPMENT

The previous sections have outlined the changes that took place in the 1980s in the way the Fund has been pursuing its multifaceted activities. As mentioned earlier, by focusing exclusively on Fund-supported programmes and on *published* information about them, critics have presented an incomplete picture. The previous sections have attempted to show the growing concern that the Fund has shown for the potential impact of its advice on the poor. Thus, the criticism that the Fund ignores the poor, or worse, that its programmes are anti-poor, is not valid. This section addresses another criticism, namely that Fund-supported programmes, which presumably use short-term policy instruments, have negative effects on long-term development. Table 4.4 provides some information on programmes now in force in Africa.

Table 4.3 Public sector wages and salaries, selected sub-Saharan African countries, 1980-91 (as % of GDP)

	1980	*1981*	*1982*	*1983*	*1984*	*1985*	*1986*	*1987*	*1988*	*1989*	*1990*	*1991*
Benin	6.6	8.1	7.6	10.3	9.3	8.6	9.9	11.2	10.1	9.2	8.7	8.5
Botswana[a]	10.5	11.8	9.9	8.6	9.1	7.6	8.0	7.5	7.2	7.5	8.6	9.3
Burkina Faso	7.8	7.6	8.3	8.5	8.0	7.3	7.3	7.7	8.5	9.1	9.6	8.8
Burundi	6.5	6.8	6.3	5.9	5.4	5.1	5.7	6.1	6.4	6.5	6.8	6.4
Cameroon[b]	5.2	5.7	4.8	5.2	5.6	5.6	5.6	7.3	7.9	8.7	8.7	9.6
CAR	11.1	11.5	9.6	9.5	8.4	7.7	7.3	7.9	7.7	7.3	6.7	7.0
Congo	10.2	7.7	7.6	7.2	7.3	7.8	12.5	12.1	12.3	10.8	10.3	15.3
Côte d'Ivoire	8.3	8.9	9.5	10.0	8.8	8.0	8.3	10.9	11.6	12.0	12.6	12.4
Gabon	4.3	4.6	4.6	5.4	5.2	5.5	8.2	8.6	9.3	7.8	8.1	8.3
Gambia, The[b]	7.8	8.7	8.8	8.7	8.9	7.5	5.8	4.4	4.2	5.2	5.7	5.4
Ghana	2.9	3.1	2.9	2.0	2.0	4.2	5.1	4.8	4.7	4.4	4.3	4.5
Kenya[b]	5.7	6.1	7.1	9.8	9.9	9.4	9.9	10.2	10.2	9.7	6.0	5.7
Madagascar	7.2	7.5	7.0	5.9	5.9	5.8	5.3	5.2	4.8	4.5	4.2	4.7
Malawi[a]	5.1	5.0	5.8	5.5	4.8	5.2	5.7	5.6	4.3	4.9	4.3	4.1
Mali	9.0	8.5	6.6	7.2	7.2	7.5	7.3	6.9	6.5	6.0	5.6	6.1
Mauritania	13.8	12.5	12.7	12.8	12.0	10.8	9.9	9.5	6.4	6.0	6.3	5.9
Mauritius[b]	8.1	9.6	10.0	9.8	9.2	8.5	7.7	6.9	7.9	8.7	8.3	7.3
Mozambique	6.4	7.1	7.6	9.2	6.7	5.2	4.8	3.5	3.8	4.5	4.9	5.4
Niger[c]	3.2	3.3	3.7	3.6	4.0	3.8	4.2	4.7	5.0	5.0	5.4	6.0
Nigeria	1.9	2.0	1.8	1.8	1.6	1.8	2.4	1.9	1.9	1.3	1.3	2.1
Rwanda[b]	4.5	6.0	5.7	5.4	5.2	5.0	5.6	5.9	6.0	6.3	6.1	6.4
Senegal[b]	11.2	12.1	9.4	9.5	10.3	9.8	9.1	9.0	8.5	8.5	8.3	8.2
Sierra Leone[b]	6.3	7.8	7.7	6.7	6.4	4.5	3.0	2.8	3.2	2.5	3.2	4.2
Somalia	...	...	...	...	3.3	2.5	1.8	1.3	1.1	1.0	0.7	...
Tanzania[b]	6.5	6.5	6.8	6.6	6.6	6.7	5.7	4.7	4.3	5.5	5.8	5.4

Togo	8.5	9.2	10.1	10.2	9.1	8.4	7.9	9.2	8.6	8.3	8.5	9.4
Uganda[b]	1.8	3.6	2.1	1.5	1.9	3.2	1.4	1.0	1.1	1.3	0.9	1.4
Zaire	5.6	5.8	5.4	3.3	3.0	3.0	3.5	3.1	3.5	3.3	5.2	...
Zambia	8.2	9.4	9.9	9.6	9.1	7.6	5.1	5.1	3.7	2.8	4.0	5.1
Zimbabwe[b]	9.6	10.5	9.8	10.0	9.7	10.2	11.1	12.1	15.0	14.9	15.2	17.0
Average	7.0	7.5	7.2	7.2	6.8	6.5	6.5	6.6	6.5	6.4	6.5	7.1

Notes: [a] Fiscal year: April–March; [b] Fiscal year: July–June; [c] Fiscal year: October–September through 1988/9, calendar years from 1989.

Source: Data provided by the authorities; IMF staff estimates; Nashashibi, 1993.

Table 4.4 IMF-funded programmes in sub-Saharan Africa (11 September 1992; in millions of SDRs)

	Date of agreement	*Expiration date*	*Amount agreed*	*Amount drawn*	*Undrawn balance*
Stand-by arrangements (4)					
Cameroon	20 December 1991	19 September 1992	28.00	8.00	20.00
Côte d'Ivoire	20 September 1991	19 September 1992	82.75	33.10	49.65
Gabon	30 September 1991	29 March 1993	28.00	4.00	24.00
Morocco	31 January 1992	31 March 1993	91.98	18.40	73.58
Subtotal			*230.73*	*63.50*	*167.23*
Extended Arrangements (1)					
Zimbabwe	24 January 1992	23 January 1995	343.80	71.20	272.60
Subtotal			*343.80*	*71.20*	*272.60*
Structural Adjustment Facility (3)					
Burkina Faso	13 March 1991	12 March 1994	22.12	6.32	15.80
Comoros	21 June 1991	20 June 1994	3.15	0.90	2.25
Rwanda	24 April 1991	23 April 1994	30.66	8.76	21.90
Subtotal			*55.93*	*15.98*	*39.95*
Enhanced Structural Adjustment Facility (11)					
Burundi	13 November 1991	12 November 1994	42.70	22.81	29.89
Guinea	6 November 1991	5 November 1994	57.90	8.68	49.22
Kenya	15 May 1989	31 March 1993	261.40	216.17	45.23
Lesotho	22 May 1991	21 May 1994	18.12	7.55	10.57
Malawi	15 July 1988	29 September 1992	66.96	61.38	5.58
Mali	28 August 1992	27 August 1995	60.96	0.00	60.96
Mozambique	1 June 1990	31 May 1993	100.65	70.15	30.50
Tanzania	29 July 1991	28 July 1994	181.90	53.50	128.40

Togo	31 May 1989	19 May 1993	46.08	38.40	7.68
Uganda	17 April 1989	7 November 1992	179.28	179.28	0.00
Zimbabwe	11 September 1992	10 September 1995	200.60	0.00	200.60
Subtotal			*1 216.55*	*647.92*	*568.63*
Total			*1 847.01*	*798.60*	*1 048.41*
Rights Accumulation Program			Max. Accumulation Rights		Accumulated to date
Sierra Leone	3 April 1992	2 April 1994	87.33		10.92
Zambia	17 July 1992	31 March 1995	836.90		83.69

Note: In addition to the above arrangements, Fund Monitored Programs (FMP) are operational in Ghana and the Gambia.

Source: IMF Treasurer's Department.

The Fund enters into a programme agreement with a member country only when the country approaches it with a request for financial assistance. In other words, the Fund does not impose a programme on any country, although its surveillance responsibility requires that it strongly advise member countries to put their house in order. Furthermore, other pressures from official and commercial creditors might induce the country to seek assistance from the Fund.

When a country approaches the IMF for a programme, it is generally experiencing major economic difficulties. These difficulties often imply that the current policies of the country are unsustainable, mainly because the country would run out of foreign exchange and therefore be unable to live up to its financial obligations. In other words, it may already be in, or be sliding into, arrears towards its creditors. In general, its balance of payments is in disequilibrium, implying that the country: (a) has been borrowing too much abroad; (b) is running down its foreign exchange reserves or has already exhausted them; or (c) is progressively imposing increasing constraints on imports. In many cases, it has also exhausted its foreign borrowing possibilities.

The balance of payments difficulty is normally the result of: (a) an overvalued exchange rate, which encourages imports and discourages exports; or (b) a structure of domestic prices which is out of line with the prices in the rest of the world; or (c) a large fiscal deficit that stimulates aggregate demand including imports. Over the short and medium term, balance of payments difficulties and other macro problems can be and are indeed at times caused by exogenous shocks.[9] Often, excessive money creation results in the domestic rate of inflation being higher than the world rate, which thus renders the exchange rate progressively more overvalued unless it is being continuously adjusted by an adequate amount. It is also common that at the time that the country approaches the Fund, its growth rate has slowed down because various economic difficulties have probably reduced capital accumulation, have distorted the structure of prices, and have allocated the reduced investment toward less efficient projects. A continuation of these policies can only prompt further reductions in the growth rate.

Many of the countries that approach the Fund for programmes have been following policies that repress the financial market and particular activities. For example, real interest rates may have been maintained at negative levels and producer prices may have been kept at levels that discourage activities in those sectors.[10] These policies are pursued to promote certain sectors over others. A repressed financial market, for instance, means that those who, because of connections, manage to get credit at negative real rates do very well, but those who save and make financial investments do very badly. As a consequence, financial savings dry out and savers place their resources either in real estate and other safe but unproductive investments, or take their money out of the country.

Countries that approach the Fund are often overregulated. The pervasive and repressive influence of the government in all sorts of activities is very much felt. In these countries, government permission is often required to start investment, to import, to obtain foreign exchange for imports, to export, and to engage in many other forms of economic activities; and permission for these activities is not easily obtainable. Labour legislation is overly rigid and investment codes overly generous. Of course, overregulation brings corruption, and this is unlikely to be a factor favourable for growth. The economies of these countries are often closed as the lack of foreign exchange, associated with the various distortions mentioned above, forces the countries to restrain imports. Local activities are strangled by a lack of basic inputs. Selective and excessive import restrictions are imposed in order to provide protection for particular domestic activities. The products of these activities are produced at high costs, thus again placing an obstacle to growth. This is the situation often encountered by Fund missions when they visit a country that has requested Fund assistance in pursuing an adjustment programme.

Fund programmes have broadly the objectives of reducing the rate of inflation, when that rate is high; improving the balance of payments; raising the efficiency of the economy; and creating the conditions necessary to stimulate a faster rate of growth. The policy instruments used in the programmes are many, but the most important are:

1. *The exchange rate*: If the exchange rate is assessed to be overvalued, the programme will call for a devaluation.
2. *Opening of the market*: If the economy of the country has been too closed, the programme will aim at opening it by dismantling quotas, lowering high tariffs, and removing other restrictions on imports.
3. *Fiscal reform*: The programme will call for an adjustment in the fiscal accounts since a fiscal deficit is often one of the major causes

of macroeconomic instability or the difficulties in the balance of payments. Fiscal adjustments will normally be required on both sides of the budget. An attempt will be made to increase government revenue without affecting, or while enhancing, incentive effects. If the tariffs of the public enterprises are too low, they will be adjusted. Tax bases will be broadened, but high tax rates will often be reduced. Tax administration will receive particular attention. In general, the objective is to raise more revenue while making the tax system less of an obstacle to development, so as not to reduce growth. Most of the sub-Saharan countries which have entered into programmes with the Fund have received technical assistance in taxation. This assistance has helped them raise or maintain revenue in the face of negative macroeconomic developments, such as deteriorating terms of trade.

On the expenditure side of the budget, concern is placed on reducing various forms of 'unproductive' spending, be this in investment or in other areas. Bloated public services are slimmed down; high real wages are reduced; 'white elephants' are eliminated from the investment budget; spending of marginal value is reduced and, in general, an attempt is made to make public expenditure more effective in achieving its objectives while reducing the total. Once again, special attention is paid to ensure that the expenditure cuts do not fall disproportionately on the poor.

The adjustment in public spending often raises questions about the role of the state in the economy and thus tends to step on many toes. This is a highly controversial area since political objectives often conflict with economic objectives. It is not surprising that public spending reduction is one of the areas which has attracted great attention from Fund critics. Every vested interest whose expenditure is reduced is likely to scream and accuse the Fund. In sub-Saharan Africa, Fund technical assistance has also aimed at creating the administrative capacity necessary to scrutinise and control public spending. Lack of such capacity has been a major factor in overruns and in the continuation of questionable spending.

4. *Financial reforms*: Programmes have been paying a lot of attention to financial liberalisation and to credit expansion. The attempt to raise real interest rates is seen as necessary for channelling resources to more productive uses. Evidence available indicates that the African countries that have entered in programmes with the Fund have generally succeeded in raising interest rates to positive levels. *Credit expansion* receives a lot of attention because of its

close connection with the behaviour of prices. Thus, limits on credit expansion, and on credit absorbed by the public sector, are found in most programmes.

5. *Price reforms*: Fund-supported programmes pay substantial attention to price reform since price controls in important sectors often distort resource allocations in major ways, thereby retarding growth. Agricultural producer prices are also often repressed to provide cheap food to the urban areas, which are politically much more vocal. As a result, agricultural production declines, food imports increase, and migration to the cities rises which exacerbates both poverty and environmental problems. Fund-supported programmes try to remove these distortions so that the signals that prices send to both producers and consumers reflect more closely the real opportunity costs of producing and consuming those goods.

All of the instruments described above have short-term adjustment effects, but they are also basic conditions for long-term growth. In fact, it can be argued that Fund programmes attempt to reduce the negative effect on growth that comes from economic distortion or poor policy. Recent work has attempted to estimate econometrically the impact of these distortions on long-term growth. It is difficult to see how removing these distortions could have negative effects on growth as some critics seem to imply.

It is difficult to assess the impact of Fund programmes on growth because the only valid test would compare the countries' performance with the Fund counterfactual test; but this is never possible. In sub-Saharan African countries, the test is made particularly difficult by the sharp deterioration in the terms of trade experienced by many of these countries over the programme period. We are, therefore, left with the always questionable before-and-after test. This test is questionable because, as indicated earlier, the fact that the countries need a programme is a clear indication that their policies had become unsustainable. In other words, the performance before the programme is too good to be sustainable in the absence of a programme or without the countries themselves making needed reforms. The time element is also important. The real test should not be how well or how badly the countries perform during the programme but how they will perform in the medium and longer run, assuming that they continue to follow the policies recommended by the programme. Keeping these caveats in mind, it is comforting to report that real GDP growth generally improves for countries that adhere to the agreements in a Fund programme and that do not experience exceptional deteriorations in their terms of trade.

VI SURVEY OF SOME EMPIRICAL STUDIES

Several studies have attempted to assess the impact of adjustment programmes on economic performance. On the whole, they conclude that adjusting countries are better-off even in the short run. While fiscal adjustments may require reductions in public expenditure, they are unlikely to represent a major social or economic problem if the cuts are made wisely and are complemented with revenue-enhancing measures. For example, in Mexico the fiscal adjustment largely reflected a sharp reduction in inefficient public sector investment. Furthermore, it bears repeating that cuts are not made because of the programmes, but because the current levels of spending cannot be maintained any longer. Statistical evidence indicates that, on average, the share of total public expenditure in GDP in sub-Saharan Africa declined only marginally over the decade of the 1980s (see Table 4.5).

In a 1993 paper, Nashashibi shows that adjustment requires an appropriate macroeconomic mix of reinforcing policies (for a more general discussion of these issues see Tanzi, 1989). In particular, Nashashibi demonstrates that an appropriate exchange rate is critical in protecting fiscal revenues because of their dependence on imports and the traded goods sector. Since sub-Saharan African countries are subject to wide swings in terms of trade, a flexible exchange rate policy is necessary to preserve the competitiveness of domestic production and the tax base. Sustaining fiscal revenues through a flexible exchange rate policy relieves the authorities from painful cuts in expenditures which, under other circumstances, would adversely affect social areas. In the CFA franc zone in Africa, a number of Central and West African countries experienced a sharp deterioration in their terms of trade after 1985, in conjunction with an appreciation of their real exchange rate. The resulting fall in income and widening of the fiscal deficit put pressure on their governments to sharply reduce expenditures, including those in social areas.

The theoretical underpinnings of SAPs and the core policies needed to implement economic reforms are set down in an article by Johnson (1992). He points out that, apart from exogenous disturbances, the failure to fully implement adjustment programmes in the African context results largely from a lack of political support and from poor

Table 4.5 Total public expenditure, selected sub-Saharan African countries, 1980-91 (as % of GDP)

	1980	*1981*	*1982*	*1983*	*1984*	*1985*	*1986*	*1987*	*1988*	*1989*	*1990*	*1991*
Benin	25.2	26.0	32.6	32.1	30.9	25.9	23.8	23.9	22.3	20.0	19.9	18.7
Botswana[a]	40.1	43.8	40.5	36.3	39.1	31.6	37.2	37.4	35.9	37.7	41.6	42.7
Burkina Faso	34.7	32.7	34.0	36.1	30.5	20.7	26.1	29.0	25.6	23.2	19.0	21.2
Burundi	24.0	25.4	27.6	30.6	25.7	23.4	24.5	30.3	26.7	27.8	28.9	26.4
Cameroon[b]	16.5	21.7	24.7	23.6	23.3	22.1	23.1	32.0	24.2	21.9	23.1	24.7
CAR	18.1	18.9	15.9	16.9	22.3	27.0	25.5	28.2	26.1	23.3	24.1	23.5
Congo	40.5	38.6	49.2	46.1	40.5	38.5	43.0	32.5	37.0	33.8	31.1	35.8
Côte d'Ivoire	40.1	38.3	40.2	40.9	35.7	34.6	31.9	33.7	40.3	40.6	36.5	35.8
Gabon	24.6	25.3	25.8	32.8	34.2	37.0	48.0	31.4	32.8	26.8	28.6	27.6
Gambia, The[b]	31.7	36.2	36.3	29.5	34.1	33.5	26.2	36.6	37.1	26.0	29.9	24.0
Ghana	11.1	11.0	11.2	8.2	10.2	14.0	14.3	14.3	14.3	14.4	13.9	14.9
Kenya[b]	32.2	34.9	33.4	28.2	27.6	29.7	29.7	30.2	28.1	30.2	30.6	30.3
Madagascar	29.6	24.4	19.6	17.9	17.9	17.2	16.2	18.7	17.1	20.5	16.9	16.3
Malawi[a]	39.4	35.7	29.5	28.7	28.2	32.2	34.2	29.2	27.9	28.6	25.7	23.8
Mali	23.3	27.0	22.1	26.6	23.3	30.2	30.4	26.3	25.3	27.1	25.4	27.8
Mauritania	28.8	29.1	30.9	27.9	27.3	24.9	23.7	25.7	26.1	29.4	27.4	24.9
Mauritius[b]	32.1	36.4	34.0	32.5	29.6	28.8	26.5	25.2	25.8	27.6	27.0	26.0
Mozambique	30.2	38.4	39.3	49.1	41.4	27.8	31.2	37.2	44.7	47.6	51.9	51.3
Niger[c]	18.9	17.6	19.7	19.1	19.6	20.4	20.1	20.3	20.9	20.9	23.7	18.4
Nigeria	25.3	23.9	20.6	21.0	14.4	13.6	20.1	24.9	23.6	21.4	23.1	25.2
Rwanda[b]	9.5	19.7	19.3	19.2	17.1	18.6	20.9	23.7	21.7	21.0	22.8	25.4
Senegal[b]	28.4	31.9	23.9	26.1	25.2	23.5	21.7	21.4	20.1	20.8	21.3	19.8
Sierra Leone[b]	28.9	31.3	26.8	21.8	17.3	18.9	19.1	25.3	16.0	17.2	20.7	21.0
Somalia	23.1	18.1	18.6	18.1	17.2	20.4	30.7	33.6	28.8	55.9	36.4	...

continued on page 92

Table 4.5 continued

	1980	*1981*	*1982*	*1983*	*1984*	*1985*	*1986*	*1987*	*1988*	*1989*	*1990*	*1991*
Tanzania[b]	37.8	33.3	34.5	29.1	29.5	27.1	23.1	24.6	24.7	27.9	27.4	26.8
Togo	32.5	33.2	32.1	35.4	36.1	36.1	37.6	33.1	28.7	28.9	28.6	22.3
Uganda[b]	5.9	9.8	17.8	15.2	17.8	17.7	12.2	9.4	13.0	10.1	12.5	16.0
Zaire	12.8	22.6	23.0	17.2	24.7	25.4	23.5	25.0	32.4	25.2	25.9	...
Zambia	44.4	37.0	38.7	33.9	30.0	36.8	53.3	32.9	30.4	27.0	32.9	37.1
Zimbabwe[b]	35.4	36.3	35.6	40.6	40.8	42.4	44.3	46.2	45.7	46.9	45.5	48.6
Average	27.5	28.6	28.6	28.0	27.1	26.7	28.1	28.1	27.4	27.7	27.4	27.0

Notes: [a] Fiscal year: April–March; [b] Fiscal year: July–June; [c] Fiscal year: October–September through 1988/9, calendar years from 1989.

Source: Data provided by the authorities; IMF staff estimates; Nashashibi, 1993.

policy management, in the face of transitory adjustment costs. Specifically, he stresses that the policies and measures to minimise certain distributional consequences must be in place *prior to* implementation of the programme. Moreover, in sub-Saharan Africa, the lack of a legal and institutional framework for a proper transition towards a market economy seems to have raised the short-term adjustment costs. Finally, Johnson maintains that without a strong mandate from the society, it may be difficult to successfully implement adjustment programmes. In other words, if the programmes do not fully live up to hopes, do not blame them.

An important OECD study (Bourguignon and Morrisson, 1992) took a sample of seven developing countries (Chile, Côte d'Ivoire, Ecuador, Ghana, Indonesia, Malaysia and Morocco) which underwent structural adjustment to tackle exogenous interest rate and terms of trade shocks in the early 1980s. Some common features of the adjustment programmes are singled out in the study. It found that, on the whole, short-term costs of adjustment depended on the initial conditions of the economy, on the timeliness of applying corrective policies, and on the nature of the adjustment. For example, adjustment costs are less intense in an economy when it has strong legal and institutional frameworks, flexible prices, and is less vulnerable to external shocks. The study points to Ghana as an example of delayed adjustment. Regarding the nature of the adjustment, measures such as price liberalisation resulted in net social gains, while policies implemented to restructure and reform public sector employment tended to have large social costs, thus requiring properly targeted safety net programmes.

The study urges donors to actively involve themselves in persuading countries to adjust on a timely basis if adjustment costs are to be minimised. With reference to fiscal measures, while per capita public expenditure seems to have declined in all countries this was mainly due to cuts in wages and salaries rather than expenditures on public services. Indeed, net public transfers actually increased in all countries except for Côte d'Ivoire. The paper also presents simulation exercises showing that *in all cases any adjustment (full or partial) is preferable to no adjustment for both growth and equity considerations.*

Sahn (1992) examines the trend of real government expenditures in 29 sub-Saharan African countries that implemented a variety of structural adjustment programmes, and concludes that the data do not support the hypothesis of widespread and systematic decline in total expenditure. He found that in 19 of these economies, the level of real total discretionary spending actually increased during the adjustment years of 1987–90. In contrast, budgetary contraction occurred in non-adjusting countries such as Swaziland and Liberia. With regard to allocations for social services, these increased during the adjustment period in most of the countries reviewed. However, government spending for higher education and hospitals exceeded the outlays for primary education and preventive and basic health care.

A World Bank study (1992b) compared three groups of developing countries which received adjustment lending during the 1980s and those which did not. While growth and stability objectives have, on the whole, been achieved, albeit with some lag, the study acknowledges that the temporary decline in the welfare of the urban poor and the delay in the recovery of private sector investment have been problematic, particularly in low-income countries. With regard to the slump in private investment, the study points to the need for financial sector reform and the promotion of confidence in the economic adjustment as important prerequisites. Also, in recognition of the need to support social sector spending to the vulnerable groups during the transition, the study provides statistical evidence as to the increasing use of World Bank adjustment loans to contain this problem. Nevertheless, it is emphasised that the poor would be worse off if there were no adjustment at all. The study also found that the bulk of the deficit reduction achieved in adjusting countries resulted from increases in revenue. On the expenditure side, as a result of improved public investment management, there has been a decline in capital relative to current expenditures. On the other hand, the study reveals that real per capita social sector spending did not decline, and in about 60 per cent of the cases under study it actually increased. However, the need to improve the delivery of basic social services to rural areas and to the urban poor by restructuring social expenditure has not been fully addressed.

VII CONCLUDING REMARKS

The main objective of this chapter has been to describe the evolving nature of IMF work. The Fund is a living institution that reacts to, and shapes, economic developments in the world. The 1980s witnessed various intellectual developments which inevitably had an impact on the organisation. For example, the rediscovery of the supply side of the economy and the renewed optimism concerning the role of markets affected the Fund's attitude toward structural changes. The renewed interest in income distribution and concern for the poor led to more explicit attention being paid to poverty. The increasing attention dedicated to the environment and to 'good governance' in general were echoed within the Fund. Of course, there is a limit to the objectives that can be taken into account by Fund programmes since each new objective requires additional staff attention, and thus additional staff, which may make it difficult for the Fund to remain focused on its fundamental objective.[11]

The chapter has also indirectly addressed two common criticisms against the Fund: first, that its programmes are damaging to the poor; and second, that they are damaging to the growth prospects of a country. As to the first of these criticisms, the chapter has tried to give an idea of IMF's attempts to protect the most vulnerable groups. Although it would be foolhardy to argue that Fund-supported programmes never negatively affect these groups, it is safe to maintain that the critics' view – namely, that these programmes almost routinely damage the standard of living of those at the bottom end of the income distribution – is simply untrue. More often than not, Fund-supported programmes are likely to raise the standard of living of the poor, or, at worst, to stop its decline. And, as argued, when Fund-supported programmes result in cuts in public spending, it is because the current level of spending has become unsustainable. But by providing some financial resources and by urging policies that protect the poor, the net result is often less damaging to the poor than it would have otherwise been had no programme been introduced.

As to the second criticism, the chapter has argued that the frequently used *before and after* criterion for testing this conclusion is not a relevant one since the situation prior to the introduction of a programme is introduced is not sustainable. If it was sustainable, the country would not have approached the Fund. However, the more valid *with and without* criterion is never feasible. Nonetheless, several analyses of countries with Fund-supported programmes have concluded that, at worst, the growth rate may have slowed down in the first year of the programme, but *if the country's authorities abided by the directives of the programmes*, growth prospects improved subsequently, though it occasionally took some time to convince those responsible for private economic decisions that the changes were there to stay. When the institutions are weak, the quality of governance poor, and the country's economy is very distorted, the results quickly generated by programmes are unlikely to be as desirable as one would like. But then the blame should not be placed on the programmes. In these cases, nothing will work unless the type of governance is changed.

The chapter has shown that in recent years Fund-supported programmes have used far more instruments than those which critics focus on. They have, for example, recommended tax reform to make the tax systems more efficient; expenditure reform to weed out wasteful public expenditure; financial reform to increase the efficiency with which financial saving is used and to raise the level of financial saving; foreign trade reform and adjustment of the exchange rate to better integrate the country with the world economy, and so forth. These are not changes that would reduce the rate of growth. Many of these recommendations have been made in close collaboration with the World Bank.

Finally, the chapter has stressed that the involvement of the IMF with the countries extends beyond the negotiated programme and the instruments mentioned in the letters of intent. For example, the Fund technical assistance work has been growing in importance and in scope. This work is primarily aimed at helping countries establish strong economic institutions for sustainable policy formulation and implementation. Technical assistance is coordinated closely with financial programming work, but it extends beyond programme countries. The Fund's surveillance role also has longer-term implications. It aims at promoting globally consistent sustained economic stability and growth in the developing and industrial worlds, as well as in economies in transition. It also aims at helping sustain good policies. It is thus in a sense comparable to *preventive* health care, while financial programmes are, at times, more comparable to *curative* health care. The results of the surveillance activity are not always immediately visible but over the longer run they are as important as those of financial programmes.

The Fund is continually questioning its own *modus operandi* in order to make it more efficient and responsive to major concerns. It recognises that mistakes have occasionally been made and that there is always scope for improvement. In fact, the changes that occurred throughout the 1980s are strong indications that the Fund is not the rigid institution assumed by its critics.

NOTES

1. During this period, what had been called stabilisation programmes were gradually renamed *adjustment* programmes to reflect the change in emphasis.

2. Having lived through the Great Depression, the founding fathers had been acutely aware the economic instability was not consistent with prosperity.
3. At this time the concern was with income distribution rather than with the very poor.
4. Critics seem to believe that, for example, reductions in imports or in public spending occur because of Fund-supported programmes, not because their level has become unsustainable.
5. Of course, a country might not come to the Fund for a programme, but it might still pursue a strong adjustment programme on its own. In this case, the instruments used would probably be largely the same, but the country would not have the benefit of the additional financial resources that accompany a Fund programme. Thus, the required reduction in imports and in public spending would be larger.
6. It was, however, recognised that it would not always be possible to protect the most vulnerable groups, especially in situations in which major distortions required drastic measures. In some cases, the institutional set-up to introduce programmes aimed at helping these groups would not be available and could not be introduced in the short term.
7. In recent years the Managing Director of the Fund has been advocating the pursuit of 'high quality growth', by which he means growth that takes into account the social, political and environmental implications of economic change.
8. It has been argued, for example, that by backing devaluations the Fund may be encouraging the excessive exploitation of natural resources, including forests and minerals. By the same token, however, failure to introduce a devaluation, when this is necessary, may bring poverty and other kinds of environmental problems.
9. For example, deterioration in the terms of trade and a sharp rise in real interest rates contributed to the deterioration of the macroeconomic situation in the early 1980s in many developing countries. However, when the shocks extend over the longer run, the countries need to adjust to them.
10. For example, farmers are often forced into subsistence farming by the low prices they received on their cash crops.
11. This means that there will always be some group or some special interest that will blame the Fund for not paying adequate attention to the group's particular concern.

5 Are Short-term Policies Consistent with Long-term Development Needs in Africa?

Frances Stewart*

I INTRODUCTION

Stabilisation and adjustment policies dominated policy-making in African countries throughout the 1980s. Given the persistence of the problems most countries are facing, it is likely that this situation will continue for the rest of the century. Most of the adjustment policies were formulated in collaboration with the major international financial institutions. During the 1980s, 34 countries had agreements with the IMF or the World Bank (UN/ECA, 1989). As the Vice President for the Africa region of the World Bank, has stated, 'the Bank has, however unintentionally, assumed the dominant intellectual role on African issues' (Jaycox, 1993b). The policies agreed with these institutions, particularly those associated with the IMF, were largely short-term in their main focus. Yet they have had important medium- and long-term implications, especially since they have been adopted over such a prolonged period. Thus, some countries had IMF agreements almost continuously throughout the 1980s, while many had two or more during the decade. Despite their medium-term implications, there appears to have been a tendency to neglect Africa's longer-term needs in formulating adjustment policies. In some respects, indeed, it appears that the policies being pursued are *actually moving African economies away from a desirable medium-term path.*

This chapter aims to elucidate the potential conflicts and com-

* This chapter draws heavily on a research project conducted at Queen Elizabeth House. The papers from this project were published in Stewart, F., S. Lall and S. Wangwe (eds), *Alternative Development Strategies for Sub-Saharan Africa* (London: Macmillan, 1992). I am grateful to the participants in the project, and especially my fellow editors, for many ideas contained in this chapter.

plementarities between the adjustment policies being adopted and long-term development needs. The next section briefly reviews the content of the adjustment policies. Section III considers longer-term development needs in sub-Saharan African economies and some of the policy implications which follow. Section IV discusses the consistency between the adjustment policies and policies appropriate for long-term development. Section V reviews alternative short-term policies that would be more consistent than the current set of policies with long-term development needs.

II STABILISATION AND ADJUSTMENT POLICY REFORMS ADOPTED IN THE 1980S

In the 1980s the reforms put forward by the Bank and the Fund set the parameters of policy change in Africa; though, of course, the extent to which particular countries consistently followed the whole package of reforms varied.

In principle, one should distinguish between *stabilisation* policies of the Fund and *structural adjustment* policies of the World Bank. The former aim to reduce short-term disequilibria, especially budget deficits, balance of payments deficits and inflation, while the latter are concerned to reorient the structure of the economy towards greater efficiency in the medium term. In practice, however, the distinction has become blurred because Bank programmes are never instituted unless a Fund programme is in place, and because the two institutions have recently undertaken joint programmes.

There has been considerable homogeneity in Fund-supported programmes in different countries. Three categories of policy have formed part of almost every programme: *demand* restraint, *switching* policies and policies relating to *long-term supply* or *efficiency*. The demand restraint element consists in policies aimed at reducing demand in the economy, with the objective of curtailing expenditure on imports and releasing resources for exports. Relevant policy instruments include reductions in government expenditure (or in its rate of increase) and in the budget deficit, controls over the money supply and credit creation, and real wage cuts. Switching policies aim to shift resources from non-tradables to tradables by changing incentives. Devaluation and exchange rate unification are the main policy instruments, accompanied by wage control and changes in domestic prices, especially in agriculture. Long-term supply policies are designed to secure a more market-oriented economy, subject to fewer restrictions and less segmentation. Reforms include trade liberalisation, financial reforms to raise interest rates in the formal sector and to integrate credit markets, and price reforms.

Analysis of the composition of Fund programmes for 1980–4 shows that demand restraint policies were implemented in almost every case, while switching and long-term policies were adopted in a somewhat lower proportion of cases (Cornia et al., 1987). Examination of World Bank structural adjustment loans (SALs) shows that the philosophical basis and values, being strongly market-oriented, were the same as Fund programmes. 'Like the IMF it stresses monetary and fiscal orthodoxy, appropriate real exchange rates, positive real interest rates, and liberal approaches on external account' (Helleiner, 1988).

Categorisation of the major SAL policy instruments suggests four major elements (Mosley, 1987): mobilisation of domestic resources through fiscal, monetary and credit policies; improvements in the efficiency of resource use – in the public sector measures include reform and privatisation, and in the private sector they largely comprise price decontrol, reduced subsidies, competition from imports and credit reform, and encouragement to direct foreign investment; trade policies, with emphasis on import liberalisation and improved export incentives; and finally, institutional reforms to improve the capacity of the public sector and to develop institutions to support the productive sectors.

III LONG-TERM DEVELOPMENT OBJECTIVES AND STRATEGY

In the Lagos Plan of Action (OAU, 1981), African heads of State and Government defined their long-run development objectives as:

- the alleviation of mass poverty and improvement in the standard of living of the people;
- self-sustained development;
- national and regional self-reliance.

There is an interesting contrast between these and the World Bank objectives put forward by Jaycox (1993b), as 'a consensus – in Africa and between Africa and the donor community – on Africa's development objectives'. The 'consensus' objectives are:

- to stimulate growth and encourage people and businesses to be productive and efficient;
- to develop Africa's human and institutional capacities;
- to increase agricultural productivity, reduce population growth rates and protect the environment;
- to achieve greater development results through improved project implementation and expanded and enhanced policy dialogue, economic and sector work and donor coordination.

The World Bank objectives underline efficiency and policy dialogue, while the African objectives emphasise poverty reduction, welfare improvement and self-reliance. Conflicts and complementarities between the two sets of objectives are to a certain extent mirrored in similar conflicts and complementarities between pro-development short- and medium-term policies and the orthodox policy set advocated by the international financial institutions, as discussed in Section V of this chapter.

The objectives put forward by the African heads of States are defined in very general terms. More concrete goals need to be articulated for policy-planning. Vital contributory objectives are the attainment of a viable balance of payments, with adequate foreign exchange for economic and social needs, and without undue reliance on aid or borrowing; the achievement of sustained growth in agricultural and industrial production, with relatively faster growth of industry over the medium term; full participation of the labour force in productive activities, with adequate remuneration; and comprehensive access of the population to basic needs, including basic health care, basic education, food, water and sanitation.

On the basis of this sketch of objectives, it is possible to identify seven major elements which form an essential part of any strategy likely to achieve these objectives. We shall briefly discuss each of these elements and their policy implications.

(A) Agrarian-focused strategy

Probably the single most important policy mistake of the 1960s, 1970s and early 1980s was the neglect of agriculture, especially food agriculture. Despite its importance in total output and employment, in the first half of the 1980s, agriculture received less than 10 per cent of total government expenditure (Table 5.1). In particular, small-scale agriculture suffered from a total lack of technological modernisation

Table 5.1 Indicators of neglect of agriculture, selected sub-Saharan African countries

	Agriculture as % of GDP 1987	*Agriculture as % of labour force 1980*	*Share of govt. expenditure going to agriculture average 1980, 1985*	*Fertiliser cons. (100s gm per hectare) 1986*	*Irrigated land as % arable and permanent 1984–6*
Botswana	3	70	9.8	5	0
Burkina Faso	38	87	4.9	61	0
Côte d'Ivoire	36	65	9.7[a]	83	1
Ethiopia	42	80	9.6	66	1
Ghana	51	56	9.2	50	6
Kenya	31	81	9.4	518	2
Madagascar	43	81	7.6	23	27
Malawi	37	83	9.3	131	1
Niger	34	91	4.5	7	1
Nigeria	30	68	4.9	94	3
Senegal	22	81	4.3[a]	40	3
Sierra Leone	45	70	3.8	22	2
Tanzania	61	n.a.	8.6	77	2
Zambia	54	73	16.9	148	0
Zimbabwe	11	73	8.9	571	6
SSA	34	71	7.3	85	n.a.
All low–income economies	31	71	n.a.	706	n.a.

Note: [a] 1980 only.

Source: World Bank, 1989a; UNDP/World Bank, 1989.

Table 5.2 Indices of consequences of neglect of agriculture, selected sub-Saharan African countries

	Food prod. per capita	*Cereal imports (vol.) 1990*	*Agricultural production % p.a. growth*		*Children under 5 malnutrition 1980–91*			*Calorie supply as % requirements*
	1988–90 (1979–81=100)	*(1974=100)*	*1965-80*	*1980-90*	*a*	*b*	*c*	*1988-90*
Botswana	75	414	9.7	–4.0	15	n.a.	n.a.	97
Burkina Faso	114	146	n.a.	3.3	n.a.	n.a.	n.a.	94
Côte d'Ivoire	101	292	3.3	1.0	12	17	20	111
Ethiopia	84	582	1.2	–0.1	38	19	43	73
Ghana	97	190	1.6	1.0	27	15	39	93
Kenya	106	1 253	5.0	3.3	14	5	32	89
Madagascar	88	161	n.a.	2.4	33	17	56	95
Malawi	83	676	4.1	2.0	24	8	61	88
Niger	71	55	–3.4	n.a.	49	23	38	95
Nigeria	106	129	1.7	3.3	36	16	54	93
Senegal	102	157	1.4	3.1	22	8	28	98
Sierra Leone	89	203	3.9	2.6	23	14	n.a.	83
Tanzania	88	18	1.6	4.1	48	n.a.	n.a.	95
Zambia	103	108	2.2	3.7	25	10	59	87
Zimbabwe	94	148	n.a.	2.4	12	2	31	94
SSA	94	186	2.0	2.1	31	13	44	93
All low– and mid–income economies	115	172	2.9	3.2	36[d]	144[d]	48[d]	107[d]

Note: [a] % underweight
[b] % wasting (12–23 months)
[c] % stunting (24–59 months)
[d] All developing countries

Source: World Bank, 1992a; UNDP, 1993b.

and poor access to inputs. As a result of this insufficient public expenditure – as well as of deficient credit markets, inappropriate pricing policies and low savings – levels of irrigation and fertiliser use remained substantially below the level of low-income economies (see Table 11.5 and Chapter 12). Poor agricultural performance followed, with adverse consequences for food availability, nutrition and the balance of payments (see Table 5.2 and Chapters 11 and 14).

It must be emphasised that the agrarian-focused strategy proposed is not one of *agricultural promotion at any cost and of any type*. It is essential that it be reasonably egalitarian, that it focuses on food crops, especially crops produced and/or consumed by poor people, and that non-traditional, high-value, exportable crops be encouraged if the benefits are to be equitably distributed. Experience suggests that such strategy should be *smallholder*-based, in order to avoid the inequities associated with large-scale plantations and the inefficiency of most socialist forms of agriculture in Africa. The policy implications of this analysis include:

- *Land reform*: land tenure systems should be reviewed in each country to assess their implications for efficiency and equity. In countries that already exhibit severe land inequality (Ghai and Radwan, 1983), such a review might argue for an immediate land redistribution; in others the institution of land ceilings may instead be required. As inequalities may develop rapidly in the context of smallholder agriculture once full private property rights are instituted (see Chapter 11), periodic reviews, possibly leading to land redistribution or other measures, are likely to be needed.
- *Extended access to inputs*: in almost every country, improved R&D efforts on the crops produced by small farmers are required, and there is a strong need to improve extension, supply of inputs and access to credit. This will entail institutional reforms as well as a substantial increase in resource flows to this sector.
- *Price reforms*: the current reforms rightly aim to improve the rural terms of trade, but the focus is biased towards export crops. Food crops – particularly traditional food crops – need similar price support.

(B) Support for rural non-agricultural production

Potentially, rural non-agriculture – especially modern activities – could play a very important role in medium-term development by increasing rural employment, raising rural incomes and allowing a more regionally balanced type of industrial development (Page and Steel, 1984; Haggblade et al., 1990). They would also contribute to raising agricultural production by bringing to the countryside the goods, services and information likely to stimulate agricultural production (Ranis et al., 1990). To achieve such a dynamic, a growing and relatively egalitarian agriculture is needed. In addition, it is necessary to improve supply conditions by developing rural infrastructure as well as energy and technology dissemination, by enhancing technical education, and by creating or strengthening credit institutions directed towards small-scale borrowers.

(C) Industrial development

Industrialisation is an essential aspect of long-term development. As Lall (1992) states, 'In nearly all economies, manufacturing industry has been the critical agent of the structural transformation that marks the transition from a primitive, low productivity, low income state to one that is dynamic, sustained and diversified.' For many sub-Saharan countries, however, most of the 1980s were years of industrial stagnation or even *deindustrialisation* (Table 5.3). Many countries were thus moving away from the long-term goal of industrialisation and diversification, in clear conflict with longer-term development needs.

The pursuit of greater industrialisation does not mean, however, that it is desirable to reproduce the industrialisation patterns of the past. Reviews of the experience over the last 30 years clearly reveal that, for the most part, those patterns were inefficient by every measure: they were highly protected, highly import-dependent, had very low linkages with the rest of the economy and were associated with very low levels of export (Lall, 1987, 1992; Riddell and Associates, 1990).

Unlike the large-scale formal sector, where examples of successful industrial development have been few and far between, the small-scale sector has been notably more successful (Page and Steel, 1984). This sector adopts labour-intensive technologies, manufactures products in demand by many low-income households and easily exhibits social benefit-cost ratios which exceed one and are invariably higher than those of the formal sector (Liedholm and Mead, 1987).

The high degree of public ownership in African industry is often blamed for much of the observed inefficiency. In 1980, for example, the net losses of public enterprises in Niger and Mali amounted to 4 and 6 per cent of GDP; the large public investments in Kenya pro-

Table 5.3 Deindustrialisation in sub-Saharan Africa in the 1980s

	Countries showing negative or no change in industrial output % p.a., 1986–9
Liberia	–6.0[a]
Niger	–4.3[a]
Mozambique	–4.1
Sierra Leone	–1.5
Nigeria	–1.2
Tanzania	0
	Countries with growth below 2.0% p.a.
Côte d'Ivoire	0.3
Togo	0.3
Zambia	0.7
Somalia	1.0
Madagascar	1.2
Rwanda	1.2
Swaziland	1.9
Total SSA	2.0

Note: [a]1980–7.

Source: World Bank, 1989a, 1992a.

duced a rate of return of only 0.2 per cent (Knight, 1992); in Tanzania, public enterprises have consistently exhibited high capital intensity and low capacity utilisation (James, 1985).

Privatisation, together with greater reliance on direct foreign investment (DFI), is advocated by the World Bank as a means of enhancing industrial efficiency and of helping the capital account of the balance of payments (see Chapter 10 for a full discussion of this topic).

However, past experience shows that in Africa the direct impact of DFI on the balance of payments has generally been negative, with outflows of dividends exceeding new capital inflows in recent years. In addition, DFI has largely been concentrated on import substitution; only in Malawi, Botswana, Zimbabwe and Senegal has it been associated with a significant increase in manufactured exports. Also, the technology used in DFI appears to be capital-intensive and import-dependent (see the evidence of Mytelka, 1992; Cockcroft, 1992; and Ohiorhenuan and Paloamina, 1992). Thus, experience suggests that DFI cannot be relied on as a substantial support for the balance of payments, nor as a panacea for the efficiency problems of African industry, while prospects for increasing DFI in the current environment are also poor. Experience with joint ventures suggests instead that nominal control (through ownership of capital) does slowly bring about indigenisation of directorships and management, leading to greater local control over decision-making than is possible with undiluted DFI, without any obvious efficiency cost (Barba Navaretti, 1992).

It is difficult to devise policies likely to increase efficiency while permitting the development of African capabilities, because for the former strong external competitive pressures may be needed, while for the latter protection, at least for a limited period, may be essential. The dual objectives of developing efficient industrialisation and building up African capabilities suggests the following policy conclusions.

1 Ownership patterns: developing African capacity

In view of the weakness of the indigenously owned private medium- to large-scale sector, wholesale privatisation is neither desirable nor politically feasible. Analysis of the limited results achieved in Malawi and Zimbabwe confirm that in most of Africa privatisation will, for the time being, remain of marginal significance (Adam et al., 1992; see also Chapter 10). Given the objective of building up African capabilities, new forms of foreign investment, such as joint ventures, are generally a better vehicle for the transfer of technology and management skills than DFI in most contexts. Special tax and foreign trade incentives to DFI are only justified where it is likely to play a key role in promoting non-traditional exports.

The main emphasis of an industrialisation strategy should be on increasing the efficiency of public enterprises and on the development of industrial firms owned and managed by Africans. As noted earlier, the existence of an efficient small-scale African industrial sector provides a potential basis for this.

2 Structured markets

The frequent discrimination against the small-scale sector (Wangwe and Bagachwa, 1990; Ndlela, 1990) needs to be reversed. The introduction of unfettered markets, however, does not by itself secure resources for the small-scale enterprises which typically lack collateral and cannot compete with large firms in unstructured credit markets. In Zambia, the market solution led to virtually *all* foreign exchange being allocated to large firms (Ncube et al., 1987).

Structured markets are needed: this means reserving a proportion of resources – credit, foreign exchange, and so on – for the small-scale sector, and thus ensuring that a 'market' solution generates adequate resources for the sector. Structured markets of this kind were successfully implemented, for instance, in India, where the requirement that 1 per cent of credit be allocated by the major banks to the small-scale sector led to the establishment and successful management of the Self Employed Women's Association. The need to 'structure' resource allocation also applies to government expenditure on infrastructure, technology, and so on.

3 Selective protection

If African industrial capacity is to be established, some protection is essential in the short to medium term. However, policies of the 1960s and 1970s offered excessive protection (in extent and duration). For the future, protection should be *milder* (with greater use of tariffs rather than quotas), of *shorter duration* (i.e., not more than 10 years), and *selective* (only applying to industries where comparative advantage can be developed over a 10-year period). In addition, while regional trade agreements should be promoted (see below), protection should be granted in the context of export promotion policy and should be complemented by selective interventions in factor markets to ensure that the skills, knowledge, infrastructure and institutions needed for competitiveness are forthcoming.

(D) Regional trade and import substitution

Most African economies are too small for efficient import substitution. In many industries, import substitution on a *regional* basis is therefore the only way that a minimum efficient scale of production can be realised. In addition, by extending the market size, production on a regional basis allows for division of labour, specialisation and competition, all of which are essential to efficient growth.

As Chapter 18 elaborates, despite the initiation of over 200 regional agreements on trade and finance, regional trade in Africa still accounts for only about 5 per cent of total official trade (or 10 to 12 per cent if unrecorded trade is included). Persistent foreign exchange problems, the limited effectiveness of regional payments arrangements in a situation of chronic lack of hard currency (Hardy, 1992), fears of economic domination by subregional powers, political problems between countries and, finally, poor transport infrastructure have all contributed to this disappointing outcome. Yet the potential advantages of regional trade, especially in manufacturing, make it essential to overcome these obstacles, as the Lagos Plan of Action recognises.

Policies to promote regional trade in manufactures should include:

- investment in transport and communication links between African countries;
- extension of regional payments arrangements, especially those providing mutual credit for trade between African economies;
- trade liberalisation on a regional basis, i.e., reduction of tariff and non-tariff barriers on a regional basis, while maintaining restrictions on trade coming from outside the region, as necessary for infant industry protection (see Hardy, 1992, and Chapter 18 of this volume for further policy suggestions).

(E) Diversification of exports

Unlike in South Asia – where the share of primary products fell from 63 per cent to 36 per cent between 1965 and 1990 – during the same years the structure of African exports remained heavily concentrated on a few primary products (Table 5.4). A few countries, notably Zimbabwe, Botswana and Mauritius, however, did see a major transformation of their exports away from primary products, showing that significant diversification is possible.

The continued specialisation on primary products severely handicaps development efforts, mainly due to the adverse trends in the terms of trade and in price fluctuations experienced by primary products (MacBean, 1966). Specialisation on primary products, furthermore, offers less in the way of economies of scale and learning than manufactured exports, while the large share of world exports of African economies in certain commodities – coffee, cocoa and tea (see Table 5.5), characterised by low income and price elasticities of demand (Islam and Subramanian, 1989), means that simultaneous expansion in output by all or many of the African countries results in less than proportionate increases in earnings. Indeed, the decline in commodity prices which took place during the early 1980s may be due less to the downturn in the OECD countries than to overexpansion of aggregate export supply (ibid.).

Structural adjustment policies – which are simultaneously being adopted in a very large number of countries and which each focus on

Table 5.4 Structure of exports, selected sub-Saharan African countries (% of exports)

	Primary products			*Manufactures*	
	1965	*1980*	*1990*	*1965*	*1990*
Ethiopia	99	99	97	1	3
Zaire	92	94	93	8	7
Malawi	99	89	95	1	5
Tanzania	87	84	89	13	11
Burkina Faso	95	89	89	5	11
Mali	97	83	98	3	2
Zambia	100	99	97[a]	0	3[a]
Sierra Leone	39	44	70	61	30
Kenya	94	84	89	6	11
Nigeria	97	99	99	3	1
Ghana	98	98	99	2	1
Senegal	97	85	78	3	22
Zimbabwe	85	71	60[a]	15	40[a]
Côte d'Ivoire	95	90	90	5	10
Congo	37	94	97	63	3
Botswana	96	30	37[a]	4	63[a]
Mauritius	100	71	70	0	30
All SSA	93	96	92	7	8
South Asia	63	30	30	37	70

Note: [a]1987.

Source: World Bank, 1992a, 1989a.

Table 5.5 Demand elasticities for selected commodities

Commodity	*Income elasticity**	*Price elasticity**
Coffee	+0.47	–0.27
Cocoa	+0.18	–0.18
Bananas and plantains	+0.58	–0.40
Tea	+0.52	+0.06
Pineapple	+1.59	–2.67
Tomatoes	+1.63	+0.17

Note: * Preferred estimates.

Sources: Islam and Subramanian, 1989.

the expansion of supply of traditional exports – are thus in part responsible for the worsening terms of trade experienced in the 1980s, and will lead to continued deterioration if the same policies are followed in the 1990s. It follows that diversification away from traditional primary commodities and into manufactures and other crops with higher income elasticities (and for which price elasticities are also likely to be relatively high) should be a very high priority. For example, the income elasticity of tomatoes and pineapples is well above one (Islam and Subramanian, 1989). This leads to the following policy implications:

- Production and exports of traditional crops should *not* be encouraged where elasticities are low; a first priority is for collective action among producers of these commodities to *restrict* supply by reducing price incentives, imposing taxes or by production quotas. Without such collective action, individual countries which restrict production may suffer a loss or double loss of earnings since their supply will fall, while world prices may also fall as other producers increase production. The international financial institutions should avoid encouraging excessive production of such commodities and support collective action to restrict supply. Research and development efforts on traditional crops should be devoted to increasing *demand* by improving quality and end uses, and *not* to increasing supply.
- Diversification into non-traditional crops should be encouraged by R&D, extension, infrastructure and marketing support, as well as price incentives.
- Diversification into manufactured exports should be encouraged by appropriate policies towards investment, human capabilities and incentives, as discussed earlier.

(F) Development of human capabilities

African economies are potentially rich in human resources; yet people are badly educated and in poor health while their capacities remain frequently underused. The consequence is low labour productivity and lack of competitiveness despite the low wages prevailing in most African economies (Helleiner, 1988).

The poor development of human resources in Africa has its origin in colonial history, which left Africa with a markedly worse educational structure than any other area in the world (Lall, 1992, Table

5.1). Since then most African countries have made considerable progress, but in 1986 the *gap* between sub-Saharan Africa and the rest of the developing world was still as large as it was 20 years earlier.

Developments in the 1980s in many respects involved a *reversal* of earlier progress. Real per capita expenditure on education and health *fell* in around two-thirds of the countries. Between 1980 and 1986 the percentage of children enrolled in primary education fell from 79 to 73 per cent for SSA as a whole (secondary education, however, maintained its momentum), calorie availability per head declined in 19 countries, while health conditions generally deteriorated (see Chapters 13 and 14).

In Africa, large improvements in productivity may be attained through improvements in human development: it has been shown that a 1 per cent increase in calorie consumption can lead to a 0.5 per cent increase in productivity among low-income workers (see Strauss's 1986 study on Sierra Leone); by reducing malnutrition among children, child feeding programmes can improve welfare and physical productivity in adulthood (see Cornia and Stewart, 1993, for a summary of evidence); human development can also generate high social and economic externalities through improved health and reduced fertility (see Griffin and Knight, 1989, for a review of evidence).

Yet the stabilisation policies of the 1980s have seen a slowdown or even reversal in the already relatively weak achievements in this area. Resumed and accelerated progress in developing human resources must be placed at the very forefront of a strategy for sustained development in African countries.

(G) Participation and institution building

Participation in the political, economic and social sphere is important both as an end and because it increases the equity and efficiency of development. Indeed, participatory patterns of development empower poor people and ensure that the benefits of development reach them. Past political and economic development has generally been weak in each dimension of participation. Governments have been relatively centralised and undemocratic, with weak or non-existent local government. Economic participation has been limited by the domination of foreigners and the state, while women have been largely excluded from political and economic decision-making. Even most development projects have not been participatory by these criteria, though there have been some examples of successful participatory projects in African countries (see Ghai, 1988, for an excellent analysis of participatory development). One such example is the Six-S movement in Burkina Faso, 'a large-scale, self-help movement, with numbers running into 200,000 and extension into other Sahelian countries' (ibid.), undertaking a variety of income-generating, community activities providing credit to support single projects which are also financed by savings funds from members.

Policies likely to increase participation include: democratisation; decentralisation of the government machinery, and introduction of local government based on local democracy; structured markets (see above) to ensure that resources are available for low-income groups; support for group organisations; reform of aid structures to support participatory projects.

IV ARE PRESENT ADJUSTMENT POLICIES CONSISTENT WITH LONG-TERM DEVELOPMENT NEEDS?

The consistency of present policies with long-term needs can be assessed within two dimensions: first is the issue of whether the present policies are succeeding to restore non-crisis conditions, in terms of the balance of payments and the domestic economy so that growth of investment, public expenditure and imports can be resumed without causing a critical foreign exchange shortage; secondly, there is the question of whether the policies are moving countries toward an appropriate structure for long-term development objectives. As the main purpose of this chapter is to consider the consistency of short-term policies with long-term needs, this section will deal with the issue of short-term effectiveness rather briefly.

(A) Are the policies returning African economies to a viable short-term position?

Despite considerable controversy over this issue, the evidence suggests that the policies are *not* succeeding in restoring viable conditions.[1] Table 5.6 summarises developments. Using the World Bank/UNDP (1989) classification, it can be seen that GNP per capita fell throughout the 1980s for all SSA countries, with smaller falls registered for 1986–9 than for the rest of the decade, and this pattern was shared by countries with 'strong' and 'weak' programmes. Real domestic investment also fell sharply, as did export earnings. The fiscal

Table 5.6 Indicators of short-term policy response in sub-Saharan Africa

	Change per annum			
	1973–80	*1981–5*	*1986–9*	*1990–2*
GNP per capita	+0.1	−1.1[a]	−0.4[a]	−1.9[a]
Inflation rate	+6.8	+23.1	+21.1	+21.4
Investment change	+4.0		−4.3 (1980–90)	
Export earnings (US$bn)	+0.2	−3.0	+3.3	+2.2
Import volume	+2.6	−4.3	+1.5	+0.2
	1981	*1985*	*1989*	*1992*
Investment ratio, %	20.9	18.2	17.7	17.8
Govt. deficit as % GDP	−6.9	−5.4	−7.7	−5.9
Current a/c balance (US$bn)	−9.6	−7.1	−6.3	−7.1
Outstanding debt (US$bn)	56.2[b]	96.2	143.2	n.a.

Notes: [a] GDP per capita; [b] 1980.
Source: World Bank, 1989a; IMF, *World Economic Outlook* (various issues); World Bank, *World Debt Tables* (various years).

deficit continued to be large. Debt continued to accumulate, doubling from 1981 to 1989. The current account deficit remained very large, despite declining imports: in 1992 it was over US$ 7 billion. An analysis by Mosley and Weeks (1993) concludes that 'the evidence indicat[es] that recovery did not begin in the mid-1980s and that there was no significant difference between "adjusters" and "non-adjusters" (or among adjusters, "strong", "weak", "early-intensive", etc.)'.

There is legitimate controversy over who or what is responsible for the failure to restore viable conditions. Exogenous events – worsening terms of trade and drought – played a role (from 1981 to 1989 the terms of trade deteriorated by 3.3 per cent per year, while drought caused major problems in the mid-1980s and again in the early 1990s). Moreover, countries did not carry out the policies recommended as consistently or toughly as the international financial institutions might have desired. But irrespective of the cause, the 'bottom line' is that the policies have not been succeeding in meeting their short-term objectives, and are consequently undermining growth potential.

(B) Consistency of short-term policies and long-term development objectives

The review of development strategies summarised in the earlier part of this chapter suggests that there are serious conflicts, as well as some complementarities, between the adjustment policies being adopted and long-run development needs. From this perspective the adjustment policies fall into three classes: contradictory policies which directly conflict with long-term objectives; policies that conflict with the long-term strategy but, with some amendments, could support it; and additional policies necessary for the long-term strategy which are not included in the usual adjustment package (see Figure 5.1).

1 Contradictory policies

Direct conflicts are most evident in four areas: cuts in public expenditure, decline in investment, indiscriminate import liberalisation, and the focus of incentives on the expansion of primary product exports.

The large cuts in public expenditure, as may be seen in Table 5.7, invariably affect items which are essential for long-term development, notably human resource development (i.e. health, education and training), research and development in priority areas, and infrastructure, especially in the rural areas. Cuts in these areas inevitably make it more difficult for countries to develop in the medium term, handicapping African economies where they are already especially weak. The expansion of physical and human investment is of the greatest importance for long-run development. The stagnation and even reversal of the modest achievements in education is particularly harmful.

Another direct conflict arises from the fall in investment that has accompanied adjustment policies. Gross investment as a proportion of GDP fell in SSA as a whole from 20.9 per cent for 1973–80, to 17.8 per cent in 1992. The investment ratio fell in 25 countries and rose in 13 over the 1980s (Helleiner, 1992c, Table 2.11). In real terms, investment per head fell by nearly half between 1980 and 1990. Curtailment of credit, falling GDP and the poor climate for foreign investment were mainly responsible. The significant rise in interest rates following financial reforms did not lead to an increase in domestic savings and seems to have choked off borrowing for investment in Ghana, Malawi, Tanzania and Kenya (ibid.).

Indiscriminate import liberalisation has been partly responsible for the industrial stagnation. This is most clearly seen in Ghana, which

Figure 5.1 Policy matrix adjustment policies and long-run needs

Long-run strategy	*Appropriate policies*	*Current stabilisation and adjustment policies*		
		Contradicts	*Needs amendment*	*New policies needed*
A. Agrarian strategy focused on small farmers	Land reform Improve terms of trade Infrastructure Inputs	 Cuts Cuts	 To include food	Land reform
B. Support for rural non-agriculture	Dynamic and egalitarian agriculture Improve supply conditions	Cuts	As in A. Above	New credit and technology institutions
C. Industrial development	Support industries with potential dynamic comparative advantages Develop capabilities (see F. below)	Undifferentiated import liberalisation	Selective protection	
D. Regional import substitution	Tariff reform Monetary arrangements Other moves towards economic integration, including improved infrastructure		Selective liberalisation	Institutional development
E. Export diversification	Selective tariffs	Indiscriminate liberalisation		

	Industrial and agricultural policy Incentives	Cuts		Industrial policy
F. Development of human capabilities	Expansion of education and training at all levels Build up industrial experience Support for local entrepreneurs	Cuts Reduced through cuts and trade liberalisation Similar to above plus encouragement of foreign investment		
G. International policies	Debt forgiveness More soft aid Coordinated commodity policies	(Encourages competitive expansion)	Insufficient Insufficient	Debt write-off Support for commodity prices

Table 5.7 Government expenditure, sub-Saharan Africa

	1980	*Most recent date*	*No. countries rising*[a]	*No. countries falling*	*1990 per capita as index 1980*[b]
GDP per capita, $ constant prices	380.0	340.0 (1990)	11	36	0.89
Govt. expenditure as % of GDP	30.6	31.0 (1987)	20	18	0.91
Percentage of govt. expenditure going to:					
General public services	19.9	18.2 (1985)	7	17	0.85
Defence	12.1	10.0 (1985)	7	18	0.75
Education	14.9	13.0 (1985)	12	17	0.85
Health	5.1	4.9 (1985)	13	16	0.87
Economic services	26.4	22.5 (1985)	15	14	0.76
Agriculture	7.9	6.8 (1985)	13	12	0.79
Interest payments	5.8	13.4 (1986)	35	1	2.10

Notes: [a] Number of countries varies according to data availability.
[b] Calculated by applying ratio of most recent date to 1980 data for GDP per capita and government expenditure ratio.

Source: World Bank, *World Development Report* (various years); UNDP, *Human Development Report* (various years).

has gone furthest towards accepting complete import liberalisation and where the industrial sector signally failed to revive along with the rest of the economy. Import liberalisation policies have not differentiated at all between other economies in the region and the rest of the world, and consequently has not encouraged regional trade.

Improved incentives for primary products have led to competitive supply expansion, which is partly responsible for the worsening terms of trade. Cocoa provides the clearest example: Ghana succeeded in substantially increasing cocoa output, but revenue hardly changed as a result of the falling cocoa price. The incentives expanding primary production (through devaluations, producer price increases and other improvements in production conditions) combined with the disincentives to industrial production following import liberalisation account for the persistently high specialisation in primary product exports over the period.

2 *Adjustment policies needing amendment*

A number of policies in the adjustment package have both positive and negative effects in the medium term: positive because they correct past distortions and encourage efficiency, but negative because they do not provide essential complementary changes or because they are too market oriented and undifferentiated which makes it impossible for African economies to build up their own capability in new areas. Examples are to be found in policies towards agriculture, trade and foreign exchange, credit, foreign investment and parastatals. In each of these areas, major amendments are needed to the policy reforms in adjustment packages to bring about desirable long-term consequences.

Taken as a whole, the adjustment packages are supposed to improve the efficiency of resource use, by replacing controls with free prices, permitting greater foreign competition from imports and privatising public sector enterprises. As a result, resources should be allocated according to comparative advantage, while competitive pressures should ensure greater X-efficiency. But this policy package leads to static rather than dynamic comparative advantage (in other words, the colonial trade structure). A much needed emphasis has been restored to agriculture, but almost exclusive attention has been placed on the export of traditional crops. Furthermore, the complementary policies towards inputs and institutions in agriculture which are essential for effective price reforms have not been adopted on an adequate scale (and indeed conditions in these respects frequently worsen because of the cuts).

In industry, competitive pressures from imports may encourage competition, but as noted above they may also lead to deindustrialisation. While displacement of parastatals by foreign investment – if it occurs – probably raises efficiency, it also reduces the possibility of developing African capabilities in running industries efficiently. The marketisation of credit and foreign exchange does not increase the resources going to the efficient small-scale sector because small enterprises lack the resources to bid effectively in such a market, but rather, as the experience of Zambia shows, increases resources going to large-scale and foreign enterprises. In summary, the adjustment package may increase short-term 'efficiency' of resources in use, but it tends to diminish African control and experience, and reduces the possibility of building up dynamic comparative advantage in non-traditional areas.

The record of the 1960s and 1970s, summarised above, shows that policy reforms were needed. The strategy adopted in these two decades was a dead-end one, from which the current impasse emerged. However, policies being adopted are too simplistic to achieve the difficult objective of combining efficiency of resource use with the build-up of local capabilities.

While some of the changes proposed move economies in the desired direction, many need amendment in order to bring about sustainable long-term development. To summarise the policy conclusions derived earlier in this chapter:

- While a more market-oriented approach is desirable, markets should be *structured* to ensure the allocation of foreign exchange and credit to the small-scale and rural sectors. A similar structuring of government expenditure is necessary to ensure that priorities are met in rural infrastructure and the social sectors.
- Price reform in agriculture must be supported by increases in inputs and improved institutions; all reforms must extend to food and non-traditional exports.
- Coordinated policies are essential in relation to traditional exports, with cutbacks rather than the promotion of production, as at present, for commodities with low elasticities.
- Some import liberalisation is desirable, as stringent controls have served neither efficiency nor equity. But import liberalisation should be *selective*, so as to promote capacity build-up in industries where dynamic comparative advantage is a realistic possibility in the medium term. Most economies should aim to build up a sizeable capacity in manufacturing exports over the next five to 10 years.
- Regional trade liberalisation should be a priority to enable coun-

tries to combine some protection from outside Africa with greater competition and exploitation of economies of scale within the region.
- New forms of collaboration with foreign investors should be encouraged; DFI should only be promoted where there is a direct and immediate link with the expansion of non-traditional exports.
- Privatisation should play a role where possible; elsewhere, the reform of parastatals should be a high priority, by reducing and, where possible, eliminating direct government regulations and government subsidisation, increasing competition and allowing parastatals to go out of business if they fail; new forms of parastatals should be encouraged, involving small decentralised units.

3 Additional reforms

Policy changes are needed for long-term development in some areas that do not presently feature in the current adjustment packages. For the most part, these would aim to increase equity and participation, objectives that tend to be neglected in adjustment policies. The most important are:

- land reform to prevent the emergence of high rural inequality and the growth of rural poverty;
- policies to reform institutions or the creation of new ones so that they serve the small-scale and low-income sectors; this includes R&D institutions, technology dissemination, and credit for small-scale enterprises;
- institutional reform (including reform of government machinery) to improve participation of the poor in decision-making, and to increase their power to exert an influence over decisions through group organisation;
- policies to provide support for the most vulnerable, particularly through well-designed food subsidies, employment schemes and income creation schemes;
- policies to create and improve regional institutions.

V ALTERNATIVE SHORT-TERM POLICIES

The main purpose of this chapter has been to analyse the consistency between Fund and Bank (described below as 'orthodox') policies and the long-term development needs of African countries. Some complementarities have emerged, but so too have significant conflicts. The focus of the previous section was on medium-term policies for development, although there were strong implications for short-term policies. This section will identify, in summary form, short-term policies that would be more conducive to long-term development, which we shall call 'pro-development' short-term policies.

(A) Pro-development short-term policies for Africa

The following are the most important elements of a pro-development approach, as compared with orthodox policies. For the purposes of brevity, they are itemised in a rather categorical and dogmatic way; they should be treated as an agenda for discussion rather than as a conclusive list. The policies are also summarised in Figure 5.2.

1 Fiscal policies – macro

- a less rapid reduction in the fiscal deficit;
- tolerance of a moderate fiscal deficit (2–3 per cent of GDP, and not more than 5 per cent) unless inflation is very rapid;
- emphasis on *revenue expansion* rather than *expenditure reduction* as a way of reducing the budget deficit.

2 Fiscal policies – meso

- equity considerations should play a major role in determining the tax structure; this is liable to mean adequate taxes of corporations (including foreign corporations), of income and of assets (land and other wealth); a progressive indirect tax structure, with high rates on luxury consumption goods, and exemption of basic foods and energy used by low-income households;
- allocation of government expenditure should emphasise maintaining/increasing expenditure on economic infrastructure (especially rural), on the social sectors, and on relief schemes (employment, social support, food subsidies);
- improvements, wherever possible, in priority ratios within sectors (i.e. towards rural infrastructure, primary health and education, low-cost sanitation schemes for rural and low-income urban areas);
- food subsidies should be reformed so as to be more pro-poor, not abolished, with care taken that 'targeting' is designed to reduce F-errors (i.e. failing to reach poor groups), as much as E-errors (reaching the non-needy) (see Cornia and Stewart, 1993);

- any cuts in expenditure should be directed at government functions that do not serve social and economic priorities: these include defence and security; subsidies to airlines; subsidies to middle/high income consumers of electricity, telephones, and so on; some industrial subsidies;
- payments of international interest to be held to 'reasonable' levels (the interpretation of this would obviously vary according to the country, but the point is that cuts in priorities should not be forced by excessive interest payments);

3 *Monetary policies*

- aggregate credit should be controlled, but not excessively restricted, so as to maintain productive investment;
- excessive interest rates should be avoided (in real terms, interest rates between -2 and +2 per cent are reasonable, given the objective of maintaining investment levels);
- a structured credit market should be adopted, in which certain areas are allocated a proportion of credit (small-scale firms and farms, agriculture, micro-enterprises), while the market is left to allocate the credit within the broad allocations;
- new institutional forms need to be created to help lending to the small-scale sector and low-income groups.

4 *Exchange rate*

- realistic and stable exchange rates (i.e. not excessively overvalued, as indicated by trade performance and parallel markets);
- dual exchange rates may be appropriate in resource-rich economies;
- foreign exchange allocation should be carried out in the framework of a *structured* market, with certain allocations to priority areas including social sectors, small-scale, agriculture.

5 *Trade regime*

- import liberalisation should be selective, and permit continued protection for industries that can be expected to acquire a dynamic comparative advantage over time;
- manufactured exports should be encouraged through special incentives, including credit allocations, foreign exchange retention schemes, and so on, along the lines of the Korean and Taiwan models (Amsden, 1989; Wade, 1990);

Figure 5.2 Comparing alternative short-term policies

Policy area	*Pro-development policies*	*Orthodox policies*	*Reason for differences*
FISCAL POLICIES – MACRO	Gradual reduction in fiscal deficit Deficit not normally to exceed 3% of GDP (5% maximum) Emphasis on revenue raising	Rapid reduction in fiscal deficit Aim to eliminate deficit Emphasis on expenditure reduction	Pro-development policies aim to maintain or increase government expenditure on social and economic priorities and sustain economic growth
FISCAL POLICIES – MESO	Emphasise equity in tax structure Allocation and priority ratios to be improved Defence, non-priorities elsewhere, and external interest payments to be cut Food subsidies reformed to be more pro-poor	Emphasise efficiency structure Priority ratios to be improved Usually leave this to government, with strong emphasis on paying external interest. Recently some talk of defence cuts Food subsidies eliminated or narrowly targeted	Greater emphasis on equity and poverty reduction in pro-development policies External debt situation not to be allowed to prevent social and economic development
MONETARY POLICIES	Credit control, not too stringent Avoid v. high interest rates Structured credit market to get allocations to priority areas	Stringent credit controls 'Market' rates of interest; positive real rates required None	Pro-development policies aim to raise investment and reallocate resources towards small-scale and priority areas

	New institutions to lend to small-scale sector	None: any structure goes against market philosophy	
EXCHANGE RATE	Realistic exchange rates; sometimes dual rates Foreign exchange allocation via structured market	Market rates; no dual rates No structuring permitted	Structured market and dual rates may be needed to ensure priorities receive allocations and manufacturing sector advances
TRADE REGIME	Selective liberalisation Encourage manufactured exports Regional trade liberalisation Restrict exports of low elasticity commodities	Complete liberalisation the aim No restrictions or selectivity	Dynamic comparative advantage and intra-SSA trade need to be promoted for long-run development
PRICING POLICIES	Price controls retained on essentials supported by supply policies No user charges for primary education and health	No price controls User charges encouraged	Need to control some prices to ensure food security of low income and access to social services
INTERNATIONAL POLICIES	Debt write off Commodity price support Increase resource flows	Debt rescheduling None let market determine prices	Need to improve international conditions to make other policies possible

- trade liberalisation to be promoted within regions in Africa, and ultimately for SSA as a whole;
- production and pricing policies for low-elasticity exports should be controlled in coordination with other producing countries.

6 Pricing policies

- some price controls should be retained over basic commodities essential for low-income earners, while other prices should be liberalised. The two major commodities for which continued control is likely to be desirable are the basic staple food and energy sources used by the poor; the aim should be to ensure that supply expands sufficiently for these commodities so that price controls do not lead to shortages and black markets;
- some government interventions in agricultural producer prices may be needed; here it is important that the prices of food crops be maintained, and that excessive incentives are not given to low-elasticity exports, as argued above.
- user charges for primary education and basic health care should *not* be introduced.

(B) International policies

The focus above has been on policy changes in African economies. But there is no question that changes in the world economy during the 1980s were severely deleterious to African countries and played a major role in their economic plight. The worsening environment affected the current account, as a result of deteriorating commodity prices, and the capital account with the build up of debt. Terms of trade losses over the 1980s amounted to as much as 13 per cent of GDP in Ghana, 29 per cent in Nigeria and 17 per cent in the Congo. According to Helleiner (1993), the worsening terms of trade was more than offset for five countries by increased ODA resource inflows. But for eight countries, the terms of trade loss exceeded the additional ODA inflow.

Debt accumulated during the 1980s rose from $56 billion in 1980 to $170 billion in 1990, or from 97 per cent of total exports to over 300 per cent. Net transfers on capital account which were $5.7 billion in 1980 had fallen to $1 billion in 1990 and minus $0.9 billion in 1991 (World Bank, 1993b). The cumulative deterioration in the external position in 1990 amounted to an annual average of over $17 billion in terms of trade and $5 billion on capital account, or a total of $23 billion – which is equivalent to 14 per cent of SSA's 1990 exports.

Adoption of some of the policies discussed above – especially the more gradual approach to deficit reduction and the maintenance of investment levels – will not be possible unless the deterioration in the external account is reversed. Countries that have succeeded in combining adjustment with growth have done so because they have better external conditions than the average: Ghana, for example, enjoyed very large inflows of resources from bilateral and multilateral sources and Botswana had revenue from diamond sales which permitted a rapid growth of imports. The IMF and World Bank have failed to acknowledge that external factors played more than a minor role in the *cause* of Africa's problems, and have therefore avoided facing up to the changes needed in the international economy.

Changes required include:

- debt write-off, by the private sector, bilateral donors and the international financing institutions;
- support for commodity price agreements, to be achieved through limits on production by all producing countries;
- greatly increased resource flows to African economies over the next 10 years, amounting to at least double current flows.

These changes are all within the competence and financial resources of the international financial institutions, with the support of the major donors. Without them it is highly unlikely that the present downward path of most African economies can be reversed.

VI CONCLUSION

The stabilisation and adjustment policies advocated by the Fund and the Bank and widely adopted in Africa have not succeeded in restoring growth in most countries; indeed, in many cases they have been accompanied by continued economic deterioration. One reason for this is the continued deterioration in the external environment. In some important respects the policies are pushing African economies away from a desirable long-term structure of development, especially because they are running down African capabilities and are reorienting the economies back to a heavy specialisation on export agriculture (or other primary products), without stimulating (or even permitting in the case of industry) a build-up of dynamic comparative advantage in non-traditional agriculture and industry. While policy reform was clearly needed at the end of the 1970s, the present package is not satisfactory from a long-term perspective.

The above discussion has sketched out suggestions for more pro-development short- and medium-term policies than the orthodox policies promoted by the international financial institutions. Conflicts are particularly sharp with the stringent requirements of the IMF; it is doubtful that the Fund can play a helpful role in African economies, given the heavy emphasis on credit and expenditure control in its programmes. There are some conflicts too with the World Bank, many of which stem from the differences in objectives between the Bank (as elucidated by Jaycox, Vice President for the Africa region) and African Heads of State. In particular, from this account the Bank appears to be almost exclusively concerned with efficiency, and therefore sees human resources as a means; in contrast, the Lagos Plan of Action puts forward poverty reduction, improved living standards for the mass of the people and self-reliance as the major objectives, with efficiency a means rather than an end. While the Bank has recently emphasised poverty reduction elsewhere as an important objective, this has not yet been properly incorporated into policy design (see, for example, Stewart, 1991a) and self-reliance has not been accepted as a legitimate objective.

NOTE

1. The World Bank/UNDP (1989) claim that the policies are working, in the sense that among countries subject to less severe shocks those which have adopted reforming policies show somewhat less negative results than those with weak or no reforming policies. But deterioration in major variables is shown in all groups of countries, while the choice of countries and the use of statistics in the World Bank/UNDP report has been much criticised, by UN/ECA (1989) among others.

6 Beyond Structural Adjustment: Policies for Sustainable Growth and Development in Africa

Oladeji Ojo

I FROM CRISIS TO ADJUSTMENT

It is now almost a decade since the first structural adjustment programme (SAP) was introduced in Africa. As of today, as many as two thirds of the countries in sub-Saharan Africa are implementing these programmes. While their rationale is rooted in the economic crisis which surfaced in the late 1970s, the last ten years have signalled an unabated slide into deep distress. From one report to the other, and from all available economic and social indicators, the story is the same – continuing economic retrogression and social deprivation. Cyclical fluctuations are normal features of economic systems, but the duration and depth of the current African economic crisis suggest that we are not witnessing different phases of economic cycles. Instead, we are confronted with a retrogression that probably has few precedents in economic history. During the 1980s, per capita incomes declined by over 25 per cent. Balance of payments and financial difficulties also worsened and the external debt burden became a major obstacle to growth and recovery.

Analysis of the African crisis showed that external shocks (such as terms of trade losses) as well as internal factors (including the pursuit of inappropriate economic policies) were all to blame. When the adjustment and policy reforms were being put in place, external factors were considered exogenous, meaning there was very little that African countries could do about them. Some international initiatives were however launched to address aspects of the external environment: these included the IMF's Compensatory and Contingency Financing Facility (CCFF) and the Enhanced Structural Adjustment Facility (ESAF); the

EC's STABEX and UNCTAD's Integrated Programme on Commodities. Internal factors, particularly economic policies, were thought to be within the control of African countries. Hence, the formulation of stabilisation and structural adjustment programmes, the major objectives of which were to reform economic policies as a precondition for the resumption of growth. These programmes are financed largely by the World Bank, the International Monetary Fund and the African Development Bank.

Three categories of policies have formed part of almost every reform programme in Africa: demand restraint, switching policies and policies related to long-term supply or efficiency. The demand restraint element consists of policies aimed at reducing demand in the economy, with the objective of curtailing expenditure on imports and releasing resources for exports. Policy instruments include reductions in government expenditures and in the budget deficit, controls over the money supply and credit creation; and policies aimed at shifting resources from non-tradables to tradables, by changing incentives. Devaluation and exchange rate unification is the main policy instrument, accompanied by changes in domestic prices, especially in agriculture. Long-term supply policies are designed to secure a more market-oriented economy, subject to fewer restrictions and less segmentation. Reforms include trade liberalisation, financial reforms to raise interest rates in the formal sector and to unify credit markets, and price reforms.

However, the magnitude and persistence of the crisis in SSA indicate that the present programmes, anchored as they are on structural adjustment and stabilisation policies, require critical evaluation and possible modification if Africa is to escape from the present 'trap' of underdevelopment and launch itself on the path to self-sustaining growth. This chapter aims to call attention to the adverse consequences of certain aspects of the current development strategy being pursued in most African countries, with a view to suggesting an alternative approach to the problem.

II FROM ADJUSTMENT TO SUSTAINABLE DEVELOPMENT

Theoretically valid as the policies of structural adjustment may be, concern is now being expressed about the implications of some of these measures for long-term development. While it is true that in a few countries (Botswana, Mauritius, Ghana, for example), one can talk of the success of SAP, in most SSA countries it appears that there is no end to, or even relief from, the economic stagnation and/or retrogression. Indeed, the very foundations of long-term growth are being gradually eroded, as the following discussion clearly illustrates.

1 Devaluation and liberalisation of the trade regime

Theoretically, trade liberalisation should lead to a worldwide optimal allocation of resources. But this 'optimum' is in the context of prevailing or existing industrial structures and technological levels of various countries. The existing comparative advantage of each country is thus taken as given. In the case of developing countries, that comparative advantage lies in the production and export of primary products. However, as also noted in Chapter 5, the essence of economic development consists in the transformation of an agrarian economy into a modern industrial economy, with the industrial sector rather than primary production taking on the leading role.

In Africa, the massive devaluation of most national currencies and the liberalisation of the trade regime inherent in current policies are not geared toward an alteration of the existing comparative advantage. Indeed, they are favouring the indiscriminate importation of cheap foreign goods, while at the same time national industries are operating below capacity because of the devaluation-induced high domestic currency costs of imported raw materials and other restrictive policies. As a consequence, local industries cannot compete with these imports, and the stage is being set, rather unwittingly, for a gradual process of 'deindustrialisation' in most African countries.

Economic history can produce virtually no evidence of a country that has successfully industrialised by completely opening its doors to unrestricted imports from abroad. Most developed countries have had to resort to some protection in order to allow a viable export industry to develop. The present development strategy in Africa requires modification to permit some 'selective' protection of key or leading industries. As the choice of such industries cannot be left to the arbitrary decisions of bureaucrats, studies should be commissioned at each national level to determine which industries should be protected and the appropriate duration and magnitude of such protection. While the implementation of multiple exchange rates is not being advocated here, the use of fiscal policy in the process of 'protection' may need to be considered.

2 *Financial deregulation*

Financial deregulation is in principle desirable because it enhances efficient resource mobilisation and utilisation. In sub-Saharan Africa, however, deregulation is resulting in prohibitively high nominal rates of interest such that only few investment projects can now be justified on profitability grounds. The decline in the investment ratio in the region can be attributed in part to this phenomenon. In an underdeveloped financial setting such as obtains in Africa, a market-determined interest rate may not be capable of clearing the market for funds. Without retreating to the older views, which elevate financial repression as a desirable instrument of public policy, there may be a need for subsidised interest rates for some leading sectors of the economy. Decisions regarding which sectors should be subsidised will need to be based on comprehensive national studies which identify, according to certain parameters, suitable industries.

A further problem with financial deregulation is its timing and sequencing. Where the macroeconomic environment is unstable, financial deregulation would compound that instability to the point that financial collapse may be inevitable. The prohibitively high nominal rates of interest (and inflation-induced low real interest rates) which accompany financial deregulation is in part a symptom of this instability. It may first be necessary to stabilise the macroeconomic environment, particularly the inflation rate, before embarking on financial deregulation, for it is only when the macroeconomic environment is stable that the interest rate can clear the market for funds without provoking excessive disruption. Successful developing countries have combined domestic price stability with substantial – even if regulated – nominal rates of interest on both deposits and loans.

3 *Cuts in public expenditures*

The large cuts in public expenditures typical of structural adjustment programmes almost invariably affect items essential to long-term development: notably expenditure on human capabilities (on health, education and training, for instance), on research and development in priority sectors, and on infrastructure. Cuts in these areas inevitably impede the chances of medium-term development, thus handicapping African economies where they are especially weak. There is clearly a need to prioritise cuts in public expenditures such that long-term development prospects are not undermined.

4 Privatisation of public enterprises

Under the current development strategy, the privatisation of public enterprises is recommended largely because of poor performance in the past of those enterprises. In principle, this move is desirable as it could reduce the claim of these enterprises on the government budget. But large-scale, and sometimes indiscriminate, privatisation may lead to a situation whereby the public sector is completely decimated, stripped of all powers of economic control and management. There is, as it were, a danger of throwing the baby out with the bath water. The issue is not and should not be the size of government but rather its efficiency. While there can be 'market failures' in an economy (and this is a major justification for government intervention in the economy), there can also be 'government failures'. What is therefore required is an optimal balance between the private and public sectors of an economy. In this context, country-by-country studies of the factors responsible for the poor performance of the public sector might cast light on those enterprises which may appropriately be privatised and those that may benefit from reform.

Even when a policy of privatisation is promoted, care must be taken to avoid indiscriminate selling as this could lead to problems of income distribution and social tension, particularly if the purchase of government enterprises is monopolised by those currently holding economic power (Chapter 10 discusses this issue in greater detail). If enterprises were sold to non-nationals, problems would arise concerning foreign control and ownership as well as the repatriation of profits. Present privatisation strategies may thus need to be modified on a country-by-country basis to allow governments to maintain a certain percentage of ownership of public enterprises in 'trust' for future generations, as well as to selectively limit areas where foreign ownership may be permitted.

Apart from structural adjustment measures, another policy response of Africa to the ongoing crisis is the adoption of a strategy of economic integration. The aim of this strategy, discussed further in Chapter 18, is to bring together the small and pristine African economies so that economies of scale can be reaped, both in production and consumption. Through the coordinated approach to economic development and structural change which it offers, economic integration is expected to contribute to the growth of African economies.

To a large extent, the two strategies have been pursued independently of each other. On the one hand, structural adjustment programmes are national in character; they are designed and implemented without considerable concern for their regional or subregional consequences. Economic integration, on the other hand, is being pursued among groups of contiguous countries, again, often without reference to the national macroeconomic policies. A reform of existing policies ought to include measures that could facilitate the interaction of these strategies. For instance, if a subregional structural adjustment programme were possible, its implementation could assist the countries involved in their mutual trade liberalisation schemes. By liberalising their trade regimes and granting regional tariff preferences, subregional structural adjustment programmes would facilitate intra-regional trade and economic integration. Similarly, a well-articulated subregional adjustment programme could also incorporate measures aimed at harmonising national macroeconomic policies. Further areas where interaction between these strategies could be useful include the convertibility of national currencies, coordinated investment decisions and cross-border investment (ECA, 1989).

These examples should not be interpreted as a critique of structural adjustment programmes. There is obviously no substitute for sound macroeconomic management, for without sound policies there can be no resumption of growth (see Chapter 4). However, the point that is being made is that some aspects of current policies need to be brought closer in line with the goals of long-term development of Africa. In its *Alternative Framework*, the ECA (1989) has voiced similar concerns. This document reviewed the present policies and made some suggestions for their improvement. Two major shortcomings, however, have made the ECA's recommendations unattractive. First, the proposals all seem to urge a return to the use of administrative controls in economic management – a development strategy that is by now thoroughly discredited. Secondly, and related to the first, the recommendations ignore the financing aspects of adjustment programmes. By emphasising administrative controls in the management of the macroeconomy, the document has not proved attractive to the financiers of adjustment programmes (World Bank, IMF and other donors) whose policy prescriptions are anchored on market-oriented adjustment policies.

III CONCLUSIONS

From the above discussion, it would appear that there is a need to reform current development policies and make them more growth-oriented. Reforms should aim on the one hand to eliminate aspects of present policies which tend to undermine or contradict long-term growth, while on the other hand policy reforms should continue to be emphasised as a prerequisite for the resumption of growth. Before the donor community accepts and implements these emerging ideas, Africa ought to input into them. It is worth recalling that Africa had no input into the theoretical formulation of SAP and the IMF's stabilisation programmes. (This might partly account for the half-hearted manner in which some countries accepted and implemented these programmes.) If there should be a review of present policies, Africa ought to have a loud and forthright say this time round. The major sponsors of structural adjustment programmes, notably the World Bank and the IMF, are so deeply committed to market reforms that they may be unwilling to support such changes. Any attempt to reform present policies must therefore take these institutions into account.

In its latest report on Africa, the World Bank (1989a) admitted that policies for sustainable development should go beyond current structural adjustment policies to include technological change, institutional strengthening, infrastructure development, improved education and health standards including reduction of population growth, land reform and other institutional constraints to development. This twist in thinking can be interpreted as an indication of the Bank's willingness to accommodate changes in its current policies. Before valuable research time is expended on activities that may not receive the required financial backing (as was the case with the ECA's *Alternative Framework*), efforts should be made to sensitise the leadership of the World Bank and the IMF on the shortcomings of present policies. A proposal could then be put forward for a joint African/World Bank/IMF research team to study current policies and propose credible alternatives, which would attract the required financing and, more importantly, put Africa back on the path of long-term sustainable development.

The proposed approach has two major advantages. By involving the donors in the preparation of a new strategy, it would secure their implicit support for it. By participating in the formulation of a new strategy, Africa would be ensuring that its long-term development concerns are taken into account. Furthermore, the sense of ownership implied by such participation would most likely lead to region-wide support for the strategy.

The implementation of this proposal may be fraught with difficulties, particularly in terms of persuading the donors to accept that present policies have shortcomings and then to agree to participate in the formulation of a new strategy. However, the bleak prospects for African economies under present policies require that an all-out effort be made to convince these institutions. Africa, through its regional institutions, must be prepared to invest sizeable resources in the research effort.

7 Macroeconomic Adjustment, Uncertainty and Domestic Private Investment in Selected African Countries*

T.W. Oshikoya

I INTRODUCTION

During the late 1970s and early 1980s, many African countries embarked on economic policy reforms and adjustment programmes to correct macroeconomic imbalances, short-term internal and external disequilibria, and to meet the challenge of restoring long-term economic growth. Adjustment policies to restore macroeconomic balances focused on bringing the level of aggregate demand and its composition into line with the level of aggregate output and available resources. The key areas of macroeconomic policy stabilisation are fiscal and credit restrictions.

In addition to demand management policies, comprehensive supply-enhancing policy instruments were initiated. The most common areas of structural and sectoral reforms include: exchange rate and trade policy, agricultural policy, public enterprise reforms, and tax and expenditure policy. The focus, in the longer term, of the adjustment programmes adopted by these countries is on creating more appropriate incentives and the framework for domestic private sector develop-

* This chapter draws on the paper, 'Macroeconomic Determinants of Domestic Private Investment in Africa: An Empirical Analysis', in *Economic Development and Cultural Change* (1993) published by the University of Chicago Press. The author wishes to thank O. Ojo, J. Otieno, T. Kouassi, G. Woldu and participants at the UNICEF seminar on 'Adjustment and Development in Sub-Saharan Africa: Is The Current Approach Satisfactory? Is There Another Way?' for their stimulating comments. The views expressed in this chapter do not necessarily reflect those of the African Development Bank or its affiliated institutions.

ment as the basis for achieving sustained growth (see Chapters 2 and 5).

However, restoring private investors' confidence poses a major challenge to African governments as the structural adjustment and policy reform efforts of most African countries have not been matched by a sufficient recovery of private investment. Private investment response remains weak and inevitably lags even when considerable progress has been made in reducing policy distortions, in correcting internal and external imbalances, and in restoring short-term growth. Without an adequate recovery of private investment, a sustained medium- to longer-term economic growth may be jeopardised. Thus, the sustainability of adjustment efforts in the region may be endangered. The increased macroeconomic uncertainty associated with the credibility and sustainability of policy reforms, macroeconomic instability, external shocks and high debt service obligations may have contributed to the slow recovery of domestic private investment in many African countries.

This chapter examines domestic private capital formation between 1970 and 1988 in eight African countries with a view to deriving policy implications that would enhance higher levels of investment essential to long-term growth. Section II reviews recent trends in private investment in selected African countries. In Section III, the determinants of private investment are empirically analysed, taking into consideration macroeconomic policy reforms and uncertainties. Section IV summarises the main policy implications of the empirical results, and Section V contains the conclusions.

II RECENT TRENDS IN DOMESTIC PRIVATE INVESTMENT IN AFRICA

This section provides preliminary evidence on domestic private investment behaviour in the selected African countries: Cameroon, Kenya, Malawi, Mauritius, Morocco, Tanzania, Tunisia and Zimbabwe. Table 7.1 presents data on private investment and public investment and selected macroeconomic indicators for the eight African countries in the period 1970–88.[1] This data reveal two distinct patterns. For the middle-income African countries in our sample – Cameroon, Mauritius, Morocco and Tunisia – private investment rates generally fell in the early 1980s, but subsequently increased in the period 1984–8. In Cameroon, private investment decreased slightly from 9.05 per cent of GDP in 1970–9 to 8.51 per cent in 1980–3, but recovered to 10.5 per cent in 1984–8. In Mauritius, the private investment rate fell from

Table 7.1 Private investment and macroeconomic indicators in selected sub-Saharan African countries, 1970-88

Country	*Private investment rate*	*Public investment rate*	*Gross domestic savings rate*	*Real GDP growth rate*	*Per capita GNP (in US$)*	*Inflation rate*	*Foreign debt–GNP ratio*	*Debt service ratio*	*Terms of trade*
Cameroon									
1970–9	9.05	10.11	16.08	5.52	691	1.29	19.34	5.47	138.0
1980–3	8.51	14.35	22.48	9.72	995	12.55	36.15	15.67	158.0
1984–8	10.48	12.78	26.50	1.36	1 106	7.00	35.20	28.82	125.0
Kenya									
1970–9	12.70	7.84	20.19	7.27	227	10.91	20.97	5.14	128.3
1980–3	12.13	9.30	19.05	3.25	395	14.40	56.80	29.80	113.4
1984–8	11.50	7.98	21.04	5.24	334	8.14	71.84	41.20	115.0
Malawi									
1970–9	9.07	13.77	14.44	6.3	183	6.26	40.40	9.57	16.5
1980–3	5.31	11.11	13.20	0.35	167	13.46	74.00	31.55	136.8
1984–8	4.37	8.50	11.84	2.84	160	16.44	97.10	41.00	113.4
Mauritius									
1970–9	17.40	7.05	20.21	6.53	1 118	10.98	11.98	2.00	103.4
1980–3	12.90	7.43	14.45	1.10	1 145	18.37	50.40	17.10	83.1
1984–8	14.12	6.88	24.36	7.88	1 456	5.08	51.02	18.36	91.9
Morocco									
1970–9	10.04	10.14	14.00	5.18	634	6.80	24.0	10.60	131.3
1980–3	10.10	11.88	13.55	3.83	725	9.65	80.6	31.90	98.0
1984–8	13.60	6.80	17.28	5.26	778	6.78	125.8	32.64	97.3

continued on page 140

Table 7.1 continued

Country	*Private investment rate*	*Public investment rate*	*Gross domestic savings rate*	*Real GDP growth rate*	*Per capita GNP (in US$)*	*Inflation rate*	*Foreign debt–GNP ratio*	*Debt service ratio*	*Terms of trade*
Tanzania									
1970–9	11.60	8.10	15.82	3.41	206	11.56	26.9	6.29	133.0
1980–3	9.20	9.40	10.98	0.90	152	27.97	49.7	23.4	103.0
1984–8	6.20	9.24	3.06	4.16	138	32.58	101.3	39.7	107.5
Tunisia									
1970–9	10.50	14.30	21.14	7.56	918	5.24	32.7	10.76	109.8
1980–3	14.40	16.90	22.50	4.28	1 225	10.37	46.6	16.30	134.9
1984–8	10.90	13.80	19.14	3.42	1 206	7.16	65.6	25.44	106.1
Zimbabwe									
1970–9	11.24	7.24	19.50	4.07	472	7.28	9.2	1.46	148.5
1980–3	10.62	7.90	14.92	6.83	830	13.07	25.6	15.10	108.5
1984–8	7.50	8.90	22.66	0.80	604	12.58	49.5	31.70	100.8

Source: See note 1 to this chapter.

a historical high of 17.4 per cent in 1970–9 to 13 per cent in 1980–3, but increased slightly to 14 per cent in 1984–8. In Morocco, private investment remained steady at 10 per cent between the 1970–9 period and 1980–3, and subsequently increased to 13.6 per cent in 1984–8. Tunisia is the only exception to this observed pattern in private investment rates among middle-income countries: the rate there increased from 10.5 per cent in 1970–9 to 14.4 per cent in 1980–3, but declined to 10.9 per cent in 1984–8.

Private investment rates fell substantially during the 1980s among low-income African countries in our sample – Malawi, Tanzania, Kenya and Zimbabwe. In Malawi, private investment fell from 9.07 per cent in 1970–9 through to 5.31 per cent in 1980–3 to 4.37 per cent in 1984–8. The same declining trend is observed in Tanzania as the private investment rate fell from 11.6 per cent in 1970–9 through to 9.2 per cent in 1980–3 to 6.2 per cent in 1984–8. The comparable figures for Zimbabwe are 11.24 per cent in 1970–9, 10.62 per cent in 1980–3 and 7.5 per cent in 1984–8.

In the middle-income countries, the average public investment rate increased from 10.4 per cent in 1970–9 to 12.7 per cent in 1980–3 before falling to 10 per cent in 1984–5. This pattern is observed for all the countries in the middle-income categories. Among the low-income countries, public investment rates increased in the early 1980s and subsequently fell during the 1984–8 period in Kenya and Tanzania. In Malawi, public investment fell from 13.8 per cent in 1970–9 through to 11.1 per cent in 1980–3 to 8.5 per cent in 1984–8. On the other hand, it increased from 7.24 per cent through to 7.9 per cent to 8.9 per cent for the three respective periods in Zimbabwe.

The share of private investment in total investment fell slightly from 53 per cent in 1970–9 to 51.4 per cent in 1984–8 for the eight countries in the sample. The share of private investment in total investment was generally higher in Kenya, Mauritius and Zimbabwe in both periods. A higher share of public investment in total investment is observed in Tunisia, Malawi and Tanzania. The average resource balance deficit for the eight countries, defined as the difference between domestic investment and domestic savings, increased from 2.8 per cent of GDP in the 1970–9 period to 4.4 per cent of GDP in 1980–3 before declining to 2 per cent of GDP in 1984–8. Finally, domestic savings rates increased substantially in Mauritius and Zimbabwe in 1984–8, while the savings rate in Tanzania fell from 16 per cent of GDP in 1970–9 through to 11 per cent of GDP in 1980–3 to an extremely low 3.1 per cent of GDP in 1984–8.

Table 7.2 Correlation coefficient between private investment and selected macroeconomic variables

Variables	*All countries*	*Middle-income*	*Low-income*
GDP growth rate	0.2074	0.0284	0.2919
Public investment	–0.0907	–0.1451	–0.2219
Credit to private sector	0.1886	0.8363	0.3373
Inflation	–0.1084	–0.2343	–0.2924
Terms of trade	–0.0466	–0.0194	–0.0658
Debt service ratio	–0.3574	–0.1767	–0.4784

The preliminary evidence in Table 7.2 points to a positive relationship between private investment and GDP growth rates. Private investment was discouraged by the slower economic growth in most countries in the sample between 1970–9 and 1980–3. However, the increase in real GDP growth in the 1984–8 period was not matched by strong private investment recovery in either the middle-income countries or the low-income countries. Indeed, as already observed, private investment declined further in low-income countries.

The slow response of private investment to economic recovery during the 1984–8 period in the countries of the sample may partly reflect continued underlying macroeconomic uncertainties. First, inflation remains high for most of the countries in the sample and is negatively correlated with the private investment rate in low-income countries (Table 7.2). Second, the ratio of external debt to GNP was more than double that of the 1970s. Indeed, for the low-income countries in the sample, the debt service ratio increased by a factor of more than 5. Further, the terms of trade, though experiencing a slight recovery in the 1984–8 period, remained substantially depressed compared to the historically high levels observed in the early 1970s for most countries. Both the debt service ratio and the terms of trade are negatively correlated with private investment in the low-income countries as well as the middle-income countries (Table 7.2). Finally, private investors' fears about the credibility and sustainability of structural adjustment programmes adopted in these countries may be undermining private investment.

III EMPIRICAL RESULTS

In this section we examine this evidence more systematically by specifiying and estimating a private investment function for the eight African countries. The specification of the private investment function draws on recent theoretical and empirical literature on investment behaviour, taking into consideration policy reforms and macroeconomic uncertainty in these countries. The following equation is specified and estimated:

$$IP = f(GR, GI, BC, CPI, TOT, DSR, DGR, V) \tag{1}$$

where

IP = the ratio of private sector investment to GDP
GR = the percentage change in real GDP
GI = the ratio of public sector investment to GDP
BC = the change in credit to the private sector
CPI = the percentage change in consumer price index
TOT = the change in terms of trade
DSR = the lagged ratio of external debt-service payments to exports of goods and services
DGR = the lagged ratio of external debt to nominal GDP
V = the coefficient of variation of key policy and macroeconomic variables.

It has been postulated that real output growth is positively related to domestic private capital formation (Jorgenson, 1967). This relationship between output growth and private investment is very important in the context of adjustment programmes as restrictive monetary and fiscal policies are likely to impact negatively on output growth in the short run, while the supply-side policies are intended to enhance the allocation of resources and response of private investment. Increases in the volume of bank credit are also suggested to have a positive impact on private investment in developing countries (Tun Wai and Wong, 1982).

In contrast, an increase in the degree of economic instability/uncertainty proxied by an increase in the debt service ratio; the ratio of external debt to output; an increase in inflation; an adverse terms of trade shock; or increased variability of policy instruments would exert a negative influence on domestic private capital formation (Pindyck,

1991; Rodrik, 1991; Serven and Solimano, 1992a; Greene and Villanueva, 1991). On the other hand, the effect of the public investment rate is, on an *a priori* basis, ambiguous (Balassa, 1988; Blejer and Khan, 1984; Aschauer, 1989).

The domestic private investment function is estimated using data on the eight African countries whose experiences with macroeconomic adjustment and trends in private investment were outlined in Section II. Given the small number of observations on any single country, we have pooled the data to investigate private investment behaviour in the empirical context of these eight African countries in 1970–88. For the 1970–9 period, we encountered a data problem on credit to the private sector in Zimbabwe. Two sets of estimates were therefore obtained as follows: the first estimate excludes Zimbabwe from the sample; the second estimate includes Zimbabwe but excludes the credit availability variable. The estimated results, as shown in Table 7.3, should be interpreted cautiously given the paucity of reliable and consistent data on private investment in African countries.

Columns I–III in Table 7.3 provide the estimate for 1970–88 in which Zimbabwe is included, but change in the bank credit variable is excluded. The total observation number is 152. With the pooled data, most of the hypotheses put forward in this section are confirmed by the empirical results. Real output growth has a strong positive effect on private investment after a one year lag. Real growth rate of GDP has a positive sign that is statistically significant at the 5 per cent level. Further, public investment has a strong positive impact on private investment after a one year lag at the 1 per cent significance level. The result suggests that complementarity between public investment and private investment dominates in our sample.

The estimated results indicate that the inflation rate is negatively related to private investment at the 5 per cent level of significance. Changes in the terms of trade have a negative, but moderate impact on private investment; the coefficients of the terms of trade are not statistically significant. The debt–service ratio has a strong negative impact on private investment activity, as suggested above. The debt service ratio has a negative and highly statistical significant sign at the 1 per cent level. In contrast, the debt–GNP ratio has a positive, but insignificant, sign.

The results provided in Column IV, derived from the pooled data on 133 observations in 1970–88, are basically similar to those in Column III. The estimated results confirm that credit availability has a strong positive impact on private investment activities in the selected Afri-

Table 7.3 Estimates of private investment on pooled data, 1970-88

Variable	*I*[a]	*II*[a]	*III*[a]	*IV*[b]
Intercept	9.5360	9.7935	9.1036	9.7974
	(12.2650)	(13.1914)	(13.1850)	(10.9326)
GR–1	0.0865	0.0888	0.0923	0.0947
	(2.1485)	(2.2078)	(2.3055)	(2.0305)
GI-1	0.1418	0.1412	0.1458	0.1393
	(2.4166)	(2.4043)	(2.493)	(2.1653)
CPI	0.0142	–0.0167	–0.0148	–0.0249
	(–1.4866)	(–1.8042)	–(1.6355)	(–1.8369)
TOT	–0.0142	–0.0088		
	(–1.0994)	(0.9390)		
DSR-1	–0.0721	–0.0538	–0.0532	–0.0474
	(–3.2568)	(–3.6594)	(–3.6221)	(–2.8835)
DGR–1	0.0121			
	(1.1062)			
BC				0.0009
				(1.7993)
ZC	–1.7512	–1.8833	–1.8792	–1.9063
	(–2.6056)	(–2.8453)	(–2.8411)	(–2.7417)
ZK	1.9244	1.8351	1.8362	1.6157
	(2.9867)	(2.8685)	(2.8715)	(2.3447)
ZM	–3.7165	–3.6239	–3.6304	–3.6045
	(–5.7375)	(–5.6374)	(–5.6512)	(–5.3335)
ZU	5.1571	5.0788	5.0984	4.9898
	(7.6712)	(7.5909)	(7.6272)	(6.7679)
R^2	0.5097	0.5089	0.5091	0.5526
SEE	2.461	2.463	2.462	2.518

Notes: The dependent variable is the ratio of private investment to GDP, in per cent. t-statistics are in parentheses. R^2 is the adjusted R^2 and SEE is the standard error of the estimate.
[a] 152 observations.
[b] 133 observations.

can countries in our sample. The coefficient of the change in bank credit to private sector is positive and statistically significant at the 1 per cent level. As previously hypothesised, uncertainty may have a very strong impact on private investment. From a policy perspective, instability of the overall economic environment as well as the credibility of policy stance may be as important as the level of available credit, public expenditure, tax incentives or interest rate in influencing private investment behaviour.

Table 7.4 presents reported estimates of the impact of uncertainty

Table 7.4 Impact of macroeconomic uncertainty on domestic private investment

Variable	*1970–88*	*1970–9*	*1980–8*
Intercept	13.3256	–3.856	16.634
	(2.6771)	(–7.663)	(5.1674)
VGR[a]	–1.2521	2.0321	–4.3292
	(–0.2969)	(1.3059)	(–1.6110)
VER[b]	–1.5439	104.155	–3.6367
	(–0.4821)	(2.5645)	(–1.0804)
VMS[c]	–1.0542	12.6467	0.5258
	(–0.1118)	(2.0822)	(0.1194)
R^2	–0.600	0.4866	0.2178
SEE	2.686	1.969	1.649

Notes: The dependent variable is the mean of the ratio of domestic private investment to GDP, in per cent. t-statistics are in parentheses.
[a] coefficient of variation of real GDP growth.
[b] coefficient of variation of nominal exchange rate.
[c] coefficient of variation of money supply growth.

in the overall macroeconomic environment and instability of key policy measures on the private investment ratio. The proposed measures of uncertainty and instability are the coefficients of variation of the real output growth, nominal exchange rate, and money supply growth. Real GDP growth variability serves as a proxy for uncertainty in the overall economic climate; while the volatility of exchange rate and money supply growth proxied the stability, consistency and credibility of policy stance of the government.

The sample for the estimated results in Table 7.4 is only 8 observations. Nevertheless, suggestive remarks on the impact of uncertainty on private investment in selected African countries can be inferred from the estimated results. In 1970–88, the variability of output, exchange rate and money supply have a negative effect on private investment, but the coefficients of the uncertainty measures are not statistically significant and the overall explanatory power of these variables is small. However, the estimated results improved considerably when the equation was re-estimated for two subperiods: 1970–9 and 1980–8. In 1970–9, the uncertainty measures, in all cases, have a positive and significant impact on private investment. The results suggest that the nominal exchange rate volatility, which was very small in the 1970s, impacts positively on private investment.

These results contrast sharply with the estimated results for the subperiod 1980–8. During the 1980s, changes in nominal exchange rate, which exhibit wide swings and high volatility, influence private investment negatively. Moreover, the uncertainty surrounding the overall economic climate in the selected countries was heightened in the 1980s. The variability of real output has a strong negative impact on private investment. On the other hand, the variability of money supply growth was minimised through stabilisation policies and this tended to have a positive, albeit weak, impact on private investment in the 1980s.

IV POLICY IMPLICATIONS

We acknowledge that broad generalisations on policy implications of the empirical results for all African countries should be avoided. Only eight of 51 countries in Africa are included in our sample owing to data constraints. Further research on private investment behaviour could be carried out on a larger sample of African countries as more data become available in the future. Nevertheless, the empirical results do shed some light on policy discussions on domestic private investment behaviour in the region.

(A) Stable and credible macroeconomic environment

The empirical result suggests that a high degree of price stability that provides a consistent incentive structure to entrepreneurs is needed to ensure a strong recovery of domestic private investment in several African countries. High and erratic domestic inflation rates, an important indicator of macroeconomic instability, are negatively related to private sector investment in the study. Macroeconomic policies aimed at sustaining moderate rates of inflation may have a salutary and positive impact on private investment and promote long-term growth. However, policies that result in erratic and unpredictable inflation rates may compound macroeconomic instability with consequential adverse effects on private investment activity. An adjustment package may itself increase instability and uncertainty, and undermine investors' confidence in the short run if the perceived probability of a future policy reversal is strong. A predictable and credible macroeconomic policy environment is, therefore, a *sine qua non* for recovery of private investment and restoration of long-term growth.

(B) Sustaining adjustment programmes

The econometric results obtained in this study confirm that real output fluctuations constitute a major determinant of domestic private investment in African countries. This empirical result has an important policy implication for the sustainability of structural adjustment programmes. On the one hand, structural adjustment reforms, often preceded by absorption-reducing monetary and fiscal policies, are likely to have an adverse short-run effect on private investment because of the initial decline in output growth and slowdown in economic activity. On the other hand, without a sufficient recovery of investment, the resumption of long-term growth in many African countries may be jeopardised if the SAPs adopted by many countries in the region are not sustainable.

In general, structural adjustment programmes and policy reforms require a comprehensive approach. However, experience suggests that an appropriate sequencing of reforms must take into account the limited and specific institutional capacity, as well as the different speeds of adjustment in goods, factor and financial markets of individual African countries. The adjustment strategy and lending should concentrate on measures to restore sustainable long-term growth in regional member countries that have made substantial progress in removing distortions, in creating a stable macroeconomic framework, and in ensuring a credible policy and enabling environment.

Further, the refinement of the adjustment strategy to increase its contribution to investment and growth recovery will be appropriate. The transition from adjustment to growth of production requires a sustained recovery of the level and productivity of investments. In addition to providing economy-wide structural adjustment lending, sectoral adjustment loans from the multilateral financial institutions to key sectors will be appropriate. In the past, trade, agriculture and industry sectors have been the main beneficiaries of such sectoral adjustment loans. The findings of this study suggest that sectoral lending to support public expenditure restructuring and financial sector rehabilitation will be essential for the recovery of private investment.

(C) Public expenditure restructuring

A positive impact of public sector investment on domestic private sector investment is confirmed by the empirical results. This suggests that for most countries in the sample public investment is complementary to private sector investment. In an attempt to achieve fiscal balance and external account balance many African countries curtailed public expenditures in the 1980s. Several African governments were reluctant to reduce public expenditures on consumption because of political constraints and the perceived immediate short-term consequences. Fiscal adjustment, therefore, often takes the form of reduced expenditures on public sector investment. However, public sector investment in human capital and infrastructural facilities that are complementary to private sector investment is required to put these economies back on higher long-term growth paths. Expanded restructuring of public sector expenditures for institutional and infrastructural development may also be required to achieve this goal. The efficiency of resource use in the public sector is also as important as the level of investment.

(D) Financial sector rehabilitation

The direct role of credit availability in private investment in several African countries is confirmed in the empirical study. Two distinct policy implications are suggested by this result. First, credit restrictions are often required as part of macroeconomic stabilisation programmes. In the context of African countries, credit restriction policy should be designed to limit the banking system net claims on the public sector and to prevent the private sector from bearing a disproportionate effect of overall credit restrictions. Both the theoretical hypothesis and the empirical evidence provided in this chapter suggest that the squeezing of credit to the private sector will result in a reduction in the level of private investment with adverse impacts on the long-term productive capacity of the private sector.

Further, the institutional structure of financial markets in African countries affects the financial intermediation process and the transmission mechanisms of credit policy in these countries. Indeed, there is deep crisis in the financial sector in several African countries: the banking system has become virtually illiquid in some countries. The pressing need in these countries is to reestablish an operational banking system. In other countries, the financial intermediation process needs to be deepened through the strengthening of the fiscal, legal and institutional framework conducive to mobilising and allocating financial resources. In most countries, domestic commercial banks with a traditional emphasis on short-term trade finance are reluctant to lend for long-term investments. Changes in their perceptions will need to be induced. In well-developed banking systems, such as in Kenya, Morocco and Nigeria, innovative financial instruments that ensure a diversity of money and capital markets should be deepened.

(E) External resources transfer

Sustained domestic private investment recovery requires mobilising domestic financial resources as well as external financial resources. Thus, the macroeconomic uncertainty associated with a high debt burden among African countries needs to be underscored. Lower private investment is associated with increased external resource transfer from African countries in this study. High debt service payments reduce the funds available for investment and the financing of essential capital goods imports. Total debt service payments on medium- and long-term external debt for regional member countries was more than US$20 billion in the 1980s. The ratio of debt service payments to exports of goods and services was about 30 per cent in the late 1980s.

The continent is saddled with a stock of debt in excess of $270 billion, representing, on average, over 90 per cent of GDP. Reducing the debt burden and its adverse impact on private investment depends on several internal and external factors: increased debt relief through appropriate debt rescheduling and forgiveness mechanisms, lengthening debt maturities, lower world real interest rates, favourable terms of trade increases in purchasing power of exports, stable real exchange rates, and competitive trade policies. Adequate external financial support will also lend credibility to adjustment programmes aimed at laying the foundation for private sector development.

V CONCLUSION

The transition from adjustment to sustained growth in Africa requires adequate recovery of the level and efficiency of private investment. The focus in the longer term of adjustment programmes is on creating more appropriate incentives to increase the efficiency of investment and on providing the framework for private sector development as the basis for achieving sustained growth of African economies.

This chapter has demonstrated that restoring private investors' confidence and raising the level of domestic private investment will depend on a predictable and stable macroeconomic environment, credible adjustment programmes and low perceived probability of policy reversal, increases in complementary public sector investment, financial sector rehabilitation, and adequate external support.

NOTE

1. The main sources of the data used in this study are as follows:
   (1) Data on private investment rates and public investment rates in Kenya, Tunisia and Zimbabwe were obtained from Pfeffermann and Madarassy (1989); in Malawi, Mauritius and Tanzania, they were obtained from national sources; and in Morocco, from Horton (1990).
   (2) Data on real GDP growth rates and terms of trade are taken from World Bank (1990).
   (3) Data on debt-service ratios and debt–GNP ratios are from World Bank, *World Debt Tables* (Washington, DC: World Bank, several issues).
   (4) Data on consumer price index, GDP deflator and credit to the private sector were obtained from IMF (1990).

Part II

Political Dimension of Reforms

8 Adjustment, Political Conditionality and Democratisation in Africa

Thandika Mkandawire

African states are, in an unprecedented manner, buffeted by a wave of pressures from both domestic and external forces calling for wide-ranging and profound economic and political reforms. The economic reforms envisaged are usually in the form of structural adjustment programmes almost invariably drawn up by international financial institutions, while the political reforms proposed usually take the form of multiparty democracy. The economic reforms have been taking place for close to a decade now, while the movement for political reform is of quite recent origin. However, whatever their sequence and differences in start-up time, the two types of reforms are now linked in the minds of both the general public and specialists. Or, at least, each now serves as the backdrop to the other, so that no coherent discussion of the prospects of one is possible without consideration of the other.

The link between economic and political reform is sometimes made in a causal manner in that reforms introduced in one sphere have provoked calls for reform in the other, or by the suggestion that certain economic reforms can only take place if specific political reforms are made and vice versa. In other cases the link between the two types of reform is seen as merely contingent: the SAP happens to take place at about the same time as the democratisation process, which was set off by events not related to the economy – the 'demonstration effect' of 'Glasnost' in Eastern Europe, the 'political conditionality' imposed by donors as a result of domestic pressures from human rights movements in their respective countries, the rise within African countries of social movements with new economic and political demands, and so forth.

Yet no matter what the source of the linkage is, the simultaneous occurrence of SAP and democratisation processes calls for careful and systematic exploration. There is a need to examine the compatibility and contradictions of the various economic reforms with the political programmes of the emergent political actors in the African political economic scene. More specifically, one should seek to answer such questions as: What are the implications of the simultaneous pursuance of SAPs and reforms toward multi-party democratic rule? How compatible are these objectives? What weights do different groups attach to these economic and political reforms? What are the domestic and foreign interests behind these changes and what content do these interests give to these reforms? What is the balance of forces between the groups pushing the different political and economic agendas and what, given the constellation of social forces in a specific country, will be the final 'mix' and its stability?

This chapter will attempt to address some of these questions, if only in an exploratory manner since the process is still unfolding and subject to rapid and unprecedented shifts in both content and direction.

I THE DOMESTIC ORIGINS OF POLITICAL REFORMS

The domestic sources of calls for political change are twofold: on the one hand, the changed political scene and the emergence of a whole range of social movements which are making demands on the political system in a manner that is unprecedented since the heyday of the struggle for independence; on the other hand, the impact of the economic crisis on the political perceptions of the state by these forces. Only a year or so ago one would have been hard put to identify social movements whose responses to the crisis were addressed not only to a set of specific policies, but also to the nature of the state itself and the processes of policy formation in Africa. Indeed, the rather passive way in which obviously painful austerity measures were received in much of Africa had begun to persuade some analysts that the political dangers of unpopular measures to the state had been 'overblown'(Bienen and Waterbury, 1989). Presumably, the long-suffering African societies could be forced to swallow more of the bitter pill without fear of widespread protest. And if there was any protest it would assume the 'exit' rather than 'the voice' option, to use Hirschman's terminology (Hirschman, 1970), or would be so diluted by all kinds of parochial schisms and patron-clientalistic commitments and loyalties as to be rendered politically impotent. Indeed, prior to the resurgence of social movements calling for democracy, there was a fascination on the part of certain groups for 'withdrawal' from the terrain in which the state was preponderant towards other areas far from the reach of the state – association life, parallel markets, ethnic associations, and so on. Considerable attention was focused on 'survival strategies' of households or social groups outside the reach of the state and the consequences of such withdrawal on the state structures. For some, the existence of such space for escape regrettably weakened the state (Hyden, 1980), while for others such a possibility of escape was evidence of the vibrancy of African civil society (Chazan and Rothchild, 1987). In both cases, however, such escape suggested the absence of social forces within civil society that would pursue democratic struggles in the arena that really mattered – the political arena.

During the last few years there has been an upsurge of movements which not only protest against the effects of adjustment policies, but are also calling for greater democratisation of their societies, greater accountability in the management of national affairs, and an end to corruption and waste, leading some to talk of an 'African Spring'. The social base of these movements remains unclear. However, one common feature is that thus far they have been basically urban-based and largely drawn from the 'formal' sectors. Contrary to some predictions, these social movements are quite 'traditional'. Trade unions, university staff associations, student movements, professional associations and urban church groups have in one way or another and in various degrees been involved in these upheavals.

In addition, demonstrators and rioters have included the ubiquitous and amorphous urban 'unemployed'. In a surprising number of cases, these movements have demonstrated remarkable resilience in the face of violent military repression. The Malian and Togolese movements are outstanding examples in this respect. Four days of rioting in Mali in 1990 in the face of an army that opened fire, killing 160 people and wounding 1000, led to a coup d'état and the overthrow of Moussa Traore. Since then the country has held democratic elections.

The political clout of these movements is reflected in the fact that they have dramatically changed the political landscape of a number of African countries. In most countries, the governments have retreated or indicated a willingness to reexamine the political structures of their countries, especially the one-party rule that has characterised most states. In some important cases these urban groups have constituted themselves into powerful electoral coalitions that have emerged victorious after general elections. This has been the case in Zambia, Benin and Cape Verde, where the one-party regimes have been abandoned, free elections held and the incumbents have accepted defeat. In Côte d'Ivoire and Gabon, multipartism has been rather grudgingly accepted and the opposition sits in the national assemblies, albeit uneasily. Kenya, Niger, Angola, Nigeria and Mozambique have all promised to hold free elections. In a number of countries, however, the process has been stalled due to the resistance and machinations of the incumbents: this is the case in Cameroon, Zaire, Togo and Burkina Faso where, as one member of the opposition has pointed out, an 'assassinocracy' still rules. In a typically British way, the former British colonies of Uganda, Ghana, Sierra Leone and Tanzania are going about the whole business in the roundabout and superfluous way of Commissions of Inquiry whose terms of reference are tantamount to sounding out the public on whether or not they seek to be free. There are, of course, some deafening silences in countries such as Sudan, but the general direction is toward some kind of democratisation of African societies.

The problems of the economy and the policies adopted to deal with the crises have contributed to the resurgence and cohesion of these otherwise disparate movements. They have also exposed the weakness and undermined the legitimacy of the state. There is no presupposition here that there is a monotonistic relationship between economic policies and political manifestation. Rather, the point is that the economic conjuncture has fuelled the various struggles for a wide range of goals, including some which are not necessarily directly linked to the economy – human rights, ethnic identity, and so on. First, macroeconomic crises have brought to light long-hidden micro-inefficiencies and have highlighted the blight of corruption, especially as it has continued to provide enormous wealth to some while the majority is called upon to 'patriotically' shoulder the burden of austerity. Under periods of rapid economic growth, various forms of microeconomic inefficiencies in economic management can be lived with and overlooked. Indeed, they may even receive theoretical justification as essential engines of capitalism's macroeconomic dynamism à la Schumpeter. However, in times of crisis these same sources of dynamism become unendurable 'distortions', which are blamed for all that has gone wrong and cast light on a whole range of inadequacies hitherto neglected or condoned.

Secondly, the adjustment programmes have led to losses of post-independence gains in welfare which were part of the populist-nationalist programmes. The working class has witnessed a drastic reduction in real wages, which has been exacerbated by the removal of subsidies on wage goods, the introduction of 'user charges' on a number of public services and widespread retrenchment in the parastatal sector.

In the most politically provocative cases, the state has simply not paid salaries over unbearably long periods of time. This has happened most frequently in countries belonging to the Franc-zone where the state does not enjoy the right to issue its own currency and cannot therefore resort to the printing press to pay salaries. The political and bureaucratic importance of regular payment of salaries, even in monies whose value has been scandalously eroded, should not be underestimated. Failure to do so not only undermines the credibility of the state but interferes with the sense of routine that is so important to bureaucratic perception.

Thirdly, SAPs have contributed to the erosion of the populist programmes forged by nationalist movements after independence. The various coalitions that have provided a modicum of peace in much of post-colonial Africa were based on a complex web of redistributive policies, including food subsidies, pan-territorial pricing, regional planning and subsidised social welfare services. The political significance of these measures has been denigrated through being lumped together with or seen as tantamount to corruption ('rent-seeking', clientalism, patronage, and so on). But this is the stuff that political legitimation everywhere includes.

Finally, the package has dramatically compromised the position of the state as the bastion of national sovereignty and has revealed its weak and dependent character *vis-à-vis* foreign powers and institutions. It has raised the question as to whom the state is accountable. The assumption by foreign experts of key functions that have long been 'indigenised' is the most dramatic manifestation of this process. The African middle classes have had to suffer the indignity and humiliation of witnessing the reversal of indigenisation programmes as expatriates have reassumed certain key positions in government, the indigenisation of which had symbolised greater sovereignty by African states. This reversal has raised in a most dramatic way the issue of sovereignty and the real danger of multilateral recolonisation of Africa.

II EXTERNAL PRESSURES: POLITICAL CONDITIONALITY AND ADJUSTMENT

The most direct expression of foreign pressure on African states has been in the realm of economic policy. For more than a decade now African countries have been implementing SAPs, almost invariably designed and imposed by the international financial agencies. While those advocating these reforms claim that they are tailored to the particular needs of each country, they have generally involved devaluation of national currencies, drastic reduction in state expenditure, privatisation of state-owned enterprises and liberalisation of the trade regime.

While in the early years of the imposition of SAPs it was taken for granted that these programmes would be unpopular and would therefore require regimes that were insulated from popular pressures or had the 'political will' (to use the current euphemism for political callousness and insensitivity) to ride roughshod over such interests (Lal, 1983), there has been a sudden shift towards a position that links structural adjustment to democratisation. So in addition to the 'economic' conditionality that plagued Africa during much of the 1980s, we now have 'political conditionality'.

It is important to emphasise that the external view on the necessity or appropriateness of democratic rule is very recent. It has been conventional wisdom that some form of authoritarian rule is a necessary, albeit painful, step towards development. It was part of the hard-headed 'No Easy Path' to development syndrome that reconciled many policy makers to authoritarian rule.

The turnaround in the West has been conditioned by a broad range of experiences, not all of which directly emanate from Africa. The first relates to the sweeping changes in Eastern Europe where economic and political liberalisation have appeared simultaneously on the agenda, in sharp contrast to the case of China where only economic liberalisation has been officially encouraged. It has therefore seemed only natural that Africa's own brand of 'perestroika' (structural adjustment policies) should be linked to 'glasnost'. Second, the parlous state of authoritarian governance in Africa has made a mockery of any form of economic assistance, as waste and corruption have eroded the basis for a rational economic use of resources. This state of affairs has been blamed on the lack of 'accountability' on the part of the authoritarian or patron-clientalist state. Hence the calls for some form of accountability that does not necessarily have to be democratic. It is also this that has forced international financial institutions and aid donors to address the question of 'governance', albeit in what is largely a technocratic manner. In its 1989 annual report, the World Bank clearly identified governance (defined as 'the exercise of political power to manage a nations affairs') as a central preoccupation. Although implicit in its pronouncement is a notion of democratisation, central to its preoccupations is the technocratic aspect of governance stressing 'capacity building' and economic growth. This has led Bratton and Rothchild (1991) to conclude: 'To date, the World Bank's fledgling governance programme concentrates on reducing the size of government, privatising parastatal agencies, and improving the administration of aid funds.'

Third, the growth of human rights movements in the donor countries has contributed to this recent turnaround in the West. These movements have striven to inject human rights issues into both bilateral and multilateral aid programmes and have therefore called for some kind of political conditionality. In a number of countries, governments have been forced by these domestic movements to begin to link continued economic assistance to better performance in the political realm, including a shift towards multipartism, respect for human rights, and so forth.

Fourth, and undoubtedly most importantly, have been the political upheavals in Africa itself. A number of donors have been shaken by the realisation that the regimes they have thus far backed are on shaky grounds. To curry favour with the new movements, some donors have had to make sharp turns in policies. In some cases, the turn-about has been mainly aimed at recapturing the political initiative.

Finally, changes in intellectual perceptions have been important in the development of views on the appropriateness of democratic rule. More specifically, there is an accumulating number of (statistical) analyses suggesting that there is no evidence of an unambiguous relationship between political regime type (democratic or authoritarian) and economic growth (Sorensen, 1991). This evidence has been used to question the related argument that authoritarian regimes are more capable of initialling the kind of economic reforms entailed by SAPs. It has also led the World Bank (1991c) to conclude: 'On the whole the evidence suggests that the democratisation-authoritarian distinction itself fails to explain adequately whether or not countries initiate reform, implement it effectively or survive its political fall-out.'

It is, from an intellectual history point of view, interesting to note that this 'evidence' is invoked and has apparently become most persuasive during the current political climate when it indeed seems most urgently needed. This coincidence should in itself cast grave doubts upon the association of democracy to specific economic aggregates for it suggests great political malleability of statistical analyses. It also points to the danger of allowing economic metaphor to dominate political discourse as well as the potentially ephemeral nature of commitment to democratic governance when it is tethered to a particular economic model.

III POTENTIAL SOURCES OF CONFLICT

At first sight, it would seem that the calls for democratisation by the internal forces dovetail neatly with the demands by the donor community for greater accountability and democratisation. Recent World Bank reports have been hailed as signalling a major shift in the donors' perspectives away from a preference for technocratic-authoritarian regimes toward an endorsement of the need for greater accountability of African states to their own people and greater democratisation of decision-making processes. Yet, as we will argue, things are not that unambiguous.

One should not take the commitment of all donors to democratisation at face value. There are at least three factors that will tend to blunt their commitment: the inertia of habit; the nature and the imperatives of economic interests of major donors in particular countries, and; the political economy informing the donors' perception of policy-making in Africa.

(A) Inertia and the loss of sovereignty

On the inertia side, there is in Africa what is euphemistically known as 'informal governance' by international institutions, which has been intensified by the loss of sovereignty by African states due to the exigencies of structural adjustment. Key ministries have been literally hijacked by these institutions, placed out of the reach of domestic politics. Not surprisingly, given past practice, there is apprehension on the part of international financial institutions about democratic management of economic affairs. There is concern about public scrutiny of aid programmes and the behaviour of aid agencies. For the major financial institutions, their ideal remains that of a ministry of finance that is insulated from the democratic processes and conducts 'policy dialogues' with the outside world unencumbered by domestic politics. Writing on one country whose performance has been widely hailed in the development establishment, Hutchful (1989) points to the erosion of national sovereignty, the 'depoliticisation' that has occurred, and the 'displacement of popular participation and mobilisation by a narrowly-based, bureaucratic management'. He argues:

> . . . it is clear that there is a fundamental inconsistency between the market ideologies of the ERP/SAP and mass mobilisation, and between the highly secretive conditions of the programme's negotiations and the exercise of democratic participation. Ghana has been turned into a laboratory for extensive neoclassical experimentation, unencumbered by the distractions of popular democracy.

There is no need to belabour the point that such 'hijacking' of key elements of the state will conflict with the democratisation processes taking place in Africa. At best it will yield a highly truncated version of democracy by denying domestic political forces access to important spheres of national life. Experience from Latin America is enlightening. Writing on the case of Bolivia where a democratic regime has pursued a highly orthodox economic adjustment programme, Malloy (1991) notes that the reality of economic crisis and its attendant need to create an insulated, autonomous, decision-making capacity produces a strong authoritarian bent:

> What we see emerging in Latin America . . . is a new kind of regime that will not conform to pre-existing concepts of 'liberal democracy'. Rather we see a hybrid regime evolving in which an outward democratic form is energised by an inner authoritarian capacity especially in the realm of economic policy.

That donors in Africa aspire to this brand of truncated democracy is not a very far-fetched proposition. The preference for such an arrangement is so obvious to the new regimes that they tend to appoint technocrats from international organisations as prime ministers and finance ministers and seek to assure donors that these technocrats will be accorded autonomy in their management of the economy.

(B) The economic interests of donors

As far as the commitment to democratisation by donors in specific countries in Africa is concerned, this has already provoked serious disappointments in some parts of Africa. The British have tended not to take the matter seriously, confining themselves to 'quiet diplomacy' without much success. France, which made a high-profile commitment to democratisation and distanced itself from authoritarian rule at the Baule meeting of June 1990, has raised the most expectations and provoked the most disappointment among the new leaders of democratic movements. Madagascar has made accusations against France for not disavowing Didier Ratsiraka and for not forcing him out of power; the Togolese, whose new Prime Minister invited French troops to dislodge the military supporters of Eyadema, were shocked to learn that the French troops who had moved to neighbouring Benin would only intervene to save French lives; and the Prime Minister of the transitional government of Congo was jolted to realise that France would not pick up the salary bill. A *Jeune Afrique* editorialist noted the ambivalence or even contradictory positions of the democratic movements which, while decrying France's constant interventions in their nations' affairs only yesterday, were now calling for French troops and the underwriting of budgets in a manner reminiscent of neocolonialism in its worst form. The editorialist went on to condemn these movements for the 'pernicious tendency, inherited from those against whom they have fought' to always turn to France.

These may be harsh words for embattled regimes such as that of Togo, but they raise a question which in some cases is leading to serious divisions among democratic movements themselves. The conflict arises from the difficulties of reconciling national sovereignty and the need for external support, even for such basic things as monitoring elections or keeping soldiers off the back of the new democracies. The case of Togo has dramatically dramatised this problem. The army's constant blackmailing of the new civilian regime there has tempted the opposition to call for France's intervention from its contingent in neighbouring Benin.

As for conflict of interests, it should be recalled that there are some powerful private economic interests in the donor countries which are closely tied to the predatory practices of the past and are understandably wary of the new democratic turn of events. These interests may enjoy enough political leverage or support to be able to exert sufficient pressure on their home governments to dilute their commitment to democratisation. The case of France in Gabon, Congo and Cameroon is suggestive of this phenomenon. It appears that ELF-Aquitaine, a major French oil company, has been involved in the disappearance of billions of dollars of oil revenue from these countries. Opposition movements in all of these countries have called for audits of the deals involving this company. This eventuality must have given French interests cold feet and may account for France opting for either cosmetic change, drawn-out processes of democratisation or even simply the status quo.

(C) The donors' perception of policy-making in Africa

Finally, the political conclusion that democratisation would be necessary or compatible with major economic programmes for African countries supported or imposed by both bilateral and multilateral donors contradicts the political analysis underlying the perception of economic policy by the donor community. To the extent that it is possible to impute an analytical framework to the World Bank's understanding of the politics of economic policy-making in Africa, one should note that this framework has changed over the years (Gibbon, 1994). In the 1960s, the Bank tended to treat the state within a basically 'modernisation' paradigm, in which the state played an essentially benign, developmental role. And in any case, the Bank's confinement to projects did not necessitate a more complex view of the state than this. In the early 1980s, the view changed. Macroeconomic policies were then perceived as being so fundamentally misguided as to make any project financing meaningless. If projects were to be economically viable, macroeconomic policies had to be favourable. The Bank initially worked on the 'basket case' view that because African states were in dire straits, the Bank could introduce 'shock treatments' without much opposition from the recipient states. However, the reluctance of many states to accept the treatment and the recidivism of those who had accepted the package compelled the Bank towards some more explicit political analysis. It accepted the 'urban bias' thesis advanced by Michael Lipton to explain the persistence of poverty in the underdeveloped countries. With this thesis one could understand why it was politically rational to persist with what were obviously economically irrational policies. Politically, it opened up the vista for the Bank to seek out political coalitions that would be supportive of its policy recommendations.

Failure to identify, let alone constitute, such coalitions has forced the Bank to once again change the political-economy paradigm informing its understanding of political processes. The current view of the Bank is informed by a relatively new approach variously labelled 'rational choice', 'the public choice', the 'new political economy' or 'neoclassical political economy'. Developed by trade theorists to explain various protectionist policies that led to 'market distortion', the 'political economy of rent-seeking societies' posits interest groups that engage in 'Directly Unproductive' (DUP) activities to capture various rents generated by state activities. Common in all of these is a methodological approach which assumes rational individual behaviour in pursuance of self-interests as the cornerstone of political alliances and interest groups.

Intellectually, this political analysis carries the epistimological advantage of consistency and parsimony with respect to assumptions used since it merely extends to politics the methodological individualism and rationality derived from economic analysis. People maximise their utilities in politics just as they do in the market. This consistency and parsimony has, however, been gained at the cost of the empirical vacuity of assertions about how policy is actually made in Africa.

The salient point about this approach is that for policy analysis, the state is seen as essentially a rent-allocating agent. By definition, any involvement of the state in productive activities is simply an expression of its distributive functions. If it is involved in production at all, it is either to create employment for the bureaucracy or to facilitate the economic activities of certain interest groups, but not for economic growth. In either case, state activities create 'distortions' which lead to the loss of static allocative efficiency (while much has been blamed on these 'distortions', empirical measures of losses caused by them have turned up embarrassingly low figures). The political conclusion of this perspective is that good governance in the poor countries would require freeing the state from the demands of different domestic groups or, where this is not possible, a dramatic reduction of its role in the economy.

For a number of years, several North American scientists have used this approach to explain policy-making in Africa (Bates, 1981; Rothchild and Curry, 1978). Indeed, the plausibility of their explanation has been such that it has now entered the conventional consensus about politics and policy-making in Africa. What presumably makes matters worse in Africa is that the state (or, at least the 'State class') is itself a rent-seeker and a highly advantaged one at that.

There are at least three political problems with this interpretation of policy-making in Africa and elsewhere, for that matter. The first is that, pushed to its logical conclusion, it has a strong authoritarian predilection and anti-political penchant for it cannot relate to those activities that are inherent to democratic politics. Seeking as it does a state that is autonomous of various domestic interest groups, it is an analysis that admires the 'political will' of a militaristic Rawlings and condemns the lack of spine of those regimes which have to relate to a whole range of interests in an essentially political way. It is also a view that justifies extensive intervention of foreign institutions, which are putatively not implicated in the debilitating 'DUP' activities. A consistent pursuance of this approach will therefore tend toward a cynical view of and disdain or trivialisation of politics, which are treated as largely pathological (Beckman, 1991; Grindle, 1991). More precisely, it leads to the denigration of or, at least, attempts to circumvent the institutional arrangements and political processes that are central to liberal democracy. The reasoning is that if all the politically active and well-organised groups are involved in rent-seeking activities, it is necessary to either bring in foreign powers or to seek a domestic 'Leviathan' that transcends local politics. The next step is a negation of democratic politics.

The second problem with this perception is that the social groups that are now pushing for democratisation in Africa have usually occupied leading positions in the political 'demonology' of international financial institutions and have been considered to be the ones responsible for the disastrous policies pursued by African states since independence. Even more significant is that it is opposition to structural adjustment rather than support for it that has mobilised these social groups in their struggles for democratisation. In the words of Beckman (1991), 'it is resistance to SAP, not SAP itself, that breeds democratic forces. SAP can be credited with having contributed to this development, not because of liberalism but because of its authoritarianism'.

Now if such are the roots of democratic struggles and if such is the likely content of democratic programmes in Africa, it is not clear how the political ascendancy of this 'urban bias', 'labour aristocracy' or 'rent-seeking' coalition can be reconciled with the economic adjustment programmes. Either the material interests of this coalition have been wrongly identified with pre-SAP policies and their control of state policies exaggerated, or the state is so autonomous of these rent-seeking groups or so beholden to foreign interests that local interest groups count for naught; or the 'rational choice' assumed to underlie policy-making is not as determinant as the theory suggests. It is only by accepting the last presupposition that one can justify the patrician calls by the donor community for the elites that have hitherto constituted the nefarious 'rent-seeking' coalitions to behave more disinterestedly and to thus countenance the sacrifice of some of their interests.

Even more confounding is the fact that among those countries which have received the highest accolades for being 'strong adjusters' in Africa, the majority have not needed democracy to introduce adjustment programmes, much to the Bank's satisfaction. Ghana, Nigeria and Malawi, to name only a few, are authoritarian regimes. Indeed, historically, the 'laboratory conditions' for neo-liberal economic policies was Pinochet's Chile where the 'Chicago Boys' could inflict 'shock treatments' without the encumbrance of interest groups or democratic politics.

To reconcile the imperatives of adjustment and the political exigencies of democratisation, there is now the presupposition that democracy can legitimise a set of policies that are admittedly unpopular. It can also improve governance which would presumably improve state capacity to implement adjustment programmes. This is how the World Bank (1991c) puts it:

> Democracies, conversely, could make reform more feasible in several ways. Political checks and balances, a free press, and open debate on the costs and benefits of government policy could give a wider public a stake in reform. The need to produce good results in order to be reelected could help, rather than hinder, economic change: it increases government's incentives to perform well and keeps predatory behaviour in check.

Of course all this does not prove that the policies adopted will or should be compatible to the SAP process unless one believes that free discussion, absence of corruption, and broad participation in policy-making will ineluctably lead to consensus around adjustment. This is the conclusion that a monistic view of politics leads to; since there is only one 'right' theory, there can be no scope for conflict on what is desirable for society (Amadeo and Banuri, 1991). The World Bank (1991c) is, to its credit, aware that this may not happen:

> Democratic governments are not necessarily more adept at managing reform either. Transitional democratic governments, perhaps because their political base is still fluid, appear to be particularly fluid . . . On the whole the democratic authoritarian distinction itself fails to explain adequately whether or not countries initiate reform, implement it effectively, or survive its political fall-out.

The Bank seems to accept the argument that democratic rule may have long-term growth and equity advantages over authoritarian rule:

> . . . there is suggestive evidence that links features of democratic systems positively with overall aspects of development and welfare. A further result emerges from the empirical literature on the

relation between economic performance and political system: by developing human resources and more particularly, by investing in education, countries have been found to strengthen the basis for open systems. Some studies suggest that for a given level of income, improvements in social indicators are associated with freedom and liberty (ibid.).

But there is a catch here. These advantages of democracy are a result of the pursuance of a whole range of policies that structural adjustment programmes scorn. The cuts in expenditure on social services which democracies need for political survival and for which they are lauded clearly suggest that structural adjustment and democratic rule are not easily reconcilable.

The third problem of the approach relates to the fact that it cannot accommodate or explain changes in policy. Since the rational behaviour of individuals pursuing self-interests inevitably leads to a specific set of policies, there are no endogenous forces that can be identified with an entirely different set of policies or that are capable of exerting policy in a direction that would not inevitably lead to another set of distortions. As Grindle (1991) notes:

> . . . if one is locked into an ahistorical explanation of why things are the way they are and the notion that existing situations demonstrate an inevitable rationality, it is hard to envision how changes in such situations occur except through catastrophic events or the exogenous introduction of wise statesmen or technocrats who are above petty political rationality.

IV CONFLICT BETWEEN FORMAL AND SUBSTANTIVE DEMAND

In much of Africa, the formal expression of demands for democratisation is multi-party democracy. However, as has been made clear during the numerous 'national conferences', the new movements also have substantive demands which reject structural adjustment or blame it for the decline in the material well-being of their countries. The widespread understanding of these movements is that the democratisation process will create the political foundations for addressing the substantive demands of the emergent democratic forces. Together with the call for democratic form, there are therefore demands against 'immiserisation'. Quite bluntly, these social forces expect some visible changes in their economic well-being, if not immediately after elections then surely soon after. However, in Africa as elsewhere, formal political reform has generally proved easier than substantive economic reform. Structural adjustment envisages a passage through 'a vale of tears' before settling on a course of sustained growth. Initially, the valley was thought to be narrow and swiftly traversed. Now it is widely admitted that it may be much wider, perhaps taking decades to cross (see Chapters 13 and 14 in this regard). How does one ensure the coexistence of the economic trough and political liberty? How is the economic logic of structural adjustment to be reconciled to the political logic of democratisation? For economists the nemesis of intelligent policies, the ghost in the machine, is what is known as 'macroeconomic Populism', which Dornbusch and Edwards (1990) disfavourably define as:

> . . . a policy perspective on economic management which emphasizes economic growth and income redistribution and de-emphasizes the risks of inflation and deficit financing, external constraints and the reaction of economic agents to aggregate non-economic policies.

Pressures on the new democratic regimes to lean towards some kind of 'macropopulism' are enormous. So far, this has not taken place in Africa. Part of this prudency arises from the expectation on the part of the new governments that 'good behaviour' will be rewarded with an inflow of funds to cushion some of the social effects of adjustment and to stimulate growth and employment. It also stems in part from a genuine belief of the new democratic movements that technocratic solutions may be closer to the solution than the highly subjective and arbitrary decisions of their predecessors.

It has for years been conventional wisdom that orthodox political measures demand authoritarian rule. The removal of subsidies on goods and services consumed by supposedly strong interest groups (the urban population), and the removal of activities upon which certain groups have earned rents would require a strong state with the 'political will' or 'courage' to override popular pressures. Pinochet and the Chicago Boys are the almost legendary coupling of authoritarian rule and orthodox adjustment programmes. The link between popular demands for democracy and adjustment would, therefore, seem to fly in the face of historical experience. Adjustment programmes, to the extent that international financial institutions will not relent on getting their monies repaid, will pose severe strains on the new democratic regimes that may emerge from the present political impasse.

The problem is not confined to Africa. In Latin America the problem of 'debt and democracy' has been a major preoccupation of political and social movements (Stallings and Kaufman, 1989). In Eastern Europe democratisation has had to confront the problems of a generalised decline in economic well-being during what is expected to be a transient phase of movement from central planning to market economies. Noting the 'exceptionally contradictory' process of democratisation in the Soviet Union, Gavriil Popov, an advocate of the free market, notes:

> I see the main problem in the relationship between, on the one hand, populism and, on the other, the tasks that must be carried out if the economy and society are to be transformed. Clearly, we could not have overthrown the powerful totalitarian system without the active participation of millions of ordinary people. But now we must create a society with a variety of different forms of ownership, including private property; and this will be a society of economic inequality. There will be contradictions between the policies leading to denationalisation, privatisation, and inequality on the one hand and, on the other, the populist character of the forces that were set in motion in order to achieve those aims. The masses long for fairness and economic equality. And the further the process of transformation goes, the more acute and the more glaring will be the gap, between those aspirations and economic realities.

V THE QUESTION OF NATIONAL SOVEREIGNTY

Given the widespread corruption in Africa and the gross mismanagement that some of the economies have been subjected to, it is tempting to accept any 'benevolent' foreign intervention in the political affairs of African countries. The temptation is even greater when some of these regimes have been set up or bolstered by foreign powers that now advocate democratisation. And indeed a number of Africans have called upon foreign governments and international financial institutions to exert more financial pressure on African countries to move towards political reform or to even intervene militarily in defence of democratic change. It should, however, be clear that democratic governance in Africa will have to address itself to issues of sovereignty and the extent of foreign involvement in the day-to-day affairs of African countries. Foreign institutions will be fundamentally mistaken if they assume that the rejection of incumbent national governments and calls by nationals for solidarity in the form of 'political conditionality' are an option for foreign domination. If anything, the confrontation with the local states is likely to be a prelude to the confrontation with foreign powers as these continue to exercise powers outside the legally and democratically constituted institutions and to demand repayment of debts from countries which cannot account for where the monies went or seek to impose policies which hurt large sections of the population.

VI CONCLUSION

The quest for democracy that has swept across much of the world has not left Africa untouched. The one-party state is now a beleaguered colossus whose collapse has either taken place or is imminent. One-man rule is disappearing rapidly, sometimes terribly as in the case of Liberia and Somalia. Yet, all is not well. First, in a number of cases the concessions to democratic demands have been no more than window-dressing to outmanoeuvre opponents or to hoodwink international agencies who are increasingly demanding some form of democratisation as a precondition for their financial support.

Second, the new democratic regimes are inheriting crisis-ridden economies and are being saddled with economic conditionalities that are placing severe strains on their political energies by undercutting their political base. Chances are that if the democratic movements pay the least attention to their domestic constituencies, they will not meet the stringent demands of their external constituencies – foreign financial institutions. They will soon be seen to be lacking, in the strange language of structural adjustment, the 'political will' to ride roughshod over popular demands.

The third cause for concern is that democratisation is taking place at a time when the sovereignty of African states has been gravely compromised. Adjustment has given foreign decision-makers political leverage that is not compatible with democratic practice. Democratisation in Africa risks obtaining foreign assistance that may eventually restrict its competence in both the economic and political spheres. The point here is not to deny foreign solidarity to democratic struggles in Africa, but to warn against 'political conditionality' that would dilute democracy by holding individual states to both economic and political ransom. But even more crucially it is to caution against the naive expectations of democratisation riding on the tanks or being shielded by the pockets of foreign powers. Processes of democratisation have been largely unleashed by internal forces against undemocratic rule, violation of human rights and gross mismanagement of resources by internal forces and the imposition of deflationary economic policies by outsiders. If the process is to be firmly anchored in African societies then we should insist that the initiative towards democratisation remain in the hands of domestic forces. External support that is an expression of solidarity, and not the usual meddlesome condescension, is most welcome.

A fourth problem is the prevalence of a dogma that severely narrows the economic options and unwarrantably ties democratisation to one economic practice or model. In much of the discussion on the politics of adjustment it is simply assumed that the economic prescriptions of the World Bank, while painful, are the *only* way out. And so the debates evolve around how societies can be made to swallow this bitter but only known cure and still remain democratic. However, the obvious absence of any sustainable success after nearly a decade of 'adjustment', despite the Bank's feverish search for such cases, the unravelling of neo-liberalism in such countries as the USA and Great Britain, and the discrepancy between the historical experience of what are touted as 'successful market economies' such as Japan, South Korea and Taiwan and the diktats of structural adjustment, suggest that the perception of adjustment as the only cure has more to do with the tenacity of a misplaced abstraction or dogma than economic logic or historical evidence. In any case, the complete foreclosure of debate on such key issues as taxation, intratemporal and intertemporal distributional issues, and the protection or promotion of particular economic activities or markets does not augur well for democracy since it drastically reduces the range of issues upon which democratic governments can pronounce themselves. As Amadeo and Banuri (1991) note, the failure of the state does not derive from its refusal to adhere to a theoretical dogma. Rather, 'it derives, in the short run, from its abandonment of the goal of governance in favour of theoretical certitudes; and in the long run, from its inability or unwillingness to create or modify institutions to facilitate the management of conflicts which are forever changing in form and intensity'.

9 Adjustment Programmes and Politico–Economic Interactions in Developing Countries: Lessons from an Empirical Analysis of Africa in the 1980s

Christian Morrisson, Jean-Dominique Lafay and Sébastien Dessus

Many developing countries undertook severe adjustment programmes in the 1980s, on their own initiative or under pressure from the international organisations. The technical or distributional aspects of these programmes have been extensively discussed. By contrast, their political consequences have seldom been systematically studied.

Most of the stabilisation and adjustment measures run the risk of causing political trouble. Cuts in subsidies, tax increases, privatisation of public enterprises or removal of commercial protection threaten the income and employment of either large numbers of people or of well-organised groups (see Chapters 13 and 14). This may result in violent reactions (strikes, demonstrations, riots, coups d'état, and so on). In turn, these reactions may lead to deep policy changes: indeed, several structural adjustment programmes (SAP) have been repealed or radically modified under such pressure. As a consequence, the formulation of a SAP cannot be a purely technical exercise; it has to be framed within a full politico–economic model. The central question, then, is how political and economic variables interact in the adjustment process. This chapter sums up some results drawn from a tentative answer to this question on the basis of the experience of 23 African countries in the 1980s

A general framework for a politico–economic model suited to the less developed countries (LDC) is presented in Section I. It describes the interactions between the economic situation, economic measures, including IMF interventions, the political situation and political measures. Section II focuses on the data problem. The lack of adequate data is a major difficulty in all the empirical studies carried out on LDCs. The problem here is magnified by the need to gather information on both the political and economic dimensions. This section shows how the problem was solved for the African countries of the sample. Section III presents some preliminary empirical results, and Section IV concludes with a discussion of the consequences of these empirical results for the adjustment strategies promoted by the international financial organisations.

I A SIMPLE POLITICO–ECONOMIC MODEL FOR THE LESS DEVELOPED COUNTRIES

Research undertaken during the last 25 years has greatly improved our knowledge of politico–economic interactions in the industrialised countries, on the basis of concepts such as popularity and vote functions, politico–economic reaction functions, politico–economic models, and so forth.[1] On the contrary, there are very few studies concerning the LDCs, with Frey and Eichenberger (1992) being a notable exception. This lack is all the more detrimental as rough statistical evidence clearly illustrates that economics and politics strongly interact in the LDCs:

- during the 1960s, 32 of the 38 poorest countries suffered serious conflicts (MacNamara, 1969);
- Africa has become the region *par excellence* for coups d'état, in large part as a result of the negative economic situation (Johnson, Slater and McGovan, 1984; O'Kane, 1981);
- the exacerbation of civil conflicts and the increase of political violence during the 1980s on the African continent is clearly linked to the simultaneous deterioration of the economic situation (for example, 22 distressed sub-Saharan countries experienced a mean 16.6 per cent decline in their per capita output from 1980 to 1986 (Todaro, 1989)).

The need to study politico–economic interactions in LDCs is also justified by the unexpected violent reactions which have accompanied some stabilisation or IMF programmes. IMF interventions have been regularly accused of increasing or promoting political instability because of the overly severe 'conditionality' associated with its balance of payments assistance. However, no empirical justification has yet been attached to this criticism (Sidell, 1988). Finally, the strong dysfunctionings of several LDC states appear to have significantly amplified the politico–economic interactions, and there is now greater awareness among economists that the problems of these countries cannot only be studied from a narrowly economic point of view (see Lafay and Lecaillon, 1993, for a recent survey of the literature). A recent World Bank report is most revealing of this change in attitudes (World Bank, 1991b).

The theoretical model used in this chapter is in large part directly inspired by the models built for developed countries. Its main specificity concerns the influence of IMF, foreign aid, and the policy conditions which generally accompany it. The objective is to represent in a simplified manner the essential relationships between measures and events, both political and economic, in an LDC during the adjustment period.

The risk of political reaction to unpopular economic measures differs significantly according to the groups concerned or the nature of the measure. For example, some preliminary empirical analyses have shown that, on the basis of African experience, wage cuts lead more often to strikes while price hikes for consumption goods more often result in demonstrations or riots. It is also clear that rural groups do not behave in the same way as urban ones when, for instance, subsidies are cut for primary goods.

Basically, the model distinguishes three decision-making units: the government, the population, and the IMF (and other public aid-giving institutions or national governments), and two categories of variables: economic or political *policy instruments*, and economic or political *events*. Policy instruments are controlled by the national government; events are not (according to this definition, variables concerning the IMF and other public aid-giving institutions or governments are to be considered as events).

The governmental set of policy instruments can be summarised by four aggregated variables:

- popular economic measures, which can worsen the future economic situation but which improve the present political situation;
- unpopular economic measures, which can improve the future economic situation but which worsen the present political situation;
- political repression (i.e. unpopular political measures);
- political liberalisation (i.e. popular political measures).

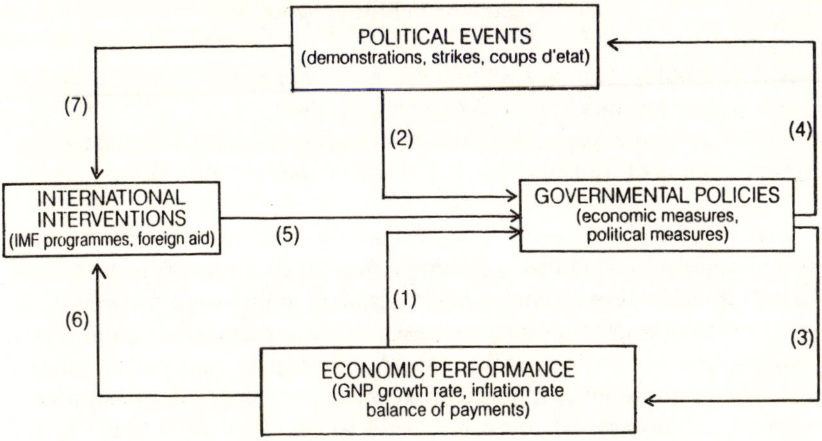

(1) Economic influences in governmental reaction functions (how economic and political measures change in response to the economic situation).
(2) Political influences in governmental reaction functions (how economic and political measures change in response to the political situation).
(3) Influences of governmental economic and political measures on the economic situation (multipliers for policy instruments).
(4) Influences of governmental economic and political measures on the political situation (multipliers for policy instruments).
(5) Influences of international aid and IMF conditionality on national economic and political policies.
(6) Influences of the national economic situation on international aid decisions (IMF decisions are supposed to be exogenous).
(7) Influences of the national political situation on international aid decisions (IMF decisions are supposed to be exogenous).

Figure 9.1 General schema of politico-economic interactions

The government uses its policy instruments to control certain strategic events of an economic or political nature, such as social troubles (demonstrations, strikes and coups d'état).[2]

Figure 9.1 represents the main interactions that the model intends to capture. One of the concerns of the model is to evidence the kind of *politico–economic cycle* that may lead to the introduction of an adjustment programme: a deep deficit in the balance of payments, the country's debt that no longer allows borrowing on international markets, and/or a rocketing inflation rate are factors which prompt governments to take highly unpopular stabilising economic measures. The IMF is often involved in the introduction of these measures, as it poses such conditions for obtaining low-cost lending from it.[3] The measures generally fall into broad categories, including:

- cuts in current and investment public expenditures;
- restrictive monetary policy;
- public employment and wage policies (decrease in real public wages, decline in the number of civil servants, etc.);
- increase in the price of consumption goods and oil products (by suppression of subsidies or increases of indirect taxes).

Due to their unpopularity, these economic measures typically prompt strikes and demonstrations, initiating a process which tends to be cumulative. In their turn, social troubles lead to repression. However, in most of the countries studied, repression is not permanent. After some months, the government takes measures of political liberalisation: universities are reopened, political prisoners are freed, suspended newspapers are reauthorised to publish, and so on. This process is typical of many of the African regimes during the studied period, which were indeed more authoritarian than democratic, but not totalitarian.

The political liberalisation policy which results from a period of repression is often accompanied by measures of economic easiness. For example, public expenditures are increased, monetary policy is weakened, initially suppressed subsidies to consumption goods are reestablished. This new popular economic policy often leads, in turn, to changes in the cabinet in order to improve government popularity and credibility: the ministers responsible for restrictive economic policy and for the political repression leave and new ministers are placed in charge of the implementation of a new economic course. In some cases, the unpopular stabilisation measures are rejected before the disequilibrium is cleared, which means that the original economic problems tend to reappear; the country is then back to its initial problem.

How does the IMF intervene in this politico–economic cycle of adjustment? On the one hand, through 'conditionality' it certainly commits the government to a more sustained stabilisation approach, and this helps to mitigate the cycle. On the other hand, the financial aid it provides may help to soften the unpopularity of several measures, and in some cases even to postpone the restoration of economic equilibria. Moreover, when social troubles occur and lead to severe repression, the IMF is pushed to increase its aid in exchange for greater respect of human and civil rights. All in all, whether the IMF's contribution mitigates or not the politico–economic adjustment cycle remains an empirical question.

II EMPIRICAL DATA

It is difficult to assert the importance of politico–economic interactions without empirical analysis. As the model contains important dynamic interactions between the economic and the political sphere, tests on time-series are essential. Hence, existing studies, generally based on cross-sectional comparisons (exploring, for instance, the link between political violence and different national economic situations in different countries at a given time), do not provide much information. It is fair to say that the databases containing time-series for LDCs are not as well supplied or accurate as those serving the main industrialised countries. For African countries, data availability makes it necessary to limit the period to the 1980s. Then, in order to preserve a sufficient number of degrees of freedom, pooled data should be utilised. The empirical tests are based on such a data set, running from 1980 to 1990 for 23 African countries (N = 23): Algeria, Burkina Faso, Cameroon, Central African Republic, Congo, Côte d'Ivoire, Egypt, Gabon, Ghana, Kenya, Madagascar, Mali, Mauritania, Morocco, Niger, Nigeria, Rwanda, Senegal, Sierra Leone, Tanzania, Togo, Tunisia and Zambia. As we have collected data for semi-annual periods, we have $23 \times 21 = 483$ observations (22–1 because some variables are lagged).

For most of the policy measures, for demonstrations, for strikes and for coups d'état, no quantitative data are available on a homogeneous basis for all the 23 African countries making up our sample. For this reason, we have built proxy indexes based on qualitative information gathered from specialised journals. Our basic source has been *Marchés tropicaux*, which gives detailed news each week, in a page or two, for each African country, including North African ones.

In order to build the required indexes, relevant policy measures and politico–economic events have been coded, when necessary, according to a four-step scale (nothing, weak, medium, strong). Indeed, some measures, such as the closing of a university or the imposition of a state of emergency, are intrinsically binary: intensity has no meaning in such cases, which have been arbitrarily rated to one.[4] Annex 1 presents the detailed list of measures and events as well as the coding table. It should be noted that policy measures are exclusively considered from the perspective of their short-term impact on popularity. For example, the privatisation of a public enterprise is considered as an unpopular measure because of its potential effects on employment in this enterprise.

This coding procedure has two evident weaknesses: it gathers only rough information, and its results depend on the subjective choices of the people who do the coding. But these weaknesses are not to be overestimated for two reasons. First, the obtained political indexes are mainly used to explain governmental reactions and governments do not possess much more sophisticated information when they take their decisions. In other words, the roughness of the indexes clearly parallels the limited character of information available to decision-makers. And secondly, as the coded information is rough, the subjective bias in coding is greatly reduced.[5]

Once the detailed events and policies have been coded on the three-step schedule, there is an aggregation problem to be solved. It concerns the relative weight to be given to intensity in comparison to frequency. Suppose that, during a six-month period, a large demonstration occurs, rated 3, and that, in another period, three small demonstrations occur, each of them rated 1. How to establish the trade-off? It was decided to retain the simple sum solution: 3 events rated 1 within a six-month period are assumed to be equivalent to one event rated 3. This solution has some justification in the absence of additional external information.

In a second step, the variation margin has been reduced, following this scheme:

Indicator Value	Sum
0	0
1	1
2	2 and 3
3	4 and more

III EMPIRICAL RESULTS

This section studies the links between economic and political events or measures on the basis of rank correlations.[6] Coefficients under 0.09, i.e. not significant at 5 per cent level, are not reported; coefficients above 0.11 are significant at a 1 per cent level.[7] The results clearly confirm that adjustment follows a politico–economic cycle. The different steps of this cycle can be analysed on the basis of Tables 9.1 to 9.6.

In Table 9.1 the effects of IMF conditionality clearly appear. IMF interventions create, in the same semester or one semester later, a decline in current public expenditures and transfers, an increase in consumer good prices, a more rigorous monetary policy, devalua-

Table 9.1 Interventions and stabilisation measures

	c501	*cr501*	*c502*	*cr502*	*c503*	*cr503*	*c504*	*cr504*
m201	0.14			–0.10			0.13	
m202			–0.11	–0.09	0.14			
m203	0.12	0.12		0.11				
m204	0.10							
m205	0.17					0.13	0.09	
m207			–0.09			0.20		0.13
m208	0.09				0.09		0.10	
m209	0.11						0.10	
m210					0.11			
m211		0.11			0.11			
m212	0.12		0.12		0.10			
m213		0.09						
m214			0.12					
m215				–0.09				
m216	0.13		0.13	0.09			0.11	
p215	0.11	0.13	0.11	0.13				

Note: *r* means a one period lag for every variable.

tions and cuts in public employment. This simply reflects the common content of stabilisation programmes. It can be noticed, in passing, that only two measures associated with IMF interventions are popular: increases in agricultural prices (taking the farmers' point of view) and import liberalisation.[8]

The *sine qua non* condition of rescheduling agreements is the prior acceptance of IMF conditions. The positive correlation between stabilisation measures and debt rescheduling (at Paris and London clubs) is then not surprising.

World Bank lending is positively associated with some stabilisation measures and negatively with others. A possible explanation of this paradox is as follows:

- during periods of accelerated growth – and of general expansion of the public budget – the World Bank lends more willingly for investment projects, hence the negative correlations with some of the (fiscal) stabilisation measures;
- the World Bank also gives financial aid, together with the IMF, in adjustment periods. This second aspect explains the positive correlation observed for some other types of stabilisation measures.

Table 9.2 Stabilisation measures and troubles

	Demonstrations	*Strikes*
m201		0.10
m204	0.15	0.10
m205	0.14	
m207		0.10
m209	0.09	
m211	0.09	0.13
m213		0.12
m214	0.12	
m216	0.11	0.11
mr207		0.09
mr208	0.10	
mr209	0.11	
mr210	0.11	
mr211	0.09	0.10
mr212	0.14	
mr215	0.11	
mr216	0.11	

Table 9.2 considers strikes and demonstrations. The numerous positive correlations between stabilisation measures and demonstrations (in the same period or a semester later) confirm that economic adjustment is a politically risky venture. For more than half of the cases, a one-period lag is observed between the policy announcement and demonstrations. This suggests that losing groups more likely react to the implementation of unpopular decisions than to their publicisation.[9] As expected, all the measures which have an impact on the price of consumption goods (cuts in subsidies, devaluation, increases in government-controlled prices or in tariffs) are strongly correlated with demonstrations. They seem to be an inescapable reaction of poor or rather poor urban populations to a sudden and dramatic decline in their purchasing power, particularly when the affected goods constitute a high proportion of the expenditures of poor families. These reactions of despair are all the more difficult to control when there is no provision for the holding of elections in the near future. Then, any serious crisis will become a regime crisis.

Restrictive monetary policy and privatisations also seem to provoke demonstrations, according to rank correlations. Monetary policy belongs to the general bundle of stabilisation measures and this provides one explanation for the observed positive correlation. A second explanation is that restrictive monetary policy increases unemployment. Privatisation generally causes massive lay-offs in the formerly public enterprises, because, for political reasons, these suffered from chronic overemployment. Massive lay-offs have a significant chance of triggering demonstrations because they take place during a period of recession, i.e. a period where there is a low probability of finding a new job.

Measures that result in price increases or which directly hurt wage-earners may also lead to strikes, but the correlation is generally much lower than for demonstrations. Many poor people are either independent workers or wage-earners in small firms (most of which belong to the informal sector). In such a context, going on strike has no real meaning or effect. The only option left in the face of price increases is street demonstrations. The only exception concerns the public and parastatal sectors, where budget squeezes directly reduce the salaries of employees and are likely to lead to strikes.

The most important result reported in Table 9.2 concerns the lack of correlation between demonstrations and cuts in public investment or current expenditures. This means that the different adjustment measures may present very different degrees of political risk. It is clearly much less dangerous to decrease public investment than to cut subsidies on agricultural goods. Governments clearly know this as they always prefer the first measure to the second, even if the IMF pushes forcefully for the opposite position. Indeed, from the economic point of view, a cut in investment threatens future growth, and direct income transfers to poor households would be more efficient than price subsidies. But governmental decision-making is grounded on political motivations. Restrictions on subsidies generate social troubles while the effects of investment cuts are spread all over the country on the small and medium-sized building industries.

Table 9.3 corresponds to the third step of the politico–economic cycle. It deals with suppression measures, which in some cases may result in large numbers of people wounded or killed. The most severe reactions are observed for coup attempts and demonstrations: firing at masses, summary shootings, death penalties and capital executions. For coups d'état or coup attempts, these reactions are not surprising; similar responses have been observed in developed countries during the few cases where these types of events have taken place. On the contrary, suppression of demonstrations is much more violent than in developed countries. The lack or dysfunctioning of electoral institutions and the weakness of the administrative machine mean that governments do not or cannot accept a resolution of crises by going to the

Table 9.3 Troubles and repression

	Demonstrations	*Lagged demonstrations*	*Strikes*	*c341*	*cr341*	*c344*	*cr344*
c420	0.16		0.15			0.32	
c421	0.24	0.17	0.17	0.13			
c424	0.10				0.19		
c425				0.20	0.12		0.15
c426	0.12	0.17	0.18				0.12
c427	0.17		0.10				
c428	0.42		0.21	0.14			
c429				0.11		0.10	0.10

polls or by allowing the opposition to peacefully publicise its point of view. Thus, any conflict turns into a dispute over the legitimacy of the regime, rather than remaining focused on a particular government within undisputed institutions as occurs in democratic countries. This explains why governments tend to react quickly and severely to public demonstrations.

By contrast, strikes are not linked to such severe reactions as firing at masses, summary shootings or executions. Governments apparently consider that they express basic material needs, without directly threatening political stability. This important difference aside, all other forms of repression (state of emergency, arrests, prohibition of demonstrations, political meetings and newspapers, closing of schools and universities) are correlated with both demonstrations and strikes. Governments tend to use all available instruments to put an end to these phenomena as quickly as possible, before they become cumulative. It is a real fact that a strike in one industry may have contagious effects in other industries and that people or students on strike have free time to participate in demonstrations.

Tables 9.4 and 9.5 are highly instructive from a political point of view: they show that, according to the sample, the African regimes are more authoritarian than dictatorial. Repression is quickly followed by measures of political liberalisation (with a lag of less than a semester). In contrast with severe dictatorships, the mean regime in the sample (relatively) rapidly releases political prisoners, abandons judicial pursuits, lifts prohibitions on meetings and newspapers, and so forth. Some observed correlations concerning connected measures are notably high. For example, the lifting of a state of emergency implies that this state was established prior to the emergency situation. This

Table 9.4 Political liberalisation and repression

	c450	*c453*	*c455*	*c456*	*c457*	*c458*
c420	0.34	0.20			0.19	0.15
c421	0.22		0.12	0.13	0.20	0.14
c423	0.21					
c424	0.33	0.21			0.71	0.22
c425			0.10	0.18	0.11	
c426	0.12		0.13		0.28	0.25
c427		0.13				
c428				0.16		0.44
c429	0.10					

Table 9.5 Political liberalisation and lagged repression

	c450	*c451*	*c453*	*c455*	*c457*	*c458*
cr420	0.37					
cr422		0.17				
cr423	0.22					0.13
cr424	0.33					
cr425		0.11				
cr426	0.13					
cr428						0.25
cr429	0.10		0.20	0.11	0.24	

is similarly the case for the closing and reopening of a university, initiating and abandoning judicial pursuits, the sentencing and rehabilitating of individuals, and so on. Significant links also exist, however, between variables which are not so mechanically connected. This means that repression and political liberalisation represent two globally interdependent packages. The mean government is a weak one; it makes use of all the instruments at its disposal when it is threatened, but gives up most of them when the political situation becomes calm again.

The rationale underlying this behaviour is grounded on two bases:

- organising long-term and large-scale repressive systems, as in totalitarian regimes, requires much capital and considerable human resources;

Table 9.6 Lagged liberalisation and popular economic measures

	cr451	*cr453*	*cr455*	*cr456*	*cr458*
p201		0.16			
p203					0.14
p204	0.10				
p206	0.13				
p207			0.13	0.11	
p208					0.09
p211					0.13
p215					0.09
p218	0.13				

- the costs of repression quickly increase with time. Developed countries may retaliate by postponing their aid, or even by cutting off their commercial exchanges with the country. This threat is especially decisive for countries with a relatively high degree of external opening and dependence on foreign aid. Moreover, because there is no equivalent of the 'iron curtain', there can be no control of emigration of persons and capital.

Table 9.6 corresponds to the last step of the politico–economic adjustment cycle: the return to easier and more popular economic policies, when political liberalisation has been achieved. Growth in investment, current expenditures, wages and employment are once again witnessed in the public and parapublic sectors. Subsidies are restored and monetary policy becomes less stringent. There are numerous significant correlations between political liberalisation and the softening of economic policy. The effect is generally observed in the same period, though a one semester lag exists in some cases. The reasons for this behavioural change are both political and economic:

- it is more dangerous to maintain unpopular economic measures, because political liberalisation gives greater leeway for social protest;
- previous stabilisation measures, decided at the beginning of the politico–economic cycle, may have produced their effects.

Empirically, all the stabilisation measures are not removed after a political liberalisation period, but several significant changes in public investment, current expenditures and some subsidies are observed.

Concerning wages, governments seem to give up more directly, without following each of the steps of the cycle, i.e. repression, then political liberalisation, then economic softening. There are direct links between wage increases and strikes. This result fits well with our analysis of repression. Governments are reluctant to use hard repressive measures after strikes, and even when they choose to react violently, in the face of demonstrations or coup attempts, they tend to supplement these actions with wage increases.

IV CONCLUSION

This chapter presents only the first step of a more global research project on the political feasibility of adjustment programmes. Despite its preliminary nature, some useful information for the framing of adjustment programmes can be derived.

Adjustment was initially seen as merely a technical problem. However, experience has shown, sometimes tragically, that this view was far too narrow. A first attempt to correct this fault was to explicitly introduce the 'social dimension' in adjustment programmes (see the discussion in Chapter 1 in this regard). The aim was to achieve a fairer distribution of the stabilisation costs in an already deprived population. Although this gave clear acknowledgement of the original failures, it also led to people thinking that the central problem was of a 'social' rather than political nature.

Even if the social cost aspect is an important one, the true priority of governments and the international organisations, whether explicit or implicit, is very different: their aim is to define and implement programmes which, in addition to their long-term efficiency, will limit the risk of severe social troubles and/or political instability. From an analytical point of view, this issue cannot be effectively addressed if the economic and political spheres remain artificially isolated from each other. As the reported rank correlations show, politico–economic interactions exist, they are strong and numerous, and can be either positive or negative. Although this rough statistical picture can only be a poor preliminary version of a full estimated model along the theoretical lines suggested in the first section of this chapter, it can offer several useful policy lessons.

First, the observed politico–economic cycle carries a strong justification for IMF conditionality. It can be considered as a means of committing the national government to not give up its restrictive policies at the political liberalisation step of the cycle, before financial and economic stabilisation has been completed. Without that commitment, the politico–economic cycle can continue without end. This assumes that the IMF is still able to enforce the previously agreed upon conditionality when the first signs of deficit reduction appear.

The second lesson concerns the framing of a politically acceptable programme. Some measures proposed by the IMF are clearly politically dangerous, and the reluctance of many national governments to institute them is understandable. It was shown that the political costs in terms of strikes and demonstrations vary deeply according to the economic measure. This therefore points to the need to define politically efficient adjustment programmes, i.e. a policy mix that minimises the probability of social trouble for a given economic efficiency (the same given reduction in macroeconomic deficits, for example). Such a programme would minimise the costs in terms of poverty and inequality only by chance, i.e. it would certainly be very different to a socially optimal adjustment programme.

Indeed, social justice and political efficiency are at variance with each other. Complementarities may exist: a cut in subsidies for basic products, for instance, has both a social and a political cost. But there are a great many possibilities. Some measures, such as wage cuts for the police and military, may be politically dangerous but without great social costs; others, such as a reduction in public investment in disadvantaged rural areas, may simultaneously present high social costs and no significant political risk.

From the point of view of the government, political priorities clearly dominate social ones. Whatever the dimensions of the so-called 'scapegoat effect' attributed to IMF interventions, the government will always assume a much larger share of responsibility in adjustment decisions. Moreover, the political consequences of a jointly agreed programme will always be borne by the government alone. While international organisations are bound to attach greater weight to economic and social consequences, they cannot ignore the the political effects of interventions.

Annex 1 Coding list of events and measures[10] (negative values = unpopular (m), positive values = popular (p))

I ECONOMIC MEASURES

201	current spending	−3 – 0 – +3
202	investment spending	−3 – 0 – +3
203	subsidies (consumption goods)	−3 – 0 – +3

204	subsidies (other)	–3 – 0 – +3
205	money supply	–3 – 0 – +3
206	income or wage taxes	–3 – 0 – +3
207	wage policy	–3 – 0 – +3
208	employment (public sector)	–3 – 0 – +3
209	privatisation, restructuration (negative values) or nationalisation (positive values)	–3 – 0 – +3
210	import duties	–3 – 0 – +3
211	rationing or liberalisation of imports	–3 – 0 – +3
212	devaluation (negative values) or revaluation (positive values)	–3 – 0 – +3
213	indirect taxes (consumption goods)	–3 – 0 – +3
214	taxes on petrol	–3 – 0 – +3
215	producer prices (in agriculture)	–3 – 0 – +3
216	consumer prices	–3 – 0 – +3
217	exchange control	
218	subsidies to unemployed	0 – +3
219	rationing	

II POLITICAL TROUBLES AND COUPS

310 strike (sector unknown)
311 strike (public sector)
312 strike (parapublic sector)
313 strike (transport)
314 strike (manufacturing)
315 strike (services sector)
316 strike (schools, universities)

If the information is available, we give the strike's intensity (+1 – +3), and the number of deaths.

321 demonstrations in towns
322 demonstrations in schools, universities
323 demonstrations in villages

If the information is available, we give the intensity (+3 if riots and pillages), and the number of deaths.

341 attempted coup
344 coup

If available, we give the intensity (+1 – +3) and the number of deaths.

III POLITICAL MEASURES

Unpopular

420	state of emergency	
421	arrests, incarceration, number of people under arrest if available	+1 – +3

422	supplementary means for police, army, supplementary means for censorship, propaganda (newspapers, television)	+1 – +3
423	hardening of regime's policy (adjournment of legislative assembly, prohibition of a political party)	+1 – +3
424	violence and on-the-spot executions	+1 – +3
425	criminal trials and executions (if available, number of death penalties)	+1 – +3
426	prohibition of strikes and demonstrations	
427	prohibition of all political debate or meetings, of newspapers, of parties or trade unions	
428	closing of school, university	
429	forced demonstrations	

Popular

450	lifting of state of emergency	
451	release of political prisoners	+1 – +3
453	measures in support of political parties and human rights	+1 – +3
455	abandoning of judicial pursuits, rehabilitation, return of the exiled	
456	lifting of a prohibition to strike or demonstrate	
457	lifting of a prohibition to meet, of newspapers, of parties or of trade unions	
458	opening of school, university	
501	IMF Interventions	
502	World Bank Interventions	
503	Debt Rescheduling (London Club)	
504	Debt Rescheduling (Paris Club)	

NOTES

1. Recent surveys in this area can be found in Alesina, 1988; Schneider and Frey, 1988; Mueller, 1989; Borooah and Schneider (eds), 1991; Norpoth, Lewis-Beck and Lafay (eds), 1991; Nannenstadt and Paldam, 1992.
2. For simplicity, coups are considered here as exogenous, despite the fact that several studies have shown that this kind of event can be explained endogenously, i.e. considered for a large part as 'the drastic response to an unstable and sometimes hopeless economic situation' (O'Kane, 1981).
3. But not necessarily, in several countries in our African sample (in Nigeria for example) the government has undertaken a stabilisation programme on its own, without any previous agreement with the IMF.
4. The arbitrariness of that choice is partially erased by the fact that the binary measures are seldom taken in isolation.

5. Previous tests, with several persons coding the same sequence of political events, have experimentally confirmed this evident point. The more you go into details, the more the subjective interpretations diverge.
6. The computation of a rank correlation coefficient is similar to that of a simple correlation coefficient, except that (1) the rank of an observation in the total sample is taken instead of its value, and (2) the mean rank is substituted for the mean value. $R_s = \Sigma(\text{rank } X^i - X) \cdot (\text{rank } Y^i - Y) / \sqrt{\Sigma(\text{rank } X^i - X)^2 . \Sigma(\text{rank } Y^i - Y)^2}$, with X = mean rank of X and Y = mean rank of Y. The significance of R_s is tested by using the same statistics for the simple correlation coefficient.
7. The low absolute value of some coefficients, between 0.09 and 0.20, is explained by the large number of observations (483) and by the rank nature of the correlations. They are in no way a sign of weak links.
8. A price increase in farm products will be popular in rural ares and unpopular in urban areas, if this increase is passed on to consumer prices.
9. Paldam (1993) confirms this point on the basis of six stabilisation cases in Latin America. Social troubles take place between four to eight months after the announcement of unpopular measures.
10. Based on summaries published in *Marchés Tropicaux*.

10 The Political Economy of Privatisation in Africa

Thandika Mkandawire

I INTRODUCTION

'Privatisation' has become one of the magic wands in the brave new world of structural adjustment and stabilisation in Africa. Privatisation means a lot of things: the transfer of public sector assets to the private sector; the creation of a private sector through the provision of an 'enabling environment' by liberalisation of the economy; encouragement of the private sector to provide hitherto publicly financed goods. All of these versions or components of privatisation are taking place in Africa. In a considerable number of countries, governments have put up for sale parastatals or public enterprises that had previously assumed the 'commanding heights' of the economy. Never mind that these heights were never dizzying. The private sector is being actively courted by governments and economies are being liberalised to give greater play to market forces. Evidence so far is that privatisation is not producing the expected results and there is considerable debate in both academic and official circles on why privatisation has not fulfilled its promise. The problem seems to be not privatisation *per se*, but the ideological and policy context within which this process is occurring. Privatisation is taking place as part of the stabilisation and structural adjustment programmes which constitute the dominant policy initiatives of the Bretton Woods institutions in Africa. It is also occurring within a political context in which there are increased demands for transparency and accountability in the management of national affairs. This chapter seeks to bring to the fore some of the implications that this context has on privatisation in Africa.

II OBJECTIVES OF PRIVATISATION

Privatisation is intended to achieve at least three things. First, it is supposed to contribute to the bridging of the fiscal budgets and rationalisation of public finances by unburdening African economies of over-extended and corrupt state and parastatal structures that have putatively wrought havoc on public finances. The sale of public property is expected to contribute to state revenue and reduce expenditures on subsidies, at least in the short run. Second, privatisation is expected to lead to greater efficiency in the allocation of resources, to generate less inflationary pressures, to stimulate more competitiveness of African economies, all of which are expected to contribute to greater total factor productivity in the economy. Third, privatisation is supposed to free both domestic and foreign private capital from the tentacles of corrupt and inefficient bureaucracies so that it can be productively engaged in those activities that have thus far been monopolised by the state or have been off-limits to the private sector. The creation of such an 'enabling environment' is expected to attract badly needed foreign capital in the less onerous form (from a debt management point of view) of direct foreign investment. Its diligent implementation is expected to reverse the decline and stagnation that have been induced by 'statist' practices of the past. Much of this is stated as a matter of faith, the case for associating privatisation with better overall economic performance being on a much weaker empirical footing than is often asserted (Yoder, Borkholder and Friesen, 1991; Nunnekamp, 1986; Kirkpatrick, 1991).

In sum, privatisation is supposed to pave the way for capitalism and all the dynamism historically associated with it. It is important to highlight this particular feature in contrast to the anodyne and not always informative notion of the 'market system'. The 'market system' is essentially an algorithm for allocating resources in decentralised systems which need not be capitalist. The capitalist system uses this algorithm, albeit not in the textbook form, and contains within it quite specific rules on property relations, the nature of competition and the outcomes of such competition. It also has implications on the role of the state in regulating markets.

III ACHIEVEMENTS OF PRIVATISATION

What has been the record of privatisation thus far? In some of the more journalistic writings there are suggestions that the privatisation programmes are 'working'. The barrage of propaganda on its virtues and the carefully orchestrated campaign by international financial institutions on 'success stories' in privatisation conceal a number of problems that privatisation faces and raises in African economies. First, the liberalisation programme has failed to reverse the decline of investment in Africa. Overall investment declined sharply from 18.4 per cent of GDP in the period 1975–81 to 15.4 per cent in the period 1982–8. The fall in investment was so severe that seven African countries were eating into their capital stock as they were not able to fully replace depreciating capital. This decline was not only due to a drop in public investment (something which SAPs often sought to achieve) but was also a result of the failure of private investment to respond to the incentives introduced by the liberalisation programmes. In a survey of private investment and macroeconomic adjustment, Serven and Solimano (1992a) conclude that in many countries adjustment has not improved the response of private investment. 'Even when substantial progress has been made in correcting imbalances and restoring profitability – often through drastic cuts in real wages – the effect on private investment has been weak and slow to appear.'

This was a survey of all developing countries. The situation in Africa more than confirms this observation. In Chapter 7 of this volume, Oshikoya shows that while private investment fell for the 'middle-income' countries in the early 1980s, it subsequently increased in the period 1984–8. For the low-income countries category to which the majority of African countries belong, private investments fell substantially through the two periods (see Table 10.1).

One expectation of adjusting governments was that with the stamp of approval of the Bretton Woods institutions, an inflow of foreign direct investment (FDI) from abroad would be generated. This has not taken place for many reasons. While liberalisation has positively influenced the flow of FDI to the newly industrialising countries (NIC), such policies have had virtually no positive effects on FDI inflows for the less developed countries (United Nations, 1992). According to this report, the flow of FDI to Africa fell to $2.2 billion in 1990 – slightly more than the amount that Portugal received in that year – a decrease of 50 per cent from 1989. The sharpest fall was in the oil-exporting countries, which historically have been the recipients of most of the FDI in Africa. The non-oil exporting countries received less than $0.5 billion per year during the second half of the 1980s – roughly the amount that Papua New Guinea alone attracted during the same period. The report notes:

> The low levels of FDI flowing to Africa underline the increasing marginalisation of the region. Continuing uncertainty regarding pros-

Table 10.1 Trends in private and public investment in selected sub-Saharan African countries (as % of GDP)

	1970–80	*1980–3*	*1984–8*
Mauritius			
Private	17.4	12.9	14.1
Public	7.1	7.4	6.9
Cameroon			
Private	9.1	8.5	10.5
Public	10.1	14.4	12.8
Malawi			
Private	9.1	5.3	8.5
Public	13.8	11.1	8.5
Tanzania			
Private	11.6	9.2	9.3
Public	8.1	9.4	9.3
Kenya			
Private	12.7	12.1	11.5
Public	7.9	9.3	8.0
Zimbabwe			
Private	11.3	10.6	7.5
Public	7.3	7.9	8.9

Source: Oshikoya (1992).

pects for economic development have deterred investments by TNCs from the major home countries as those companies favour countries with high growth rates and large domestic markets.

In the case of British and French capital, which are very important for much of Africa, there has been rapid disengagement from the continent despite the favourable attitudes of African governments toward the private sector and despite the prevalence of SAPs (Bennell, 1990). The poor response of FDI to new policy initiatives affects even those countries that are considered to be ideologically open to private capital and as having met key demands of the international financial organisations through radical structural adjustment and stabilisation policies. Thus, Ghana, the show case for structural adjustment programmes in Africa, showed only 'meagre' results in its divestiture programme (Gyimah-Boadi, 1991). And in Côte d'Ivoire, while ideology has always favoured private investment and state enterprises were established in lieu of the private sector with the clear intention of their being sold off to the private sector, there have nonetheless been few takers (Marcel, 1991). Nigeria had expected to raise as much as N3000 million by June 1992, but was only able to raise about 10 per cent of this amount (N275 million) by the beginning of the year (Chiejena, 1992).

IV GENERAL PROBLEMS OF PRIVATISATION

To understand the difficulties that privatisation encounters in Africa, one has to recall that it is taking place within a particular policy framework of stabilisation and structural adjustment. These policies have not only created a new trade and investment regime but have also generated specific political responses and demands. As suggested by research on Africa and elsewhere, it is the general economic and political environment and the political stability of a country coupled with fundamental market and cost considerations that are the most critical factors influencing private investment, especially the currently much coveted form of foreign direct investment (Guissinger, 1985; on Africa, see Bennell, 1990).

(A) Economic constraints

The standard structural adjustment programme includes the reduction of government expenditure, high interest rates, liberalisation of the trade regime (through devaluation, removal of import substitution policies) and reduction of domestic consumption. The economic and political conditions generated by these policies have undermined the process of privatisation, or at least, made it much less productive and dynamic than it was meant to be.

1 Retreat of the state

The state is both directly and indirectly a major contributor to aggregate demand in African economies. Reduction of state expenditure has therefore had an immediate effect on the levels of aggregate demand, reducing the already Lilliputian markets for industries that suffered from excess capacity due to the smallness of the domestic markets.

In the early years of structural adjustment in Africa it was simply assumed that state investment 'crowded out' private investment by using up or having privileged access to scarce resources which could have been better used by the private sector. This of course goes against

Table 10.2: Determinants of real private investment (as % of GDP)

Effect on private investment of a 1 % point increase in:	*Percentage point*
Ratio of public investment to GDP	0.257
Ratio of foreign debt to GDP	–0.065
Real GDP growth	0.151
Inflation stability	–0.001
Real exchange rate stability	0.003

Source: Serven and Solimano (1992b).

one of the major tenets of economic history, namely that among 'late industrialisers' the state plays a crucial role in stimulating private investment - the state 'crowds in' the private sector. It also goes against considerable evidence that public investment has a positive effect on private investment. In a recent study, Serven and Solimano (1992b) confirm the 'crowding in' hypothesis. They regress real private investment on the ratio of public investment to GDP, ratio of foreign debt to GDP, real GDP growth rate, inflation stability and real exchange rate instability. The results of the econometric analysis are reproduced in Table 10.2. These clearly show that the largest effect corresponds to public investment: an increase in the ratio of public investment to GDP by 1 per cent raises the private investment ratio by over one fourth of a point.[1] A number of econometric studies suggest that while the effect of aggregate public sector investment on private investment may be consistent in some cases with the 'crowding out' hypothesis, the substitution coefficient between public and private investment is quite small and not significantly different from zero. When public investment is further disaggregated by type of public sector investment, the studies show that an increase in the infrastructure component of government capital formation raised private investment (Blejer and Khan, 1984).

A possible retort to this would be that whether or not the public sector crowds out private investment, it is an inherently less efficient user of resources (Khan and Reinhart, 1990). Again, however, the evidence is more complex. Even for Africa with its countless examples of egregious mismanagement of public enterprises, the equation of private with efficient and public with inefficient is not unambiguously borne out by empirical evidence, (Millward, 1988; Grosh, 1988).

Most studies suggest that what is important is not ownership as such but the market conditions in which a particular enterprise operates. One of the unstated assumptions about privatisation is that it will lead to increased competition which, in turn, will lead to a greater efficiency in the use of resources and, therefore, higher growth rates. This, however, need not follow. First, in theory, the benefits of liberalisation are static, a one-off effect. Theory is silent on the effects of liberalisation on growth. The factors conducive to growth may not always be enhanced by liberalisation. It is for this reason that Rodrik (1990) suggests that 'the eradication of allocative inefficiencies through liberalisation may sometimes have to play a secondary role when it threatens policy stability. Illiberal policies which do not damage overall stability of the economic system are on the whole preferable to liberal policies which are inherently unsustainable and engender instability.'

Second, the contraction of the state need not lead to a competitive market. It can create a precarious vacuum that may be filled by anti-competitive and other forms of rapacious behaviour. In a number of cases, where the state stepped in to break trading monopolies during colonial times, privatisation has led to the re-emergence of these monopsonistic trading houses (Reusse, 1987). In the more politically explosive cases, privatisation has led to predatory commercialisation, with 'market forces' unleashed largely through essentially traditional hierarchies relying on extra-economic compulsions and with no protective measures for the poor. Furthermore, to the extent that most state enterprises are loss-makers, divestiture is only likely to take place if it is accompanied by a whole range of incentives which would tend to militate against increasing the level of competition. In many cases, privatisation has been accompanied by measures to 'fatten the calves' before selling them to the private sector, which often demands retention of a number of monopolistic or market privileges. Under such conditions, conversion of public monopolies into private ones would not solve the problems of inefficiency (Commander and Killick, 1988). In Senegal, the programme of massive privatisation only took off after the government reintroduced the protective measures it had removed as part of its structural adjustment programmes.

In addition, it should be recalled that state policies are not the only source of monopolistic practices in Africa. Many theories suggest that capitalist accumulation in the developing countries will be congenitally monopolistic for a whole range of reasons other than state interventionism: technological dependence, market size, economies of scale, 'product cycles' and so forth (see for instance Felix, 1974; Vernon, 1966; Merhav, 1969). The implications of much of this literature and the structural features that they highlight have been lost due to the implicit or explicit assumption that, left to itself, the market conforms to the textbook competitive models (Lessler, 1991). One obvious source of monopoly is technological dependence, which determines the scale of production and, in the absence of capital goods, necessarily leads to the imitation of techniques evolved in the advanced capitalist economies with their vastly larger markets (Merhav, 1969). And given the size of the African markets, only a few firms will dominate the production of a given commodity and the economies will be characterised by relatively higher levels of technical concentration than would be accounted for by their overall levels of economic development.

Another important factor in establishing the link between the economies of the 'centre' and those of the 'periphery' is the form of capital movements. In models where such capital movements are viewed in the context of the conventional trade theory and where periphery economies are viewed as competitive economies, the flow of investments is not linked to the monopolistic trends in the periphery. However, for a long time now there has been a body of theories arguing that the flow of capital is best viewed in the framework of monopoly. With the shift from portfolio to direct investments in the immediate post-Second World War period, it became necessary to formulate new theories of investment and internationalisation of capital. One of the more widely used theories is Vernon's 'product-cycle' theory, which states that direct investments by transitional firms follow the export of the product from the centre to the periphery (Vernon, 1966). In the initial stages of production of a commodity, the firms at the centre enjoy full technological monopoly and can, therefore, rely on the export promotion of their product without fear of any new entrants. However, as the product 'matures', periphery countries begin to have a comparative advantage in production, mainly through cheap labour enter into licence contracts with companies based in the centre, learn the new operations and compete effectively in international markets. In the usual case, however, the transnational firms may themselves carry out direct investments in the periphery. The impression given by Vernon is that during the 'product-cycle' the product is produced by several countries or firms. If this view is accepted, then there is nothing in Vernon's theory which suggests that direct investments inherently lead to monopoly at the periphery.

However, other interpretations question this in-built dilution of monopoly in the course of the 'product-cycle'. Vaitsos (1974) argues that the fruits of monopoly in the final market enjoyed early in the 'product-cycle' can be partially or totally preserved in later periods by the institutional mechanisms of 'package' or collective product and factor flows in the FDI model. This is particularly so since the 'product-cycle' theory itself suggests that foreign investment is, to a large extent, undertaken as a defensive strategy to maintain already established market positions and to prevent potential competitors from displacing the original exporters or licences. Vaitsos argues that in this sense the process of foreign investment retards competitive force and is directed towards the preservation of monopoly positions; a technological monopoly is thus transformed into an institutional one.

It should also be recalled that the large monopolies in Africa have been created as joint ventures between the state and transnational corporations (TNC). Historically, the rise of joint ventures has not always been due to state initiatives. Private firms, especially TNCs, have sought out the state to jointly cover the costs, to ensure a foot in the decision-making processes of the state, or to spread the risks of investing in unknown economic climates. There is evidence to suggest that in Africa private firms are inclined to invest in the highly protected sector (for Kenya, see Grosh, 1988). Indeed the import substitution policies that produced such protection of the domestic market may have been the primary incentive for investing in such economies. A sudden move from such a strategy towards one of export promotion is likely to be so disruptive as to undermine any other private investment, including that which is supposed to benefit from the new policy package. The 'deindustrialisation' caused by the sudden opening up of the market can have the effect of destroying the preconditions for any future industrialisation that may have been acquired during the import substitution phase – namely, trained manpower and infrastructure.

Once these 'structural features' are taken into account, one cannot but agree with Sylos-Labini (1969) when he states that:

> . . . imperfect laws and, generally speaking, artificial elements do not, in modern economies, create but merely buttress oligopolistic market power which has structural and ultimately technological origins. It would be an illusion, therefore, to place too much hope of this variety [i.e. policies calling for artificial restoration of competition].

It should therefore come as no surprise that privatisation in Africa has tended to lead to uncompetitive monopolistic markets, even when accompanied by the liberalisation measures of SAP. It should be noted that even in the developed countries with governments avowedly committed to the 'free market', competitive conditions have not generally followed denationalisation because (a) privatisation has not led to changes in the size of the enterprises; (b) 'barriers to entry' are real, and; (c) the major enterprises have been privatised as 'single' entities so as to attract public interest in flotation of a potential monopoly as well as to avoid confrontation with the top management of the enterprises who do not appreciate the 'parcelling out of an empire' (Ramadhan, 1989). These arguments would *a fortiori* hold even more tightly in Africa.

Given the above discussion, it should be obvious that privatisation gives to the state new regulatory roles (which may include breaking up monopolies, monitoring the behaviour of the private sector, and so on). As such vital roles obviously cannot be performed by an administratively incapacitated state, efforts are needed to strengthen the capacity of African governments to effectively manage privatisation (Vernon-Wortzel and Wortzel, 1989).

Such counsel stands starkly against the practices which have hitherto accompanied the privatisation process in Africa. Indeed, here we encounter a major paradox in the process of privatisation in Africa. While most of the reforms have to be carried out and ensured by the state, the dominant process involves the emasculation of the state which is essentially viewed negatively. Privatisation, one should recall, is essentially a state activity. One implication of this is that if a government has been corrupt or if policy-making and implementation have been bedevilled by the pursuit of private agendas by interests groups or bureaucrats, the process of privatisation is unlikely to escape the impact of these sources of 'government failure' (Vickers and Yarrow, 1991).

Both domestic and foreign capital need state guarantees. These guarantees include not only market protection but also the provision of supportive measures on the supply side: human and physical capital. The collapse of education systems and the neglect of existing infrastructure only compound the risk and uncertainty faced by the assiduously courted foreign capital. The laissez-faire attitudes that the privatisation syndrome entails do not assure the private sector of the reliability of state guarantees. Experience with such policies shows that for the state to gain credibility for its commitment to privatisation, it must adopt a positive, activist stance towards the private sector.

One of the arguments for privatisation is that by unburdening the state of unprofitable enterprises, privatisation will contribute to the amelioration of the fiscus. In practice, however, because of the dogmatic and undiscriminating nature of the process, privatisation has often completely ignored the financial costs of the process to the state. State investment may have been financed through domestic and foreign borrowing which has still to be repaid. The selling-off of public firms at highly undervalued rates may aid the state budget in a one-off manner, but it leads to losses by the state that further undermine state finances in the medium and long runs by leaving it with a worse portfolio consisting of firms for which there are no private buyers. It should be borne in mind that the parastatals which the private sector finds attractive are in most cases those that are money-making (Jacquemot, 1988). In many cases, state enterprises have been grossly undervalued, particularly those with poor profit-making track records, while their divestiture has required a whole range of activities to 'fatten the calf'. These include writing off debts, retrenchment of labour force and payment of redundancy money, guaranteeing pension rights, and so on (Ghai, 1985).

2 *Monetary policy*

The tight monetary policy is intended to achieve two things: fight inflation and subject savings and investments to market forces. With respect to the latter, the international financial institutions have been guided by the McKinnon-Shaw view that 'financial repression' has deterred economic growth. The hypothesis states that financial liberalisation would raise interest rates which, in turn, would boost the volume of domestic savings and hence the equilibrium rate of investment (McKinnon, 1973; Shaw, 1973). Furthermore, high interest rates would contribute to an efficient use of resources by ensuring that only those economic activities with high returns receive funds, thus presumably reversing the wasteful allocation induced by artificially low interest rates. Experience so far has confounded these expectations. Greene and Villanueva (1991) show that while the rate of private investment is positively related to economic growth, the level of per capita GDP and the rate of public sector spending, it is negatively related to real interest rates and the ratio of debt to GDP. Their study shows that the estimated coefficient of real interest rate was negative and statistically significant. A 1 per cent point rise in the real interest rate would reduce the investment rate by less than a 0.1 percentage point. High interest rates serve to deter investment by raising the user cost of capital rather than to promote investment by increasing the volume of saving.

In addition, the contraction of public investment has reduced the attractiveness of a whole range of investment activities. It should be recalled that although high interest may well lead to a portfolio shift from unproductive assets to bank deposits, assets may also lead to a move away from capital goods (Morisset, 1993). This trend will be reinforced in a situation of macroeconomic instability where, as suggested by McKinnon (1988), liberalisation accompanied by high interest rates will tend to push banks towards highly risky investment. The prospects for this type of investment are of bonanzas should they turn out good and low losses should they turn out bad, due to state guarantees on deposits, and so on. In such a situation, the potential savings surplus that may have been induced by high interest rates will be unmatched by high investment demand and will vent in the form of reduced commodity purchases or speculation (Taylor, 1988). In the African case this has shown up in speculative investments in real estate, capital flight, and so forth. On the other side of the demand-supply equation, high interest rates have not always induced higher savings. This is not surprising, given the considerable amount of evidence suggesting that the overall saving rate does not react to the rate of interest (Giovannini, 1985). Finally, removing interest rate ceilings frequently puts the financial sector in a frenzy and ultimately causes it to crash (see for instance Wagao, 1992). The usual situation is that with high interest rates, working capital costs are pushed up. This in turn leads to bankruptcies and the collapse of credit demand, leaving the banks with excess liquidity. Crises faced by the banking sector in most African countries have only added to the uncertainty about the economic environment and have further discouraged private investment.

3 *Trade regime*

One of the major components of trade policies is the devaluation of local currencies. The impact of such devaluations on aggregate investment will depend on the structure of the economy. For countries highly dependent on imported and intermediate goods, one immediate effect of devaluation is an increase in the real cost of imported inputs. Another is the depression of investment in non-tradable goods. This may be the desired objective of trade policies on the assumption that the increased investment in tradable goods will more than compensate for the decline in investment in the non-tradables, which means that there will be an increase in aggregate investment. There is little evidence, however, to suggest that on the aggregate this is what has happened in African economies. Indeed, the unfavourable terms of trade and many other exogenous constraints on exports have imposed enough uncertainty as to blunt the incentives to the tradable goods sectors stemming from devaluation.

The foreign exchange squeeze induced by austerity has impacted on privatisation by making it difficult to import crucial inputs. With widespread excess capacity in the economy, the inducement to invest and the attractiveness of privatisation for state firms have been compromised. While market liberalisation would in principle lead to easier access to foreign exchange, structural adjustment programmes have resulted in massive currency devaluations which have slashed the foreign exchange values of remittances and the market value of existing foreign capital.

Another effect of changes in the trade regime has been the removal of protection which has hitherto accounted for the viability and profitability of state enterprises and joint ventures. The removal of various 'hidden' subsidies and protective measures that have thus far sustained the private sector has undermined the private sector's viability (Bennell, 1990). 'Opening up' of the domestic markets has radically changed the prospects of a number of enterprises.

A key element of the trade regime under structural adjustment is the transfer of more resources abroad to service debt. To achieve this, demand management dominates stabilisation and structural adjustment programmes. By their very nature, these measures seek to redress trade imbalance by, among other things, reducing domestic consumption or forcing the economy to 'live within its means'. The contraction of demand takes place following the reduction of public consumption and through shifts in income distribution in favour of profit and reduction of the real product wage. All this has adverse effects on the size of the domestic market.

The ratio of foreign debt to GDP has exerted a significantly adverse effect on private investment. This was compounded by exchange rate instability and higher international interest rates (Serven and Solimano, 1992b). Developing countries have tended to export more capital in the form of debt repayment in the forlorn hope that such good conduct would attract private investors. This has not come to pass, largely due to the fact that, contrary to the impression given by their real and imagined importance in our economies, the Bretton Woods institutions have very little control in the international financial markets. While they have now assumed the leadership for official aid and can thus influence the perception of a particular country's standing in the eyes of the donors, they do not have the same clout in the financial institutions that matter so far as private capital is concerned. Consequently, while disapproval by the institutions may close doors to foreign finance (both public and private), a stamp of approval by these institutions does not open the doors to foreign private investment. If anything, it has provided an opportune occasion for disinvestment. Convertibility of currencies and the free flow of capital have merely facilitated capital flight (Mosley, Harrigan and Toye, 1991).

4 Economic policy instability

The effects of adjustment on privatisation ultimately hinge on the nature of the underlying investment function and which arguments enter into such a function. Following the move away from simplistic neo-classical theories of investment to more realistic and complex ones, the problems of uncertainty now occupy a central place in the study of responses of private investors to adjustment (see for instance Rodrik, 1991). As argued by Rodrik, the rise of private investment requires a 'sustainable policy environment', the key components of which are: (a) stable macro policies, chiefly a small fiscal deficit and a realistic exchange rate policy; (b) a credible and predictable set of microeconomic incentives; (c) the absence of sharp distributional changes that would create political pressures to reverse down the line problems of credibility of policy reforms (Rodrik, 1990). Virtually all the key components of SAPs tend to undermine the sustainability of the policies pursued to attract private investment. Such variables as openness to trade or interest rates are either 'considerably less impressive' or statistically insignificant as explanatory variables for the inflow of private investments. Most studies stress uncertainty about key economic variables such as the volatility of interest rates, uncertainty about the foreign debt and its implications on real exchange rates and other adjustments to facilitate the transfer of incomes to foreigners (Serven and Solimano, 1992a).

One should add here that the very process of policy-making in Africa has added to uncertainty and instability. The comings and goings of delegations from the international financial institutions are a source of rumours and speculations about impending currency devaluations, suspensions or resumption of standby arrangements, debt rescheduling or changes in the ministries of finance. The uncertainty about who 'owns' particular policies further compounds the uncertainty regarding policy measures, both in terms of their content and eventual sustainability. In addition, SAPs have assumed a 'stop-go' character which is as much caused by African governments as it is by the international financial institutions. The usual process has been characterised by long drawn-out negotiations resulting in programmes which prove to be outdated by the time they are adopted. In most cases, predictions about international commodity prices and responses of economic agents may have been totally misrepresented, resulting in the failure to meet agreed upon 'targets' and in the suspension of the standby arrangements. The usual response of the African state is to tighten import controls in order to conserve its radically diminished import capacity. This only makes things worse in the eyes of the donors, who will demand even more painful remedies the next time around. The case of Zambia is a classic example of this process (Seshamani, 1992).

(B) Political constraints

One major source of uncertainty is the political response to structural adjustment programmes. As has been argued in a number of studies, SAPs have tended to undermine the legitimacy of the state and its capacity to govern (on the political consequences of SAPs see Chapter 9 of this volume, and Mkandawire and Olukushi, 1994). The effect of this is to undermine the political credibility and sustainability of the adjustment policies and to thus discourage private investment. The adoption of measures that lead to 'IMF riots' only convinces the private sector of the 'political instability' of the country, which then nullifies the attractiveness of such incentives as low real wages, 'equilibrium exchange rates', macroeconomic stability, and so on. In some cases the measures adopted under these programmes may be simply deemed 'too good to last'. African countries are engaged in what is tantamount to 'beggar my neighbour' policies to attract foreign investment. Investment codes are being revised to make the countries attractive to foreign capital. The incentives being offered by the African states are in most cases so sumptuous as to not be politically or even economically supportable, which only adds to the scepticism of private capital. The fact that these incentive structures are imposed by foreign agencies does not improve matters.

Structural adjustment programmes have got the politics of adjustment wrong largely by failing to identify the nature of the state and society within which public enterprises are situated. In most cases there has been no national consensus on privatisation. Politically key social groups have almost invariably opposed structural adjustment. Labour, the student movements and increasingly professional groups have voiced their opposition to structural adjustment programmes. It is true that the processes of this transformation may entail a transformation of ideological perspective, with 'the sons of fierce nationalists' often becoming faithful liberals (Singer, 1985).

In practice, the nascent capitalists expect greater support from the state against labour, foreign capital and other elements that may be an encumbrance in their struggle for ascendancy (Kennedy, 1988). Not surprisingly, they have expressed their displeasure with the new programmes (Gyimah-Boadi, 1991). Bangura (1991) notes that the Nigerian entrepreneurs have combined their 'statist outlooks' with passionate calls for the privatisation of public enterprises. 'Major sections of this group insist on state protection and adjudication on how enterprises should be distributed.'

One source of the political blind spot on the politics of privatisation is a rather narrow interpretation of why nationalisation took place in African countries. It is generally assumed that nationalisation is either a strategy of the 'patrimonial state' to acquire instruments for pursuing its patron-clientalistic politics or is an outcome of the rent-seeking bureaucracies which use the state apparatus to facilitate their 'DUP (directly unproductive profit-making activities)' (see, for instance, Sandbrook, 1988). Such a perspective fits in with the current cynical view of the state and seems plausible in light of flagrant cases of corruption and fraud. However, it only captures part of the truth. Nationalisation or state ownership of industry was a historical and political background that can only be ignored at the risk of undermining the political basis of the privatisation exercise (for a useful typology of trajectories toward state participation in the economy, see Sobhan, 1979). In a large number of cases, the new states in post-independence Africa did *not* nationalise existing industry, simply because not much industry existed at independence. What they did instead was to set up new industries either as wholly owned parastatals or as joint ventures. This often followed the failure to attract foreign private investment. The 'African socialism' that provided the ideological or rhetorical scaffolding to state interventionism was essentially a way of making virtue out of necessity. Nationalisation, which was at times couched in socialist language, was part of the nationalist desire to assert control over the national economy. In the absence of a national bourgeoisie, the state was the only national institution capable of assuming this nationalist role, especially in the large-scale enterprises. Consequently national industry, no matter how tattered and dilapidated, tends to be viewed as 'national patrimony' and its sale to foreigners is viewed negatively. In many countries 'privatisation' is a 'dirty word' since it would still mean foreign control for a large number of economic activities. And this is still a sore point in Africa, especially now that 'debt fatigue' has begun to set in and when foreign investment is associated with the repayment of debts (through debt-equity swaps) that were dubiously incurred by corrupt and dictatorial regimes.

One should add here that the negative experience with previous attempts at privatisation and a number of dubious deals in the privatisation process in African countries do not make matters easy. Indeed, one major problem with privatisation has been the lack of transparency of the process itself. In the case of Cameroon, Kamguem (1992) observes that the process of privatisation is characterised by '*un flou artistique*' (soft-focus effect): choice criteria, the methods of evaluation, the conditions for sale, and the list of enterprises to be sold are only known to a small group of individuals 'considered to possess innate knowledge' about such matters. Tenders are parsimoniously publicised and, in most cases, the takers will already have been chosen. Because of the corrupt practices involved – the kickbacks – there is a preference for foreign capital. The Cameroon case is not an exception. In the case of Ghana, previous experiences with privatisation created considerable political furore because public opinion held that the government was selling property too cheaply (Tangri, 1991). In Côte d'Ivoire, the disinvolvement of the state from parastatals ended up in the privatisation of these enterprises to the same people closely connected to the Houghueut Boigny family group while retaining the same, although now more informal and arm's length, privileged access to public financial networks. In Mali it was widely felt that the privatisation carried out by Moussa Traore's government was meant to transfer state assets to his friends or relatives. Such doubt on the probity of the deals entered into by the state partly reflects the objective difficulties of evaluating state assets in economies with so thinly developed capital markets and partly points to the deeply-rooted mistrust by the general public of both the African government officials and foreign financial institutions orchestrating these privatisation exercises. The fact that those who are buying run-down state enterprises are precisely the same 'Big Men' who may have manned these same enterprises or have accumulated their capital from them only makes the suspicion stronger. Scepticism is further fuelled by the lack of transparency in the inherently secretive authoritarian regimes that have overseen the privatisation process. Not surprisingly, the new democratic movements in Africa have often called for a re-examination of the privatisation deals entered into by their authoritarian predecessors.

It is important to recall that much of the privatisation in Africa is occurring at the same time as calls are being made for greater democratisation in African political life. In the eyes of the private sector such regime changes may be considered as destabilising. The implications for FDI are brought out in one of the rare glimpses of the private sector's attitudes towards democratisation in Africa given by a survey conducted among a cross-section of European private sector companies (Blakey, 1993). It showed that these firms placed a high priority on political stability. They were not only worried about non-democratic change but even about democratic ones. In particular, it was felt that the encouragement of good government and democratic rule may have negatively affected foreign investment.

In a number of countries that are ethnically divided, let alone racially pluralistic, nationalisation was induced by the need to ensure a politically viable control of property. The expansion of the state was therefore linked to a number of distribution measures whose purpose was to redress certain historical imbalances. In such situations privatisation may touch upon a whole array of political sensitivities and arrangements. More specifically, as Herbst (1990) notes, a rolling back of the state may lead to 'status reversal provoking greater ethnic consciousness' so that ethnic groups that have been consciously discriminated against for years to please the majority may suddenly become conspicuously wealthy from government-instituted reform packages. And so in most countries in Africa privatisation may lead to greater control by ethnic or even racial minorities: a control whose results can lead to the nightmares of Idi Amin's Uganda. Examples of such potentially explosive outcomes abound. In Kenya, domestic savings are considerable enough to facilitate high levels of privatisation, but the distribution of these savings has been such that the Kenyan government, despite its basically pro-capitalist ideological leanings, has been reluctant to embark on extensive privatisation (Adam et al., 1992). Thus, the fear that the privatisation of maize marketing would likely have benefited Asians led to strong opposition by the government to the World Bank proposal for privatisation (Mosley, 1988). In Sudan, privatisation of the grain markets and banks was 'tailor-made' to suit the interests of the fundamentalist National Islamic Front (Elmekki, 1992). In a country such as Tanzania where religious conflict was said to be non-existent, there is increased concern over the emergence of growing numbers of Muslim property owners. In Nigeria, it is presumably the 'Northern establishment' which is opposed to privatisation, as this 'would deliver the economy into the hands of the much larger, richer, and better organised Southern bourgeoisie' (Diamond, 1988). Perhaps even more telling is the rush towards privatisation that one witnesses in South Africa today. There the Whites see privatisation of the vast state structure spawned over the years by Afrikaner nationalism as a way of ensuring White dominance in the economy of post-apartheid South Africa.

Both the lack of support of key social groups and the blindness of the privatisation programmes to the historical roots of state enterprises have tended to jeopardise the stability of the programmes and therefore to reduce their credibility. Politically, privatisation has been seen as selling collective property cheap to well-placed nationals or worse, as 'selling the national patrimony' to foreigners.

V PRIVATISATION AND THE EMERGENCE OF A NATIONAL BOURGEOISIE

In much of the writing from both the Right and Left it is assumed that privatisation will, for better or worse, usher in an era of growth of capitalist production in Africa. On the Right, the expectation is that the current wave of liberalisation will remove the many barriers that both colonial and post-colonial statism has raised against the growth of private capital. On the Left, the dominant position is that international financial institutions will accelerate the capitalist penetration of African economies. This penetration will be dominated by foreign capital, while domestic capital will play a compradorial role. However, little research has been carried out to establish either of these propositions for while the creation of an environment favourable to the private sector may be necessary, it is far from sufficient in order for capitalism to gain a firm footing in Africa. To confound matters further, there is uncertainty as to what is the appropriate environment to arouse 'the animal spirits' of capitalists. As noted, exhortations to foreign capital to come and benefit from a changed and more favourable environment or even a demonstrated willingness to relate to foreign capital in a supine position have not always yielded the expected response.

Both the global flows of foreign investment and the exigencies of the development of national economies place the largest burden of private investment on domestic capital. It is the author's contention that if capitalism is to be politically viable in Africa, it will have to have some national anchoring based partly on the capacity of the indigenous 'capitalist classes to direct state policy toward their gaining access to labour, land and capital, toward limiting the role of foreign capital, and toward nurturing indigenous capitalist investment by facilitating institutions of stabilising capital-labour relations and supplying technical services and physical infrastructure. For political legitimacy the capitalist class will have to convince critical sections of the nation that its 'project' of capital accumulation is in the national interest.

Here one can benefit from a distinction used by Marxists regarding two styles of integration of periphery economies into the world capitalist system. This can take place either through a general 'compradorisation' of the economy or the establishment of a national bourgeoisie. The former refers to a situation where national capital is largely confined to export-import trading activities while the latter refers to the implantation of national capital into directly productive activities in industry and agriculture. Nationalist policies geared toward the development of a national bourgeoisie are usually also aimed at the creation of such an anchoring through indigenisation policies, expansion of a domestic market, the protection of national industries, the opening of foreign markets to national producers and the restriction of foreign economic penetration. This should be contrasted to a 'compradorial model' in which the economy is 'open' and local capitalists are largely confined to such mercantile activities as managing imports of foreign goods and exporting largely primary commodities. It is the former model that has historically sustained the development of capitalism at the national level. The usual nationalist expectation is that privatisation will eventually lead to the emergence of a national bourgeoisie. Most of the 'radical leaders' who carry out policies of privatisation politically premise their policies on this objective and constantly urge national capital to move away from compradorial activities and to assume its patriotic role of building national productive capacity. It is also assumed that in the transitional period foreign capital, in the form of direct investment, may play a central role.

Although the mandate of the Bretton Woods institutions is to defend the interests of the global capitalist system, the privatisation programmes they are pushing through are not likely to contribute to the emergence of a vibrant indigenous capitalist class in the African countries. Indeed, structural adjustment programmes have the overall effect of undermining the emergence of anything like a national bourgeoisie. The opening up of the economy and the removal of state support places the nascent national capitalists in untenable positions *vis-à-vis* transnational capital. The rolling back of the state disarms the national bourgeoisie in their struggle for ascendancy over the domestic market. Were this to be accompanied by growing productive investment by transnational firms, the story might be economically different. However, the situation thus far is that adjustment has sustained compradorial activities which historically have undermined the emergence of capitalism at the national level and have failed to attract private capital into industry.

VI CONCLUSION

This chapter has not set out to argue against all privatisation *per se*. To the extent that African economies will remain capitalist for at least some time to come, they will have to have a vibrant private sector. Rather, the point argued is that, as currently conceived, privatisation is neither growth-oriented nor likely to generate politically sustainable structures of ownership. It also cautions against naive expectations about the ease and the virtues of the current styles of privatisation. Failure to get the politics of privatisation right exposes the process to such uncertainty as to render it a non-starter. Privatisation has thus far taken a rather ad hoc form, largely because it has been carried out in response to fiscal crises, balance of payments problems and external pressure, especially from Bretton Woods institutions. It has not been part of a systematic strategy to reduce the state or to restructure its role and promote the private sector in accordance with some perception of the long-term developmental exigencies of the economy. Seen as a long-term strategy of capitalist development, privatisation would obviously not have been accompanied by a laissez-faire view of the role of the state. Instead, it would combine various state initiatives with support to what is obviously a nascent capitalist class. This would involve protection of the domestic market, joint ventures with domestic capital, selective divestiture with preferential treatment for domestic investors and support to export efforts by national industry. This, and not the Sunday-school tale of free markets, is the real lesson from the successful NICs. The inactivity of the state in compliance with external pressures only undermines the credibility of the programmes as the state is seen as not doing anything to ensure the success or irreversibility of its programme.

Even more importantly, this chapter has argued that the role of the state in the industrialisation of Africa is far from exhausted. The development of private capital is unimaginable in the absence of a state that 'governs' the market. Indeed as Felix (1992) argues: 'For political and economic reasons the centre of gravity of economic policy will over the long term remain a mixed economy with a large interventionist public sector, rather than the small open competitive economy that rationalises the current push to roll back the state.' We have also sought to underline the fact that while there may be a general set of policies for the worldwide development of capitalism, the development of capitalism within a particular nation-state depends on national policies that are reflective of that country's economic structures, position in the international division of labour, natural and human resource endowments and political and social history. This will call for imaginative choices and the creation of new institutional arrangements to ensure economic growth. Such nostrums as 'privatisation' are too general to address themselves to the specific ills of different African economies.

And finally, the great question in Africa will be how to ensure privatisation under democratically accountable regimes. Neo-liberals usually conflate the market with society and simply assume that liberalisation of the market is equivalent to liberalisation of the polity and civil society. Given the penchant of private capital to favour authoritarian rule in the Third World, will democratisation in Africa be seen as increasing uncertainty and therefore be considered a hindrance to private capital accumulation?

NOTE

1. Several WIDER studies on African economies suggest that public investment, even in its aggregated form crowds in private investment (Mkandawire, 1990; Ndulu, 1990b; Oyejide and Reheem, 1990; Rattso and Davies, 1990).

Part III

Agriculture and Social Impact: Key Issues

11 Neglected Issues in the Decline of Africa's Agriculture: Land Tenure, Land Distribution and R&D Constraints

Giovanni Andrea Cornia*

I THE NATURE OF SSA's AGRICULTURAL CRISIS

(A) The decline in production

Despite the region's wealth of natural resources, food production across sub-Saharan Africa has grown more slowly than population growth since the late 1960s, leading to a worsening food crisis that has occasionally reached famine proportions. The growth rate of agricultural production, which averaged between 2 and 3 per cent annually during the 1960s, slowed down during the 1970s before rising modestly in the 1980s and early 1990s. During the 1970s, 13 SSA countries suffered *absolute declines* in agricultural production, while between 1980 and 1992 (year of a particularly severe drought) another eight countries witnessed further declines in food production despite numerous policy efforts aimed at giving a new impulse to the sector (see Chapters 2 and 5).

Even for those countries that have experienced some revival of the agricultural sector over the last decade, the recovery of food production has generally not been able to keep up with population growth.

* The author would like to thank Nikos Alexandratos and Gerald K. Helleiner for their comments on an earlier version of this chapter, FAO's Agrostat database (in particular, Mr Chikhani for the computation of the data in Tables 11.1 and 11.2), Mr Roseboom and Mrs Mazzucato of ISNAR for providing relevant bibliographic material and for sharing their views on some R&D issues in Africas as well as Anny Bremner for the editing of the text and Patrizia Faustini and Andrea Manuelli for their assistance with the survey of the literature. Naturally, any remaining errors are the author's.

Average per capita food availability – which had declined by 15 per cent between the early 1960s and 1980 – dropped therefore by another 10–11 percentage points between 1980 and 1992 for SSA as a whole, or by 5–6 points if the period 1980–91 is considered (FAO, 1992a, Table 4).[1] There have been some notable exceptions to this rule. In Benin, Burkina Faso, Mauritius and Nigeria, food production per capita rose by between 17 and 30 per cent between 1980 and 1992, while other countries, such as Chad, Ghana, Kenya, Senegal and Uganda, were able to broadly increase food production in line with population growth (ibid.).

(B) Shifts in the structure of production

The slow growth of agricultural output in sub-Saharan African countries has been accompanied by a *shift in the structure of the crops produced* (Table 11.1). The general pattern observed shows that the per capita production of African indigenous food crops, i.e. sorghum, millet, local brands of maize, roots and tubers, has declined more rapidly or grown more slowly than the production of rice, wheat and hybrid maize and of a number of export crops such as tobacco or natural rubber. However, the production of other export crops, including oilcrops, tropical beverages and cotton, has also grown as slowly or even more slowly than that of African indigenous food crops (Table 11.1). This pattern is clear for the first two of the three subperiods considered (and particularly for the second), while the data for 1988–92 are clouded by the effects of the 1990–2 drought (as the indigenous food crops, which are more adapted to a regime of low and unstable rainfalls, were affected less than proportionally).

The trend towards a relatively worse performance of African traditional food crops is broadly confirmed by the data on changes in yields (tons per hectare) by main crop types (Table 11.2). During the 1960–80 period, yields of sorghum, millet and tubers rose less rapidly than those of wheat, maize and rice, and broadly in line with most export crop yields. During the second and third subperiod, the growth rate of sorghum and millet (and maize) yields remained consistently below that of wheat, rice and most export crops, though the yields of roots and tubers improved somewhat.

These differential trends would tend to suggest that smallholders – many of whom are women specialising in low-risk, low-input, low-yield indigenous crops – have been affected by the production crisis of the last two decades far more severely than commercial farmers

Table 11.1 Growth rates of production per capita by major crop types in sub–Saharan Africa, 1961–92

	*Wheat, rice, maize**	*Sorghum, millet*	*Roots, tubers*	*Coffee, tea, cocoa*	*Nuts, oil crops*	*Fibre crops*	*Tobacco leaves*	*Natural rubber*
1961–80	0.1	–2.0	–0.4	–1.5	–2.3	–2.9	–1.1	–0.9
1981–7	0.7	0.6	–0.3	–1.0	–0.7	2.8	2.2	1.4
1988–92	–6.0	–4.6	1.6	–5.0	–3.0	–5.2	8.9	–4.7
1961–92	–0.7	–1.8	–0.1	–2.0	–2.1	–2.0	1.1	–0.9

Note: * Includes both local and hybrid varieties.

Source: Computed on the AGROSTAT data base of FAO.

Table 11.2 Growth rates in yields by major types in sub-Saharan Africa, 1961-92 (tons per hectare)

	Wheat	*Rice*	*Maize**	*Millet, sorghum*	*Roots, tubers*	*Coffee, tea, cocoa*	*Nuts, oil crops*	*Fibre crops*	*Tobacco leaves*	*Natural rubber*
1961–80	3.0	0.5	1.6	0.4	0.6	0.5	0.3	–1.3	0.9	–0.9
1981–7	0.7	3.0	–0.4	0.2	1.1	1.8	1.4	–0.8	1.8	3.9
1988–92	3.9	–0.2	–5.7	–3.0	0.7	–1.8	1.7	–0.1	4.0	–5.5
1961–92	2.6	0.7	0.1	–0.2	0.7	0.5	0.8	–1.0	1.5	–0.2

Note: * Includes both local and hybrid varieties.

Source: Computed on the AGROSTAT data base of FAO.

Table 11.3 Broad characteristics of the main types of Zambian farms, in 1980

Criteria	*Subsistence*	*Emergent*	*Commercial*
Crops grown	Cassava, millet, sorghum, maize groundnuts	Cotton, tobacco, maize sunflower	Maize, sunflower, tobacco
Inputs used	Some fertiliser	Pesticides, certified seed, fertiliser	Fertiliser, certified seed, pesticides, herbicides
Main source of cash	Occasional food surplus sale, fishing, beer, charcoal	Production of cash crop surplus for sale	Production of cash crop for sale
Production of new cash crops (cotton, sunflower, soyabeans, tobacco)	None	Some	Some
Power source	Hand hole and tools	Hand hole, oxen, few tractor hire or ownership	Tractor and few oxen
Labour source	Family, communal, some casual	Family, communal, casual and few permanent labour	Permanent and casual labour
Size of farms	Usually 5 acres* (up to 13 acres)	Usually 13 acres to 50 acres	50 acres to 1,500 acres
Estimated number of households	500 000 (80%)	120 000 (19%)	6000 (1%)
Share of total land owned*	(23%)	(34%)	(43%)

Note: * One hectare is equal to 2.5 acres.

Source: Mwape (1989).

and the estate sector, even though estate production of some export crops has also been negatively affected. If this is the case, these data would further indicate that the agrarian dualism typical of African agriculture has become more acute. The main features of this dualism are illustrated in Table 11.3 (see also Jha and Hojjati, 1993, who confirm this picture on the basis of 1985–6 data).

II DOMINANT EXPLANATIONS AND NEGLECTED ISSUES REGARDING THE DECLINE OF SSA's AGRICULTURE

By and large, the dominant explanation for SSA's agricultural crisis has focused, especially in the early-to-mid-1980s, on the negative effects of various 'price distortions' which have characterised African agriculture over the last two decades, particularly during the 1970s and early 1980s (World Bank, 1981; Cleaver, 1985). This view has emphasised the negative influence on aggregate agricultural supply of artificially low food prices, excessive interference by parastatals in the commercialisation of food and cash crops, pan-territorial pricing, overvalued exchange rates, and the excessive implicit or explicit taxation of export crops. These factors, according to the proponents of this view, resulted in the development of parallel markets and smuggling and, when these options were not available, in the contraction of supply as the opportunity cost of leisure exceeded the remuneration of the crops produced.

Econometric analyses of the effects of price distortions during the 1970s indicate that, while important, 'price distortions' accounted for less than a third of the observed decline in agricultural supply (Cleaver, 1985) and that aggregate supply responses to price increases were fairly small both in the short and long term (Beynon, 1989; Bond, 1983). More recently, several commentators have focused on the negative effects of infrastructural constraints (see among others World Bank, 1989b), which are said to inhibit the ability of farmers to fully respond to higher prices and thereby discourage an increase in agricultural production. Indeed, public action and investment in roads, irrigation, electrification and adult literacy have been shown to trigger larger supply responses than is the case for price increases (Binswanger, 1990).

Demand factors have also been underlined, particularly in explaining the poor performance of traditional food crops. These include the shifts in consumer preferences induced by urbanisation, increased imports (or food aid) of wheat and rice and by the low income elasticity of demand for African crops as well as the marketing constraints and adverse pricing policies affecting these crops (Pearce, 1990). Typically, low retail prices for wheat, rice and maize have stimulated the consumption of these staples, thereby crowding out cassava, millet and sorghum, particularly in urban areas.

These 'dominant' explanations of the decline of SSA's agriculture are highly relevant and underscore some of the policy changes necessary for a lasting and sustainable recovery of food production in sub-

Saharan Africa. They are, however, neither able to fully explain the extent of the observed decline in agricultural production nor to provide a reasonable explanation for the differential performance of traditional food crops. Furthermore, they are not able to incorporate into their respective theoretical frameworks the profound changes which have occurred, and are still occurring, in the 'institutional framework' of SSA's agriculture, particularly with regard to land distribution, tenure systems and agricultural research systems of the vast majority of the countries of the region (Jazairy et al., 1992).

Without denying the importance of other complementary explanations, this chapter will attempt to provide answers to these neglected issues. In a nutshell, the main thesis presented can be summarised as follows:

1. Contrary to the received theory, traditional tenure systems are not being spontaneously and frictionlessly replaced by an efficient private agriculture with a fairly equal distribution of the operated land.
2. While traditional tenure systems are showing considerable adaptability to new conditions, land, credit and insurance market imperfections are instead pushing SSA's agriculture towards a system characterised by growing differentiation in access to land and to other factors of production. Considerable landlessness and quasi-landlessness have already emerged in a number of extreme cases and are expected to intensify substantially over the next 30 years.
3. In addition, in the absence of adequate institutional structures, tenancy insecurity as well as transaction and litigation costs are increasing.
4. As medium and large farmers are able to maintain control of an important share of available farmable land, and as the urban elites acquire an increasing share of this land as an edge against inflation or for reasons of prestige, the production of traditional food crops is gradually declining (in relation to that of wheat, rice and maize), wealth and income distribution and food security are worsening, and major efficiency losses are becoming inevitable. These trends are observed clearly, for instance, in Malawi and other Eastern African countries (Dickerman and Bloch, 1991).
5. The decline in the traditional food crop sector is compounded by the only limited improvements in the field of agricultural research and extension regarding traditional food crops.
6. While other contributory factors concur with the crises of African agriculture, and therefore need to be dealt with in an appropriate

manner, important policy reforms are required in the field of land distribution, tenure reform and R&D in the traditional food crop sector.

III LAND TENURE AND LAND CONCENTRATION: DOMINANT VIEWS ON THEIR IMPACT ON EQUITY AND EFFICIENCY

Two views have so far dominated the debate on land tenure and land distribution in sub-Saharan Africa, namely the neo-classical view and the neo-institutional view.

(A) The neo-classical 'private property right paradigm'

According to this paradigm, 'institutions', i.e. the legal framework regulating production and exchange in agriculture as well as the type and nature of property rights, constitute a given. Property rights should be certain and stable. Whenever distortions of various kinds (owing, for instance, to obsolete cultural traditions, political interference, 'rent-seeking behaviour' or other factors) alter this 'optimal situation', the policy maker should correct the distortions through appropriate interventions.

While many sub-Saharan African countries have moved from a situation of land abundance to one of land scarcity, traditional land tenure systems still prevail in most of them. Such tenure systems, however, reflect outdated institutional arrangements, causing disincentive problems and an inefficient allocation of resources. In particular, traditional land tenure systems are responsible for:

- an unclear definition of property rights. Efficiency requires that rights are clearly assigned to an individual, that they are easy to identify and verify, and that they provide certainty of legal tenure. The greater the ambiguity in property rights the higher the *transaction cost*, i.e. the cost of arranging a contract *ex ante* and of monitoring and enforcing it *ex post*. Under such a system, therefore, contracts are not legal or easily enforceable and the costs of litigation are high. High transaction costs in acquiring the land and in maintaining clear property rights reduce its value and therefore discourage the most efficient allocation of land among producers.
- lower investment in the land. Under communal tenure not all *costs*

and benefits of individual action are fully internalised, thereby creating considerable 'free rider' and incentive problems. This leads to a decline in investment incentives as well as in the demand for loanable funds, as the risk that the benefits of one's investment and efforts will be internalised by others grows. At the same time, the inability to offer the land as collateral on a loan reduces the supply of credit.

According to the 'private property right paradigm', the existing distribution of land is based on merit and the land market functions as an 'optimal allocator' of farmable land to the most efficient producers. Thus, land distribution should not be modified through land reform or other redistributive measures. In situations like those prevailing in SSA, where a land market does not exist or is not fully developed, public policy should aim at creating one or at strengthening it. In addition, a distribution of land which assigns a considerable share of the total to large farms is justified by their greater efficiency in relation to small farms. Indeed, the production cost curve in agriculture is U-shaped, with a very long declining left arm.

In the SSA context, the neo-classical paradigm therefore recommends the creation/expansion of an unconstrained land market, the granting and registration of individual land rights, the demarcation of boundaries and the development of a land cadastre. Such an approach therefore generates several specific *testable hypotheses* on the *effects of individualisation of land rights* and the production efficiency of large farms. The individualisation of land rights would be expected to:

- increase tenure security by reducing transaction costs;
- increase private investment in the land. The demand for loanable funds would be expected to rise because of lower transaction costs and greater security. There would also be a greater supply of credit due to the higher value of the land and the possibility of using it as a collateral.

(B) The neo-institutionalist perspective

While the neo-classical paradigm assumes (but does not explain) existing institutions and ignores their evolution, neo-institutional economics treats institutions or 'economic structures' (rules, contracts and institutions *strictu sensu*) and land distribution as *endogenous*. Both of them evolve *spontaneously* in response to changes in technology and factor endowment so as to minimise the transaction cost. The main features of such an approach are (see, for instance, Binswanger et al., 1989):

- In most of SSA, agrarian structures were initially characterised by communal land ownership. Land was allocated to the members of the community by the council of elders on the basis of household size. Cultivation was geared to subsistence needs and was carried out with long fallow periods, making exclusive use of family labour. Capital accumulation was non-existent, the technology extremely simple and the credit market sharply limited. Output could thus be increased only through greater land and labour inputs. Land was in almost unlimited supply, thus reducing the scope for social differentiation within the rural sector.
- As population density increases, progressively more intensive systems of land use are adopted in response to shifts in factor prices. Agricultural technology (defined by the length of fallow, method of cultivation, choice of tools and use of complementary inputs) then shifts and the (exogenously given) stock of improved technology is drawn upon.
- Population growth also induces important institutional changes, including a shift from collective to individual land rights and an '*induced technical and institutional change*' (Hayami and Ruttan, 1985). According to this view, changes in the relative scarcities of resources induce a derived demand for technological innovations to facilitate the substitution of the relatively less scarce and cheap factors for more scarce and expensive ones. In a land-scarce economy, for instance, yield-increasing high yield varieties (HYV) and fertilisers are substituted for land.
- The intensification of production therefore increases the demand for credit, while the shift from collective to private titles tends to increase the supply of credit as the land can be used by the individual borrower as collateral. Capital market imperfections, however, mean that land purchases can only be financed from self-generated funds. This would tend to make any initial distribution of landholding more unequal. Money-lenders also acquire land pledged as collateral by defaulting farmers. The distribution of landholdings therefore tends to become more unequal over time.
- However, as institutions also evolve in relation to market imperfections or the lack of given markets, sharecropping becomes a response to the lack of an insurance market and to the need to minimise

transaction and supervision costs. While the distribution of landholdings becomes more unequal, the distribution of operated holdings remains instead fairly egalitarian.

- The persistence of large holdings – despite growing population pressure – is justified by the economies of scale that they enjoy on the capital market and in product processing, marketing and storage as well as by their role *vis à vis* the smallholders in the fields of risk insurance, credit provision and technical innovation.
- Thus, if unimpeded by government policies, growing land scarcity and the consequent shift in the relative prices of land and labour will lead to the evolution of the African tenure system in an efficient manner, with the gradual assignment of private rights (ultimately including complete alienability) to the individual cultivator. This encourages, in turn, the emergence of a land market through which land is to be transferred to the most efficient cultivator.
- As institutions evolve endogenously over the long term in an optimal way, there is no need for government intervention which could even be harmful.

V EMPIRICAL EVIDENCE AND CRITIQUE

(A) Land tenure and efficiency

Most of the arguments developed by neo-classical economics (NCE) and neo-institutional economics (NIE) about land tenure systems, their evolution and their impact on economic efficiency are of a purely theoretical nature. They therefore face the risk of reaching erroneous conclusions due to the omission of important variables or for relying on overly restrictive assumptions. In these two theoretical approaches, the following pitfalls can be distinguished.

1 Confusion of property regimes and underestimation of the flexibility of customary land tenure systems

A careful distinction should be made between situations of open access in which a good is nobody's property and those where such goods are the common property of a group in which rules of access, exclusion and use are strongly regulated and sanctions for misuse or use by non-members are enforced (Platteau, 1992). Furthermore, mounting pressures towards the privatisation of property rights do not necessarily mean that the management rules of common-pool resources cannot be adjusted to the new situation nor that private property is superior to other property regimes. Indeed, traditional systems have shown a considerable flexibility and adaptability to new conditions without immediately losing their basic features. In general, one observes a gradual process of wrestling the land from the lineage, to the sub-lineage, then to the extended family and, finally, to the nuclear family.

2 *Coexistence of various types of property rights and methods of land acquisition*

Most of the literature indicates that even in highly populated areas different types of property rights coexist and that the majority of land is still acquired through non-market methods. In a study of eight regions of Ghana, Rwanda and Kenya, representing a variety of situations with respect to land scarcity and commercialisation of agriculture, Place and Hazell (1993) found that 70–80 per cent of the parcels had been acquired through *non-market methods*, i.e. through inheritance, gifts, government allocation and clearing of forest land, thus negating the hypothesis of spontaneous privatisation of land rights due to growing land shortage. Even in the most land-scarce areas, only between 18 and 29 per cent of the parcels had been acquired *through the market* (Table 11.4). Similar results were found in studies of Cameroon, Nigeria and Togo (Lawry and Stienbarger, 1991), of the Zaria region of Nigeria (Ega, 1984) and of South Ghana (Dei, 1990). These studies also showed that even under conditions of rapid population growth, the shift from common property regimes to private regimes takes place very slowly, if at all. A longitudinal study of the structure of property rights in South Ghana (Dei, 1990) indicates, for instance, that the proportion of land acquired through purchases increased from 18 to only 21 per cent between 1982 and 1989. At this speed, a fully privatised agriculture would be reached only towards the end of next century, by which time the overall structure of the economy is likely to have changed.

3 *Underestimation of the ability to dispose of the plots under traditional tenure*

The Place and Hazell study found that land rights were highly transferable, including in those cases in which the land had been acquired through non-market methods. Indeed, except for one of the eight areas surveyed, the producers had *complete rights* on the land in 45 to 81

Table 11.4 Prevalence of land rights in Ghana, Rwanda, Kenya, 1987-8 (per cent)

		GHANA			*RWANDA*		*KENYA*	
Land rights	*Anloga*	*Wassa*	*Ejura*	*Ruhengeri*	*Butare*	*Gitarama*	*Madzu*	*Kianjogu*
All parcels								
Limited transfer	52.4	6.0	21.0	15.5	36.7	21.1	26.2	23.6
Preferential transfer	2.1	29.1	6.6	3.1	16.5	21.3	6.3	67.9
Complete rights	45.4	64.9	72.4	81.5	46.7	57.6	67.5	8.5
Permanently held parcels								
No right to sell	23.3	29.7	17.5	2.4	28.2	22.4	30.9	91.3
Right to sell with approval	14.0	55.6	73.5	19.7	37.3	10.6	39.0	4.9
Right to sell without approval	62.7	14.7	9.0	77.8	34.5	67.0	30.1	3.9
Parcels held permanently	59.2	92.3	86.3	83.1	64.9	78.9	97.7	97.2

Source: Place and Hazell (1993).

per cent of the cases. *Preferential transfer rights* (including the preferential right to bequest the land) were found in 3 to 29 per cent of the cases, while *limited transfer rights* were prevalent in 30 to 50 per cent of the cases. With only two exceptions, the proportion of parcels that could not be sold at all oscillated between *only* 17 and 31 per cent. Finally, it should be noted that while land markets have emerged with an increase in land scarcity, the majority of land transactions – including sales – occur under the traditional system and are not sanctioned by the existing formal legislation.

4 *Underestimation of the security of tenure of traditional systems*

Dualistic systems prevail in the majority of African countries. Though apparently inappropriate, particularly for situations of intensive cultivation, traditional systems generally provide high tenure security for family plots and lower security for extensive cultivation which remains under communal jurisdiction. However, evidence shows that the proportion of family-held plots against the total tends to increase with land scarcity. The Place and Hazell study (1993) demonstrated, for instance, that tenure stability was very high, as the parcels held permanently (either with complete rights, preferential transfer rights, or long-term use rights) varied from 60 to 97 per cent, regardless of whether the land had been acquired through market or non-market mechanisms. These data tend to negate the validity of the 'private property right paradigm' according to which tenure security increases with the individualisation of titles to the land.

5 *Land tenure and economic efficiency*

There are only few quantitative analyses of the relation between individualisation of property rights and the extent of credit and input use, propensity to invest in the land, and land yields. Place and Hazell (1993) showed that individualisation of land rights was significantly correlated with informal and total credit use (but not with use of formal sector credit) only in one of the eight regions analysed. In the others, this relationship was either not significant or negative, or could not be tested for lack of data.

Land improvements appeared instead to be positively correlated with tenure security. Indeed, land improvements were the least likely in the case of parcels with short-term use rights and most likely for those with long-term tenure security. The most significant association, however, was found with the right to bequest and not with that to sell.

Similar results were found in a study on Cameroon, Togo and Nigeria (Lawry and Stienbarger, 1991) where the propensity to adopt land-improving farming practices was not found to be significantly different among people with long-term tenure security, regardless of whether the latter was acquired through purchase, gift or inheritance. Land improvements were instead least likely in the parcels of those farmers with short-term tenure security. Finally, no significant relationship was found in the Place–Hazell study between the individualisation of property rights and land yields.

All in all, the literature reviewed above provides little support for the conclusions of the private property right theory regarding the presumed greater economic efficiency of privately-owned land and related proposals for massive land registration and titling programmes. Similar conclusions are drawn in an *ex post* review of the credit and investment effect of land registration programmes carried out in Kenya, Uganda and Zimbabwe (Barrows and Roth, 1989). On balance, the study found little evidence for the argument that registration increased demand for credit and investment in agriculture, while identifying crucial constraints to credit use in the limited overall volume of credit to agriculture, complicated procedures and excessive cost of credit for the small farmers and the biases of the credit market in favour of the larger farmers. Even when titled farmers were shown to exhibit higher productivity than non-titled farmers – as in the Njoro District of Kenya – the analysis demonstrated that this apparent superiority was in fact due to the greater average farm size, mode of access to the land and preferential access to credit and input markets of the titled *vis à vis* the non-titled farmers (Carter et al., 1991).

6 *Misconceptions about the effects of land registration programmes*

When a communal tenure system is abruptly transformed into a prevailingly private property regime, as in the case of ambitious land-titling programmes, the transition in tenure systems is generally characterised by losses of short-term security and considerable equity and efficiency costs.

To start with, the issuing of individual land titles may lead to an increase in tenure security over the long term. However, in the short term it often actually decreases because of a surge in land disputes caused by the costs and inequities arising from the *de facto* dual system of land rights which will prevail for several years. In addition, in most of the programmes experimented so far the high costs associated with land registration and the lack of familiarity with government bureaucracy have discouraged registration itself and have depressed the demand for titling by small farmers (Besteman, 1990; Carter et al., 1991; Williams, 1992).

Second, the introduction of land registration and a new property regime may also cause considerable *equity costs*. It may indeed bring about the displacement of the rights of weak or politically marginalised groups and the allocation of public land to the estate sector, thus increasing the control over the land by the urban elites and other powerful groups. As a result, tenure insecurity for those unable to register their land grows, while land concentration may worsen. Examples of such equity costs are to be found in many African countries: in Kenya, where the land reform of the early 1960s dispossesed several Kikuyu of their land (Barrows and Roth, 1989); in Somalia, where the Land Law of 1975 *de facto* offered town dwellers the opportunity to establish property rights, through land registration, on land belonging to the rural communities (see Besteman, 1990); in Nigeria, where the Land Use Decree of 1978 led to the preferential issuance of certificates of land occupancy to the government class and the business community. The equity costs associated with land-titling programmes can be further exacerbated by the courts which frequently rule in favour of the rich who can better afford the risks implicit in the legal process, the litigation costs and – if necessary – the bribes.

Third, tenure reform can also cause considerable *efficiency costs*, in the form of income foregone as tenure insecurity discourages new initiatives, investments and new sales of land. Efficiency also suffers because of the high transaction costs entailed by the need to gain or maintain direct control of the land and because of the high costs of litigation over ownership of land and demarcation of the parcels.

7 *Lack of induced technical innovation or 'autonomous agricultural intensification'*

As has been seen, the neo-institutionalist approach maintains that changes in technology and relative factor prices should also lead to a more intensive type of farming, with higher fertiliser inputs, greater irrigation, higher cropping intensity and improved yields. However, available information shows that in the case of Africa this type of spontaneous, market-driven, 'technological transition' is facing considerable problems. The data in Table 11.5 show unambiguously that the input intensity of production and land yields vary only marginally

Table 11.5 Agricultural inputs and yields in sub-Saharan Africa and South-East Asia, 1982–4

Country	*GDP per capita 1987 US$*	*Arable land per agric. worker (ha)*	*% Irrigated land on arable land*	*Fertiliser consumption (kg) per ha*	*Yields of cereals (tonnes/ha)*
		A. Land-rich Sub-Saharan Countries			
Cameroon	970	3.0	0	12	1.0
CAR	330	5.5	0	1	0.5
Zaire	150	1.9	0	2	0.9
Average	480	3.5	0	5	0.8
		B. Land-scarce Sub-Saharan Countries			
Burundi	250	0.4	1	2	1.1
Ethiopia	130	1.0	0	5	1.2
Kenya	330	0.7	1	27	1.6
Lesotho	370	0.5	0	24	0.8
Malawi	160	1.1	1	18	1.2
Nigeria	370	1.4	0	9	0.7
Rwanda	300	0.3	0	1	1.2
Somalia	290	0.8	4	3	0.6
Uganda	260	0.9	0	0	1.7
Average	270	0.8	1	10	1.1
		C. Land-scarce South-East Asian Countries			
Bangladesh	160	0.5	16	41	2.0
India	300	0.9	25	38	1.5
Indonesia	450	0.7	26	65	3.3
Nepal	160	0.4	24	13	1.6
Pakistan	350	1.4	–	62	1.6
Sri Lanka	400	0.7	28	73	2.8
Vietnam	–	0.4	17	44	2.5
Average	300	0.7	23	45	2.2

Source: Cornia and Strickland (1990).

between land-rich and land-scarce countries of SSA (panels 1 and 2). The data also show that fertiliser use and the proportion of arable land irrigated in the land-scarce Asian countries, i.e. countries with comparable average amounts of arable land per agricultural worker and with a similar level of economic development, are, respectively, four and 22 times greater than they are in the land-scarce countries of Africa south of the Sahara (Cornia and Strickland, 1990). The technological transition appears particularly problematic in the 'coarse grain and cassava belts' of Western and Central Africa, where the consumption of fertiliser per hectare barely reached 4.9 and 1.4 kg respectively as opposed to a regional average of 7.2 kg (Pardey et al., 1991, Table A6.1).

(B) Land distribution and efficiency: the 'inverse relation' in SSA's agriculture

1 The evidence

The conclusions reached by the NCE and NIE regarding the presumed superiority of large farms, the role of 'optimal allocator of land' played by the market and the spontaneous evolution of land distribution (and the attendant implication of the potentially harmful nature of government interventions in the land market) are contradicted by the existence of a clear '*inverse relation*' between farm size and land yields in several sub-Saharan countries, particularly in those countries where surplus labour is considerable.

A study by Cornia (1985) provides evidence of this relation for five SSA countries, namely Ethiopia, Uganda, Nigeria, Tanzania and Sudan (Table 11.6). The analysis is based on farm-level data collected in the mid to late 1970s by the Farm Management Division of FAO for countries characterised by different land scarcity, agro-geological conditions, farming practices, use of intermediate inputs and hiring of non-family labour. Despite this variety of conditions, gross output per hectare was found to be inversely related to farm size in all five countries. 'Small farms' had between three to five times higher yields than 'large farms'. The inverse relation was found to hold *a fortiori* when yields were measured in terms of value added per hectare. Similar results have been found in other countries affected by some measure of land scarcity, such as Rwanda, Burundi, Malawi, Zimbabwe, South Africa, Ethiopia, Côte d'Ivoire, northern Nigeria and a growing number of countries in Southern and Eastern Africa and in coastal West Africa. A study by Heyer et al. (1976) in settlement areas of Kenya found that farms of less than four hectares had a gross output per worker about seven times greater than farms of 32 hectares or more. Place and Hazell (1993) also showed that holding size was inversely related to yields in Rwanda, Ghana and Kenya, while Carter et al. (1991) found that output and family income per acre first declined and then rose with the increase in farm size.

Not all quantitative analyses for land-scarce countries provide immediate evidence of this 'inverse relation'. A recent analysis (Lele and Agarwal, 1989) covering Kenya and Malawi showed, for instance, that yields per hectare were consistently higher on the large estates than on small holdings. When computing the value of all resources used in the production of one unit of output, smallholders showed

Table 11.6 Selected farm indicators by farm size in selected sub-Saharan African countries, (mid-1970s)

	CLS	*GO-WO*	*GO-MD*	*MD-LN*	*GO-LN*	*VA-LN*	*KA-LN*	*VA-GO*	*LUI*	*OFLI*
Ethiopia	< 1.0	11.4	0.21	339.7	74.6	69.8	245.3	0.93	0.52	0.00
	1.0–1.5	35.5	0.64	246.0	159.3	144.3	320.4	0.90	0.91	0.02
	1.5–2.0	9.9	0.16	220.0	36.4	25.1	56.7	0.69	0.78	0.00
	2.0–2.5	26.4	0.59	97.0	57.7	47.3	136.4	0.81	1.00	0.15
	2.5–3.0	22.9	0.46	136.7	63.6	51.2	149.6	0.80	1.24	0.05
	3.0–3.5	31.2	0.53	185.0	98.1	88.2	240.0	0.89	1.00	0.04
	3.5–4.0	20.1	0.40	126.7	51.8	42.0	134.8	0.81	0.92	0.03
	4.0–5.0	37.9	0.88	62.6	55.3	46.6	75.9	0.84	0.87	0.11
	5.0–6.0	27.4	0.81	51.6	42.2	33.3	59.4	0.78	0.80	0.01
	6.0+	41.6	1.49	6.1	9.2	8.2	2.7	0.89	0.63	0.00
Nigeria	< 0.5	40.8	5.44	138.4	753.7	595.8	814.5	0.79	1.36	0.26
	0.5–1.0	48.2	3.23	167.5	542.2	408.5	509.9	0.75	1.29	0.39
	1.0–1.5	66.0	4.63	133.5	479.4	365.6	319.4	0.76	1.57	0.37
	1.5–2.0	37.1	2.59	146.7	389.4	286.3	509.5	0.75	1.57	0.31
	2.0–2.5	79.6	8.44	66.9	393.0	321.1	341.9	0.81	1.55	0.38
	2.5–3.0	144.3	8.46	56.2	478.0	370.4	149.7	0.77	1.61	0.54
	3.0–3.5	161.0	6.90	45.7	315.9	170.3	165.6	0.53	1.35	0.64
	3.5–4.0	112.3	6.97	53.8	375.8	265.7	177.9	0.70	1.66	0.44
	4.0–5.0	140.3	8.48	41.9	356.1	270.1	190.8	0.75	1.34	0.47
	5.0–7.0	175.9	6.90	52.9	388.5	254.8	156.6	0.69	1.82	0.58
	7.0–10.0	217.1	8.34	44.0	367.2	274.2	173.0	0.74	1.62	0.59
	10.0–15.0	208.5	8.64	39.1	338.5	274.4	64.8	0.81	2.01	0.71
	15.0+	210.4	7.84	15.8	124.6	77.9	494.2	0.62	0.86	0.46
Uganda	< 1.0	9.8	0.86	255.7	221.4	194.6	109.5	0.87	0.79	0.07
	1.0–2.0	15.4	1.10	192.8	212.5	191.0	160.9	0.89	0.78	0.06

	2.0–3.0	27.6	1.27	115.5	146.8	129.3	86.5	0.88	0.67	0.03
	3.0–4.0	29.3	1.45	77.4	112.7	98.6	91.2	0.87	0.54	0.01
	4.0–5.0	18.8	1.23	91.7	94.5	83.5	140.2	0.86	0.51	0.05
	5.0–6.0	23.9	1.20	60.6	73.3	65.8	57.0	0.88	0.39	0.01
	6.0–8.0	24.1	1.18	45.8	54.1	48.5	23.0	0.89	0.35	0.02
	8.0+	13.0	1.00	35.5	35.5	31.8	28.1	0.89	0.33	0.07
Tanzania	< 0.2	35.7	0.76	1378.2	649.8	904.8	2199.9	0.86	1.43	0.00
	0.2–0.4	29.9	0.87	415.6	361.9	340.8	1616.9	0.94	1.29	0.00
	0.4–0.6	38.7	1.24	208.1	259.9	250.5	390.9	0.96	1.03	0.05
	0.6–0.8	66.6	1.37	238.7	329.4	299.6	636.1	0.96	1.02	0.00
	0.8–1.0	39.7	1.14	172.3	196.7	186.5	332.9	0.94	1.03	0.01
	1.0–1.5	48.3	1.35	123.6	168.0	157.8	384.5	0.93	0.96	0.01
	1.5–2.0	31.5	1.34	114.0	153.6	146.7	180.7	0.95	0.97	0.04
	2.0–2.5	56.1	1.39	105.3	147.0	139.8	157.6	0.95	0.95	0.04
	2.5–3.0	65.5	1.03	130.7	135.0	131.8	81.4	0.97	0.97	0.05
	3.0–4.0	73.5	1.55	78.3	122.1	117.8	75.6	0.96	0.96	0.01
	4.0–5.0	43.1	0.82	74.2	61.0	58.6	91.3	0.96	0.85	0.05
	5.0–6.0	9.8	0.98	60.2	59.2	57.8	49.4	0.97	0.93	0.13
	6.0–8.0	83.8	1.58	53.4	84.5	82.3	30.5	0.97	0.94	0.04
	8.0–10.0	72.6	1.05	47.7	50.2	49.5	82.9	0.98	0.97	0.10
	10.0–15.0	99.1	1.55	54.1	83.9	83.0	47.1	0.99	0.95	0.26
	15.0+	220.7	5.99	19.5	117.0	117.0	18.1	1.00	1.00	0.42
Sudan	< 0.5	14.1	0.61	328.2	203.2	198.9	115.2	0.97	1.00	0.02
	0.5–1.0	15.1	0.41	206.5	85.0	82.9	344.2	0.97	1.00	0.11
	1.0–1.5	24.1	0.59	160.0	94.5	93.0	60.2	0.98	1.00	0.15
	1.5–2.0	36.5	0.90	161.3	146.8	142.1	219.1	0.96	1.00	0.19
	2.0–2.5	29.2	0.86	78.9	64.0	62.0	67.3	0.96	1.00	0.18
	2.5–3.0	30.1	0.60	114.7	69.8	67.6	87.0	0.96	0.98	0.24

continued on page 236

Table 11.6 continued

CLS	*GO-WO*	*GO-MD*	*MD-LN*	*GO-LN*	*VA-LN*	*KA-LN*	*VA-GO*	*LUI*	*OFLI*
3.0–4.0	37.7	0.85	87.8	75.4	73.4	66.3	0.97	1.01	0.18
4.0–5.0	36.8	0.79	88.6	70.8	68.6	52.1	0.96	0.99	0.29
5.0–6.0	46.4	0.89	66.6	59.7	57.7	64.3	0.96	1.00	0.25
6.0–7.0	48.8	0.73	96.9	71.6	68.9	26.8	0.96	1.00	0.29
7.0–8.0	31.1	0.55	52.0	28.7	27.5	21.1	0.95	1.00	0.24
8.0–10.0	50.6	1.14	41.9	47.9	46.7	80.4	0.97	1.00	0.34
10.0–15.0	36.6	0.58	60.2	35.1	33.7	36.5	0.96	0.99	0.36
15.0+	69.3	0.73	51.8	38.2	36.6	32.9	0.96	1.00	0.50

Notes: All values are expressed in 1970 US dollars; land figures are expressed in hectares. The meaning of the symbols: CLS = farm size (intervals expressed in hectares; GO-WO = gross output per worker; GO-MD = gross output per man-day; MD-LN = man days per hectare; GO-LN = gross output per hectare; VA-LN = value added per hectare; KA-LN = capital stock (land excluded) per hectare; VA-GO = value added/gross output rate; LUI = land use intensity; OFLI = per cent of off-farm labour.

Source: Cornia (1985).

greater efficiency than the estate sector in the case of coffee production in Kenya and maize and tobacco production in Malawi. Similarly, Berry and Cline (1979) demonstrate, on the basis of Malawian data for 1968–9, that the apparent superiority of large farms over small farms in terms of cash income per acre is reversed when total (as opposed to marketed) output is taken into account. Hence, the inverse relation becomes more meaningful if adjustments are made when computing the size of farms and the value of output (Lipton, 1993). Land ought to be measured in hectares of land of the same quality, while output should also include that part which is consumed by the producers themselves, should be netted of the costs of intermediate inputs, and should be valued at shadow prices so as to correct for the possible distortions introduced by pricing policies (as in the case of the indigenous food crops mentioned above).

2 *Explanations of the 'inverse relation'*

It needs to be stressed that this inverse relation is *not* due to intrinsic 'decreasing returns to scale' related to an increase in the size of output (in general, returns to scale in agriculture are found to be constant). It is due instead to a 'second inverse relation', i.e., between farm size and labour inputs, even more pronounced than the first relation. The data in Table 11.6 show, for instance, that the intensity of this relation is far stronger than for the farm size/yield relation. In turn, the higher labour input per hectare observed on the small farms is due to their higher ratios of farmed/owned land, to their greater recourse to double-cropping, to their choice of higher value added (and labour-intensive) crops, and to their higher labour inputs per unit of land cultivated with the same crop.

The key issue then concerns this observed greater labour intensity in small-scale farming. Two main explanations have been proposed (Sen, 1966; Berry and Cline, 1979; Platteau, 1992), which may be summarised as follows.

The first explanation focuses on factor market imperfections and, in particular, on the *'labour market dualism'* (Berry and Cline, 1979; Ellis, 1988), by which the market wage rate paid to agricultural labourers by large farmers exceeds the marginal opportunity cost of family labour. Somewhat less frequently, this explanation also focuses on the lower capital costs borne by large farmers in relation to smallholders.

The 'imputed' labour cost is thus lower in the small farm sector because most people prefer to work on their own farm. This reduces the disutility of work as it more easily allows the internalisation of the benefits of one's own work, thereby leading to a better utilisation of land (as well as of capital). In some countries, working on one's own land also allows an important amount of labour to be provided by women and children who, for cultural reasons, are forbidden to work outside the family farm's boundaries. Finally, working on the family's land also facilitates the coordination of farm work and domestic chores, thus making a greater supply of female labour possible.

A second cause of the observed discrepancy between the prevailing wage rate and the opportunity cost of family labour is that while large farms employ labour until its *marginal* productivity equals the wage rate, small farmers employ labour until their *average* productivity equals the (implicit) wage rate. Still another explanation focuses on the limited probability of finding employment outside the family farm. When preference for leisure is low and survival needs acute, the effective wage for which the small farmer is willing to work is equal to his/her marginal productivity multiplied by the probability of finding employment. If the latter is very low, the quantity of work imputed to small farms will be very high.

The second explanation for the greater labour intensity of small-scale farming is based on the *lower transaction costs faced by smallholders* (Platteau, 1992). Basically, smallholders face a zero cost of screening and supervision, which on the other hand can be substantial for large farms if the landlord wants to ensure an adequate monitoring of his employees' labour effort and prevent a dilution of incentive. The cost of supervising hired labour (which entails considerable managerial diseconomies of scale) is substantial since 'quality labour' and, hence, close monitoring is essential in agriculture.

The inverse relation has been verified in several labour-surplus economies characterised by limited employment opportunities outside agriculture, but tends to become weaker, or to disappear altogether, when the opportunity cost of family labour exceeds the marginal productivity of labour in the small farm sector. Several authors have suggested that this inverse relation also breaks down when the modernisation of agricultural practices (as in the case of the 'green revolution') is accompanied by substantial imperfections in the *credit market*. This renders the purchase of modern inputs more difficult or proportionately more expensive for smallholders, who are therefore unable to benefit from the potential increases in yields brought about by technological modernisation. In such a situation, the disadvantage of small farmers would be compounded by the inability of the *insurance market* to provide insurance at affordable prices against the risk of crop failure. The smallness of farms, however, does not significantly impede *per se* the adoption of, or success with, improved varieties of seeds and related inputs because modern inputs are highly divisible and the 'green revolution' technology is basically scale-neutral. A more socially efficient solution can be obtained instead through an elimination of imperfections in the insurance and credit markets.

Similar arguments on breaking down the 'inverse relation' have also been made in relation to the introduction of indivisible labour-saving technologies (such as tractors) or whenever considerable 'economies of scale' exist in the commercialisation of agricultural products. Also in these two cases, however, more socially efficient solutions could be achieved through the development of a tractor-hire market as well as some kind of 'collective action' (as in the case of commercialisation consortia among small producers).

V THE LACK OF 'INDUCED INSTITUTIONAL INNOVATION' AND LIMITED PROGRESS IN R&D FOR TRADITIONAL AFRICAN FOOD CROPS

One of the striking features of the African situation is the discrepancy between the received theory on 'induced institutional innovation' (Hayami and Ruttan, 1985) and the limited progress in creating R&D institutions capable of contributing to the intensification of production through a more widespread adoption of modern varieties (MV).

As indicated in Table 11.7, while rice and wheat account for 71 per cent of the total food production in South-East Asia, they represent a mere 9 per cent of total food production in SSA. In the latter region, the mainstay of food production is represented by millet and sorghum and root crops, the first two accounting for 26 per cent of total food output and the third, 60 per cent. However, the proportion of arable land planted with modern varieties in SSA is considerably lower in the case of coarse grains and root crops. According to Matlon (1990) 'After several decades of research, probably less than 5 per cent of total sorghum and millet areas (in the West African semi-arid tropics) . . . is sown to cultivars developed in modern crop improvements programs'. Or, as noted by Lipton and Longhurst (1989), with the exception of hybrid maize, traditional ' . . . food crops in SSA are not the classic MV breakthrough crops'.

Table 11.7 Production structure of food crop production in Africa and South-East Asia, 1988

	Africa		*S.E. Asia*	
	m.m.t.	*%*	*m.m.t.*	*%*
Total cereals	62.7	39.6	339.3	83.3
Wheat	6.7	4.2	59.2	14.5
Rice paddy	7.6	4.8	230.4	56.5
Barley	5.6	3.5	2.6	0.1
Maize	19.2	12.1	26.3	6.4
Millet/sorghum	22.3	14.1	20.5	5.0
Other	1.3	0.1	0.3	0.0
Root crops	95.8	60.4	68.1	16.7
Potatoes	4.4	2.7	16.7	4.1
Cassava	57.4	36.2	44.4	10.9
Other	34.0	21.5	7.0	1.7
TOTAL	158.5	100.00	407.4	100.00

Note: m.m.t = million metric ton.

Source: FAO (1989).

Some authors (see for instance Mosley, Chapter 12, this volume) attribute the limited adoption of MV for sorghum, millet and cassava to factor market imperfections, and in particular to credit market imperfections. An alternative explanation of the limited development and adoption of modern varieties of sorghum, millet, maize and root crops underlines instead the problems affecting agricultural research in Africa and, in particular, the unbalanced allocation of R&D resources among various crops, and the low efficiency with which these resources are used.

The 'agricultural research gap hypothesis' requires an examination of trends in R&D expenditure both at the international and at the national level. The data in Table 11.8 show that between 1971 and 1988 sorghum and millet consistently received a very low share of the total (between 3.1 and 5.0 per cent) of the international research expenditure. Roots and tubers also received a limited share of the total worldwide research expenditure of the Consultative Group on International Agricultural Research (CGIAR), while wheat, barley, maize, legumes and, above all, rice and livestock received, in contrast, much larger shares. The data also show that this allocative pattern has not substantially changed over time. As other data on the distribution of CGIAR expenditure by commodity and region (see Table 9.7 in Pardey et al.,

Table 11.8 Worldwide commodity orientation of CGIAR core research operating expenditure

	1971–5 %	*1976–89* %	*1981–5* %	*1986–8* %
Rice	21.5	17.2	17.3	17.2
Wheat, barley & triticale	13.8	10.9	10.3	9.1
Maize	19.5	9.3	7.2	7.3
Sorghum & millet	3.1	3.3	4.8	5.0
Subtotal, cereals	57.9	40.6	39.6	38.7
Potatoes	4.6	7.0	6.1	6.8
Other roots & tubers	6.8	5.4	4.8	4.5
Legumes	8.1	11.4	11.2	12.9
Subtotal, crop research	77.4	64.4	61.7	62.9
Livestock	10.2	19.8	19.1	19.7
Subtotal, commodity research	87.6	84.2	80.8	82.6
Farming systems	12.2	11.7	9.9	8.5
Food policy	0.1	2.0	3.1	3.7
Genetic resources	0.1	2.0	4.2	2.8
NARS capacity building	0.0	0.0	1.9	2.4
Subtotal, other research/activity	12.4	15.8	19.2	17.4
Total	100.0	100.0	100.0	100.0

Note: The 1971–85 shares are based on core operating research expenditures exclusive of an administrative component. This administrative component was included, apparently on a prorated basis, in the 1986–8 data. Total may not sum due to rounding.

Source: Pardey et al. (1991).

1991) indicate that since 1983, 39 per cent of its research expenditure has been allocated to international agricultural research centres operating in SSA, one can conclude that in 1986–8 only about 2.5 per cent of the total CGIAR core operating research expenditure was allocated to R&D on sorghum and millet and 2 per cent to roots and tubers. In contrast, during the same period SSA-based agronomic research on rice, maize and livestock received respectively 4.8, 3.1 and 13.4 per cent. Even wheat – whose cultivation in SSA is severely limited by agro-geological constraints – received a share of global CGIAR resources similar to that of cassava.

Unfortunately, there is no readily available international compilation of data on the commodity orientation of the expenditures of National Agricultural Research Centres (NARs) in SSA, which account for approximately four fifths of total R&D in the region. Even national data are extremely difficult to come by. Data from INRAN (the main agricultural research institute of Niger), for instance, show that between 1976 and 1980 research on millet, sorghum and cowpeas absorbed 63 per cent of the total research expenditure, a fairly balanced share in view of the fact that about 90 per cent of the land cultivated during the rainy season is planted with a combination of these three crops. This proportion declined however to 46 per cent over 1981–5, to 44 per cent for the subsequent five years and to 39 per cent in 1991 (Mazzucato et al., 1993).

In the absence of adequate information, one may argue, however, that several NARs have suffered since independence from an export crop bias. Data from the early 1970s show that research expenditure in developing countries was concentrated primarily on export crops (such as cotton, cattle, coffee and sugarcane) or on wheat, rice and maize. While research on sorghum had received some non-negligible resources, millet and cassava had been basically neglected (Pinstrup-Andersen, 1982, Table 3.5). Even assuming a reorientation of national research over the last 10–15 years, such a 'lagged response' to the real research needs of Africa is responsible for the delay in the achievement of that 'critical mass' of research needed to achieve meaningful results (CGIAR, 1992). As an indication of the relative youth and weakness of national sorghum and millet research programmes in West Africa, Matlon (1990) underscores, for instance, that in 1986 there were only 11 national scientists involved in sorghum breeding throughout the region.

The African NARs, in addition, suffer from a series of institutional and management problems which, in view of the dominance of the traditional food crops in total output, affect *in particular* the R&D on these crops, even when research resources are allocated in a balanced manner. Firstly, the African NARs were established much later than similar institutions in Asia and Latin America. Furthermore, most of them have *de facto* continued to be controlled by the former colonial powers and are unevenly distributed across Africa. The NARs from Nigeria, Côte d'Ivoire, Kenya, Mali, Sudan and Tanzania account for about half of the regional total, while in at least 10 countries they do not reach the minimum size for carrying out research in an efficient manner.

The African NARs still face huge problems of 'capacity building'. Despite rapid growth between the early 1960s and the mid 1980s, the research staff is proportionately smaller than in the other developing regions, they still depend on expatriates for a third of their employees, comprise many national staff with only little research experience and are affected by a considerably higher turnover (Pardey et al., 1991). A recent evaluation of African NARs found that they were poorly funded, carried out research programmes with little relevance to the agricultural needs of smallholders and did not cooperate with each other. None of them was found to be up to present Asian standards and only nine of the 46 centres scrutinised met minimum acceptable levels despite large annual expenditures (Cleaver, 1993).

These various problems tend to create a situation in which the already relatively modest expenditures of SSA's NARs generate even fewer successes in developing improved varieties relevant to the needs of the smallholders.

VI POLICY CONCLUSIONS

The foregoing analysis has shown that the prevailing orthodoxies dominating the debate on land tenure, land distribution and technological innovation come up against considerable theoretical and empirical problems in the SSA context, that the policies implemented on the basis of their conclusions have seldom produced the expected results, and that there is a need for a broader model of land distribution, tenure and registration, as well as for a different approach to agricultural research. The following policy recommendations derive from the analysis.

(A) Land tenure types and land registration

While attempts to suddenly and radically modify traditional tenure systems into systems based mainly on private property rights should be discouraged, in the presence of growing land scarcity and tenure conflicts there are many good reasons to issue formal land titles, provide official and *affordable* registration and guarantee the protection of clearly defined land rights. This is a particularly urgent task whenever the indigenous tenure systems are weak or non-existent, the incidence of land disputes high and when the land rights of vulnerable groups are being eroded, as, for instance, in areas of new settlement, immigration and project interventions requiring the privatisation of land rights (Migot-Adholla et al., 1991).

While in some cases *individual property rights* should be given precedence, it does not follow that they should be the only ones to be granted. *Group titles* – including family, clan, sub-lineage, village and cooperatives titles – should also be issued, registered and equally guaranteed by the law, particularly if the communities themselves make such a request. As the above review of the literature has shown, many different types of property rights provide similar tenure security and incentives to economic agents.

Indeed, while it can cause incentive and 'free rider' problems, group titling often presents considerable advantages over other types of property regimes (Platteau, 1992). It allows, for instance, reductions in the budgetary and 'political' costs of registration which, as this chapter has shown, has discouraged demand for registration among smallholders and allowed encroachment by urban elites on their land. If accompanied by appropriate management, group titling also allows greater flexibility in patterns of land use, greater scope for specialisation in production, as well as greater economies of scale in the procurement of inputs, the commercialisation of output and in the use of indivisible inputs such as agricultural machinery, as well as in surveillance and guarding, boundary demarcation and walk-to-work time.

Group titling also allows for an equitable distribution of income and does not require the imposition of land ceilings or continuous efforts to avoid restratification among various groups of farmers, as in the case of a tenure system based exclusively on individual rights. Furthermore, the pooling of incomes provides better insurance against the risk of crop failure.

(B) Completely free or regulated land market?

The above review of the literature found that a continuous spectrum of transfer rights existed in all countries analysed. While secure property rights (whether private or collective) offer considerable incentives, it is not obvious that an entirely unconstrained land market would come up with a 'socially optimal allocation of land', given the conditions of unequal distribution of political and economic power and of pervasive factor and product market imperfections characterising most of rural Africa.

Even assuming no political interference in the allocation of land, a free land market can generate strong disequalising tendencies and exacerbate landholding and income inequality due to the play of both demand and supply side factors. To start with, land is not demanded only as a factor for agricultural production but also as a financial investment (particularly if investment opportunities are limited and capital markets underdeveloped), as an edge against inflation or as a source of political prestige for urban elites. Land will not necessarily be allocated therefore to the most dynamic profit-maximising entrepreneurs but to those with greater financial resources and political patronage. On the supply side, capital market imperfections and unsustainable consumption expenditures (for dowries, funerals, marriages, taxation, fees, droughts, or due to adverse movement in relative prices) may cause distress sales by defaulting small farmers.

Particularly in situations where land scarcity is very acute, it is desirable therefore to grant land titles that, while ensuring the security of tenure (providing in this way adequate investment and production incentives) do not allow completely free transfer rights. This can be achieved through the granting of long-term leases or use rights (including the right to bequeath) but not full transfer rights, or through the granting of land rights conditional to the prior approval of the group in case of sale, mortgage or lease of the land. In extreme cases, an excessive restratification in the distribution of land can be prevented by forbidding the sale and mortgaging of land and through the imposition of ceilings on ownership (Migot-Adholla et al., 1991).

(C) Land redistribution and land reform

Under both private and communal property systems, unequal access to the land has been identified as a major factor underlying poverty among smallholders and the landless as well as the poor performance of traditional food crops in sub-Saharan Africa. The evidence on the existence of an 'inverse relation' in SSA indicates furthermore that the unequal land distribution prevailing in a growing number of African countries imposes a considerable efficiency cost on agriculture as a whole. There is a strong case therefore for redistributing land to the landless and land-deficient farmers in all those countries with surplus land in the estate, large farmer and state sectors or under unallocated communal tenure and where a considerable proportion of labour resources would remain idle because of such skewed distribution of land.

The extent of redistribution and the way it should be accomplished are however open to discussion and should be determined on a case-by-case basis. In any event, redistribution ought to be carried out in an '*incentive compatible*' and '*power compatible*' way (Lipton, 1993). For instance, unless factor, insurance, credit and product failures can be simultaneously removed and efficient markets created (or 'collective action is undertaken') for those activities for which economies of scale do exist (tractorisation, storage and commercialisation of products), land redistribution should lead to a situation in which small-scale and *some* large-scale farm units coexist. Indeed, the latter can play a second-best, but positive, role as intermediaries-providers of services (credit, fertilisers, technical innovation, and so on) for the small farms. In addition, market and tax incentives should be used (together with more traditional methods) to obtain control of the land. The taxation of land, particularly if left idle, and the desubsidisation of inputs would make the divestiture of land more feasible from an economic perspective.

In order to respect the principle of 'horizontal equity', the burden of land reform should be shared among all high-income groups in society. Part of the resources to be utilised for compensation for land reform ought, for instance, to be mobilised through the taxation of the high-income urban settlers who, under the traditional land reforms, would not suffer any loss.

Land reform, finally, should be decentralised to local level by making use of the information and political support of the local political movements and of the NGOs who have more information on surplus land and on who the poor are.

(D) New approaches to R&D on the crops of the poor

National research programmes on traditional food crops must be considerably further strengthened. Three arguments justify this proposal. Firstly, a very large proportion of the African population depends on them for survival. Cassava provides a major source of dietary energy to 160 million people in the subhumid tropics, while millet and sorghum contribute about two thirds of caloric intake and close to half of the proteins in semi-arid Africa (CGIAR, 1992). Second, the history of research on such food crops is still short and the related national research programmes remain weak. Third, potential payoffs from research in this field appear substantial (ibid.). Thus, resources for NARs also need to be substantially strengthened.

Research will have to take into greater account the local factor endowments, agro-geological conditions, population density and farming practices. Particularly in semi-arid areas, farming systems research ought to focus on the development of low-resource, low-risk production systems. The development of yield-stabilising, stress-avoiding and drought-resistant varieties will be a key component of these systems, but low-cost soil and water conservation measures will be equally important. Research on the development of appropriate high-input packages will be relevant, particularly in densely populated areas but its adoption will depend heavily on the ability to remove distortions in both good and factor markets.

It will also be necessary to give greater attention to the specific needs of small farmers. There are, for instance, several HYV on shelf which are not used by the small farmers as they do not answer their needs. The key to the solution of this problem lies in the adoption of a farmer participatory research approach to enable an understanding of their circumstances, strategies and decisions on resource allocation (which are often ignored). In this way, their perspective on priority problems and on new appropriate techniques to solve them may be effectively integrated into new packages.

NOTE

1. Although production data may fail to adequately record subsistence production and may underreport levels even for commercially marketed crops (due to parallel market activities, cross-border smuggling, and so on), the gravity of the food crisis can be grasped by the notable increases in food imports and food aid.

12 Policy and Capital Market Constraints to the African Green Revolution: A Study of Maize and Sorghum Yields in Kenya, Malawi and Zimbabwe, 1960–91*

Paul Mosley**

I THE PROBLEM

As is well known, one element in the continuing underdevelopment of sub-Saharan Africa *vis à vis* other parts of the Third World is the continuing poor performance of the agricultural and, in particular, the food crop sectors. Both in *per capita* and per acre terms, food crop yields in Africa lag well behind performance elsewhere, and in *per capita* terms, food production at the beginning of the 1990s is actually lower than it was ten years ago (see Chapter 11). There can be few more urgent development priorities, whether in terms of relieving pressure on the balance of payments, releasing resources from the food-producing to the tradables sector, or promoting equity by raising the incomes of poor rural people, than finding a means of correcting this dismal performance. Most assessments of the possibility of a green revolution in Africa, however, have been profoundly sceptical, usually for some combination of the following reasons:

* A comprehensive version of this chapter, including complete data and sources, can be found in Mosley (1993b).

** The author wishes to thank Nikos Alexandratos, Lawrence Smith and Colin Thirtle for their most valuable ideas and suggestions.

- There does not exist a 'shelf' of high-yielding varieties of African crops that holds out the hope of increasing yields on anything like the same scale as was achieved in Asia in the 1960s and 1970s through the introduction of modern varieties of wheat and rice (see, for instance, Lipton, 1988).
- Because population densities are lower in Africa than in Asia, there is less *incentive* to intensify production methods, except in a few areas of high population concentration (Biswanger and Pingali, 1988).
- Soil, climate and irrigation potential are all much more hostile to the introduction of modern varieties in Africa than in Asia.

The first two of these arguments at least, however, are inadequate. A first indication of the range of available technologies in food crops has been given by Collinson (1989); this is expanded upon in Table 12.1 by providing a comparison between national average yields and those achieved in on-farm trials, both in dry and in rain-sufficient areas, for the three countries on which we shall focus later in this chapter.

So far as the second argument is concerned, a quick look at the available yield data suggests that even when population density figures are appropriately corrected for the carrying capacity of the land, the expected correlation between population density and food crop yields does not hold. As will be apparent from Table 12.2, if average grain yield levels are computed for those sub-Saharan countries defined by Biswanger and Pingali (1989) as having 'high', 'medium' and 'low' agroclimatic densities respectively, the result is the opposite to that expected, with the sample of low-density countries having on average slightly higher yields than the sample of high-density countries.

On the argument so far, then, yield increases are precluded neither by an absence of appropriate technologies nor by 'relative abundance of land', even supposing that to be an accurate description of the African condition. The fact remains, however, that performance has been poor, and we are therefore driven to look for an alternative explanation. The key to our approach will be the argument that the high-yielding technical packages described in Table 12.1 require amounts of money which local capital markets, operating under conditions of high risk, are ill-equipped to provide. Under such conditions any technical changes which occur are more likely to be policy-induced than spontaneously induced, as the conventional approach prefers, by population pressure. This argument will be pursued through detailed examination of three African countries: two towards the top end of the yield spec-

Table 12.1 Kenya, Zimbabwe and Malawi: maize and sorghum yields (tons/hectare) with different management practices

Kenya			
High potential areas:		Low potential areas:	
Kitale Agricultural Research Station		Katumani Agricultural Research Station	
Local seed	Hybrid seed with appropriate management	Local seed	Improved seed with appropriate management
Maize 2.1	8.6 (KSC511)	0.9	4.5 (KCB)
Sorghum		0.7	1.4*
Malawi			
High potential areas:		Low potential areas:	
Kasungu ARS (Average of 2 FAO trials)		Blantyre ADD average yields 1990/91	
Local seed	Hybrid seed with appropriate management	Local seed	Improved seed with appropriate management
Maize 1.1	3.0 (MH17)	0.7	2.3 (average all hybrids)
Sorghum		0.5	1.5
Zimbabwe			
High potential areas:		Low potential areas:	
		Matopos Research Station	
Local seed	Hybrid seed with appropriate management	Local seed	Improved seed with appropriate management
Maize 2.4	7.5 (SR52)	1.1	3.6 (R201)
Sorghum		0.6	2.9 (SV1)

Notes: Appropriate management is taken as: early planting, correct spacing, 40 kg. P_2O_5 and 40 Kg N per hectare, intensive weeding unless otherwise specified.

Source: Research stations as listed. Data relate to 1991 trials. Name of hybrid used in trial given in brackets. Except for Zimbabwe, Matopos, data are for on-farm trials only. In the trial marked,* unimproved seed was used with different management methods.

trum, as in Table 12.2 (Kenya and Zimbabwe), and the other, Malawi, towards the bottom, even though it is one of the most densely populated countries in Africa. These countries have been selected for analysis not only because of this contrast but more importantly because although no African country has really good crop yield data, the data for the three countries mentioned are better than the average in the sense that attempts are made to cross-check results by means of alternative estimation methods (for a full discussion of this issue see Mosley, 1993b).

Table 12.2 Grain yields in relation to population density in selected sub-Saharan African countries, 1988–90

	Grain yield per hectare (kg/ha; 1988–90 average)
'High-density countries'	
Kenya	1722
Ethiopia	1199
Nigeria	1172
Rwanda	1102
Malawi	1110
Sub-group average	1261
'Medium-density countries'	
Zimbabwe	1540
Ghana	1027
Tanzania	1391
Sierra Leone	1344
Gambia	1204
Sub-group average	1301
'Low-density countries'	
Zaire	758
Zambia	1841
Cameroon	1232
Madagascar	1918
Côte d'Ivoire	884
Sub-group average	1326

Notes: Population density is the 'agroclimatic labour density' defined as the number of agricultural workers per million calories of production potential, and is from Biswanger and Pingali (1989).

Source: Grain yield is 'average, all cereals' from FAO (1992b).

II ANALYTICAL FRAMEWORK

Consider a farm household which has three potential sources of income: growing a modern variety of food crop (Y_m), growing a traditional variety (Y_t), and off-farm income (Y_o). Total income is the sum of these three:

$$Y = Y_t + Y_m + Y_o \tag{1}$$

The factors of production are land (N), labour (L), and other inputs such as fertilisers (Z). Off-farm income is produced using labour alone,

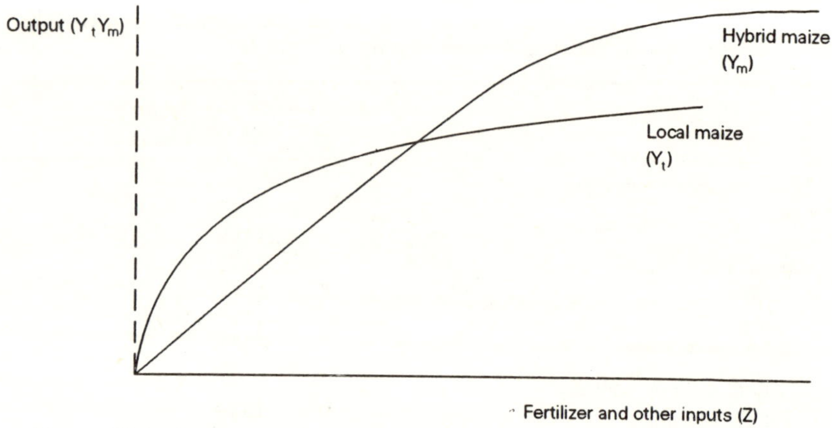

Figure 12.1 Response of traditional and modern varieties of maize and sorghum to fertilisers

Source: Alexandratas (1991).

whereas the traditional and modern varieties of the crop require all three inputs. But the production functions for the two varieties are very different. Modern varieties respond less to fertiliser and other inputs at low, and more at high, levels of application[1]. If for reasons of capital market imperfection, or otherwise, the farm household is constrained to low levels of 'other inputs', it may well find itself locked into production of the traditional variety, as in Figure 12.1.

We now consider the nature of the rural capital market, specifically as it bears on the possibility of purchasing 'recommended' technical packages such as those whose potential is illustrated by Table 12.1. The cost of these at current market prices in relation to prevailing average rural income levels in 1991 for important maize-producing areas in our sample countries was as set out in Table 12.3.

Will a farmer working 1.5 hectares – the average 'small farm' size in the countries to be examined – be able to finance such packages? For most, the answer is no. Given that the cost of planting *one hectare* of maize to modern varieties with recommended management practices, as shown in Table 12.3, ranges between one quarter and two thirds of total annual family income, the possibility of financing such purchases out of savings will necessarily be confined to a few individuals, which leaves purchases on credit as the only remaining option. Access to credit, in other words, is likely to be a crucial additional element in the production function for modern varieties. In

Table 12.3 Kenya, Malawi and Zimbabwe: cost of recommended technical packages in relation to average family income, 1991

	Cost (per hectare) of recommended technical package for maize	*Average annual rural family income 1991*
	(US$)/ha)	(US$)
Kenya (Katumani)	63	305
Malawi (Kasungu)	68	96
Zimbabwe	76	276

Notes: *Small farms* are defined as farms of less than 5 hectares (Kenya, Malawi); communal and resettlement areas (Zimbabwe).
Income in col. 2 is from all sources: gross marketed production divided by number of households, plus allowance for off-farm income and on-farm consumption.

Source: Cost of technical packages: as for Table 12.1.
Average rural incomes: Kenya: Government of Kenya (1991);
Zimbabwe, *Second Annual Report of Farm Management Data for Communal Area Farming Units, 1989/90* Farming Sector, MLARR Farm Management Research Section; Malawi, Conroy (1992).

each of the three countries investigated, and we suspect that the same applies for the rest of sub-Saharan Africa as well, the agricultural credit market comprises three parts: commercial banks who lend only to estate-owners and not to small farmers, informal money-lenders whose dealings are confined to short-term loans and often to their own village, and agricultural development banks – to which more recently have been added experimental 'quasi-formal' operations normally financed by aid donors or NGOs (on Malawi, see Chipeta and Mkandawire, 1992; on Zimbabwe, see Chimedza, 1990). Only the third of these, therefore, is a realistic option for most smallholders; but only for a minority, as agricultural development banks throughout Africa have suffered from bad project selection and chronic arrears problems, with the consequence that it has been difficult for them to sustain and develop their operations. Hence, credit is not available to all those willing to pay the market price for it.[2] In addition, such institutions will generally only lend to those possessing a secure title to their land, which immediately cuts out all those farming land in communal tenure and a majority of women farmers. Table 12.4 gives details of those taking, and wishing to take, credit for agricultural production in our three sample countries. For those willing to borrow but unable to do so, the capital market fails, and the propensity to purchase modern-

Table 12.4 Kenya, Zimbabwe and Malawi: proportion of smallholder farmers using and desiring crop loans (sample data)

	Zimbabwe	*Malawi*	*Kenya*
Proportion of smallholder farmers using credit	26	18	22
Proportion wishing to have credit	50	59	72

Source: Zimbabwe, Bratton (1986); Malawi, Conroy (1992); Kenya, World Bank (1989d).

variety packages will depend on prospective yields in relation to affordability (the gap between output and input prices), and in relation to alternative off-farm income opportunities.

The argument so far can be summed up by means of Figure 12.2. In part (a) of the diagram, individuals *FG* receive credit, but there is an excess demand *EF* for credit at the institutionally fixed interest rate: for these individuals, the credit market is 'missing'.[3] The number of individuals who have access to credit, together with the level of output and input prices, determines the position of the budget constraint, *XX*'. The optimal technology with this budget constraint is

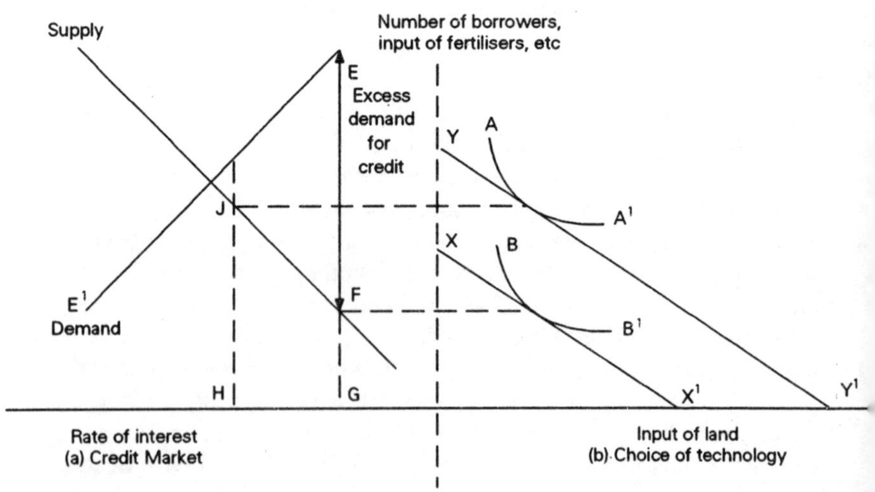

Figure 12.2 Credit market and technological choice in food crop agriculture

BB': mainly traditional varieties. Were the credit constraint to be relaxed to the extent of allowing a number of farmers *HJ* to be able to borrow – which paradoxically might be best achieved by *raising* the interest rate[4] for formal sector credit – this would move the budget constraint out- to *YY'*, and the optimal choice of technology would become *AA'*, consisting mainly of modern varieties. The same result could alternatively be achieved by *either*:

1. a relaxation in the liquidity constraint achieved through a general increase in output prices, or a general reduction in input prices; or
2. a shift in relative factor prices making 'fertiliser and other modern inputs' cheaper and land dearer (not shown in the figure), as in standard induced-innovation theory (e.g. Ruttan and Thirtle, 1989).

It will be clear from the analysis so far, therefore, that changes in relative input prices are not the only route, nor perhaps the most important, by which technical changes may be induced.

We now proceed with the formal specification of the model in order to produce hypotheses suitable for testing. The farm household is assumed to maximise total net expected income:

$$E(Y) = E(Y_t + Y_m + Y_o)$$

subject to the constraints:

Net income from
traditional varieties: $Y_t = P_o f(N, L, Z, W) - (P_n N_t + P_l L_t + P_z Z_t)$ (2a)

Net income from
modern varieties: $Y_m = P_o g(N, L, Z, C, W) - (P_n N_m + P_l L_m + P_z Z_m)$ (2b)

Off-farm income: $Y_o = h(L)$ (2c)

Cash-flow constraint
(all income to be financed from current income, savings or credit): $S + C + Y = P_n N + P_l L + P_z Z$ (2d)

where the notation employed is the following:

Y_t	output of traditional varieties
Y_m	output of modern varieties

Y_o	off-farm income
N	land acreage
$[N_t$:	allocated to traditional varieties,
N_m:	allocated to modern varieties]
L	labour input
$[L_t$:	allocated to traditional varieties,
L_m:	allocated to modern varieties]
Z	supplementary inputs capable of increasing yield [fertiliser, pesticides, irrigation water, etc.]
$[Z_t$:	allocated to traditional varieties,
Z_m:	allocated to modern varieties]
S	savings held by farmers
C	credit available to farmers
P_n, P_l, P_z	prices of land, labour and 'modern inputs' respectively
P_o	Price of grain paid to farmers (assumed constant as between modern and traditional variety)
$f(\ )$	production function for traditional varieties
$g(\ )$	production function for modern varieties

Maximising (1) subject to the constraints (2a) – (2d), the Lagrangean is

$$\theta = (Y_t + Y_m + Y_o) + \lambda_1 (Y_t - [P_o f(N, L, Z, W) -$$
$$(P_n N_t + P_l L_t + P_z Z_t] + \lambda_2 (Y_m - [P_o g(N, L, Z, C, W) -$$
$$(P_n N_m + P_l L_m + P_z Z_m)] + \lambda_3 (Y_o - h(L))$$
$$+ \lambda_4 (S + C + Y - (P_n N + P_l L + P_z Z) \qquad (3)$$

where λ_1 to λ_4 are the Lagrange multipliers attaching to the constraints (2a) to (2d) respectively. Taking partial derivatives of (3) with respect to the exogenous variables and setting them equal to zero, we reach the following first-order conditions for a maximum, assuming that an interior solution exists and that all constraints are binding:

$$\frac{\partial\theta}{\partial N} = \lambda_1 P_o \frac{\partial f}{\partial N} + \lambda_2 P_o \frac{\partial G}{\partial N} + \lambda_4 P_n = 0 \qquad (4a)$$

$$\frac{\partial\theta}{\partial L} = \lambda_1 P_o \frac{\partial f}{\partial N} + \lambda_2 P_o \frac{\partial G}{\partial N} + \lambda_4 P_l = 0 \qquad (4b)$$

$$\frac{\partial\theta}{\partial Z} = \lambda_1 P_o \frac{\partial f}{\partial N} + \lambda_2 \frac{\partial G}{\partial Z} + \lambda_4 P_l = 0 \quad (4c)$$

$$\frac{\partial\theta}{\partial C} = \lambda_2 \frac{\partial g}{\partial C} + \lambda_4 = 0 \quad (4d)$$

$$\frac{\partial\theta}{\partial W} = \lambda_1 P_o \frac{\partial f}{\partial W} + \lambda_2 \frac{\partial G}{\partial W} = 0 \quad (4e)$$

$$\frac{\partial\theta}{\partial \lambda_1} = Y_T - P_o f\,(N, L, Z, W) - (P_N N_t + P_l L_t + P_z Z_t) = 0 \quad (4f)$$

$$\frac{\partial\theta}{\partial \lambda_2} = Y_m - P_o g(n, L, Z, C, W) - (P_n N_m + P_l L_m + P_m Z_m) = 0 \quad (4g)$$

$$\frac{\partial\theta}{\partial \lambda_3} = Y_o - h(L) = 0 \quad (4h)$$

$$\frac{\partial\theta}{\partial \lambda_4} = S + C + Y - P_n N - P_l L - P_z Z \quad (4k)$$

Our ultimate objective is to find out how the variables in this system, and in particular, output per acre (Y/N) will respond when the equilibrium depicted by equations (4a) to (4k) is disturbed. We thus proceed to calculate the reduced form of the system. First, if one substitutes for all the λ terms in (4a) to (4e), (4e) becomes:

$$\frac{\partial f}{\partial N} = \frac{\left(\frac{\partial G}{\partial C} P_l - \frac{\partial f}{\partial W}\right)}{\partial G/\partial W} \quad P_o \frac{\partial f}{\partial W} \quad (5)$$

Differentiating (2a) and (2b):

$$\partial Y_m = \frac{\partial g}{\partial N} dN + \frac{\partial g}{\partial L} dL + \frac{\partial g}{\partial Z} dZ + \frac{\partial g}{\partial C} dC + \frac{\partial g}{\partial W} dW \quad (6a)$$

$$\partial Y_T = \frac{\partial f}{\partial N} dN + \frac{\partial f}{\partial L} dL + \frac{\partial f}{\partial Z} dZ + \frac{\partial f}{\partial W} dW \quad (6b)$$

Substituting from (5), and using the principle that

$$\frac{d(Y_m + Y_T)}{dN} = \frac{\partial Y_m}{\partial N} + \frac{\partial Y_T}{\partial N},$$

$$dY = \frac{\frac{\partial G}{\partial C}P_1 - \frac{\partial G}{\partial N}P_o \frac{\partial f}{\partial W}}{\partial G / \partial W} dN + \frac{\partial g}{\partial N} dN \tag{7}$$

or

$$\frac{dY}{dN} = \frac{\frac{\partial G}{\partial C}P_1 - \frac{\partial G}{\partial W}P_0 \frac{\partial f}{\partial W}}{\partial G/\partial W} + \frac{\partial g}{\partial N} \tag{7'}$$

Expression (7) is the relationship that we shall want to examine in the remainder of this chapter. In essence, it is a formalisation of Figure 12.2. Changes in income per acre of land (dY/dN) are induced not only by changes in relative factor prices and, in particular, the cost of labour, (P_l) but also by changes in the price of output in relation to purchased inputs (P_o), by the availability of credit and the response of modern varieties output to credit $\left(\frac{\partial G}{\partial C}\right)$, the productivity of hybrids in relation to traditional varieties and, of course, by weather $\left(\frac{\partial G}{\partial W}\right)$.

All of these except for the last two are potentially or actually policy variables, and to that extent, innovation can be seen as policy-induced. Table 12.5 lists these parameters with their meaning and expected sign, for future reference.

III EMPIRICAL INVESTIGATIONS

(A) The data

In Table 12.6 estimates of yield levels for the past 30 years are set out for Kenya, Malawi and Zimbabwe.[5] For sorghum, yield data are only available from the mid-1970s, but those data we have suggest that yields are almost invariably low by world standards (only surpassing 1 ton/hectare in an unusual year) and, if anything, on a declining trend

Table 12.5 Parameters that determine variation in crop yields (∂Y/∂N) in equations (7) and (7')

Parameter symbol	*Description*	*Introduced in equation*	*Expected sign of effect on Y/N*	*Empirical estimates displayed in table**
P_l	Cost of agricultural labour	(2d)	–	A-2 to A-4
P_o	Output price in relation to cost of fertiliser and other inputs	(2a, 2b)	+	A-2 to A-4
$\frac{\partial G}{\partial N}$	Yield increase derivable from modern varieties	(2b)	+	A-2 to A-4
$\frac{\partial f}{\partial W}, \frac{\partial G}{\partial W}$	Production response of traditional and modern varieties respectively to weather conditions	(4e)	+	A-2 to A-4
$\frac{\partial G}{\partial C}$	Responsiveness of modern varieties to credit	(4d)	+	A-2 to A-4

* Tables A-1 to A-4 refer to Mosley (1993b).

Table 12.6 Kenya, Zimbabwe and Malawi: maize and small grains yields (tons/hectare; five-year averages)

Period	*KENYA*		*MALAWI*		*ZIMBABWE*	
	Maize	*Sorghum*	*Maize*	*Sorghum*	*Maize*	*Sorghum*
1960–75	1.48	–	1.00	–	1.18	0.66
1966–70	1.75	–	1.12	–	(1.26)[a]	0.75
1971–5	1.90	–	1.05	–	1.84	0.69
1976–80	1.87	0.74	1.04	0.60	1.53	0.65
1981–5	1.78	0.80	1.15	0.76	1.40	0.45
1986–90	2.17	0.58	1.10	0.60	1.55	0.54
Rate of change 1986–90 in relation to 1960– 5 (% p.a.)	1.9	−2.2	0.6	0.0[b]	1.2	−1.7

Notes: – denotes data for full five-year period not available.
[a] Average of 1966 and 1970 only; [b] for intervening years, data on large farm yields only available.

Source: Mosley (1993b).

in all three countries. This finding parallels the trend reported for Western Africa by Matlon (1990). For maize, the trend is upward between the early 1960s and the late 1980s in all three countries, but in Malawi, insignificantly so. In Kenya, on the other hand, the trend growth rate of 1.9 per cent per year for maize yields rivals that achieved by India and other Asian countries during the same period. What we have, to be precise, are Asian rates of application of modern varieties in Kenya and Zimbabwe, Asian rates of productivity growth in Kenya only, but a very un-Asian and persisting differential in yields between large and small farms in all three countries. Table 12.7 shows this differential to be significant in both Kenya and Zimbabwe.

(B) Time-series regression analysis

We now examine, using regression methods, changes in yields over time in terms of the variables emerging from the model of the previous section and listed in Table 12.5. The results of this exercise are shown in Tables 12.8 and 12.9, using ordinary least squares analysis as there are no obvious simultaneities involved.

For maize, the results in Table 12.8 suggest that between 66 and 75 per cent of the variance in aggregate maize yields, according to country, can be explained by the variables included in our model, even in its present crude form without lags. Although all variables have the 'right' sign, in terms of the expectations set out in Table 12.5, the coefficients on the real agricultural wage rate and (for individual countries) the weather are insignificant. The ratio of output to input prices is significant in all three countries, as are credit disbursements to the small-farm sector in Kenya and Zimbabwe, suggesting that these policy-related variables have a role to play in explaining yields over and above the influence of relative factor prices. On the argument presented in Figure 12.2, this influence operates through the provision of liquidity which enables the farmer to overcome the obstacle of imperfection in the capital market. For sorghum, broadly the same story holds, but the equations are much less well estimated: the r^2s are below 25 per cent, and the index of sorghum prices and the ratio of hybrid to local seed yields, although of the right sign, are insignificant in all cases. Credit is a significant determinant of yields in the case of Kenya only. Indicators of input (seed and fertiliser applications) show much better correlation with the chosen independent variables than grain yields, suggesting that in some environments increased inputs of seed and fertiliser do not produce proportionate

Table 12.7 Summary table: large versus small farm yields (kg/ha), 1970–89

	Zimbabwe						*Kenya*		
	Maize			*Sorghum*			*Maize*		
	(1) *Commercial areas*	(2) *Communal areas*	(3) *Ratio (1)/(2)*	(1) *Commercial areas*	(2) *Communal areas*	(3) *Ratio (1)/(2)*	(1) *Rift Valley (mainly large farms)*	(2) *Other provinces (mainly small farms)*	(3) *Ratio (1)/(2)*
1970–4	4 103	573	7.2	873	426	2.1	2 621	1 460	1.8
1975–9	4 460	666	6.7	2 075	456	4.5	2 964	1 610	1.8
1980–4	3 620	586	6.2	2 005	342	5.8	2 517	1 460	1.7
1985–9	4 333	998	4.3	–	–	–	2 623	1 770	1.5
Whole period 1970–89	4 129	705	5.8	1 651	408	4.0	2 681	1 575	1.7

Source: Kenya: Central Bureau of Statistics. Other provinces in high potential area (col. 2) are: Central, Western and Nyanza. Zimbabwe: Government of the Republic of Zimbabwe (1989).

Table 12.8 Determinants of maize yields: results of regression analysis (dependent variable: average maize yield for each country (tons/ha) (ordinary least squares estimation)

Data set	*Period covered*	*Number of observations*	*Regression coefficient on independent variables: (Student's t-statistics under coefficient in brackets)*						r^2	*D.W.*
			Constant	*Real agricultural wage rate*	*Real maize price (index 1980=100)*	*Credit disbursements (1) (value of loans to small farmers in 1980 £'000)*	*Ratio of yields under hybrid to yields under local seed*	*Weather (average rainfall in mm at selected weather stations)*		
Kenya	1960–91	32	1.09 (6.72)	-0.0015 (0.48)	0.042* (2.17)	0.063* (2.06)	0.17* (2.12)	0.0019 (1.68)	0.75	1.5684
Malawi	1960–91	32	0.24 (2.59)	-0.013* (2.33)	0.0042** (8.37)	0.0016 (1.25)	0.13* (3.00)	0.0005 (0.05)	0.86	1.3073
Zimbabwe	1960–91	32	0.34 (1.32)	-0.012 (0.74)	0.048* (2.16)	0.018** (2.45)	0.13 (1.24)	0.0027 (0.19)	0.79	1.6004
Pooled data	1960–91	96	0.49* (4.60)	-0.013** (4.99)	0.027 (2.78)	0.08* (1.80)	0.14** (4.93)	0.004** (3.31)	0.66	(0.9426)
				relative factor prices	policy variables		biological conditions			

Notes: * denotes significance of a coefficient at the 5% level; ** denotes significance at the 1% level; A bracketed Durbin-Watson Statistic indicates that the residuals are serially correlated.

Source: Mosley (1993b).

Table 12.9 Determinants of sorghum yields: results of regression analysis (dependent variable: average sorghum yield for each country (tons/ha) (ordinary least squares estimation)

Data set	*Period covered*	*Number of observations*	*Regression coefficient on independent variables: (Student's t-statistics under coefficient in bracke's)*						r^2	*D.W.*
			Constant	*Real agricultural wage rate*	*Real sorghum price (index 1980=100)*	*Credit disbursements (1) (value of loans to small farmers in 1980 £'000)*	*Ratio of yields under hybrid to yields under local seed*	*Weather (average rainfall in mm at selected weather stations)*		
Kenya	1960–91	32	0.60*	–0.01*	0.029	0.012*	0.28	0.009	0.21	1.7781
			(2.33)	(1.97)	(0.96)	(2.17)	(2.18)	(0.52)		
Malawi	1960–91	32	–0.10	–0.031*	0.02	0.031	0.15	0.007	0.24	1.5323
			(0.38)	(1.73)	(1.29)	(1.73)	(1.11)	(0.25)		
Zimbabwe	1960–91	32	0.61*	–0.023	0.007	0.012	–0.032	0.0029	0.15	1.9632
			(2.80)	(1.61)	(0.38)	(0.60)	(0.37)	(1.05)		
Pooled data	1960–91	96	0.61**	–0.0023	0.042	–0.0012	0.012	0.010	0.06	1.6862
			(6.77)	(1.02)	(0.51)	(0.33)	(0.54)	(0.95)		
				relative factor prices		policy variables	biological conditions			

Notes: * denotes significance of a coefficient at the 5% level; ** denotes significance at the 1% level; A bracketed Durbin-Watson Statistic indicates that the residuals are serially correlated.

Source: Mosley (1993b).

increases in yields. This is a fundamental problem, and will be further taken up in a cross-section analysis below.

Two obvious econometric problems need to be corrected: the automatic and spurious correlation between those series that are not stationary (i.e. maize yields in Kenya and Zimbabwe, and credit disbursements in all the selected countries) and the Durbin-Watson statistics for Malawi and pooled data within the maize regression, which indicate the presence of serial correlation in the residuals. We tackle these problems by the simplest route, namely estimating the regression equation in first differences. If this is done, (Table 12.10) the Durbin-Watson statistics move sufficiently close to 2 to suggest that the problem of serial correlation has been eliminated. The r^2s (except for Malawi) increase also. The pattern of results is not greatly altered if the large farm areas of Kenya and Zimbabwe are excluded from the regression, except that the coefficient on the wage rate becomes (perversely but insignificantly) positive. On the superficial evidence of Table 12.10, an increase of 1 ton/hectare in maize can be produced *ceteris paribus* by either an increase of 32 percentage points in the ratio of maize to fertiliser prices or an increase of 71 000 in the number of small farmers receiving credit. But other things, of course, may not be equal: this is a single equation model, and although we have assumed no important simultaneities in the system, it would be important to ascertain the extent of feedbacks before using it as a guide to policy.

(C) Cross-section analysis: interactions within the credit market

The time-series relationships estimated in Tables 12.8 and 12.10, not surprisingly in view of the data problems involved, fall short of a desirable level of goodness of fit or, in all probability, of predictive power. It would therefore be of particular value to check them by cross-section methods wherever possible; however, this is not possible for many of the variables in Table 12.6, since, under the marketing systems prevailing in all three countries, input and output prices, at least on the official market, are the same for all farm families at any given time. However, conditions in credit markets do vary between regions and countries, hence the component of the model which deals with the capital market can be checked in this way; and if one takes a realistic view and goes beyond a simple measurement of conditions prevailing in *formal* credit markets to examine the *total* availability of credit (see Mosley, 1993b) cross-section analysis becomes a necessity, as we do not have time-series data on conditions in African

Table 12.10 Determinants of maize yields: results of regression analysis

(dependent variable: year on year change in average maize yield $\frac{Q}{A_t} - \frac{Q}{A_{t-1}}$ for each country).
Ordinary least squares estimation

Data set	*Period covered*	*Number of observations*	*Regression coefficient on independent variables: (Student's t-statistics under coefficient in brackets)*						r^2	*D.W.*
			First difference in:							
			Constant	*Real agricultural wage rate*	*Maize/fertiliser price ratio*	*Value of loans to small farmers (1980 £'000)*	*Ratio of yields under hybrid to yields under local seed*	*Weather (average rainfall in mm at selected weather stations)*		
Kenya	1960–91	31	–0.007 (0.01)	–0.003 (0.18)	0.033* (1.80)	–0.012** (3.35)	0.12* (1.61)	0.0077 (0.67)	0.69	2.0516
Malawi	1960–91	31	0.009 (0.02)	–0.01 (0.13)	0.38** (8.38)	0.048 (0.61)	0.17** (4.33)	0.0006 (0.87)	0.84	2.2168
Zimbabwe	1960–91	31	–0.0022 (0.037)	–0.0025 (0.32)	0.035* (1.54)	0.052* (1.88)	0.23* (2.11)	0.001 (0.32)	0.83	2.1416
Pooled data	1960–91	93	–0.005 (0.24)	–0.0014** (4.77)	0.031** (3.81)	0.014* (2.50)	0.27** (7.44)	0.0003 (0.33)	0.80	
Pooled data, small farm areas only[a]	1960–91	93	0.0022** (0.11)	0.002** (6.18)	0.003** (3.85)	0.015** (2.56)	0.028 (0.24)	0.0004 (0.47)	0.62	2.5225
			relative factor prices		policy variables		biological conditions			

Notes: * denotes significance of a coefficient at the 5% level; ** denotes significance at the 1% level; a bracketed Durbin-Watson Statistic indicates that the residuals are serially correlated.

[a] The data set used for this regression is: Zimbabwe, communal areas; Kenya, maize farms outside Rift Valley Province; Malawi, all maize farms (for data and sources, see Table 12.7).

informal credit markets. This section takes a few halting steps in this direction.

We begin by comparing yields in districts which have similar natural resource environments but differential access to credit. This is attempted for Malawi and Zimbabwe in Table 12.11 on the basis of cross-section data for 1990–1 and 1989–90 respectively. We discover that, for these two years, between the two smallholder regions in the high-rainfall natural region IIa of Zimbabwe, the Chiweshe area, which had better access to credit, had markedly higher yields. In Malawi, the two central Agricultural Development Divisions of Kasungu and Lilongwe had higher maize yields and better access to smallholder credit than elsewhere in the country, even though they had lower average rainfall than any other part of the country except for Ngabu in the South. These figures do not, of course, prove that access to credit is the crucial causal factor in determining yields, as other potential causes have not been held constant, but they do constitute additional evidence for the proposition that the capital market constraint should be taken seriously.

With regard to the relationship between the quasi-formal and the informal parts of the credit market, the key issue which needs to be resolved is: How is the relationship between credit flows and farmers' yields affected by the existence of a large and thriving population of rural money-lenders? The relationship between formal- and informal-sector credit volumes is not pre-determined (as is demonstrated in detail in Mosley, 1993b): the advent of a quasi-formal lender may cause informal money-lenders to shrink their volume of lending (because they 'surrender' business they have lost) or to increase it (because they decide to compete aggressively by venturing into new markets, and by reducing their profit margin among existing borrowers, and because of income effects). Which of the two effects predominates is of considerable empirical importance. Preliminary fieldwork results from Kenya and Zimbabwe suggest that in practice, the relationship may often be complementary rather than competitive. Table 12.12, derived from interviews with a small number of money-lenders in regions where quasi-formal institutions had recently started to provide credit, shows that their response was more frequently to expand their volume of business than to reduce it.

Given the small size of the sample, these results can only be taken as illustrative; our research is currently in the process of expanding the sample size. It does appear, however, that in two of the countries under examination the relationship between the quasi-formal and in-

Table 12.11 Malawi and Zimbabwe: smallholder and sorghum yields in relation to credit inflows and natural resource conditions

Malawi (1990/1 cropping season)								
Districts:	*Karonga*	*Mzuzu*	*Kasungu*	*Lilongwe*	*Salima*	*Liwonde*	*Blantyre*	*Ngabu*
Average yield: Maize	1.02	1.23	1.34	1.24	1.26	1.02	0.88	0.71
(tons/ha) Sorghum	0.48	–	–	–	0.65	0.32	0.49	0.71
% of smallholders received loans from smallholder agricultural credit administration	29	24	30	31	23	15	16	12
Average rainfall 1979/80 to 1990/91 (mm)	981	1422	848	956	1199	1054	1047	820

Source: Smallholder Agricultural Credit Administration; *Malawi Agricultural Statistics* 1992 Edition; Malawi Meteorological Office.

Zimbabwe (1989/90 cropping season)						
Sample area:	*Buhera*	*Chirau*	*Chirumanzo*	*Chiweshe*	*Nyajena*	*Zvishava*
Average yields: Maize	1.16	1.23	2.16	2.27	0.34	0.98
(tons/ha) Sorghum	0.64	–	–	–	–	–
% of householders received Agricultural Finance Corporation loan 1989/90	–	12.0	51.8	51.8	3.3	..
Natural Region	IV	IIa	III	IIa	IV	V
(Annual rainfall mm)	450–650	750–1000	600–800	750–1000	450–650	<450

Source: GRZ (1992).

Table 12.12 Two regions of Kenya and Zimbabwe: money-lenders responses to the question 'Has your volume of lending increased in the last year'?

Kenya (Chogoria)		Zimbabwe (Chiweshe)	
Yes	82%	Yes	73%
No	18%	No	27%
Among those answering Yes:		Among those answering Yes:	
Reduced interest rates	71%	Reduced interest rates	65%
Actively looked for new borrowers	56%	Actively looked for new borrowers	77%
Sample size	17		22

Notes: In both of the districts under study, a quasi-formal credit organisation (Presbyterian Church of East Africa, Zimbabwe Agricultural Finance Corporation) had set itself up or expanded its operations in 1991/2.

Source: Interviews in Chogoria (Meru district, Kenya) and Chiweshe (Central Mashonaland province, Zimbabwe), October 1992.

formal credit market may be complementary rather than competitive, and if this is true, the variable defined as C in the preceding analysis (formal sector credit disbursement) may be directly, and not inversely, related to the overall availability of credit to the rural economy.

(D) Inter-country comparisons

Although our research suggests that policy and capital market variables do exert an influence on grain productivity, that influence varies, on the evidence in Tables 12.8–12.10, from country to country, and it is important to consider why. In particular, the influence of both the maize/fertiliser price ratio and credit disbursement on maize yields is both lower and less significant in Malawi than in Kenya and Zimbabwe. Indeed, in Malawi the classical 'modernising' stimuli of fertiliser, credit and a stimulative price policy were made available on an increasing scale, as in Kenya and Zimbabwe, during the 1980s, and yet the apparent response of maize yields (Table 12.6) has been insignificant. Can the variables of our model explain this paradox?

So far as we can assess, the non-policy variables of Table 12.5 – weather, wage rates and the yield increase derivable from modern varieties – do not exhibit trends sufficiently different in Malawi from the other countries to provide a satisfactory explanation of Malawi's inferior performance. We are therefore thrown back on two possible explanations which lie 'outside' our model. The first is that the hybrids available to Malawian smallholders do not taste or mill as well as local varieties, in spite of their higher yield, so that the incentive to use hybrids is less than appears from the significant difference in productivity; this is argued with considerable vigour by Kydd (1989) and Smale et al. (1991). For this reason, hybrid utilisation is growing from a much lower base, being about 30 per cent for Malawi in comparison with over 70 per cent in both Kenya and Zimbabwe. The other is that a tendency for *hybrid* yields to rise for the reasons given by our model is counterbalanced by a falling trend in *local* maize yields caused by the declining fertility of the soil. This cuts the link between modern inputs and overall yields in countries such as Malawi where local maize usage is significant. Available data (Mosley, 1993b) show that the demand constraints mentioned by Kydd and Smale have not stopped sales of hybrid seed in Malawi from doubling between 1986 and 1991 and from growing at a faster rate than in the other two countries. Moreover, farmers growing *hybrid* maize seed in Malawi experienced increasing yields over the 1980s, by contrast with the experience of the country as a whole.[6] However, the correlations between yield and use of modern inputs (seed and fertiliser) for Malawi as a whole are much lower than in Kenya and Zimbabwe, partly because local maize does not respond to fertiliser as well as it does elsewhere but much more because the yields on unfertilised maize are falling, due to a decline in the fertility of the soil, at least as fast as hybrid yields are rising. A favourable stance of price and credit policy has not, so far, been able to override this handicap.

IV IMPLICATIONS

It is common ground that recent economic development in sub-Saharan Africa has been stunted by comparison with other regions of the developing world, and that the poor performance of the food crop sector has much to do with this. However, the arguments presented in this chapter warrant a reconsideration of the notion that Africa is doomed to low crop yields by low population density and factor price ratios which, as a consequence, are unfavourable to the adoption of high-yielding varieties (HYV). We have argued from first principles, and empirical analysis appears to provide confirmation, that in an envi–

ronment where the investment required for the effective adoption of HYVs is large in relation to the farmers' income, access to credit and the output/input price ratio will be key determinants of the adoption rate. Since both are heavily influenced by government policies and institutions, innovation should appropriately be seen as policy-induced rather than merely induced by naturally occurring input scarcities.

A major policy offensive has, of course, been recently launched across the entire developing world by the World Bank under the name of 'structural adjustment', aimed at raising productivity by liberalising output and input markets; but its results in relation to African agriculture appear to have been scanty (Lipton, 1990) and the analysis of this chapter may help us to see why: for liberalisation, in terms of the variables in Table 12.6, administers a boost by raising output prices but deals a negative shock as well by making inputs such as fertiliser more expensive for small farmers. In relation to the capital market, it simply bypasses the main problem; namely, in an inherently imperfect capital market many small farmers will not be able to acquire finance even for profitable projects. In such a market, liberalisation will not improve access at the bottom end, nor, self-evidently, will a policy of simply pumping out state-subsidised loans in the general direction of small farmers. What is needed are institutions specially designed for the function of lending to small farmers without collateral and achieving high recovery rates even in conditions of considerable climatic uncertainty. Luckily, many new institutions of this type, including some in Africa, have shown promise in walking this difficult tightrope (Yaron, 1991; Hulme, 1990).

In conclusion, it is interesting to make an explicit comparison between the countries examined in this chapter, where according to the general scholarly consensus the green revolution is still to come, and those of South Asia where it has already occurred. Such a comparison is made in Table 12.13 in respect of the independent variables featured in Table 12.6, plus one or two others. It may be noted first of all that the difference in yield growth between India and Pakistan on the one hand, and at least Kenya and Zimbabwe on the other, is not dramatic: to speak of revolution in the one place and non-revolution in the other would appear inappropriate. Secondly, there is little significant difference between the African and Asian countries considered with regard to the yield gap between traditional and modern varieties, or with regard to input/output price ratios. In these respects, it is not appropriate to speak of either 'the natural environment' or

Table 12.13 Green revolutions compared: Africa versus South Asia

	India	*Pakistan*	*Kenya*	*Malawi*	*Zimbabwe*
Growth of grain output per hectare (per annum) 1988–90 in relation to 1961–3	3.6	1.5	2.5	0.6	2.4
Output per hectare (kg) 1988–90 average	1 861	1 744	1 722	1 110	1 540
Percentage of farmers receiving institutional loans (1990)	38	–	22	18	26
MV/TV yield ratio without fertilisers	1.2:1 (wheat) 1:1 (rice)	1.4:1 (wheat)	1.3:1 (maize)	1.1:1 (maize)	1.2:1 (maize)
Area irrigated (% of area under arable and permanent crops, 1990)	25.4	78.2	2.1	0.9	7.8
Fertiliser price/maize price ratio (1988)	–	–	4.5	10.3	1.9
Large farm/small farm yields (all cereals 1987)	0.9	1.1	2.9	–	3.1

Source: Yields (rows 1 and 2) and irrigated area (row 5), FAO (1987, 1991).
Large/small farm yield ratios (row 7): India: Singh (1990).
Fertiliser price/maize price ratio (row 6): Lele et al. (1989).
Percentage of farmers receiving institutional loans (row 3): NABARD and Table 12.3.
MV/TV yield ratio (row 4): Singh (1990).

'policy' as being more favourable to technical progress in South Asia than in Africa.

There are differences between Asia and Africa, however, in respect of area irrigated, the yield differential between large and small farmers, and the proportion of farmers receiving institutional credit. Minor irrigation, HYV packages and credit are widely available to South Asian farmers; they are much less within the reach of African farmers, and such green revolution as there has been in Africa is therefore very much more confined to large farms. An appropriately financed downward extension of the credit and agricultural inputs markets would therefore appear to be a major policy priority for African governments and international aid donors in the 1990s. As is illustrated by the experience of India and Indonesia, whose agricultural prospects were widely dismissed in the 1960s but which are now net food exporters in the 1990s,[7] it is not appropriate to despair of African prospects in this area simply because past performance has been sluggish. Appropriate policies, taking due note of innate imperfections in rural finance and input markets, may yet be able to bring about a turnaround of similar magnitude.

NOTES

1. Data suggesting that yield curves may cross in this way are presented by Conroy (1992), Table 10.32 for Malawian maize, Nadar and Faught (1984) for Kenyan maize, and Osmanzai (1991) for sorghum and millet in Zimbabwe. Contradictory evidence is, however, presented by Smale et al. (1991) in respect of maize trials in Malawi, who suggested that hybrid yields may be superior at all levels of complementary input.
2. Desai and Mellor (1993, Table 3) estimate that institutional credit is only available to 4.4 per cent of African famers, by comparison with 13.5 per cent in South Asia, 34 per cent in East Asia and 23 per cent in Latin America.
3. This may result from the rationing of households in the credit market because of potential default (Stiglitz and Weiss, 1981). The demand curve, EE', is defined by the rate of return which farmers expect to be able to earn on investment in modern inputs. The curve drawn in Figure 12.2 should be interpreted stochastically, as an average of the subjective expectations of all farmers; for risk-loving farmers it will be further to the north-west than for risk-averse farmers (Binswanger and Sillers, 1983).
4. Or by reforms facilitating farmers' access to the informal credit market.
5. A full discussion of data sources containing details of the estimation methods used and a commentary on the degree of confidence that can be placed on each of them may be found in Mosley (1993b).
6. The correlation coefficients (r^2) between rates of fertiliser and overall maize yields are:
   Kenya 0.92
   Malawi 0.74
   Zimbabwe 0.91
   Data as for Tables 12.8–12.10.
7. For these his cases, see respectively Singh (1990) and Booth (1990).

13 The Impact of Macroeconomic Adjustment on Incomes, Health and Nutrition: Sub-Saharan Africa in the 1980s*

David E. Sahn

I INTRODUCTION

Most countries in sub-Saharan Africa have embarked on a process of stabilisation and structural adjustment. This has been made necessary by unsustainable balance of payments and budget deficits. The major policy instruments associated with adjustment have been devaluation of the exchange rate, restructuring of government expenditures and related fiscal restraint, monetary discipline and rationalisation of interest rates, as well as reforming (and sometimes shrinking) the state and state-run institutions. In turn, concern has been raised that such measures could have deleterious nutritional and health consequences. Specifically, it has been argued that the prospect of reduced spending on social services and subsidies enjoyed by the poor, declining wages and employment, and higher prices of tradable staple foods giving rise to falling real incomes, constitutes a threat to the most vulnerable groups. In order to address these concerns more fully, this chapter is structured as follows.

Section II begins with a discussion of government expenditure policy during adjustment. Section III then focuses on the implications of market reforms for household incomes. Recognising that the provision of state services and the level of incomes are not the only factors that

* The material presented in this chapter draws heavily on three papers: Dorosh and Sahn (1993); Sahn and Bernier (1993); Sahn (1993).

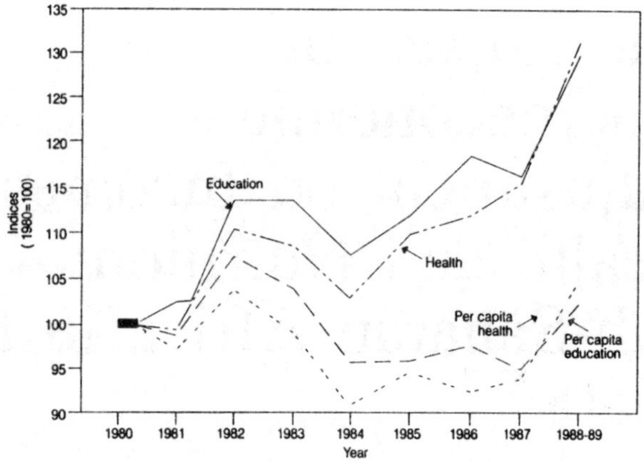

Figure 13.1 Real health and education expenditures: total per capita expenditure

Notes: Education data covers Burkina Faso, Ethiopia, the Gambia, Ghana, Kenya, Lesotho, Liberia, Madagascar, Malawi, Niger, Sierra Leore, Togo, Uganda, Zambia, Botswana, Mauritius, Swaziland, Zimbabwe, Cameroon and Nigeria. Per capita series excludes Sierra Leore.

Health data cover Burkina Faso, Ethiopia, Kenya, Liberia, Madagascar, Malawi, Niger, Rwanda, Uganda, Zambia, Botswana, Mauritius, Swaziland, Zimbabwe, Cameroon and Nigeria.

Source: World Bank (undated data set) Africa Tables: Sahn (1992).

affect health and nutritional outcomes, Section IV addresses the issue of the impact of adjustment on time allocation, income sources and income control. A concluding section presents some of the dilemmas that policy makers face in incorporating welfare concerns into what is arguably a non-discretionary process of economic adjustment.

II SOCIAL SECTOR EXPENDITURES

The state assumes a critical role in the social sector, owing to the propensity for market failures. In considering the impact of adjustment on health and nutrition, as mediated through public expenditure policy, the salient issues are how the level and efficiency of nutrition- and health-related public expenditures change during adjustment, and the role of the private sector in responding to the needs of the poor.

The actual experience of adjusting countries in Africa on these fronts is highly variable. Nonetheless, an unweighted average of social sector spending among African countries during the 1980s indicates that health and education expenditures were on the rise during the 1980s. The rapid pace of population growth, however, resulted in a stagnating level of per capita spending (Figure 13.1). The level of health and education expenditures as a percentage of GDP during the 1980s on the other hand remained stable (Sahn, 1992).

The fact that adjustment has, in general, not resulted in a declining budgetary role for the state in delivering social services, however, says little about the efficiency of such expenditures and their link with outcomes. This is due, firstly, to the overriding importance of the intrasectoral allocation of resources. In this regard, the evidence is clear: social sector services have been and continue to be skewed. Favour has been accorded to the provision of secondary and university education, and health services were biased toward secondary and tertiary health care.

To amplify on this point, Table 13.1 presents the distribution of spending by education level for the most recent year for which data were available. Some caution in examining this table is required since the shares to various levels of education were limited to those distinguishable by level; general administrative and other expenses that were not allocatable were netted out of the calculation. The underlying assumption, therefore, was that the unallocatable shares would be distributed proportionately to those that were allocatable.

The results indicate a wide variation in the allocatable shares destined for primary education. The share of total education expenditures, summing recurrent and development spending, allocated to primary education ranges from a low of 31.3 per cent in Botswana to a high of 85.9 per cent in Ghana. When this information is disaggregated, at the low end of the spectrum we find that in Uganda only 29.9 per cent of recurrent expenditures were for primary education. Guinea-Bissau's 76.3 per cent showed the highest share of recurrent expenditures destined for primary education, followed by Chad. For most countries, however, the share was between 40 and 50 per cent, including for Burkina Faso, Cameroon, Lesotho and Zambia. Furthermore, biases that existed in terms of recurrent expenditures were generally worse for investment.

Similarly, government-run health ministries in sub-Saharan Africa are often inefficient and wasteful of resources, even in the face of severe total budget constraints. One study reports that an astonishingly low $7.00 for each $100 spent on drugs is used effectively

Table 13.1 Shares of education expenditures allocated to different levels (most recent year)

Country	Type	*Distribution of allocatable shares* Primary	Secondary	Higher	Total allocated	Unallocated	Year
				Per cent			
Benin	Both	54.4	27.8	17.7	79.0	21.0	1988
Botswana	Both	31.3	45.0	23.7	96.1	3.9	1991
Burkina Faso	Recurrent	45.7	24.5	29.8	94.0	6.0	1990
Cameroon	Recurrent	42.1	25.0	32.9	100.0	0.0	1992
Cape Verde	Recurrent	65.1	(34.9)		100.0	0.0	1986
Central African Republic	Both	54.0	25.0	21.0	100.0	0.0	1990
Chad	Recurrent	68.1	28.7	3.2	75.2	24.8	1988
Côte d'Ivoire	Recurrent	52.0	32.5	15.5	100.0	0.0	1990
	Development	27.4	52.8	19.8	100.0	0.0	1990
	Both	51.8	32.7	16.5	100.0	0.0	1990
Gambia	Both	48.8	39.3	11.9	84.0	16.0	1989
Ghana	Both	85.9	(14.1)		100.0	0.0	1988
Guinea-Bissau	Recurrent	76.3	21.3	2.4	71.2	28.8	1989
Kenya	Recurrent	57.1	24.7	18.3	94.0	6.0	1990
	Development	0.0	27.4	72.6	83.5	16.5	1990
	Both	49.8	25.1	25.2	92.6	7.4	1990
Lesotho	Recurrent	44.4	32.5	23.1	86.5	13.5	1987
Madagascar	Both	(72.0)		28.0	100.0	0.0	1990
Malawi	Recurrent	58.0	16.3	25.6	81.5	18.5	1988
	Development	4.1	21.5	74.4	87.4	12.6	1988
	Both	45.7	17.5	36.8	82.8	17.2	1988
Mozambique	Recurrent – Total	37.2	42.7	20.1	100.0	0.0	1990

	Development – Total	8.2	59.9	31.9	100.0	0.0	1990
	Recurrent – Including aid	50.0	35.6	14.4	100.0	0.0	1990
Nigeria	Both	(81.2)		18.8	100.0	0.0	1984
Senegal	Recurrent	48.9	25.5	25.5	94.0	6.0	1991
Tanzania	Recurrent	62.1	24.2	13.7	91.2	8.8	1986
	Development	15.9	63.7	20.4	76.1	23.9	1986
	Both	52.7	32.7	14.7	87.9	12.1	1986
Uganda	Recurrent	29.9	51.0	19.1	89.1	10.9	1989
	Development	41.6	14.6	43.8	93.0	7.0	1989
	Both	32.9	42.0	25.2	90.0	10.0	1989
Zaire	Both	(66.0)		34.0	100.0	0.0	1986
Zambia	Recurrent	45.0	30.9	24.1	90.1	9.9	1986
Zimbabwe	Both	55.3	30.4	14.3	95.8	4.2	1990
	Recurrent	51.3	29.2	19.5	89.8	10.2	
	Development	16.2	40.0	43.8	90.0	10.0	
	Both	49.3	30.6	20.2	90.9	9.1	

Source: Sahn and Bernier (1993).

(Serageldin et al., 1992). This inefficiency comes in numerous forms. At the extreme is the pilferage and theft of equipment and supplies, particularly pharmaceuticals which are in short supply. Poor management of the health care system, however, is the more pervasive problem. This includes problems such as bypassing lower-level facilities where care should be provided, in part due to poor health care practices and in part due to the distortion of overinvesting in secondary and tertiary care facilities; inadequate procurement procedures that contribute to expiration and spoilage of pharmaceuticals; and overstaffing of facilities, especially with non-technical workers, which further inflates the wage bill relative to other forms of expenditures (Serageldin et al., 1992). But perhaps most importantly, inefficiency in the health care system derives from inappropriate priorities: emphasising curative care instead of prevention and the delivery of basic services.

To illustrate this point, Table 13.2 clearly shows that promotive/preventive care was discriminated against in most countries for which data are available. In Burundi, for example, the disproportionate share of the budget allocated to hospitals has resulted in inadequate health care staffing at the primary levels. In Chad, health centres and preventive medical care each received 19 per cent of the recurrent budget in 1988, while twice that amount went to hospitals, with an additional 23 per cent destined for management. Even in Angola during the period it was under the tutelage of Cuba and the Soviet Union, there was a marked skewing of current expenditures and investment toward hospital services, primarily in Luanda and to a lesser extent in other urban areas.

Côte d'Ivoire also shows a strong curative care bias in the public health system. Almost 54 per cent of total recurrent expenditures and 61 per cent of development expenditures were allocated to the tertiary level in 1990, compared to only 35 and 22 per cent of recurrent and development expenditures, respectively, allocated to the primary level. This contributed to a variety of problems, including technical inefficiencies such as the channelling of demand towards the highest level of the health infrastructure. The excessive number of patients seen in hospitals, often by physicians instead of more appropriate paramedics, contributed to these inefficiencies. Furthermore, the fiscal costs of such misallocation was shouldered almost entirely by the government, as less than 6 per cent of the tertiary level expenses were recovered through fees paid by patients.

Likewise, in Madagascar, during 1991, 42.7 per cent of recurrent expenditures was spent on secondary and tertiary health services, with

Table 13.2 Shares of health expenditures allocated to different levels (most recent year)

Country	*Level/type*	*Share (%)*	*Year*
Angola	Primary – Development	6.0	1992
	Secondary – Development	20.0	1992
	Tertiary – Development	28.5	1992
	Other – Development	45.5	1992
Burundi	Primary – Development	18.0	1983–7
	Hospital – Development	70.0	1983–7
	Other – Development	12.0	1983–7
	Primary – Recurrent	20.0	1983–7
	Hospital – Recurrent	80.0	1983–7
Central African Republic	Curative – Recurrent	97.0	1988
	Preventive – Recurrent	3.0	1988
Chad	Preventive – All	19.0	1988
	Primary – All	19.0	1988
	Hospital – All	39.0	1988
	Administration – All	23.0	1988
Côte d'Ivoire	Primary – Recurrent	34.9	1990
	Secondary – Recurrent	11.5	1990
	Tertiary – Recurrent	53.5	1990
	Primary – Development	22.0	1990
	Secondary – Development	17.0	1990
	Tertiary – Development	61.0	1990
Ghana	Primary – Recurrent	23.0	1990
	Primary – Development	44.1	1989
Kenya	Curative – All	50.2	1990
	Preventive – All	10.3	1990
	Hospital – All	8.2	1990
	Rural – All	18.8	1990
	Other – All	11.3	1990
Lesotho	Hospital – Recurrent	70.0	1984
	Primary – Recurrent	14.0	1984
Madagascar	Primary – Recurrent	18.3	1991
	Secondary/tertiary – Recurrent	42.7	1991
	Administration/Other – Recurrent	39.0	1991
Malawi	Preventive – All	6.8	1988
	Curative – All	73.2	1988
	Administration/Training – All	20.1	1988
Mozambique	Preventive – Recurrent	64.0	1989
	Curative – Recurrent	36.0	1989
Nigeria	Preventive – Recurrent	20.0	1985
	Curative – Recurrent	80.0	1985
Senegal	Hospital – Recurrent	42.0	1990
	Other – Recurrent	58.0	1990

continued on page 280

Table 13.2 continued

Country	*Level/type*	*Share (%)*	*Year*
Tanzania	Hospital – All	68.0	1991
	Preventive – All	6.0	1991
	Other – All	26.0	1991
Uganda	Preventive – Total – All	60.0	1989
	Preventive – Government – All	33.0	1989
	Preventive – Donor – All	83.0	1989
Zimbabwe	Administrative – All	6.6	1988
	Medical care – All	80.7	1988
	Preventive – All	12.0	1988
	Research – All	0.8	1988

Source: Sahn and Bernier (1993).

an additional 39.0 per cent spent on administration and other services. This left only 18.3 per cent of the budget designated for primary care. Zimbabwe too had a top-heavy and urban-oriented health system, with curative services comprising a disproportionate amount of the budget.

While it would be possible to recount similar experiences elsewhere, the fact is that most government-sponsored health services in Africa have been directed to patient care in hospitals, laboratory services, and related drug costs for patients. The returns as measured in terms of indicators of population-based statistics on morbidity, mortality and nutrition are low in relation to expenditures. Conversely, African governments have met with only very limited success in performing most public health services, notably health education and preventive care, including prenatal care and family planning. The possible exception is the relative success of immunisation campaigns and efforts at promoting the use of rehydration therapies in certain countries, or regions therein.

The skewness of the intrasectoral allocation of expenditures raises an important question: Has adjustment changed the priorities of the state? Reviewing the evaluation of budgetary priorities in the social sector in Africa provides little encouragement in response to this question. While there is some evidence that social sector adjustment programmes, such as in Ghana, Niger, Malawi and Zimbabwe, have been successful in reorienting social services toward the poor as a component of their efforts at economic reform, their accomplishments stand in contrast to most of the experience which demonstrates that economic reform has failed to effectively tackle the technical inefficiencies in health and education spending. The biggest constraint to massive restructuring is political, since the gains in technical efficiency will come at the expense primarily of the elite who were responsible for, and have benefited from, existing distortions. It is hypothesised that serious efforts at reform will therefore only occur when such change is incorporated into a new incentive structure of policy makers.

Indications that a reorientation of available resources is equally important – and in many cases is more critical to adjustment improving health and nutrition – as simply maintaining levels of spending, carries a number of implications. First, given our findings that government spending contributes to an overvalued exchange rate, as will be discussed in greater detail below, there is a convincing case to be made for a smaller role of the state in the economy. This argument will remain strong, at least until the role of the state is dramatically redefined and takes on a very different form than that assumed in recent years. Second, in considering how to revitalise the social sector, it is important not to lay blame on the process of adjustment for the dismal condition of the health and education systems extant in African countries. Rather, it is better to recognise the scope for, and limitations of, the adjustment process in ameliorating the institutional deficiencies in the social welfare system. Realising that the inadequacy of the social sector is the result of years of neglect and rent-seeking, and that years of restructuring will be required to rectify distortions, is the first step. Identifying the additional human and financial resources, both as part of and separate from adjustment operations, which will be required to address the limited quality and quantity of social sector services is the second step. This latter step, however, will only be feasible in a reform-minded economy where the role of the state, and its excess, have been reoriented.

A final point on the role of the state in the provision of social services is that while the level and intrasectoral distribution of government budgets are important, so too is the way that policy facilitates or impedes the role of the private sector. Evidence in this regard indicates a prominent role for privately provided health care and education in Africa. In Zimbabwe, for example, private care providers accounted for around 37 per cent of health expenditures. In Malawi, approximately 45 per cent of the country's health services are made up of church-related and other private voluntary health organisations. Vogel (1988) reports that in some countries (Sudan and Guinea, for instance) expenditures on private care actually exceeded public sector expenditures, while the value of private sector payments in Benin was greater than that of public recurrent expenditures. Another recent study by Serageldin et al. (1992) also indicated that mean private spending was substantially higher than aggregate government health expenditures in Côte d'Ivoire and Ghana. In the case of Burundi, 30 per cent of primary health care facilities were run by religious missionaries. They were in part subsidised by external charities, although user charges covered most operating costs. This was in contrast with the state-run system where only about 10 per cent of operating costs were recovered.

While evidence on the share of education expenditures assumed by the private sector is more limited than for health care, a similar story nonetheless emerges. In both health and education, however, it is important to recognise that the prominence of the private sector in part reflects the failings of the state. As a consequence, the informal and indigenous institutions grew to fill the void left by the state. Nonetheless, the challenge is to redefine an appropriate partnership, recognising the valuable contribution of the private sector and informal institutions. This suggests focusing attention not only on the reform of public expenditure policy, but on the entire legal and regulatory framework in which the complementary private sector operates.

III MARKET REFORMS

In conjunction with fiscal policy reform, the principal objective of structural adjustment in Africa has been to reduce market distortions. The primary macroeconomic instrument used to achieve this objective has been exchange rate reforms. The intent here is basically to rationalise relative prices and increase allocative efficiency, thereby promoting growth (see the discussion in Chapter 16). In addition, trade policy reform and liberalisation of domestic marketing arrangements have represented major focal points of adjustment policies. The former is intended to make prices of goods at the border of a country more representative of those on international markets. Market liberalisation is designed to remove restrictions impeding the transmission of market-determined prices to the consumer and producer. Adjustment policies are therefore expected to affect prices paid by consumers as well as the incomes of farm and non-farm households. The link between adjustment, open market prices and incomes is thus the focus of the remainder of this section.

(A) Consumer food prices

The welfare concern over the effect of reforming commercial policies on nutritional outcomes revolves around the prospect of higher consumer prices for staple foods. This is expected for two reasons. First, prior to reform, food subsidies were pervasive in much of sub-Saharan Africa. Second, since most staple grains are tradable goods, and one of the underlying purposes of adjustment is to raise the price of tradables relative to non-tradables in order to improve the balance of payments situation (i.e., through encouraging exports and discouraging imports), it is expected that open market prices for imported food and import substitutes will rise.

The evidence from a large number of countries indicates that with few exceptions, reform has not been accompanied by rising market prices for food, despite the fact that theory would suggest otherwise. This is once again explained by the characteristics of state intervention in economies prior to adjustment.

First, with regard to the role of food subsidies in promoting improved nutritional status, most of the evidence from Africa, in contrast with Asia and Latin America, shows that the beneficiaries of state intervention in commodity markets prior to adjustment were not the poor. Specifically, research from a wide variety of African countries, including Guinea (Arulpragasam and Sahn, forthcoming), Tanzania (Sarris and van den Brink, 1993), Niger (Jabara, 1991) and Mozambique (Alderman et al., 1991), presents a picture of subsidies being ineffective, not just an inefficient means of transferring income to and protecting the nutritional status of the poor. This is because subsidised goods were highly rationed, generally limited to urban areas, and even within urban areas, were biased to better-off households which were effective rent-seekers.

Indeed, in a few cases, such as Madagascar and Zambia, the subsidy did represent a sizeable income transfer to most urban households, including the poor. However, the net effect on poverty of such schemes is not necessarily positive. For example, in Madagascar, only an estimated 7 per cent of the country's poor reside in urban areas (Dorosh et al., 1990). These households undoubtedly suffered a real income loss with the end of the subsidy. However, rice producers, many of whom were among the rural poor, gained from the reduction of taxes on their output. This is not to dismiss the dislocation of the relatively small number of nutritionally vulnerable households. It does argue that the removal of the untargeted subsidy was sound economic policy.

Instead of continuing the subsidy, it would have been appropriate, however, to design a compensatory mechanism for the urban poor.

Therefore, it is generally the case that removing subsidies in Africa has small, if any, harmful effects on the nutritionally vulnerable. Instead, eliminating highly rationed, urban-based food distribution schemes adversely affected the less needy households more proficient at rent-seeking, while the vast majority of the poor, already reliant on parallel free markets, faced little dislocation.

As discussed above, the other major mechanism through which adjustment affects prices, and hence health and nutrition, is exchange rate devaluation that threatens to raise open market prices (as opposed to the rationed subsidised prices) for staple goods. In practice, however, the relationship between exchange rate reform and relative and absolute prices was often weak. This was attributable to, first, the fact that official exchange rates had often become irrelevant for the vast majority of transactions occurring long before reform commenced. Instead, the meaningful cost of foreign exchange was determined by the parallel market. Second, concurrent with reforms of exchange rates, changes in trade and internal marketing policies often overwhelmed any price effects that would be attributable to devaluation.

This phenomenon of the weak link between prices and exchange rate is illustrated by Figures 13.2 and 13.3 for Ghana and Tanzania. They show that consumer price changes did not correspond to the movements in the real exchange rate. In fact, a disconnection between consumer prices and the real exchange rate was found in a large number of other countries, including Gambia, Malawi, Niger, Guinea and Mozambique; there are exceptions, however, such as the case of rice in Kenya and Madagascar, where commodity prices follow relatively closely the direction of the exchange rate.

It is also the case that where reforms have been slow in coming, the prices of staple grains on open markets often remain artificially high. Two recent studies, one from Mozambique and the other from Zimbabwe, illustrate this point. In the case of Mozambique, traders were relegated to operating on parallel markets and were not allowed to import grain directly from inexpensive international suppliers. Instead, they had to procure commodities from Swaziland and South Africa for certain grains, paying high prices as a result of the risk premia and high transaction costs involved in such purchasing and dangerous overland transport. As a consequence, goods on the parallel market were priced far in excess of world markets plus a reasonable marketing margin. There was every reason to expect, therefore,

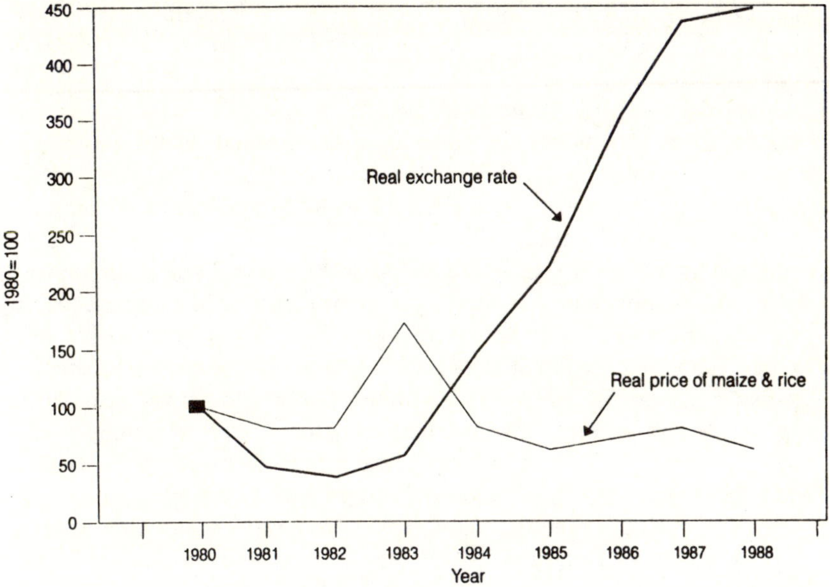

Figure 13.2 Real exchange rate and real prices of major tradable staples in Ghana

Source: Alderman (1991).

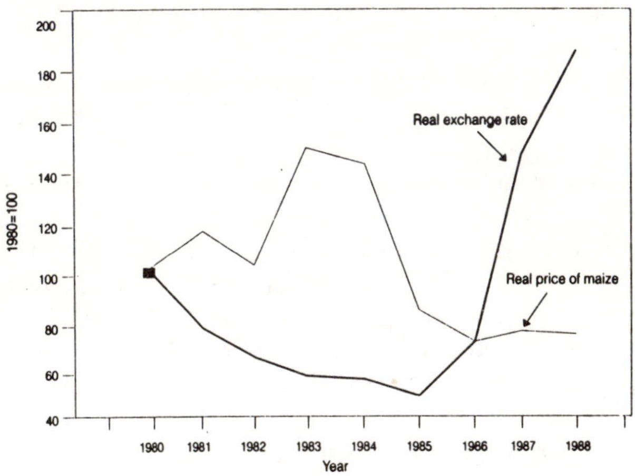

Figure 13.3 Real exchange rate and real prices of major tradable staple in Tanzania

Source: Sams and van den Brink (1993).

that legalising grain trade and removing the high transaction costs would lower open market prices of certain goods to consumers (Alderman et al., 1991).

A similar story has been told for Zimbabwe. The state control of grain markets exerted in the form of inter-regional trade restrictions and resale restrictions that block the sale of grain to low-cost, informal sector millers and traders resulted in long and circuitous marketing channels. It also limited the availability of less expensive, higher extraction maize meal that would appeal to the poor (Jayne et al., 1991).

Yet another example of this type of problem of the reluctance to liberalise trade and undertake needed economic adjustments was found in the Sahel. According to Badiane (1989), the persistent obstacles against cross-border and regional trade of food grains has been hurting the consumer. He pointed out that removing trade restrictions would be especially useful for facilitating maize imports from the humid coastal countries during the Sahel's periods of recurring droughts.

In sum, the data give no indication of generalised increases in real consumer prices in the wake of reform. This is despite the significant real exchange rate devaluation that took place in many countries. The reasons why devaluation did not bring about the expected increase in the real price of staple foods, especially tradable cereals, revolve around, first and foremost, the fact that market clearing and consumer purchases prior to reforms were taking place on parallel markets where access to officially priced foreign exchange was negligible. These markets had already adjusted to the grievous exchange rate distortions and were consequently not affected by reforms. Likewise, simultaneously with devaluation, other changes in trade policy and marketing arrangements were occurring that were often of greater importance in determining prices, again in large part because official markets had long before become highly rationed and were by and large limited to the urban and privileged consumers. As reforms in marketing took place, and systems of tariffs were rationalised, the cost of marketing fell in a number of cases, reflecting greater competition, reduced transaction costs, and so forth. All of this contributed to the moderation of free market retail prices in many of the countries examined.

(B) Incomes and producer incentives

Real incomes may be mediated through changes in earnings, state and private transfers, and prices. Measuring the evolution of incomes over time based on household data is simply not possible in any country in Africa. This is in sharp contrast to other regions such as Latin America and Asia where there are traditions of performing household surveys. In the absence of household data, three major approaches to determining the impact of adjustment on poverty are feasible, each with their own merits. These are discussed below.

First, in order to gain a better understanding of the degree to which adjustment affects real incomes, we can examine the sources of incomes, distinguishing between those goods that are tradables and non-tradables. For example, Table 13.3 shows that among the poor for a sample of African countries, agricultural income comprises between 39 and 76 per cent of the total income; of that, production for home consumption is considerably more important than income generated from market sales. More relevant, however, is that income from marketing non-traded goods, whose prices are not expected to increase as a consequence of adjustment, generally exceeds the income from sales of tradable foods and export crops. This immediately suggests that even if adjustment policies such as exchange rate devaluation brought about an increase in market prices for tradables, the short-term, first-round effects on the incomes of the poor were small, albeit significant, in countries like Côte d'Ivoire where export crops were an important component of the incomes of poor households.

When expenditure share data are examined for a number of countries we find that the share of food expenditures derived from home consumption ranges from 32 per cent in The Gambia to 88 per cent in the west and south of Madagascar (Table 13.4). In addition, market purchases were more likely to be for non-tradables than for tradable food products in most cases. These data reinforce the message that the poor have considerable scope for buffering not only any decline in price incentives, but also any increase in retail prices.

While such descriptive data are useful and help in reaching some tentative conclusions, they nonetheless fail to directly address the counterfactual – what would have happened to the incomes of the poor in the absence of economic adjustment. While few in number, there are some economic models that inform this issue.

A recent study from Malawi (Sahn et al., forthcoming), for instance, analyses the implications of, among other policies, the failure to move rapidly toward export parity prices for tobacco. The results show that as a consequence of Malawi's taxation of smallholder exports, GDP grew at an average annual rate of 4.4 per cent slower during the 1980s than it would have if it had adhered to border-pricing principles. In addition, the policy of taxing smallholder cash crops exacerbated the

Table 13.3 Sources of per capita income of poor rural smallholder households, by country and region

	Ghana		*Tanzania*	*Côte d'Ivoire*		*Malawi*	*Madagascar*			*The Gambia*	*Kenya*	*Rwanda*	*Burkina Faso*		
Income source	*Forest*	*Savannah*	*All*	*Forest*	*Savannah*	*South*	*Coast*	*Plateau*	*South*	*Regional*	*Regional*	*Regional*	*Sahelian*	*Sudanian*	*Guinean*
Agricultural income[a] of which:	0.57	0.68	0.73	0.76	0.81	0.51	0.42	0.39	0.48	0.51	0.54	0.45	0.49	0.59	0.56
Home consumption	0.37	0.54	0.50	0.31	0.40	0.37	0.25	0.31	0.37	0.20	0.40	0.33	-	-	-
Tradable foods[b]	0.05	0.11	0.20	0.06	0.15	0.27	0.10	0.11	0.16	0.10	-	-	-	-	-
Non-tradable foods[c]	0.32	0.43	0.31	0.24	0.25	0.10	0.15	0.20	0.21	0.10	-	-	-	-	-
Agricultural sales	0.20	0.14	0.23	0.45	0.41	0.14	0.17	0.08	0.11	0.31	0.14	0.12	-	-	-
Tradable foods	0.05	0.07	0.07	0.05	0.11	0.01	0.00	0.01	0.01	0.22	-	-	-	-	-
Non-tradable foods	0.07	0.07	0.13	0.07	0.11	0.02	0.05	0.07	0.07	0.09	-	-	-	-	-
Export crops[d]	0.07	0.01	0.03	0.34	0.18	0.12	0.13	0.00	0.03	0.00	-	-	-	-	-
Off-farm earned income[e]	0.40	0.31	0.25	0.21	0.17	0.13	0.55	0.58	0.49	0.22	0.42	0.38	0.20	0.25	0.38
Non-earned income[f]	0.03	0.01	0.02	0.03	0.02	0.36	0.03	0.03	0.03	0.27	0.04	0.17	0.31	0.16	0.06
Total	1.00	1.00	1.00	1.00	1.00	1.00	1.00	1.00	1.00	1.00	1.00	1.00	1.00	1.00	1.00

Notes: [a] Includes livestock; [b] Rice, maize, groundnuts, other tradable foods; [c] Millet, cassava, sweet potato, yams, other non-tradable foods; [d] Cocoa, tobacco, cotton, coffee, cola nuts, rubber, sugar, other exportables; [e] Includes wages, salaries, and own-account; [f] Includes income from transfers, remittances, and other non-earned sources.

Source: Ghana, Tanzania, Côte d'Ivoire, Malawi and Madagascar computed from sources mentioned in Sahn and Sarris (1991); The Gambia from Jabara et al. (1991); Kenya, Rwanda and Burkina Faso from von Braun and Pandya-Lorch (1991).

Table 13.4 Expenditure shares of rural poor, selected sub-Saharan African countries

	Ghana		*Tanzania*	*Côte d'Ivoire*		*Malawi*	*Madagascar*			*The Gambia*	*Kenya*
Shares	*Forest*	*Savannah*	*All*	*Forest*	*Savannah*	*South*	*Coast*	*Plateau*	*South*	*Regional*	*Regional*
Food share	0.73	0.80	0.71	0.65	0.70	0.61	0.59	0.65	0.62	0.67	0.82
Traded	0.10	0.26	0.23	0.15	0.28	0.35	0.19	0.16	0.16	0.34	0.33
Rice	0.02	0.08	0.05	0.06	0.11	0.00	0.13	0.16	0.13	0.15	0.01
Maize	0.06	0.16	0.17	0.05	0.10	0.33	<0.01[a]	0.01	<0.01	0.01	0.31
Groundnuts	0.01	0.01	0.01	0.01	0.05	0.02	<0.01	0.01	<0.01	0.02	-
Other	0.01	0.01	0.00	0.02	0.03	0.00	0.05	0.00	0.03	0.16	0.01
Non-traded	0.63	0.54	0.48	0.50	0.42	0.26	0.46[b]	0.49[b]	0.49[b]	0.33	0.49
Millet	0.00	0.16	0.04	0.00	0.03	0.01	<0.01	<0.01	<0.01	-	0.02
Cassava	0.12	0.05	0.02	0.04	0.03	0.01	0.00	-	-	-	0.45
Other	0.51	0.33	0.41	0.46	0.37	0.25	0.00	-	-	-	-
Non-food share	0.27	0.20	0.29	0.35	0.30	0.39	0.41	0.35	0.38	0.33	0.18
Total	1.00	1.00	1.00	1.00	1.00	1.00	1.00	1.00	1.00	1.00	1.00

Notes: [a] <0.01 means a positive share between 0 and 0.005; [b] The data for Madagascar did not permit us to distinguish the role of cassava versus other goods in the non-traded goods share; [c] - means not available.

Source: Ghana, Tanzania, Côte d'Ivoire, Malawi and Madagascar computed from sources mentioned in Sahn and Sarris (1991); The Gambia from Jabara et al. (1991); Kenya from IFPRI South Nyanza data set.

poverty problem. Smallholders with less than 1.5 hectares, a group that comprises the vast majority of Malawi's poor, would have seen their share of value added increase by nearly 3 per cent if export parity pricing rules had been followed. Thus, the taxation of export crops by parastatals resulted in a lose-lose situation: lower economic growth and a more skewed distribution of income.

Other recent attempts to explore the impact of adjustment on poverty and income distribution, using computable general equilibrium models for four countries, have also shown that the failure to adjust, especially in terms of the two key elements – exchange rate devaluation and liberalising agricultural markets – would have deleterious effects of the incomes of the poor. In particular, models from Cameroon, the Gambia, Niger and Madagascar were used to examine the effects of alternative adjustment policies in responding to a negative terms of trade shock and reduced foreign savings on household incomes (Dorosh and Sahn, 1993). One particularly poignant result, that of the effect of exchange rate reforms, is summarised in Figure 13.4. This figure shows the effects on the incomes of the urban and rural poor of adjusting to a terms of trade shock through exchange rate devaluation, instead of the more typical response of the 1970s and early 1980s whereby countries responded to their deteriorating balance of payments position by imposing quotas on imports and rationing the overvalued foreign exchange. Simply, the costs are high for the poor, both in rural and urban areas, of failing to rapidly move to reform economic policies in the face of a negative terms of trade shock and a deteriorating balance of payments situation. The beneficiaries of the failure to take strong reform measures are the rich, particularly in urban areas. In light of this group's disproportionate political influence, it therefore comes as little surprise that there was considerable resistance to undertaking adjustment, especially through devaluation.

A number of other findings follow from the analysis of the counterfactual use of our computable general equilibrium models. First, to the extent that the government attempts to, and succeeds in, increasing foreign borrowing in the face of a terms of trade shock, or goes on a spending boom, as was characteristic of many African countries during the late 1970s, the beneficiaries are primarily the urban households. They gain the most from increased demand for urban investment goods and for skilled labour. Second, redirecting investment so that investment goods are not so heavily concentrated in urban areas and so that greater use is made of unskilled labour will further poverty alleviation associated with increased foreign savings. Third, poli-

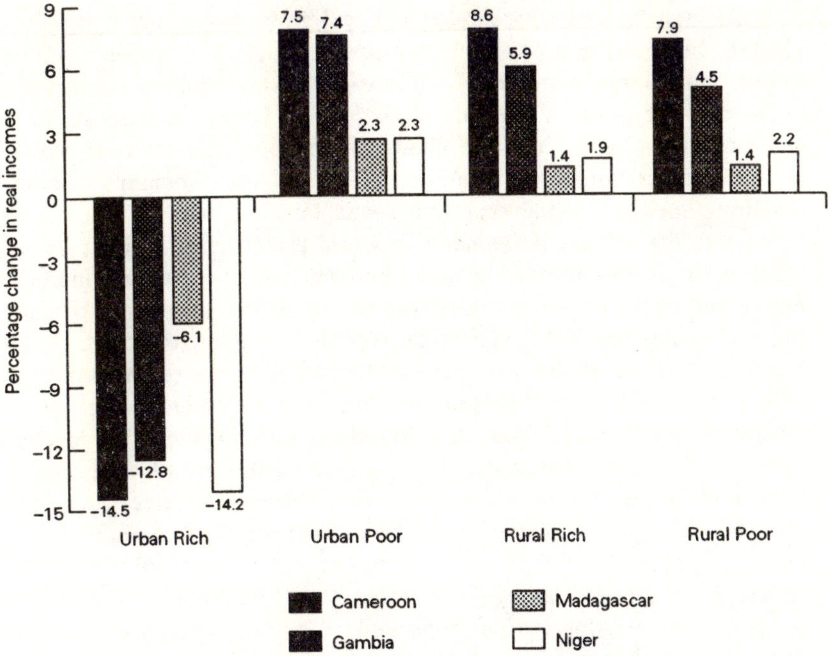

Figure 13.4 Effect of devaluation on real incomes, by income group and country

cies that tend to bring about a devaluation of the exchange rate, such as reducing capital inflows and government spending, will be distributionally in favour of the poor. In some cases where the poor are heavily involved in the export sector, their absolute incomes will rise despite an overall contraction in aggregate value added. Fourth, the ideal poverty alleviation scenario is that of raising the short-term consumption of the poor through concessional finance while carrying out offsetting macroeconomic and trade policies which ensure that there is no consequent real appreciation of the exchange rate. Indeed, policies that prevent real exchange rate appreciation may seem to be an indirect approach to poverty alleviation. They are, however, essential, if not always sufficient.

Despite this generally favourable assessment of the effect of adjustment on incomes of the poor, a number of important factors seriously dampen any enthusiasm about the reforms of the 1980s. First is that in many cases the opportunities to raise rural incomes in the short term through restoring incentives and realigning prices have been neglected. Indeed, there has been a strong reluctance to make requisite reforms in a large number of countries. This has worked against the welfare of the poor. While this is obvious in countries such as Zaire and Somalia where economic chaos has ensued, the harmful effects of a reluctance to revise misguided prices are also apparent in other countries such as Madagascar and Tanzania.

Second, the adverse movements in world prices have worked against many countries attempting to raise producer incomes through increasing prices. This phenomenon of producers seeing stagnating or falling real prices for their exports, despite the state moving to raise the producers' share of the world price, has been observed in a number of countries, including Madagascar, Ghana and Cameroon.

A third problem that has been manifest in using the price mechanism to raise incomes of the poor is that enabling factors that promote and facilitate a response to improved price incentives are often absent. In particular, the poor quality of physical infrastructure, the lack of systems for information collection and dissemination, the absence of an appropriate legal and regulatory framework, the inability to promote the adoption of improved technology because of inadequate national research institutions and extension systems, and other related factors impede the transmission of, and response to, an improved incentive structure. All this is not to suggest that restoring macro stability and removing egregious economic distortions is not essential, but that it is not always sufficient to promote sustainable growth in incomes.

1V THE IMPACT ON NUTRITION AND HEALTH

As discussed at the beginning of this chapter, the effects of adjustment on incomes are not synonymous with the impact on health and nutrition. In fact, the concerns over the impact of adjustment on the form and source of income, on who earns the income, and on decisions regarding how income is used are of great importance. So too are the effects of changing incentives to participate in market activity on household production, including time-intensive inputs into child health and nutrition. In combination these factors point to the possibility of deteriorating health and nutrition despite higher incomes, and vice versa.

In this regard, the most important point is that experience in Africa corresponds to that in other regions of the world, showing the weak relationship between national income on the one hand, and national health and nutrition aggregates on the other (Hill and Pebley, 1989; Hill, 1991). This is an important message for a number of reasons. First, it suggests a resiliency on the part of households to the failures of the state to formulate policies that promote equitable growth. Second, on the positive side, it suggests that public health measures can be instituted to reduce mortality and malnutrition, even in adverse economic conditions. This, however, requires a commitment to reorienting the distribution of health resources in a more equitable manner. Third, on a related note, even if adjustment does bring about sustainable aggregate economic growth, this will certainly not be synonymous with improved health and nutrition; raising GDP offers the potential, but not the assurance, that increased resources will be allocated to investment and recurrent spending that will improve health and nutrition.

While the data on national aggregates tell a story that health and nutritional goals can be protected, even during recessionary periods, there remain a couple of issues especially relevant to the relationship between adjustment and health that go beyond the issue of incomes. In particular, prominent in this domain of concern is the effect of shifting incentives in export crops. It has been argued that production of export crops will be at the expense of national food security by decreasing production of food crops, and of household food security by decreasing home production in lieu of cash crops. On both counts, there is little corroborating evidence. At the national level, even if food crops declined at the expense of export crops, the opportunities for imports, especially in a policy context of reduced trade restrictions, should ensure adequate food supplies. Furthermore, studies generally indicate a complementarity at the aggregate level between increased food production and export cropping (von Braun and Kennedy, 1986; Weber et al., 1988). This reflects the fact that the economic incentive structure and non-price environment for exports and food crops generally move in the same direction. Also, household-level research does not indicate any deleterious effects of income being earned from commercial crops instead of subsistence crops (Sahn, 1990; Sahn et al., forthcoming; von Braun et al., 1989).

An even more difficult issue to quantify is the extent to which the quality and quantity of time inputs into a variety of tasks, such as food preparation, breastfeeding, sanitation, and so forth, are affected by adjustment. This issue is particularly important relative to a change in the incentive structure for market versus home production activities. Women assume primary responsibility for child care, food preparation and other home production activities, all of which may be diminished by greater participation in the labour market, something that is apparently occurring commensurate with the withdrawal of the state from essential marketing functions. Some studies suggest that there are higher costs in reallocating time from direct (for instance, child care) to indirect (for instance, earning income) welfare provisioning activities for women (Juster and Stafford, 1991). However, recent data from urban Guinea indicate that this generalisation does not always hold, as both men and women have considerable leisure time (Glick et al., 1992). In the final analysis, the research in this area has been highly speculative and suffers from a lack of empirical rigour.[1] There remains a need for a fuller appreciation of the trade-offs between increased incomes and a reduction of time in home production, without which it is impossible *a priori* to resolve the effects of such changes on the nutritional status of children and women.

Another concern that has been raised regarding the effects of adjustment programmes on health and nutrition is the issue of income control (for a detailed discussion of issues regarding gender-specific income control see Collier, 1991; and Elson, 1991). Specifically, improved incentives for cash cropping in the Gambia resulted in men assuming a more important role in earning income, and thus greater control over how income was allocated (von Braun et al., 1989). This, combined with the evidence that the preference ordering of men gives a lower priority to inputs into nutrition than for women, may represent a risk to vulnerable household members. Thus, the prospect of an increase in women's market labour activities represents a risk through reducing the time available for child care; and conversely, a reduction in market activities also has its risks mediated through a loss in income control. These conflicting influences of market participation and incomes on the one hand, and child care inputs on the other, need to be sorted out on a case by case basis. They reinforce the complexity of the gender-, time-, and income source-mediated impacts of reforms on nutrition. There is clearly a need for more empirical evidence on these matters, as argued by the inconclusive nature of recent reviews (Sahn and Haddad, 1992; Haddad, 1992; MayaTech, 1991). Whether it be the fact that observed patterns of income earning by individuals within the household are not exogenous, but interdependent, or the fact that there are complex patterns of bargaining that resolve the differences in the preference ordering of individual household members, research is needed to further explore these important processes. Such research, however, will be demanding both in terms of data requirements and the models employed.

V CONCLUSIONS

The evidence presented in this chapter suggests that, on balance, the incomes and living standards of the poor changed little during the years of economic adjustment in Africa. It was also argued that a commitment to major policy reform, particularly exchange rate reforms and market liberalisation, will generally have positive distributional implications and are essential to protecting the medium- and long-term welfare of the poor in the face of an economic crisis. In many respects, however, such a conclusion begs two important questions: Are macroeconomic stability and reforms of economic policy a prerequisite to growth? And does sustainable poverty alleviation require growth? I would argue that the answer to both is a resounding yes. If that is the case, then the fact that many African countries have begun to move toward market economies and restore a semblance of fairness and orderliness to economic policy, without seriously harming the poor, is an accomplishment that differentiates them from Eastern Europe and Latin America.

The primary reason that adjustment in sub-Saharan Africa was not synonymous with falling living standards is that, unlike in Latin America, reform was not primarily characterised by demand restraint in response to severe indebtedness stemming from years of excessive and unsustainable borrowing and spending. Cuts in government spending and related contractionary measures to stem excessive inflation and burdensome debt have not been the hallmarks of adjustment in Africa. In fact, with the exception of a few middle-income countries, the adjustment experience in Africa has borne little resemblance to that in Latin America. The exceptions are cases such as Côte d'Ivoire, whose government-led investment resulted in an unsustainable overexpansion of the economy, and Cameroon where the need for and response to adjustment have similarities to other oil-producing countries such as Ecuador and Venezuela, which were hit by a fall in oil prices. But on the whole, the starting-point for policy reform in sub-Saharan Africa were countries with widespread poverty, stagnating economic growth, acute distortions, and economies where consumers and producers had already developed mechanisms to respond to the inept and corrupt intervention of the state. These included resorting to parallel markets and increasing reliance on private care providers, subsistence agriculture, on-farm storage and production of local drought-resistant crops.

The purported deleterious effects of adjustment on Africa's poor is also a reflection of the understandable albeit erroneous tendency to confuse the reforms being undertaken with the economic crisis that precipitated the need for such policy changes. An equally important weakness in much of the thinking about the negative effects of adjustment revolves around the question of who were the beneficiaries of distortions, and thus the losers when they were (or in many cases, hopefully will be) reversed. The criticisms that adjustment reduced subsidies, raised prices, slowed down increases in minimum wages, and so forth, overlooks the fact that subsidies and rent-seeking opportunities were rarely enjoyed by the poor. Rather, the politically powerful urban elite were the primary beneficiaries of distortions that both hurt the poor in the short term, as manifested in shortages of goods and services and scarcity prices, as well as in the medium and long term by retarding the pace of economic growth.

Thus, the greater the longevity of the old rules and regulations that governed the economy and perpetuated the distortions, the slower the rate at which recovery will have positive effects. In large part, this can be explained by the fact that moving rapidly and comprehensively in efforts at economic reform is important since the process of sustainable and equitable growth requires a series of key enabling factors without which recovery will falter. In fact, the failure of adjustment programmes to address the range of factors that contribute to missing, incomplete or uncompetitive markets and related structural reform impediments to growth (banking regulations and investment codes, among others) have prevented producers and consumers from fully responding to improved market signals and opportunities.

While the general conclusion, then, is that adjustment has had little to do with causing poverty in sub-Saharan Africa, it should not be expected to be a panacea either. More specifically, the reforms being undertaken, and those that are intended but not yet realised, are necessary, albeit not always a sufficient condition for growth. The measures undertaken to date are also, in general, not sufficient for alleviating poverty and meeting social welfare objectives. This suggests the need to look beyond stabilisation and adjustment programmes to a development strategy that does not compromise the hard-fought progress attributable to such reforms.

State investment in physical and social welfare, with the recognition that human capital development will have substantial, if not more difficult to measure, returns is a key component of such a growth strategy. But those investments, both in terms of programmes and infrastructure, need to be designed to encourage complementary investments by the private sector as well as community-based action to improve and protect human resources. The challenge to the state is to reorient its role away from the allocation of privileges to setting the correct legal, regulatory and incentive framework, generating requisite information and technology, and building institutional capacity in state and civil institutions in order to provide the know-how, for example, to design appropriate health and nutrition interventions based on appropriate information.

NOTE

1. See, for example, Kennedy and Bouis (1989), which shows how regional resource endowments affect the way in which changes in time use, commensurate with increased cash cropping, had differential effects on nutrition.

14 The Social Impact of Adjustment in Africa

Alessandro Pio

I INTRODUCTION

During the 1980s, 37 out of the 45 countries belonging to sub-Saharan Africa (SSA) underwent at least one (and sometimes as many as 15) adjustment programmes (Jespersen, 1992; World Bank, 1989a). In spite of this remarkable pool of real world experience, the assessment of the social and economic impact of these programmes is still the subject of considerable debate. The lack of consensus in the scientific and policy-making communities can be attributed to one ideological and two methodological problems. The ideological problem stems from the fact that some analysts already 'know' that adjustment is either good or bad for a country, and simply set out to prove their point by selectively choosing and interpreting evidence. The two methodological problems are, in turn, more difficult to deal with, even for an observer who starts out without preconceptions. They are the result of (i) the impossibility of holding 'everything else equal' during the implementation of adjustment programmes and (ii) the still unsatisfactory state of the art of methodology for such analysis.

The sharp decline in world trade accompanied by rising interest rates and falling commodity prices which characterised the 1980s provides a good example of the first methodological problem. Some of these phenomena triggered the adjustment process, others significantly affected the environment in which it took place, with different impacts on the various countries depending upon their export mix and degree of external financial exposure. It is therefore difficult to isolate the impact of the policies implemented. With regard to the second problem mentioned, one can identify four methodological approaches to the analysis of the effectiveness of structural adjustment programmes (SAP) (Khan, 1990; see also Chapter 2):

1. the *before-after* approach, which compares social and macroeconomic

performance before and after the implementation of the programme;
2. the *with-without* approach, which compares performance in adjusting and in non-adjusting countries;
3. the *econometric* approach, which makes use of regression analysis to evaluate policy performance after correcting to the extent possible for different socioeconomic and external variables;
4. the *simulation* approach, which compares the outcome of different policies (or lack thereof), making use of simplified models of the economic system under analysis.

All of these approaches are characterised by specific methodological problems, a discussion of which goes well beyond the purposes of this chapter. They do nonetheless help to explain why it is possible to obtain conflicting interpretations from analyses of the same raw empirical evidence.

Adjustment programmes (including those implemented in SSA) are normally characterised by fiscal and monetary austerity (to reduce internal demand and thus improve the balance of payments, the budget deficit and the inflation level) and by liberalisation, which broadly entails reducing the role of the state in economic activity (both in regulation and directly in production and distribution) and allowing prices (including the interest and exchange rates) to fluctuate. Much of the debate on the social impact of adjustment has focused *empirically* on the impact of fiscal austerity on spending in the 'social sector' (health and education), and *theoretically* on the distributive impact of liberalisation policies (which should, for example, benefit the rural poor to the disadvantage of urban dwellers). In Chapter 13 of this volume, Sahn argues both points, concluding that 'on balance, the incomes and living standards of the poor changed little during the years of economic adjustment in Africa'. The following comments aim to provide further evidence on the issue, partly questioning some of the conclusions reached by Sahn. The main lines of the argument may be summarised as follows.

First, the social sectors (health and education) in SSA were in fact hit less hard by fiscal retrenchment than in other areas of the world. This was the result of a combination of less deflationary internal policies and the availability of international aid flows to sustain this type of expenditure. Our analysis, however, shows that national health expenditures were reduced by both low- and middle-income countries which applied fiscal austerity measures, though they were at least partly replaced by foreign aid. The analysis also points to some econometric weaknesses of both our and Sahn's (1992) elasticity estimates, which should lead to a cautious interpretation of the results.

Second, while one can theoretically argue that the (rural) poor benefit from market liberalisation policies, there appear to be questionable asymmetries in these processes requiring further explanation. In addition, export price instability can have a negative impact on purchasing power and hence on availability of nutritional inputs.

Finally, even though input and process indicators are important in order to understand the adjustment process, the ultimate test is given by output indicators in terms, for example, of health and educational status. A review of recent, albeit scant and difficult to obtain, evidence shows that the results may be less satisfactory than one could have hoped for. It also points to the need (Section V) to develop more reliable 'cyclical social indicators' in order to monitor more closely the evolution of these socioeconomic processes.

II THE DEBATE ON PUBLIC SOCIAL EXPENDITURE

Most sources agree that the fiscal experience of SSA countries during the 1980s was mixed. If we abstract for a moment from specific adjustment programmes and consider the general evolution during the adjustment *decade*, we can see that for the 15 countries for which data are available (Table 14.1), seven had a higher central government expenditure/GDP ratio in 1989 than in 1981, two had approximately the same share, and six had witnessed fiscal retrenchment. If we look at the share of social expenditure (health + education) in total public expenditure, the results are roughly similar: seven countries with an increasing share and an equal number with a declining ratio. It is interesting to note that in only half of the cases did countries diminish or increase *both* social and overall expenditures, whereas in just as many cases the trends are divergent. When we look at the *absolute level* of real total and per capita expenditures in the social sector, we again notice that one fourth (total level) or one half (per capita figures) of the countries showed lower social expenditures in 1989 than in 1981.

The impact of fiscal adjustment on expenditures in the social sector has been estimated by Sahn (1992). His findings point to a positive elasticity of health and education expenditures with respect to total government expenditure. Such elasticity (ranging from 0.63 for health expenditure in pre-adjustment low-income countries (LIC) to

Table 14.1 Evolution of public and social sector spending in selected sub-Saharan African countries, 1981–9

	Education + health Total expenditure (%)		*Total expenditure GDP (%)*		*Education + health expenditure at 1985 prices ($ millions)*		*Education + health expenditure ($ 1985 per cap.)*	
	1981	1989	1981	1989	1981	1989	1981	1989
Botswana	27.11	24.93	37.88	45.2	66.74	161.50	70.25	127.16
Burkina F.	21.6	25.16	15.44	11.2	30.01	41.21	4.23	4.73
Cameroon	10.2	15.38	20.69	20.9	135.05	324.59	15.45	28.70
Ethiopia	13.47	16.9	26.64	39.7	162.68	416.72	4.15	8.42
Ghana	29	39.9	13.38	15.9	242.67	495.95	22.26	33.02
Guinea Bis.	–	4.09	–	–	–	–	–	–
Kenya	28.4	25.16	29.58	32.04	468.96	621.57	27.57	25.50
Liberia	23.6	–	32.8	–	80.91	–	43.04	–
Malawi	16.1	16.25	34.44	27.26	54.01	55.68	8.59	6.88
Mali	18.8	11.25	22.83	28.9	60.05	54.38	8.24	6.83
Mauritius	22.76	24.52	31.25	25.02	64.54	88.83	67.94	86.24
Niger	14.2	21.4	23.6	23.8	61.93	121.40	10.72	16.21
Nigeria	21.66	7.27	37.5	28.1	6714.95	2003.15	77.36	17.43
Tanzania	19.5	16.6	36.6	32.4	477.83	411.29	24.93	16.58
Togo	21.94	19.6	33	35.1	53.87	57.42	20.03	16.79
Zambia	18	16.31	36.66	31.2	178.21	135.13	30.36	17.32
Zimbabwe	26.4	31.08	29.35	40.8	309.00	593.49	42.86	65.94

Source: IMF, *Government Finance Statistics Yearbook* (1987 and 1991a); IMF, *International Financial Statistics* (1991b).

1.33 in education for post-adjustment middle-income countries (MIC)) is systematically higher for middle-income than for low-income countries, and is approximately 40 to 60 per cent higher *after* adjustment as compared to pre-adjustment levels.

Sahn's estimates, however, are based only on the countries which increased government spending during the period. This is a rather peculiar type of fiscal adjustment, thus raising the question of what happened in those countries which reduced public spending as a result of the adjustment programme. We have seen, in fact, that 40 per cent of the countries listed in Table 14.1 have reduced central government expenditures as a percentage of GDP. A positive and growing elasticity would therefore imply that in such countries fiscal adjustment has been accompanied by a *reduction* in social expenditure.[1]

To address this question, the same methodology can be applied to estimate the elasticity of health and government expenditure to total government expenditure separately for samples of both expenditure-

Table 14.2 Elasticity of education expenditure with respect to total expenditure

	Before Adjustment	After Adjustment
Expenditure-reducing countries		
Low-income	0.41	–0.10
Middle-income	2.42	–1.30
Expenditure-increasing countries		
Low-income	0.15	0.37
Middle-income	0.94	1.96
Memo*		
Low-income	0.66	1.08
Middle-income	0.92	1.33

Note: * Estimates from Sahn (1992).

Source: Author's estimates and Sahn (1992).

increasing and expenditure-reducing countries.[2] The results are presented in Tables 14.2 and 14.3.

Table 14.2 shows the elasticities for education. As in Sahn (1992), whose results are reported at the end of the table for comparison, elasticities are lower for low-income countries and tend to become larger after adjustment. The differences in absolute values should not be surprising, as there are differences in the country coverage between this and Sahn's sample. The most relevant finding is the existence of *negative* elasticities for expenditure-reducing countries after adjustment. This means that education has been 'protected', and has enjoyed an increase in the share of the public budget at a time of expenditure cuts. This protection has been more limited in LICs (presumably because of the more limited amount of resources available).

Not only has the education sector been relatively protected during the fiscal adjustment, but evidence suggests (Jespersen, 1992) that, especially in low-income countries, a shift of resources has taken place from secondary to primary education in the early and intermediate stages of adjustment. This finding does not necessarily contradict Sahn's assertion that secondary and higher education still absorb a disproportionately large share of this sector's budget (see Table 13.1), since he refers to the *latest figures* on relative shares, whereas Jespersen compares the *evolution* of such shares during the 1980s. The share of primary education in total recurrent expenditures grew in sub-Saharan LICs from 40 per cent in 1980 to 46 per cent in 1986-8, while it declined from 50 per cent to 42 per cent in MICs. This is probably the result of changing national priorities, as well as of the emphasis on primary education on the part of international financial institutions (notably the World Bank), which were relevant actors in the design of adjustment programmes due to their role as sources of external financing.

More difficult to assess, though also potentially more troubling, is the impact on the end users. Even though education's *share* of total expenditures may have grown, the *level* of expenditure has remained constant or decreased in real terms in several countries, which means that *per capita* outlays have in fact declined. Since teachers' salaries, textbooks and supplies have normally fallen victim of expenditure reduction, there is cause for concern that stable or increasing primary enrolment rates and decreasing resources may have resulted in lower quality education, whose negative impact on social and economic development will become evident only a decade from now. As the concluding section of this chapter elaborates, this is one reason why better and more timely indicators of social development are needed.

A similar line of reasoning can be applied to the health sector. Table 14.3 shows the estimated elasticities. What we observe in this case is that elasticities remain positive even for expenditure-reducing countries. This means that while expenditure-increasing countries have also raised sanitary spending (though at a lower rate than the overall budget, since elasticity is lower than unity), the countries which have had to reduce total outlays have also decreased spending in the health sector. The greater vulnerability of the health sector to budget cuts can be at least partly explained if we include foreign aid in the picture. Jespersen (1992) has remarked that while very little external funding was available for education, donor resources became important in the financing of recurrent health expenditures, accounting for as much as 20 per cent of such expenditures in Burundi in 1985 and 50 per cent in Mozambique in the late 1980s. It would therefore appear that we are witnessing is a phenomenon of 'expenditure diversion': since foreign aid funding was more readily available for the health sector, central governments undergoing fiscal adjustments shifted resources from health to other less 'attractive' destinations, counting on external aid to pick

Table 14.3 Elasticity of health expenditure with respect to total expenditure

	Before Adjustment	After Adjustment
Expenditure-reducing countries		
Low-income	–1.49	0.23
Middle-income	0.07	7.47
Expenditure-increasing countries		
Low-income	0.04	0.62
Middle-income	–3.01	0.19
Memo*		
Low-income	0.63	0.93
Middle-income	0.83	1.13

Note: * Estimates from Sahn (1992).

Source: Author's estimates and Sahn (1992).

up the slack. This interpretation helps explain why observed indicators (such as child mortality and morbidity) did not show any significant worsening in the face of budget cuts. One must also credit the diffusion of immunisation and oral rehydration therapy for reducing child mortality at times of acute adjustment.

While these elasticity data are helpful in guiding our interpretation of what happened during the 1980s, their accuracy should not be overestimated. R-squared values for the underlying regression estimates ranged from 0.01 to 0.23. Sahn (1992) obtained similar R-square results, ranging from 0.01 to 0.17. Since the underlying regressions explain such a small share (from 1 to 23 per cent) of total variance, it is possible that including other relevant explanatory variables would completely change the value of the estimated regression coefficients, and hence the values of the elasticities. Also, not all coefficients were significant at the 5 per cent level (a problem, once again, shared by Sahn's 1992 estimates). Low R-squared values and occasionally insignificant coefficients, together with differences in the sample composition, help explain the differences between the two sets of estimates. It is nevertheless encouraging to find that for certain types of countries and expenditures the orders of magnitude and the trends (from before to after adjustment, from LICs to MICs) are broadly similar.

The above review of the behaviour of social spending during adjustment shows that only in the case of education was the sector 'protected' even in situations of general expenditure reduction. An increase in health and education expenditures was otherwise only made possible by increasing resource availability, either of internal or external origin. This conclusion seems to indicate that less drastic internal fiscal adjustments or availability of external financial flows are needed to cushion the impact of adjustment on social sector spending. In this sense, adjustment may have been socially less painful in Africa (or at least in some African countries) than in other regions, for example Latin America, precisely because one or both of the above characteristics was verified during the 1980s.

Maintaining a given *level* of spending is obviously only part of the picture, since the intrasectoral allocation of resources (primary versus secondary education, preventive versus curative health care, rural versus urban focus) and the efficiency with which resources are used have very relevant implications for the translation of these inputs into outputs and levels of welfare, as is extensively discussed in Chapter 13. Some authors have argued that the elimination of subsidies and the introduction of user fees have not significantly hurt the poor since they had very limited access to the subsidised goods and services in the first place. While this may be true, it seems that even where some mistargeting was eliminated, not enough *retargeting* was achieved. Proceeding along this line would in fact entail redesigning the service delivery systems so as to actively reach a more substantial share of the needy population, after having made sure that the less needy are not unfairly favoured.

III THE IMPACT OF MARKET LIBERALISATION POLICIES

Much of the debate on the effect of market liberalisation policies on the poor is based on indirect evidence because data on incomes, on their intrafamily allocation, and on the composition of consumption baskets are difficult and costly to gather. The main argument (very effectively summarised in Chapter 13 by Sahn) is that the poor, and especially the rural poor, had very limited access to subsidised goods and services and hence were not significantly affected by the elimination of subsidies. The removal of exchange rate controls would also have a limited effect on the rural poor, either because home-grown and non-traded food staples represent a large share of their consumption basket or because the traded food component was already being purchased on the parallel market, at prices which reflected the liberalised (previously black market) exchange rate. Finally, an increase in the price of agricultural products (caused by exchange rate devaluation and liberalisation of marketing channels) would increase their income, providing an incentive to shift to the production of exportable commodities which would provide the cash needed to purchase food on the market. The reasoning briefly outlined above is convincing in many of its arguments, but it should be qualified by four points of caution.

First, the reasoning is based on a series of asymmetries in the transmission of price signals to the (rural) poor. The rural poor were not previously affected by price subsidies on goods, services or the exchange rate, but are expected to respond to price changes for their products induced by devaluation or the elimination of marketing boards. While this response is evident in the results of carefully developed and painstakingly calibrated models, there is reason to want to be cautious and wait for more empirical evidence on the effects actually observed in the real world.

Second, the asymmetry discussed above seems to stem from the choice that individuals have of taking part in, or retreating from, market-oriented activities. In the presence of high prices, households will mostly consume home-produced food crops and not resort to public services, whereas given the right price incentives they will orient their production and consumption to the market. If this is the case, it would be useful to investigate more closely which other elements contribute to this market orientation, in order to better be able to predict the impact from a change of incentives. It is in fact also possible that changes in price incentives will not affect individual behaviour if producers and/or consumers are isolated from markets as a result of survival strategies or long-standing traditions.

Third, excessive market orientation can be dangerous for two reasons: producers of non-tradable agricultural commodities may see the price of their products fall as a result of expenditure-switching policies, while producers of exportable goods will become subject to the wide price fluctuations which characterise international markets in the absence of some national price stabilisation mechanism, as in the case of coffee. The result would be increased uncertainty about the purchasing power of cash crops, which could undermine the expenditure-switching policies.

As a fourth, and final, point one must not overlook the impact of adjustment policies on the urban poor who represent a much lower percentage of the population in sub-Saharan Africa than in other continents (for example, Latin America), but who are nevertheless likely to be negatively affected by the improvement of the terms of trade for the rural residents. Consideration for their situation is also dictated by their potentially more vocal role in national political life, which can have an impact on the political sustainability of an adjustment process.

While the above arguments do not deny the positive social impact which structural adjustment can have by modifying income levels and relative prices, they are meant to put the spotlight on areas for research or policy design which still require considerable attention.

IV MEASURING IMPACT, NOT INPUTS

As already argued, much of the evidence on the impact of adjustment is indirect. The level (and sometimes the composition) of social spending has been measured, the weight of non-traded crops in the consumption basket has been calculated, the amount of home consumption has been estimated, and the effect of different policies on particular social or income groups has been modelled. Evidence on the final impacts – rather than on the initial or intermediate inputs – of the adjustment process is unfortunately more piecemeal and harder to come by. When such evidence is available, it paints a picture which at least partly contrasts some of the more optimistic assessments of the results of adjustment policy.

Jespersen (1992) presents some carefully asembled evidence on the well-being of SSA households. Nutritional levels (measured directly or indirectly through increases in hospitalisations and related deaths) worsened in many countries in the early phases of adjustment, and improved again in 1987–9. Educational achievement was also found to be declining, as evidenced by a reduction in the rate of increase of primary school enrolments and higher drop-out rates. No clear evidence was found on infant and child mortality and morbidity rates, partly because of a lack of comparable data.

A recent publication by UNDP and the World Bank (UNDP and World Bank 1992) provides some more information on the impact of the early stages of adjustment, though unfortunately most data stop at 1989, therefore impeding an assessment of the more recent trends. As Table 14.4 shows, the broad trends just outlined are confirmed. Over-

Table 14.4 Selected social indicators for sub-Saharan Africa

	1980	*1985*	*1989*
Life expectancy at birth	47	49	51
Infant mortality	127	118	107
Immunisation rates:			
– Tuberculosis	29	37	68
– DPT	22	26	42
– Polio	19	29	43
– Measles	33	30	45
Average daily caloric intake	2107	2040	2007
Primary school enrolment	70	68	65*
– males	82	72	71*
Changes in % of a cohort reaching the final grade of primary school. Number of countries:			
– where percentage increased in 1980–9	n.a.	n.a.	12
– where percentage decreased in 1980–9	n.a.	n.a.	12

Notes: * 1988 data.
n.a. = not applicable.

Source: UNDP and World Bank (1992) and author's calculations.

all health measures (life expectancy and infant mortality rate) show a moderate improvement, possibly attributable to the increased diffusion of immunisation and oral rehydration therapy, while nutrition and education have been negatively affected. Average caloric intake has declined, and we know that an average figure hides considerable disparities among the affected subgroups, making this indicator potentially even more disturbing. Primary school enrolment rates have also dropped (especially for males) and in approximately half of the countries for which data are available the percentage of students of a cohort reaching the final grade of primary school has declined.

The situation is of course different in the various countries, as Tables 14.5 and 14.6 show. The analysis of these data shows that there is no clear correlation between strength of the adjustment (as defined, for example in World Bank, 1990d) and social indicators. Among non-adjusting countries we observe both positive (for example, Botswana) and negative (for example, Benin) trends in social indicators, just as among adjusters (such as Mauritania and Senegal versus Madagascar and Nigeria). This finding underlines once again the relevance of the specific set of policies implemented in each country,

Table 14.5 Health and nutrition indicators for sub-Saharan Africa

	Country	*Life expectancy at birth*		*Infant mortality (per 1000)*		*Average daily caloric intake*	
		1980	*1990*	*1980*	*1990*	*1980*	*1988*
	Angola	41	46	153	129	2100	1725
NA	Benin	47	51	124	111	2005	2145
NN	Botswana	60	68	63	37	2122	2269
OAL	Burkina Faso	44	48	154	133	1790	2061
OAL	Burundi	45	50	114	68	2288	2253
NA	Cameroon	53	57	106	88	2179	2161
	Cape Verde	62	67	59	40	2433	2436
OAL	Centr. Afr. Rep	47	51	117	98	2028	1980
	Chad	42	47	147	125	1762	1852
	Comoros	51	55	113	92	2068	2046
OAL	Congo	50	54	124	113	2409	2512
EIAL	Côte d'Ivoire	49	53	109	91	2498	2365
NA	Ethiopia	43	48	155	131	1777	1658
	Gabon	48	53	116	96	2243	2396
	Gambia, The	40	44	159	136	2009	2360
EIAL	Ghana	52	55	100	84	1909	2209
OAL	Guinea	40	43	161	138	1992	2042
OAL	Guinea-Bissau	37	40	168	145	1797	2690
EIAL	Kenya	55	59	83	66	2145	1973
	Lesotho	52	57	116	93	2360	2307
NA	Liberia	51	54	159	135	2319	2270
EIAL	Madagascar	50	51	138	116	2397	2101
EIAL	Malawi	44	48	169	146	2197	2009
OAL	Mali	44	48	184	166	1695	2181
EIAL	Mauritania	43	47	142	121	1963	2528
EIAL	Mauritius	66	70	32	20	2676	2679
	Mozambique	45	49	156	135	1797	1632
	Namibia	53	58	120	99	1842	1889
OAL	Niger	42	46	150	128	2236	2340
EIAL	Nigeria	48	52	118	98	2250	2039
NA	Rwanda	46	49	135	116	1986	1786
	Sao Tome-Princ.	-	66	83	69	2258	2657
EIAL	Senegal	45	48	103	80	2373	1989
	Seychelles	-	71	-	17	2125	2179
OAL	Sierra Leone	38	42	171	146	2027	1806
OAL	Somalia	44	48	145	126	1796	1736
OAL	Sudan	47	51	123	102	2304	1996
	Swaziland	52	57	133	112	2428	2548
EIAL	Tanzania	47	50	122	110	2244	2151
EIAL	Togo	49	54	110	88	2151	2133
	Uganda	46	49	113	96	2098	2013

continued on page 310

Table 14.5 continued

Country	*Life expectancy at birth*		*Infant mortality (per 1000)*		*Average daily caloric intake*	
	1980	*1990*	*1980*	*1990*	*1980*	*1988*
OAL Zaire	49	53	111	91	2068	2034
EIAL Zambia	50	54	90	74	2174	2026
OAL Zimbabwe	55	64	82	42	2132	2232

Notes: Caloric intake is measured in Kcal. per capita; EIAL are countries that have undertaken 2 SALs or 3 Adjustment Operations or more, with the first adjustment operation in 1985 or before; OAL are other countries receiving adjustment lending; NA are countries that did not adjust although it was necessary for them to do so; NN are other non-adjusting countries.

Source: UNDP and World Bank (1992); World Bank (1990d).

Table 14.6 Education indicators for sub-Saharan Africa

Country	*Illiteracy rate*		*Primary school GER*		*% of cohort ending prim. school*		*Secondary school GER*	
	1980	*1989*	*1980*	*1988*	*1980*	*1989*	*1980*	*1988*
NA Benin	72	77	64	63	56	36	16	–
NN Botswana	–	26	92	116	90	89	21	33
OAL Burkina F.	–	82	18	31	70	68	3	6
OAL Burundi	73	50	29	70	94	87	3	–
NA Cameroon	–	40	104	111	67	70	19	27
Cape Verde	–	34	112	109	–	39	8	16
OAL CAR	67	62	71	67	47	56	14	11
Chad	–	70	–	51	29	78	–	6
EIAL Côte d'Ivoire	65	46	74	–	89	73	18	19
NA Ethiopia	–	–	35	36	50	50	9	15
The Gambia	80	73	51	61	92	96	11	16
EIAL Ghana	–	40	80	73	74	–	41	39
OAL Guinea	–	76	31	30	41	43	14	9
OAL Guinea Bis.	81	64	67	53	15	19	6	6
EIAL Kenya	53	31	115	93	61	51	20	23
Lesotho	–	–	103	112	38	52	17	25
NA Liberia	–	61	49	–	–	–	23	–
EIAL Madagascar	–	20	143	97	–	–	–	19
EIAL Malawi	–	–	60	72	32	31	3	4
OAL Mali	–	68	27	23	40	40	9	6
EIAL Mauritania	–	66	37	52	80	78	11	16
EIAL Mauritius	21	–	108	105	–	98	48	53
Mozambique	67	67	75	68	21	34	5	5
OAL Niger	90	72	27	30	79	75	5	7

continued on page 311

Table 14.6 continued

Country	*Illiteracy rate*		*Primary school GER*		*% of cohort ending prim. school*		*Secondary school GER*	
	1980	*1989*	*1980*	*1988*	*1980*	*1989*	*1980*	*1988*
EIAL Nigeria	66	49	97	62	–	–	19	16
NA Rwanda	50	50	63	64	41	46	3	6
EIAL Senegal	–	62	46	59	84	85	11	16
OAL Sierra Leone	–	79	52	53	48	-	14	18
OAL Sudan	–	73	50	-	-	76	16	-
Swaziland	–	–	103	105	63	62	38	44
EIAL Tanzania	–	–	93	66	76	71	3	4
EIAL Togo	–	57	71	101	26	52	34	24
Uganda	48	52	50	77	76	–	5	8
OAL Zaire	46	28	94	76	–	60	34	22
EIAL Zambia	37	27	90	–	83	80	16	-
OAL Zimbabwe	31	33	85	128	–	74	8	51

Notes: GER = Gross Enrolment Ratio.
EIAL, OAL, NA, NN = See Table 14.5.

Source: UNDP and World Bank (1992).

showing the limited utility of broad distinctions between 'adjusters' and 'non-adjusters'.

V THE NEED FOR SOCIAL INDICATORS

As the above discussion clearly shows, evidence on the social impact of adjustment programmes – and in fact more generally on the level of welfare in the social sphere – is fragmentary and incomplete. Contrast this situation with the availability of economic indicators. An economist who wishes to make a quick assessment of a country's macroeconomic situation will look at a few indicators, such as GDP growth, infiation, unemployment, current account and capital flow balances in the balance of payments, public sector budget deficit and money supply growth. While not exhaustive, these data will allow a rapid assessment of the overall macroeconomic environment. Frequency and comparability of these data is essential, but in most countries, including many in the developing world, the above indicators are already available on a quarterly, and sometimes monthly, basis. What is even more interesting is that in countries with severe macroeconomic imbalances (say a high level of inflation or dangerously low levels of foreign currency reserves) the frequency of available data will increase, since it becomes more important for operators to monitor the situation through accurate weekly or daily estimates of the main macroeconomic variables.

The situation is dismally different when we look at social indicators, or at economic indicators which address the issue of income distribution. Available data are often the result of censal extrapolations or averages calculated using 'comparable countries' as a reference point. Development literature (UNDP, 1991), however, has clearly shown that political will and appropriate policy design can lead to marked improvements in social indicators, even at very low levels of GDP per capita. Hence, reference to other countries is of very limited use in this case, precisely because it overlooks this fundamental consideration.

In spite of some recent and very commendable efforts (such as the World Bank's Living Standard Measurement Study project) no systematic collection of such data takes place. This can be considered a case of market failure, deriving from the very long time horizon which characterises social phenomena. The effects of inadequate nutrition, health and schooling will not become apparent for many months or years, in some cases decades, and the associated loss in welfare and output will concern society as a whole at some distant time in the future or will mostly affect some of its weakest members rather than its more economically active and politically vocal components. For these reasons, there is no immediate incentive to monitor adequately the social and distributive situation.

The problem is certainly not one of cost or of technical feasibility. Devising a relatively simple set of indicators (for example, infant mortality rates, percentage of low weight births, percentage of first and second degree malnutrition, school drop-out rates, results in national examinations or standard tests at various levels) and establishing procedures for their systematic observation and calculation are well within the technical capabilities of most countries. The cost would not necessarily be higher than that of computing GDP or the inflation rate, or unemployment statistics. The benefits of such data availability would stem from the possibility of designing rapid intervention programmes and better tailoring existing activities to actual needs (even on a geographical basis, as exemplified in UNICEF, 1990), and from the avoidance of the human capital waste currently taking place. A coordinated international research effort could provide guidelines regarding the choice of indicators and suitable methodologies, much as the UN SITC codes or national accounting guidelines provide a benchmark for national statistical activities in the area of economics. Given the importance of human capital for growth, as suggested by the most recent economic literature, such investment should easily repay itself if the results were properly employed in the better design of adjustment and growth-oriented policies.

NOTES

1. This concern is confirmed by an analysis of the sample of countries studied in Sahn's 1992 article. This shows that when we compare the 1984–6 period with 1980–3, fully 20 out of 29 countries witnessed a reduction of government spending, and that even when comparing 1987–9 with 1984–6, 10 out of the 29 countries still reduced government spending.
2. I would like to thank Marcello Burzi for his assistance in the computation of the elasticities as well as for other helpful comments on the contents of this chapter. The estimation methodology is essentially based on the one presented in Sahn (1992). The model is:

$$\left[SOCEXP_{it} - \frac{1}{t}\,\Sigma(SOCEXP)_{it}\right] = \left[\beta_0 + \beta_1^* D_1 + \beta_2^* D_2\right]*$$

$$*\left[\ln(TOTEXP)_{it} - \frac{1}{t}\,\Sigma\ln(TOTEXP)_{it}\right] + u_{it}$$

where:

i	=	countries;
t	=	years (1981–9);
SOCEXP	=	social expenditure (education or health) in percentage of total government expenditure;
TOTEXP	=	total government expenditure in percentage of GDP;
D_1	=	dummy variable equal to 0 for years before adjustment and to 1 for years after adjustment;
D_2	=	dummy variable equal to 0 for low-income countries and to 1 for middle-income countries
u	=	zero-mean normally distributed errors.

We estimated the relevant coefficients through OLS procedure, and obtained the elasticities multiplying the coefficients by the sample means calculated either for before/after adjustment years or for low-/middle-income countries. The relevant coefficients can be here summarised:

	Before adjustment	After adjustment
Low-income	β_0	$\beta_0 + \beta_1$
Middle-income	$\beta_0 + \beta_2$	$\beta_0 + \beta_1 + \beta_2$

Part IV

External Constraints and Policies

15 External Resource Flows, Debt Relief and Economic Development in Sub-Saharan Africa

Gerald K. Helleiner*

I INTRODUCTION

There is no longer much controversy as to the limited developmental impact of structural adjustment programmes in sub-Saharan Africa, at least so far. Even the most enthusiastic proponents now describe their results as disappointing. Within the World Bank, the most careful econometric tests carried out to date, using a 'modified control group' approach (which controls for external and internal shocks, and political and other initial conditions), show that adjustment programmes in sub-Saharan Africa were not associated with any statistically significant differences in growth in the second half of the 1980s. According to these studies, they were associated with significantly lower investment rates, marginally significantly lower savings rates, and significantly higher exports (Elbadawi, 1992; Elbadawi et al., 1992). The primary debate now concerns the reasons for these weak results and hence the best means of doing better.

Some argue that policy reforms have been inadequate or inappropriate or both; further policy reform and tougher conditionality on foreign assistance is therefore prescribed. This chapter argues, however, that the prime cause of disappointing performance is the insufficiently supportive external environment. African reform programmes have usually been underfunded relative to objective calculations of the requirements for better overall economic performance.

* This chapter draws, in part, upon two earlier papers: one published in *World Development*, June 1992; the other presented to a conference entitled 'From Stabilization to Growth in Africa' in Marstrand, Sweden, 6–7 September 1992. The author wishes to thank Martine Lussier for computational assistance.

II THE ROLE OF EXTERNAL RESOURCE FLOWS IN SUB-SAHARAN AFRICAN DEVELOPMENT

The World Bank's long-term perspective study (1989a) argued that sub-Saharan Africa would need to have about 9 per cent of its GDP added to internal savings (i.e. 'transferred' financially) from external sources during the 1990s in order to attain minimally acceptable growth rates (4 to 5 per cent, or 1 to 2 per cent per capita). This seemed a very conservative estimate of the requirements for such targets in light of the fact that, according to the Development Assistance Committee of the OECD, overseas development assistance (ODA) already accounted for 11 per cent of sub-Saharan African GDP in the late 1980s, during which time growth rates fell short of the targeted rates. The Bank's estimate was based on highly optimistic projections of export growth, rates of return on investment and savings rates, none of which have so far been realised. (The Bank has consistently understated African external resource requirements in the past, no doubt in order to try to induce donors to offer a little more, rather than simply throwing up their hands in despair.)

There is no escape from the need for further external resource flows for sub-Saharan Africa in the 1990s. Since the prospects for voluntary fresh bank lending, bond finance, direct foreign investment or even export credits are not very bright, ODA is the only halfway realistic possible source of significantly expanded external capital flows. ODA plays a particularly important role where fiscal constraints on key public expenditures (health, education, infrastructure, and so on), as well as savings or foreign exchange stringency, are important determinants of economic performance. However, the prospect of increased ODA flows is not a very hopeful one. Overall ODA flows to developing countries are stagnant in real terms. Aid flows to sub-Saharan Africa already rose more rapidly in the 1980s than ODA in general. The region now receives nearly 35 per cent of total world ODA, up from less than 10 per cent in 1960 (while its share of the developing countries' population is only about 12 per cent).

The highest immediate returns from expanded external flows to import-strangled economies are typically reaped from the provision of increased inputs for the rehabilitation and full utilisation of existing capital stock rather than from the creation of new capital. Increased supplies of 'free' foreign exchange in situations of savings, foreign exchange or fiscal constraints, where economic policies are broadly 'right', can yield extraordinarily high returns. At the same time, they can render many other potential investments remunerative. Growth-oriented adjustment requires investment for the restructuring of production towards tradable goods and services. There are obviously also continuing needs for the expansion of social infrastructure and the directly productive capital stock for steady longer-run development as well as for the immediate relief of absolute poverty. There can be neither private nor public incentives for such investments in the absence of assurances of adequate provision of inputs for their effective operation.

Concern over the 'absorptive capacity' of recipient African governments for increased external assistance may in some circumstances, particularly where there is war, civil strife or gross mismanagement in government, be appropriate. In the main, however, given the sharp drop in African imports (and, even more, imports per capita) below prior levels, the virtually universal phenomenon of import-related underutilisation of both social and directly productive capital, and continuing increases in population which will expand import needs, such concerns are inappropriate. This is particularly the case in those countries where adjustment programmes are in place.

Among the other most important thrusts in development and adjustment thinking in recent years is the increased emphasis now placed upon stability, policy credibility and sustained government effort (World Bank, 1990a). More important than achieving policy 'perfection' at each point in time, whatever that might mean, is the creation and maintenance of a stable overall policy environment, and the creation and preservation of credibility for and confidence in an announced adjustment and development programme. Stable incentives and politics can compensate for quite a lot of policy 'imperfection'. Only with the resulting reduction in overall uncertainty will private decision makers and public servants be able to act rationally, consistently and in the longer-term social interest. This new perception of the prime prerequisites of success has created a fresh interest in 'critical thresholds', below which very little will happen but above which much more is possible.

Among the key elements in securing policy credibility are the adequacy of finance and the assurance of its continuation. It makes little sense to strain over optimal policies if it is blatantly clear that adjustment possibilities are so tightly constrained by resources as to throttle the best of reform efforts. Once gross macroeconomic policy distortions are overcome, the greatest threat to the success of adjustment programmes is almost certainly underfunding.

While it has been very difficult to prove unambiguously that there is improved development performance in consequence *purely* of policy reform, either in Africa or elsewhere, econometric investigations, notably those undertaken within the World Bank (Faini et al., 1991), have shown that there is a positive and statistically significant correlation between increased imports and improved growth in recent years. Increased external resources evidently *are* highly productive in periods of foreign exchange stringency in the short- to medium-term, probably primarily through their effects upon capacity utilisation (Faini et al., 1991; Ndulu, 1991).

The World Bank's most recent analysis (1992b) of its adjustment lending experience appears to provide further empirical support for the proposition that increased official transfers have a significant developmental impact. Since this is still disputed by some, it is unfortunate that the details of its background studies were not presented in the published report. Its summary states that, 'Total official flows . . . have a positive, independent influence on growth in the low-income countries on average . . . in Sub-Saharan Africa such flows are positively associated with growth' (p. 19).

How large the effects of *increased external flows* were, relative to those associated with the *policy changes* in intensive adjustment programmes, cannot be discerned from the data presented in the Bank study; it is clear, however, that the latter effects were much smaller for low-income and sub-Saharan African countries than for others. The Bank study diverts attention from this critically important question by attacking a straw man: 'some critics maintain, growth has recovered in some adjustment lending countries, such as Ghana, only because official money was pouring in. The evidence refutes this contention. The positive effects of being an adjustment lending country come in addition to – and can be identified separately from – the effects of total financing . . . the policy reforms associated with adjustment lending, not just the financing, account for the improvement in economic outcomes' (ibid., p. 19). Few have ever argued that policy reforms count for *nothing*.

One *cannot* induce from this study whether, on the margin, more policy reform or more finance will be of greater benefit. Yet the study is much more specific in its recommendations to adjusting countries to 'stay the course' and to introduce 'further reforms' than it is to donors to increase external flows (pp. 25–26). In the absence of increased external assistance, it is difficult to see how these countries are to take 'action to further their long-run development – including investment in human capital, efficient expansion of infrastructure and institutional development' (p. 25) while also devoting 'more attention . . . to the alleviation of the suffering of the poor' (p. 26).

Nor is there any logic in the Bank's assertion that, because the low-income countries received larger external transfers than the middle-income countries, underfinancing does not explain their relatively poor performance (p. 18). The question should be, in the Bank's terms, how much the low-income countries received *relative to what they require to grow more quickly* (others would say to perform better in more broadly defined developmental terms), not what they received relative to what other better-equipped countries got. It goes almost without saying in this regard that low-income countries also have greater needs – consumption needs – that are unrelated to growth effects.

It is worth noting that the 1992 Bank study also notes that the lower growth rates in low-income and sub-Saharan African countries are *not* attributable to weak macroeconomic policy adjustment (or, for that matter, to larger external shocks or constraints). 'They had undertaken more, not less, adjustment' (p. 14). The Bank, sensibly, concludes that, 'The differences in average economic outcomes seem to result from differences in the level of development' (p. 14). Levels of development are not quickly changed; longer-term development requirements, including the *true* need for appropriate and sustained external resource flows, must therefore be addressed.

III EXTERNAL RESOURCE FLOWS AND EXTERNAL SHOCKS IN THE 1980S IN SUB-SAHARAN AFRICA

Unfortunately, external resource transfers to sub-Saharan Africa have failed in recent years to approach the required levels; and the requirements rose greatly in the 1980s in consequence of severe external shocks.

Table 15.1 shows terms of trade losses (gains), and increases (decreases) in ODA, by sub-Saharan African country (excluding those in which there have been major political disturbances, those for which there are not published World Bank data and Mauritius, a very special case) between 1980 and 1990. Of the 20 countries in the table, 18 experienced terms of trade losses, averaging 28 per cent. (The overall average, including terms of trade gains, was a loss of 14 per cent.[2] The median was a loss of 30 per cent.) This experience reflected, above all, developments in world primary commodity markets, as shown in Table 15.2. Tropical beverages, vegetable oilseed and oil prices

Table 15.1 Change in terms of trade and development assistance in sub-Saharan Africa, by country, 1980-90

	Terms of trade 1990 (1980=100)	*Annual terms of trade loss/(gain), 1990 (US$ millions)*	*% of 1990 GDP*	*Increase (decrease) in annual ODA, 1980–90, 1989 constant Dollars (millions)*
Low income				
Burkina Faso	98	3	0.0	(31)
Central African Republic	94	8	0.6	54
Ghana	48	800	12.8	207
Kenya	75	344	3.9	449
Madagascar	85	59	1.9	(17)
Malawi	98	8	0.3	224
Mali	109	(29)	(1.2)	34
Mauritania	93	35	9.5	(58)
Niger	69	195	7.7	86
Nigeria	57	10313	29.1	142
Rwanda	51	108	5.0	33
Sierra Leone	71	56	6.2	(73)
Tanzania	77	90	3.8	104
Togo	72	117	7.2	72
Uganda	55	124	4.1	415
Lower Middle-income				
Cameroon	63	704	6.3	52
Congo	70	484	16.9	59
Côte d'Ivoire	62	1594	16.1	305
Senegal	102	(15)	(0.3)	296
Upper Middle-income				
Gabon	63	1451	30.1	43

Notes and source: Terms of trade: derived from UNCTAD (1989) and World Bank (1992a).
Terms of trade loss: 1990 export value (World Bank, 1992a) multiplied by 100/terms of trade, 1990 (1980=100) (from previous column) minus 1990 export value.
Increase in ODA: derived from OECD (1991).
Export volume growth rate: World Bank (1992a).

Table 15.2 Annual percentage rate of change of real non-oil commodity prices, by major commodity groups, 1970–90*

	1970–82	*1982–90*
Tropical beverages	2.3	−11.0
Cocoa	3.7	−11.7
Coffee	2.4	−10.3
Tea	−2.2	−8.0
Food	−2.3	−2.5
Vegetable oilseeds and oils	−3.3	−9.5
Agricultural raw materials	−0.4	−1.9
Minerals, ores and metals	−3.2	0.3
Total	−1.8	−3.1

Note: * Deflated by the UN index of export unit value of manufactures exported by developed countries, 1980 weights.

Source: UNCTAD (1991).

plunged drastically due to expanding supplies and stagnant demand in the 1980s. Real petroleum prices (not shown in Table 15.2) fell by even more from their 1980 peak, causing particularly severe problems for Nigeria and other African petroleum exporters. An up-to-date account would show even further terms of trade losses in SSA; in late 1991, *The Economist*'s index of real primary product prices was at its lowest level since it was first created in the 1840s (*The Economist*, 11 January 1992).

Expressed as a percentage of 1990 GDP, terms of trade losses in some countries – such as Ghana (12.8 per cent), Mauritania (9.5 per cent), Nigeria (29.1 per cent), Congo (16.9 per cent), Côte d'Ivoire (16.1 per cent), Gabon (30.1 per cent) – were very great indeed; and these countries are by no means all oil exporters. The average loss of the losers was 9.0 per cent of GDP; including gainers, it was 8.0 per cent. (The median was a loss of 5.6 per cent of GDP.)

A useful way of assessing the terms of trade loss is to compare it with changes in official development assistance over the same period (also shown in Table 15.1). Leaving oil exporters out (none of whom had terms of trade losses made up by increased ODA[3]), five of the 13 (non-oil) countries (in Table 15.1) that lost from terms of trade deterioration enjoyed increases in ODA that more than compensated: Central African Republic, Kenya, Malawi, Tanzania and Uganda. The remaining eight countries did not: Burkina Faso, Ghana, Madagascar,

Mauritania, Rwanda, Sierra Leone, Togo and Côte d'Ivoire. Evidently, while the majority suffered net (of ODA) terms of trade losses, aid donors did more than compensate some. Seven of the 20 countries shown either enjoyed terms of trade improvements or ODA increases that more than compensated for terms of trade losses over the 1980s. In the majority (65 per cent) of cases, however, the aid increases of the 1980s failed even to compensate sub-Saharan African countries for their terms of trade losses.

This account has not included inward private capital flows, capital flight or debt servicing obligations, which, together, generally worsened balance of payments pressures (see Husain and Underwood, 1991, for a full account).

Recent World Bank analysis of the experience of countries receiving its adjustment loans in the 1980s tells an even more depressing story. According to its data, both the sub-Saharan African and low-income recipients of World Bank adjustment loans suffered external shocks (from terms of trade and interest rate changes) which, in total, *considerably* exceeded increases in external capital flows during their adjustment periods in the 1980s.

Table 15.3 shows the average external shock in the 1981–5 and 1986–90 periods, relative to the average experience in the 1970s, expressed as a percentage of average GDP, for two categories of countries in sub-Saharan Africa and the low-income group – those benefiting from intensive Bank adjustment lending and those receiving 'other' adjustment lending. (Table 15.4 lists the countries in the Bank's categories.) The right-hand side of the table shows the resource balance deficit (net external resource transfer) as a percentage of GDP. Adjusting sub-Saharan African countries, after a large injection of external resources in 1981–2, thereafter suffered declines in these flows in 1986–90 to lower levels than had been enjoyed in the 1970s; this occurred while they were absorbing external shocks of 4–5 per cent, on average, of their GDP relative to the 1970s. In adjusting low-income countries too, external shocks were not nearly compensated by changes in external resource flows (although those enjoying intensive adjustment lending experienced a small increase in resource flows).

Table 15.5 shows, for the record, aggregate real net resource flows and real net transfers to sub-Saharan Africa over the past decade, *without* taking external shocks into account. It is noteworthy that both real resource flows and transfers peaked in 1989. Both have dropped severely in the two subsequent years – to levels below those of 1981–2 – while real commodity prices were plunging.

Table 15.3 External shocks and resource balance deficits, sub-Saharan Africa and low-income countries, 1970s and 1980s

	Total external shock		*Resource balance deficit*			
	1981–5 vs. 1971–80	*1986–90 vs. 1971–80*	*1971–9*	*1981–2*	*1983–5*	*1986–90*
	(% of GDP)		*(% of GDP)*			
Sub–Saharan African countries						
Intensive adjustment lending (IAL)	–4.8	–5.0	7.4	11.6	6.7	7.3
Other adjustment lending (OAL)	+5.1	–4.0	9.8	13.4	7.7	7.6
Low–income countries						
Intensive adjustment lending (IAL)	–4.4	–4.5	7.9	11.5	7.8	8.4
Other adjustment lending (OAL)	+1.9	–1.9	10.7	16.5	12.5	10.1

Source: World Bank (1992b).

Table 15.4 World Bank categories for analysis of Table 15.3

IAL		*OAL*	
Sub–Saharan	*Low–income*	*Sub–Saharan*	*Low–income*
Côte d'Ivoire	Bolivia	Benin	Bangladesh
Ghana	Ghana	Burkina Faso	Benin
Guinea–Bissau	Guinea–Bissau	Burundi	Burkina Faso
Kenya	Kenya	Cameroon	Burundi
Madagascar	Madagascar	CAR	CAR
Malawi	Malawi	Congo P.R.	The Gambia
Mauritania	Mauritania	Gabon	Mali
Mauritius	Nigeria	The Gambia	Niger
Nigeria	Pakistan	Mali	Sierra Leone
Senegal	Senegal	Niger	Somalia
Tanzania	Tanzania	Sierra Leone	Sri Lanka
Togo	Togo	Somalia	Sudan
Zambia	Zambia	Sudan	Zaire
		Zaire	
		Zimbabwe	

Source: World Bank (1992b).

Table 15.5 Aggregate real net resource flows and net transfers (long-term) to sub-Saharan Africa, 1980–91 (constant 1991 US$ billions)

	1980	*1981*	*1982*	*1983*	*1984*	*1985*	*1986*	*1987*	*1988*	*1989*	*1990*	*1991*
Real net resource flows	13.6	15.2	16.4	13.3	11.7	12.3	13.9	16.0	14.8	18.1	15.8	14.4
Real net transfers	7.3	9.9	11.1	8.2	6.1	5.8	8.5	10.2	8.9	13.2	10.9	9.5

Source: Joint Bank/Fund Development Committee (1992).

IV THE NEED FOR FURTHER DEBT RELIEF

The evident need for increased official resource transfers for African development is directly related to the problem of Africa's external debt, most of which is owed to official creditors. If newly-acquired external resources must be employed for the service of external debt, they obviously cannot contribute to African social or economic development.

Sub-Saharan African countries actually directed, on average, about 6 per cent of GDP, and 20 per cent of exports, to external debt service in 1991–2. In 1991, about 36 per cent of scheduled interest and principal payments on long-term debt were added to arrears, exclusive of the rising arrears to the IMF. That is, actual debt service payments amounted, in total, to no more than 60 per cent or so of those to which these debtors were contractually obliged.

In economies that are so dependent upon key imported inputs for the utilisation of their existing capacity and external savings for their growth it is unfortunate, indeed shocking, that high proportions of available 'free' foreign exchange should have to be employed in the servicing of foreign debt. In this context, it is also shocking that 'aid donors' continue to tie so much of their assistance to particular items and/or sources that do not always coincide with recipients' needs. Writing down the African external debt, and 'freeing', as well as significantly expanding, official development assistance could make a major contribution to African recovery in the 1990s. Official flows and debt problems therefore must be considered in an integrated and consistent fashion.

It is well known that in recent years the problems created by Africa's external debt have been worsening. The overhang of African debt, still increasing in consequence of failure to fully meet current obligations, now constitutes a significant extra drag upon the prospects for African development. The constant pressure of debt-related financial negotiations deflects policy makers from the necessary and more socially productive activities of development-oriented economic decision-making. It thus both detracts from effective economic governance and reduces absorptive capacity for utilisation of further public resources, whether locally or externally mobilised, for development. African governments' absorptive capacity for further debt negotiations and extensive consultations with external sources of advice is a much greater problem, in the majority of cases, than their absorptive capacity for further resources. No less important, heavy external debt servicing obligations discourage private investors and government reformers alike by imposing a major 'tax' upon successful adjustment efforts.

Reducing the current external cash flow obligations and payments on debt accounts, particularly for those countries that are pursuing serious policy reforms and getting their macroeconomic fundamentals 'right', will thus most likely be the most cost-effective form of official external resource transfer to Africa in the 1990s. Debt reduction must constitute a major element in any serious externally supported effort to restart African development.

Although in most sub-Saharan African countries (Nigeria is a major exception) private creditors account for a relatively small proportion of external debt, failure to deal with them – through clearing arrears, rescheduling and writedowns – can be very costly in terms of more expensive or unavailable trade credit and higher-priced imports. As far as commercial debt is concerned, there is no reason, in principle, for African debtors to be treated in any way less favourably or less quickly than those already benefiting from debt reduction initiatives under the Brady initiative, or its successor arrangements.

Four Sub-Saharan African countries (Niger, Mozambique, Nigeria and Uganda) retired commercial bank debt in 1991–3 by buying it back and/or converting it to new instruments at significant discounts (18, 10, 40 and 12 per cent respectively), and several more are in preparation. Except in the case of Nigeria, which financed its own programme, the buy-backs have been financed, up to a limit of $10 million per country, by grants from a special $100 million IDA 'debt reduction facility' established (from World Bank profits) in 1990 for this purpose – the so-called 'sixth dimension' – and by official donor grants (from France, the Netherlands, Switzerland and Sweden). The complexity and time-consuming character of the necessary negotiations have impeded efforts to retire commercial debt more quickly and in more countries. The $100 million fund provided to IDA out of the IBRD's profits for this purpose is already much too small. Developed country governments that are themselves writing down their own African debt should insist, and provide inducements to ensure, that their private creditors offer no less favourable arrangements to the beneficiary debtors. Thus far they have largely, and inappropriately, stood aside from these negotiations.

Modest amounts have also been converted in debt-for-development schemes into local currency for use in environmental protection or social expenditures. By June 1992, about $80 million had been converted in sub-Saharan Africa, half of this total in Nigeria and the rest in Ghana, Guinea, Kenya, Madagascar, Niger, Sudan and Zambia. These efforts should continue to be encouraged but their aggregate importance is likely to remain relatively small.

There have already been many official initiatives in the sphere of African external debt. So far, however, they have had only minor effects upon the transfer of resources to Africa. Cancellation of debt associated with earlier ODA lending has mattered little since the debt was originally on very soft terms. Some official creditors have also cancelled, written down or converted other official loans on a bilateral basis; but the total value of such concessions has been small. The most significant official debt relief has been multilaterally agreed in the Paris Club, particularly after the Western Economic Summit in Toronto in 1988.

The so-called Toronto terms for Paris Club debt rescheduling have long been recognised as far from adequate. The terms of debt reductions, where they occurred, were too modest (averaging about 20 per cent) (World Bank, 1990b), too slow to take effect (because they applied only to servicing obligations during the 'consolidation period' rather than to the entire stock of debt), confined to too limited a share of the stock (the 'eligible' debt, contracted before the 'cutoff date', when the country first received Paris Club relief), and too costly in terms of negotiators' time. Some creditors have consistently availed themselves of the agreed option to extend maturities rather than reduce principal or interest rates.

Among the most important proposals that have been offered by non-Africans for improving Paris Club treatment of low-income African countries' debt are:

1. a one-off reduction of the total eligible debt stock (rather than continuing to reschedule only one year's maturities each year) by two

thirds, with an initial five-year period of interest capitalisation and an extension of the repayment period from 14 to 24 years for the remaining debt (Major/Trinidad, 20 September 1990);
2. total forgiveness of bilateral official debt to the poorest of the severely debt-distressed countries (the 'least developed' and other low-income countries) (Pronk/Paris, 7 September 1990);
3. a three- to ten-year moratorium on all bilateral official debt servicing with all rescheduling on IDA terms (Fraser/UN, 1990).

All of these are to be conditional on the existence of an agreed adjustment programme and additional to current or anticipated resource flow commitments (see Abbate and Tran-Nguyen, 1991, for an analysis of the effects of these proposals).

From December 1991 onwards, the so-called 'enhanced Toronto terms' have slowly been introduced to a number of African countries (Benin, Ethiopia, Guinea, Mali, Mauritania, Mozambique, Sierra Leone, Tanzania, Togo, Uganda and Zambia) by all but a few official creditors. These provide for 50 per cent reductions in the net present value of payments on the consolidated portion of non-ODA debt, a somewhat longer consolidation period (with an extension if IMF programmes are 'on track'), and a promise to consider a total 'eligible' debt stock reduction after three years (again, if IMF targets are reached). The 50 per cent figure – well short of the Trinidad terms – seems to have originated in the unfavourable comparisons so frequently drawn between the Paris Club's provisions (50 per cent writedown) for Egypt and Poland and its treatment of low-income countries. The World Bank's willingness to finance the buy-back of commercial debt at very low prices would seem to imply official approval for writedowns on African debt that are considerably larger than those that have so far been undertaken by official creditors themselves. Indeed, they are larger than the so-called 'Trinidad' terms proposed by the British Government in September 1990. The continued constipation of the Paris Club's response to low-income Africa's debt problems, in the face of virtually unanimous professional agreement and much high-flown political rhetoric, defies either political or economic explanation. Low-income debt-distressed countries urgently need much more radical official debt relief than has so far been offered, and they need it for their entire stock of debt.

Since international financial institutions' debt (making up an increasing share, now about one third of total annual actual debt servicing) will not be touched, and only about 15 per cent (in 1990) of actual sub-

Saharan African debt servicing is to the Paris Club, the improvements in Africa's cash flow emanating from Paris Club reforms, actual or proposed, will not be as great as might be supposed. Nevertheless, they can be of significant benefit to some of the low-income African countries. Unfortunately, the gains will, in some cases, be immediately deducted from bilateral ODA commitments to the beneficiary countries, leaving them literally no better off than before (except with respect to the reduced debt overhang).

Low-income debt-distressed countries' obligations to multilateral institutions are, by common agreement, best handled by refinancing at highly concessional terms; and most of the World Bank's and IMF's credit to these countries has already been treated in this manner. Some bilateral donors are also providing grants to debt-distressed African countries that are undertaking reform programmes to permit them to meet current obligations to the international financial institutions. The problem of arrears to the international financial institutions, however, is a much more difficult issue.

Arrears in African countries' repayment obligations to the IMF are unlikely to be successfully addressed in existing or newly agreed arrangements for dealing with them, all of which require major 'up front' policy change, without the prospect of supportive external resource transfers (earned through accumulation of 'rights') until much later. Such punitive approaches risk aborting recovery. Where adjustment programmes have been agreed and performance is maintained, the errors of the past should not be permitted to further cloud what is, in any case, a highly precarious economic future. IMF arrears, or at least the interest on these arrears, should be financed via the sale of IMF gold, so as not to 'waste' scarce donor resources on maintaining the IMF's already 'super-safe' balance sheet.

V INSTITUTIONAL REFORM IN THE AID RELATIONSHIP

Given that the development problems faced by African countries are now seen as being long-term in nature, their financial difficulties are not best addressed through mechanisms, such as those of the IMF, that were designed for short-term or 'emergency' circumstances. It is surely anomalous that so much in the realm of the financing of development still rests upon the shoulders of the IMF, which is both ill-equipped and hesitant to prescribe upon developmental matters, and which, for its own good reasons, has been taking resources (exclusive of increasing arrears) out of sub-Saharan Africa for a good many years.

In any case, the IMF no longer acts as a supplier of conventional liquidity to the low-income countries. Rather, it collaborates with the World Bank (and other official suppliers of longer-term finance) in the development of short- to medium-term (three year) overall economic policy frameworks and, where possible, supplies modest amounts of supportive and highly concessional medium-term finance. Not only has it been unable, despite contrary statements of intent, to prevent net aggregate repayments from sub-Saharan Africa for the past half-decade, but its contingency financing facility has failed to play any role in securing the success of those adjustment/development programmes it has supported in low-income countries.

Is it therefore not at last time to reconsider the most appropriate means for the provision of international finance to very low-income countries? The IMF's traditional role as a supplier of short-term finance is not being performed now, and apparently cannot easily be performed under existing institutional arrangements. The overwhelming need in these countries is for grants and long-term finance in support of far-sighted development programmes. It would therefore be best, in the case of very low-income (or 'least developed') countries, to build new (and workable) contingency financing arrangements into the longer-term financing programmes put together by the World Bank and other aid donors in World Bank consortia, UNDP Roundtables, and the like; and allow the IMF to retreat, in these cases, to a relatively smaller role as a source of technical advice on monetary matters.

The IMF would thereby be relieved of an 'aid' role with which it is not comfortable (see for instance Polak, 1989), the 'bad press' associated with its steady negative net transfer out of Africa as well as its inappropriate role as 'gatekeeper' for access to debt relief and external finance. The IMF's present claims on very low-income countries could either be frozen at existing levels or eliminated by using the proceeds from limited sales of IMF gold. The World Bank group would then formally take over as the international financial institution with primary, *though certainly not exclusive*, responsibility for assessing these countries' needs for external finance, and for formulating and monitoring country-specific conditions for its provision. To perform this role effectively it would be required to both encourage efforts to expand the role of independent advisors and further to develop its cooperation with other national and international development agencies, including those of the United Nations and, in Africa's case, the African Development Bank and the Economic Commission for Africa.

'Graduation' from very low-income (least-developed? IDA-eligible?) status would thereafter involve a return to 'normal' IMF membership.

Such an institutional 'reform' may not be of enormous immediate economic consequence for the relevant lowest-income African countries; but if their debt is to be satisfactorily dealt with at last, and serious efforts made both to strengthen their economic decision-making capacity and to reduce unnecessary transaction costs, it would be a useful and appropriately-timed concomitant of these other, more important, measures.

To some degree, the international financial system has already been edging in this direction. Is it not now time to shift in a more direct and visible manner? In any new dispensation it will be important, above all, to avoid the creation of any one overpowering arbiter of Africa's development requirements, such as the World Bank seems to many to have become. The object must be, rather, to assist Africans in reaching their own development decisions through the provision of multifaceted and sustained external assistance – in the context of genuine policy dialogue, and consistent and sustained domestic effort.

VI CONCLUSION

The 'disappointing' performance of sub-Saharan African countries engaged in adjustment efforts is *not* the product of insufficient policy reform. It is, above all, the product of initial conditions (low levels of development) that are more difficult to build upon than those of others, and of insufficient external support (net of adverse external shocks). Development takes longer than enthusiastic reform-mongers originally thought; it also takes more resources. (In addition, there is room for doubt as to the efficacy of some of the adjustment policies being pushed upon reforming governments, but these issues have not been addressed in this chapter.)

Increased debt relief and expanded official development assistance will be necessary if the economic performance of those sub-Saharan African countries that are getting their policies broadly 'right' is to approach acceptable and hoped-for levels. The need for longer-term perspectives and sustained external resource flows suggests a relatively diminished future role for the IMF in sub-Saharan Africa. The power of the World Bank, the obvious multilateral alternative to the IMF, is unfortunately already too great relative to that of African governments and institutions, and other sources of external assistance.

Expanded external resource flows must therefore be accompanied by improved mechanisms for policy dialogue, broader participation in it, and the development of local 'ownership' of policies and programmes.

NOTES

1. For instance, dispensaries without medicine, schools without textbooks or paper, and so on.
2. These averages are calculated on a simple, unweighted basis.
3. Niger, Nigeria, Cameroon, Congo and Gabon. All benefited from ODA increases over the 1980s, but these increases all fell substantially short of their terms of trade losses.

16 The Output and Inflationary Impact of Devaluation in Developing Countries: Theory and Empirical Evidence from Five African Low-income Countries*

Riccardo Faini

I INTRODUCTION

There are striking similarities in the recent economic history of many low-income countries with primary commodity-based economies. Typically, the 1970s brought a commodity price boom, which more than offset the terms of trade impact of the first oil shock. Around 1974–5, the price of most commodities suddenly rocketed. For instance, between 1976 and 1977 the price of cocoa almost doubled, while that of coffee, a major foreign exchange earner for many sub-Saharan African countries, tripled between 1975 and 1977. However, not all commodities showed this upward trend: mineral prices, such as copper, remained depressed for the entire decade.

While this commodity price boom brought a significant improvement in the terms of trade, it also created substantial macroeconomic complications. First, rudimentary tools of macroeconomic control did

* This chapter draws on research undertaken for UNCTAD. The author wishes to thank A. Tran-Nguyen and F. Giannotti for useful discussions and assistance with the data. The opinions expressed in the chapter are those of the author and should not be attributed to UNCTAD.

not allow policy makers to sterilise the monetary implications of the greater inflow of foreign exchange, exacerbating therefore the process of real appreciation. Second, political pressure to abandon conservative fiscal policies often became irresistible following the fiscal bonanza. In Kenya, real fiscal revenues increased by almost 50 per cent between 1975 and 1979 in the wake of higher coffee prices. It was therefore extremely difficult for the government to deny demands for higher social and economic spending. But this was not the end of the story: the surge in commodity prices led to the general expectation of further increases, with enhanced effects on export performances and fiscal revenues. Countries were therefore able to supplement their revenues with external borrowing. The need for the international banking system to recycle OPEC surpluses favoured this trend. The extent and the ease with which many SSA countries gained access to Eurocurrency markets is therefore not very surprising. Even in those (mineral-exporting) countries which did not share the commodity boom, the expectation was that mineral prices would soon return to and exceed earlier levels. Hence even these countries were able to finance increased public expenditures. When the commodity price boom failed to materialise, or when it dimmed, governments reacted by relying even more heavily on foreign borrowing. Bankers obligingly supplied further credit.

As is well known, the beginning of the 1980s marked a turning-point for many developing countries. The international financial system had grown increasingly weary of large-scale lending to the Third World. The collapse in commodity prices and more generally the dramatic deterioration in their terms of trade, the surge in interest rates and the sequence of negative (agricultural) supply shocks were more than many countries could endure. Faced with a sudden cutback in foreign lending, precisely when it was more urgently needed, many developing countries were forced to reassess their fiscal, monetary and exchange rate policies. They had to earn more foreign exchange either by exporting more or by importing less, i.e. by increasing income or by reducing absorption. Real exchange rate depreciation became an essential component of the adjustment process in developing countries. It was intended to promote both export expansion and import contraction. IMF-supported stabilisation programmes invariably included stringent conditions on devaluation. The World Bank also conditioned most of its programme lending to a more flexible management of the exchange rate. While the 1970s commodity bonanza had allowed many developing countries to overlook the difficult issues relating to exchange rate policies, the 1980s brought the need for more rigorous management to the forefront.

The insistence by international organisations on the need for currency depreciation was not however universally accepted. Many critics argued that devaluation policies could prove to be ineffective or could even have perverse effects. Theoretical and empirical studies contended that devaluation would have inflationary and sometimes even contractionary effects. Yet the fact remains that the real exchange rate in most developing countries followed a steadily depreciating trend during the 1980s. The question therefore arises: Were devaluation policies generally beneficial, or was devaluation excessive at times, breeding inflation rather than promoting adjustment? This chapter addresses this question by examining the experience of five low-income countries: Ghana, Kenya, Malawi, Senegal and Zambia.

II THE IMPACT OF DEVALUATION: A THEORETICAL SURVEY

Theoretical surveys of the impact of devaluation typically distinguish three approaches, focusing on elasticity, absorption and monetary aspects. The crucial assumptions in these models concern the level of resource utilisation and the flexibility of domestic prices. In a Keynesian-inspired model, resources are not fully utilised and output is to some extent demand-determined. Consider the simplest case where domestic prices are sticky: a nominal devaluation will lead to a corresponding real depreciation; in turn, depreciation of the real exchange rate will work by boosting demand for domestic output, both by domestic and foreign consumers, leading to increased production. As a result, devaluation will have an unambiguous expansionary effect on the economy, which will be magnified by high values of export and import demand price elasticities. Consider the case where the external disequilibrium does not prompt policy makers to devalue: the loss of reserves and the unemployment induced by the overvalued exchange rate will result in tempered wage demands and inflation, and will eventually restore the external balance. The process, however, may be long and painful due to widespread price and wage rigidities.

At the other extreme of the theoretical spectrum is the monetarist model, where resources are fully utilised and the purchasing power parity holds. Domestic prices therefore cannot fall out of line with respect to foreign prices. A devaluation will be fully reflected in raised domestic prices, with no effect on the real exchange rate. Similarly, output will stay at its full employment level. The trade balance will nonetheless improve in that price increases will reduce the real value of household wealth and, through the real balance effects, depress absorption. Contrary to the Keynesian model, even in the absence of devaluation, the full flexibility of prices ensures that the automatic adjustment mechanism will act quickly and effectively in returning equilibrium to the economy.

How useful are these two models in understanding the impact of devaluation in developing countries? The underlying assumption of fixed resource utilisation in the monetarist model is not very helpful, particularly in the developing country context where cyclical and structural factors combine to keep the economy well within its production possibility frontier. Even the Keynesian approach, however, has shortcomings, both because of a disproportionate attention to demand factors and the assumption that the country has some market power and can therefore influence its terms of trade. For most developing countries, a more palatable assumption would be that they have little or no market power and cannot influence international prices.This chapter therefore relies on an alternative approach: the (two-sector) dependent economy model with exogenous terms of trade. The economy is assumed to be small in international markets, yet its real exchange rate is well defined as the relative price of non-traded goods. Finally, both demand and supply factors can be shown to determine equilibrium in the economy. This approach, as the following discussion will demonstrate, can cast considerable light on the controversy surrounding the impact of devaluation.

Assume that the levels of production in both the traded and non-traded goods sectors are a function of labour and capital, with capital fixed in the short run:

$$Q_i = F_i(L_i, K_i) \tag{1}$$

$$i = T, N$$

where Q_i, L_i and K_i respectively denote output, labour and capital in sector i. The two subscripts, T and N, refer to the traded and the non-traded goods sectors respectively. Profit maximisation subject to equation (1) will determine labour demand, which will depend on the exogenously fixed capital and the real wage. In turn, employment will determine output through equation (1). To close the model, we need to specify the demand side. The total expenditure (Z) is assumed to be equal to real income.[1] Finally demand for good i is specified in very general terms:

$$D_i = D_i(Z, p_T, p_N) \tag{3}$$

where p_i is the price of good i. Suppose now that the nominal wage w is fixed.[2] Clearly, the economy may settle at an equilibrium where resources are not fully employed. Traded goods prices are fixed for a given nominal exchange rate. This fixes the real wage, and thus employment and output, for traded goods producers. Non-traded goods prices, on the other hand, will equate demand and supply in that market. There is no guarantee that p_N will be high enough for labour demand in the non-traded goods sector to absorb unemployment.

This simple set-up can be used to study the effect of devaluation. A currency depreciation will bring a proportionate increase in the price of traded goods, which in turn will lead to supply and demand effects for both traded and non-traded goods. It can be shown (see the Annex to this chapter for a formal derivation) that the percentage change of the price of non-traded goods will be equal to:

$$p'_N = \frac{1}{\epsilon_N(1 - \eta_N\gamma_N) + \eta_{NT}} (\eta_N\gamma_T\epsilon_T + \eta_{NT})p'_T \tag{4}$$

where γ_i, η_i, ϵ_i, and η_{NT} denote respectively the income share, the income elasticity of demand, the price elasticity of supply and the compensated price elasticity of demand for good i. A prime indicates a log-derivative.

Some interesting implications can be drawn from equation (4):

1. Devaluation is inflationary: we have both $p'_T > 0$ and $p'_N > 0$.
2. Devaluation is expansionary:[3] under the condition of money wage rigidity, the increase in p_T and p_N, will lead to higher output and employment in both sectors.
3. The balance between inflation and expansion depends crucially on the elasticity of supply. Consider two polar cases: a) $\epsilon_T = \epsilon_N = 0$. Then $p'_T = p'_N$, i.e. inflation is high, there is no real exchange rate depreciation and no effect on output levels; b) $\epsilon_N = +\infty$, $\epsilon_T > 0$. Then prices of non-traded goods will not change, the nominal devaluation will be matched by an equivalent real depreciation, and output in both sectors will increase. It is important to note that a high value of the supply elasticity for traded goods, ϵ_T, is a mixed

blessing. On the one hand, it strengthens the expansionary effects of devaluation; on the other, it exacerbates its inflationary consequences. The reason for this perhaps unexpected result is simple. A high value of $\in_T$ will lead to a substantial increase in output of traded goods following a devaluation. The consequent income effect will feed back into demand and prices for domestic non-traded goods. As noted earlier, this may be an important channel in primary exporting countries, where traded goods prices and output fluctuations have pervasive effects on the rest of the economy.

The presence of black and/or parallel markets for goods and foreign exchange may substantially affect how devaluation operates. This is a crucial consideration for one country in our sample, Ghana. The literature on this issue has grown quite rapidly in the last few years (for theoretical analyses see Dornbusch, 1986; Kharas and Pinto, 1989; Lizondo, 1987, 1991; and Pinto, 1991; for empirical applications see Chhibber and Shafik, 1990; and Islam and Wetzel, 1991). The typical assumption in models of this kind is that agents hold both domestic money and foreign assets in their portfolio. The proportions of the two types of assets is a function of the expected rate of depreciation of the black market exchange rate. An increase in the budget deficit financed by money creation will create a portfolio disequilibrium, with the excess supply of money inducing a depreciation of the parallel exchange rate. In some models, this will feed back on the real economy, provided that some current accounts transactions are conducted at the black market rate. Suppose for instance that, because of widespread foreign exchange rationing (as in Ghana, before 1984), producers buy their imported inputs from the black market. The devaluation of the black market rate will then increase intermediate input costs and lead to a real appreciation. Interestingly, in this set-up, an increase in foreign aid will not lead, as in more standard models, to a real appreciation. In fact, the increase in capital inflow will allow the government to rely less on monetary financing and, through this channel, pressure on the real exchange rate and on inflation will be reduced. Devaluation of the official exchange rate will also be effective, at least in the short run. Increasing the domestic price level will induce a portfolio imbalance, i.e. an excess *demand* for domestic money. The black market exchange rate will appreciate, with beneficial effects on inflation. Furthermore, the reduced differential between the black and the official exchange rates may encourage exporters to rely more on official channels, with positive effects on the budget deficit.

III THE EMPIRICAL EVIDENCE FOR FIVE LOW-INCOME COUNTRIES

(A) The real impact of a devaluation

The impact of a real depreciation on the real economy has been the subject of long-standing controversy, both at a theoretical and empirical level. Some of the main theoretical arguments were reviewed in the previous section. From an empirical point of view, there is consensus that for developing countries a real depreciation would lead to some improvements in the trade balance, but with relatively limited effects (Faini and de Melo, 1990). Further, a real depreciation would not, at least in the short run, elicit a substantial output response, so the burden of the trade balance improvement would fall mostly on a contraction of aggregate demand. We first test these propositions for our sample countries by running the following simple regression:

$$TB/Y = a_0 + a_1 \ln RER_t \qquad (7)$$

where Y and TB stand for real output and the real trade balance respectively. Estimation results for equation (7) are presented in Table 16.1. We rely both on an ordinary least-squares and an instrumental variables procedure, but only present the latter. For the five countries in the sample, the coefficient has a negative sign, i.e. a real appreciation will worsen the trade balance, and is statistically different from zero. Its value is however quite small (.086, against .20 for a large sample of developing countries (Faini and de Melo, 1990)). Individual

Table 16.1 Real exchange rate and the trade balance

Dep. var.:	*TB/Y*	
Sample	$\ln(RER)_t$	St. error
5 countries	−.086	.025
Ghana	−.01	.008
Kenya	−.28	.069
Malawi	−1.05	.34
Senegal	.20	.11
Zambia	−.45	.16

Note: Estimation procedure: instrumental variables (IV) (instruments: terms of trade, $\ln(RER)_{t-1}$, $(TB/Y)_{t-1}$, country dummies).

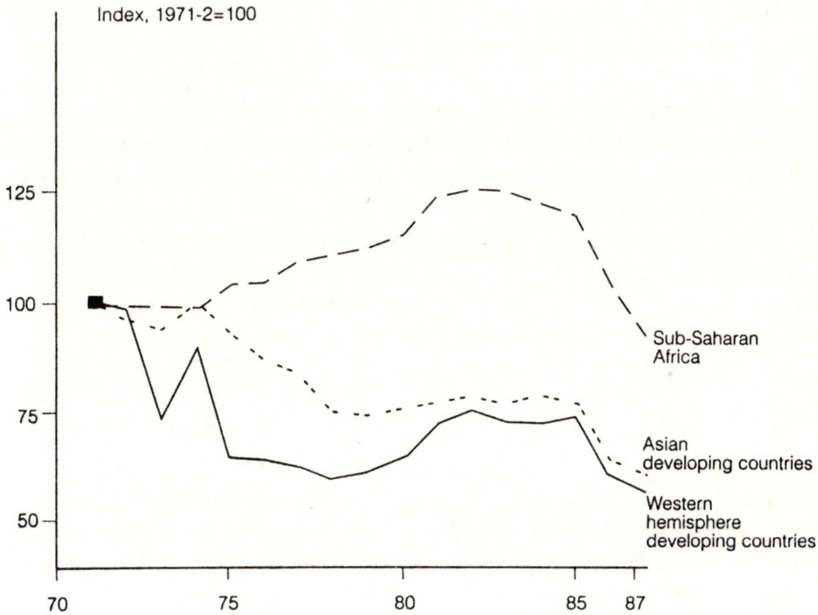

Figure 16.1 Real effective exchange rate for selected regions, 1970–87
Source: World Bank (1989e).

country results provide a broad confirmation of these results. Overall, such findings support the notion that devaluation in low-income countries will only induce a modest improvement in the trade balance.

Some comment on these results is needed. The finding that the trade balance is not very responsive to the real exchange rate seems to contradict the claim by Balassa (1989) that exports in sub-Saharan Africa are fairly elastic to relative price changes. Balassa's results are corroborated by the observation that SSA lost market shares during the 1970s when its real exchange rate was appreciating (Figure 16.1) and that these losses have largely been recouped with the recent depreciation. To reconcile these seemingly conflicting results, it need only be recalled that imports in a foreign exchange constrained economy may exhibit a perverse response to the real exchange rate. Suppose that the total import flow is constrained by the availability of foreign exchange. A real depreciation will have two conflicting effects: on the one hand, it will increase the price of imported goods; on the other, it will raise export receipts and therefore induce a higher demand for imports. Existing empirical evidence (Moran, 1989; Faini et al., 1992) concludes that the latter effect is quite strong and may account for the overall low responsiveness of the trade balance to variations in the real exchange rate.[4]

What impact does a real depreciation have on output? We take the following route to answer this question. The short-run output equation is assumed to be a log-linear function of the capital stock (K) and of the real exchange rate:

$$\ln Y_t = b_0 + b_1 \ln K_t + b_2 \ln RER_t + b_3\, t \tag{8}$$

where the coefficient b_3 captures the effect of technological progress. Equation (8) cannot be estimated as it stands, as there is no information on the capital stock. We rely on the following procedure: equation (8) is considered to be lagged one period, i.e. for Y_{t-1} and multiply it by $(1 - \delta)$, where δ stands for the depreciation rate. We then subtract the resulting expression from equation (8) and use a log-linear approximation to the capital stock identity $K_t = I_t + (1 - \delta)\, K_{t-1}$. The estimating equation then becomes:

$$\ln Y_t = b_0 + b_1 \ln I_t + b_2 \ln RER_t - (1-\delta)\, b_2 \ln RER_{t-1} + (1-\delta)\, lnY_{t-1} \tag{9}$$

Again, we apply equation (9) to a time-series – cross-section of our sample countries. All coefficients are fairly well determined (Table 16.2). In addition, the coefficient b_2 bears a negative sign, an indication that at least in this case the output response to a real depreciation is positive. The coefficient is however very small and, quite crucially, significantly smaller than the coefficient a_1 measuring the impact of the real exchange rate on the trade balance. The results are borne out by different estimation methods, i.e. by an instrumental variable procedure (column 2). Negative coefficients are also found, at an individual country level, for Ghana, Malawi and Zambia. The small, albeit positive, output response indicates that a real depreciation will

Table 16.2 Output and the real exchange rate

Dep. Var.: $\ln Y_t$		
Expl. var.	CS[a, b]	CS[a, c]
$\ln I_t$	.026	.037
	(.015)	(.020)
$\ln(RER)_t$	–.038	–.050
	(.019)	(.021)
$\ln(RER)_{t-1}$	0.24	.042
	(0.19)	(.022)
$\ln Y_{t-1}$	.92	.97
	(.029)	(0.34)
R^2	.999	.999
DW	2.02	2.13

Notes:
[a] CS: cross–section analysis (Ghana, Kenya, Malawi, Senegal, Zambia)
[b] OLS estimates
[c] Instrumental variable (IV) estimates (instruments: terms of trade, exchange rate, money supply, capital flows, lagged values of previous variables, lagged GDP deflator, country dummies).
Standard errors in parentheses. Country intercepts have been omitted.

improve the trade balance largely by compressing domestic absorption.

(B) The inflationary impact of devaluation

Besides strongly questioning the favourable evaluation of the impact of adjustment programmes on SSA countries offered by a World Bank/ UNDP study, the Economic Commission for Africa has recently argued that one of the main effects of currency devaluation in Africa has been to fuel inflation.[5] To examine this issue more closely, it is necessary to specify the determinants of inflation. Following existing literature, a distinction is made between cost-push factors (i.e. the cost-increasing effect of higher wages and input prices), excess demand (induced by unduly expansionary macroeconomic policies) and other exogenous factors (weather shocks, price decontrols). The impact of these factors will differ depending on the import and exchange rate regime in a particular economy. Drawing on Chhibber (1992), we distinguish between countries with an open capital account and fixed exchange rate (i.e. Senegal), countries with a closed capital account and a fixed but adjustable exchange rate (Kenya) and countries with a closed capital account and pervasive controls (Ghana, until 1983). It is expected that monetary policy will be relatively less influential in the first case, provided that excessive monetary growth spills mostly into capital outflows rather than into the goods market. In the second case, all factors should simultaneously affect inflation, while in the third case devaluation may have little impact on inflation (as argued in the previous section). In general, devaluation is expected to have both a direct effect on inflation by increasing import prices and an indirect effect by influencing wage-setting behaviour and monetary policy. The equation below grasps only the direct effect. Following these considerations, price behaviour is modelled in the following manner:

$$\ln p_t = \alpha + \alpha_0 \ln w_t + \alpha_1 \ln w_{t-1} + \alpha_2 \ln e_t + \alpha_3 \ln e_{t-1} + \alpha_4 \ln M_t + \alpha_5 \ln M_{t-1} + \alpha_6 \ln p_{t-1} + \alpha_7 CU \quad (12)$$

where p, w, M, e and CU denote respectively domestic prices, wages, nominal exchange rate, broad money supply and capacity utilisation. The last term is used to capture the impact of supply shocks. It is measured as the deviation of output from its trend. We expect prices to be homogeneous of degree one in their nominal determinants, i.e. an equi-proportionate increase in w, e and M should lead to an equal increase in prices. To test this restriction, equation (12) is reparametrised in the following manner:

$$\Delta \ln p_t = \alpha + \alpha_0 \Delta \ln w_t + (\alpha_0 + \alpha_1)(\ln w_{t-1} - \ln p_{t-1}) + \alpha_2 \Delta \ln e_t + (\alpha_2 + \alpha_3)(\ln e_{t-1} - \ln p_{t-1}) + \alpha_4 \Delta \ln M_t + (\alpha_4 + \alpha_5)(\ln M_{t-1} - \ln p_{t-1}) + (\alpha_0 + \alpha_1 + \alpha_2 + \alpha_3 + \alpha_4 + \alpha_5 + \alpha_6 - 1)\ln p_{t-1} + \alpha_7 CU \quad (13)$$

It can easily be verified that if price homogeneity holds, the coefficient of $\ln p_{t-1}$ should be zero. The restriction is easily accepted both for the cross-country analysis and at an individual country level, and has been imposed on the data. In the estimation, broad money supply, manufacturing wages and the special drawing right (SDR) exchange rate are used as a measure of M, w and e respectively. The dependent variable is taken to be the GDP deflator. Table 16.3 presents the long-run elasticities of prices with respect to money supply, nominal exchange rate and wages and the short-run elasticity with respect to capacity utilisation. All the equations have been estimated by instrumental variables, with the exception of Kenya for which a Hausman test did not however indicate any bias in the ordinary least squares estimates. For the cross-section sample, both the ordinary least squares and the instrumental variables estimates are displayed. The point coefficients do not differ much, but the estimates are much less precise when we rely on an instrumental variable procedure. Consider the cross-section results (row 1): first, exchange rates, money supply and, at a lower level of significance, wages, all affect prices; second, the impact of the exchange rate on prices is not exceedingly large, .31 in the long run, a value not very different to the average degree of openness in these economies;[6] third, our measure of capacity utilisation, *CU*, has a negative effect on prices, suggesting that a positive supply shock, such as a good harvest, will contribute to reduce inflation; finally, the results for wages and money supply are borne out by individual country estimates. Ghana was not included in the cross-section, given its significant behavioural differences in the inflation process. Following earlier considerations, it is essential to include a measure of both the official and the black market exchange rate in the equation for Ghana (see Table 16.4). The main finding is that the official exchange rate has no explanatory power when the black market rate is included in the equation.

Overall, these results appear to indicate that devaluation and excessive money growth were the main causes of perduring inflation. Real wages are clearly not the culprit; they exert only a modest effect on prices and, furthermore, have been steadily declining since the beginning of the 1980s. Two major implications follow. First, fixing the nominal exchange rate to fight inflation cannot be an effective strategy to the extent that money supply and the fiscal deficit (which are tightly related) are not brought under control. By pegging the exchange rate and not dealing with macroeconomic imbalances, the policy maker will walk the perilous road of over-appreciation and balance of payments crises. Second, the crucial impact of devaluation on inflation may not necessarily be the direct one, but may also work through other channels. Suppose that a devaluation leads to a higher budget deficit due to, say, higher interest payments on foreign debt. Short of alternative means of financing, the Treasury will have to rely on the printing press, which will fuel inflation. This is, as shall be seen, in many respects what happened in Zambia.

Our econometric results can be used to cast further light on inflation behaviour for the five countries during the 1980s. Table 16.5, which reports the evolution of several macroeconomic indicators since

Table 16.3 The causes of inflation

Dep. var.: ln p_t Sample	Δln$e$	Δln$w$	ΔlnMS	CU
CS[a,b]	.31	.25	.44	−.23
	(.14)	(.16)	(.05)	(.10)
CS[a]	.17	.41	.42	−.19
	(.20)	(.26)	(.07)	(.28)
Kenya	.16	.48	.37	−.17
	(.08)	(.13)	(.05)	(.20)
Senegal	−.41	.87	.55	−.14
	(1.05)	(.82)	(.33)	(.21)
Zambia[c]	.81	.89	.05	−.28
	(.44)	(.19)	(.13)	(.49)

Estimation procedure: instrumental variables.
Notes:
[a] Kenya, Malawi, Senegal, Zambia.
[b] OLS estimates.
[c] The homogeneity restriction was rejected.
Key:
CS: cross-section
Δln$e$: nominal exchange rate devaluation
Δlnw: growth of nominal wages
ΔlnMS: growth of money supply
CU: capacity utilisation

Table 16.4 Inflation in Ghana

Dep. var.: ln p_t *Expl. var.*	*Coeff.*	*St. err.*	*Coeff.*[a]	*St. Err.*
e_b	.30	(.23)	.15	(.09)
e_o			.07	(.18)
ln M/p	.47	(.18)	.38	(.07)
ln w/p	−.15	(.34)		
CU	−.31	(.99)	−1.05	(.50)
ln p_{t-1}	.13	(.12)	.56	(.17)
R^2	.76			
DW	2.33		1.35	

Notes:
[a] from Chhibber (1992).
Key:
CU: capacity utilisation (GDP in Chhibber, 1992).
w: wage rate
M: broad money supply
e_b: black market exchange rate
e_o: official exchange rate

Table 16.5 Macroeconomic indicators in five sub-Saharan African countries, 1980–8

	Year	*rer*	*e*	*infl*	*money*	*gdp*	*rb/y*	*def/y*	*a/y*
Ghana	1980	0.266	0.007	0.416	0.291	0.006	–0.007	–0.042	–0.010
	1981	0.807	–0.099	0.560	0.414	–0.030	–0.002	–0.065	–0.104
	1982	0.239	–0.066	0.238	0.210	–0.067	0.044	–0.056	0.044
	1983	0.592	0.194	0.802	0.338	–0.046	0.005	–0.027	–00.02
	1984	–1.975	2.285	0.304	0.429	0.083	0.007	–0.018	0.025
	1985	–0.308	0.416	0.192	0.380	0.044	–0.001	–0.022	0.065
	1986	–0.390	0.640	0.349	0.392	0.049	0.018	0.001	0.927
	1987	–0.167	0.613	0.335	0.427	0.043	0.003	0.005	0.054
	1988	–0.123	03.40	0.292	0.380	0.057	–0.002	0.000	0.070
Kenya	1980	–0.114	0.000	0.094	0.059	0.052	–0.114	–0.046	0.118
	1981	–0.064	0.094	0.095	0.149	0.045	0.040	0.066	0.067
	1982	0.099	0.127	0.112	0.151	0.021	0.017	–0.079	0.028
	1983	–0.019	0.166	0.122	0.093	0.010	0.056	–0.049	0.041
	1984	0.083	0.033	0.089	0.170	0.020	0.022	–0.049	0.048
	1985	–0.013	0.113	0.070	0.096	0.057	0.041	–0.063	0.027
	1986	–0.026	0.145	0.094	0.236	0.066	0.040	–0.044	0.047
	1987	–0.044	0.111	0.060	0.108	0.055	0.011	0.000	0.080
	1988	0.004	0.114	0.095	0.076	0.058	0.002	0.000	0.079
Malawi	1980	0.013	0.000	0.198	0.127	–0.001	–0.138	–0.158	0.272
	1981	0.038	0.000	0.140	0.221	–0.054	–0.102	–0.125	0.152
	1982	–0.009	0.100	0.099	0.150	0.022	–0.106	–0.076	0.113
	1983	0.032	0.075	0.097	0.092	0.039	–0.101	–0.071	0.111
	1984	0.077	0.143	0.121	0.265	0.052	–0.020	–0.052	0.040
	1985	–0.013	0.186	0.085	–0.107	0.045	–0.078	–0.084	–0.062
	1986	–0.100	0.224	0.131	0.354	0.009	–0.015	–0.098	0.040
	1987	–0.110	0.269	0.198	0.297	0.001	–0.018	0.000	0.071
	1988	0.080	0.187	0.084	NA	0.032	–0.095	0.000	0.149
Senegal	1980	–0.052	0.001	0.117	0.098	–0 .030	–0.157	0.009	0.172
	1981	–0.126	0.153	0.058	0.200	–0.008	–0.200	–0.034	0.210
	1982	0.036	0.124	0.090	0.190	0.141	–0.142	–0.062	0.105
	1983	–0.004	0.116	0.083	0.040	0.025	–0.127	–0.059	0.163
	1984	–0.021	0.095	0.120	0.051	–0.044	0.114	0.081	0.163
	1985	0.122	0.018	0.094	0.044	0.037	–0.119	0.000	0.181
	1986	0.199	–0.116	0.074	0.106	0.043	–0.084	0.000	0.159
	1987	0.050	–0.044	0.024	–0.003	0.039	–0.080	0.000	0.147
	1988	–0.066	0.030	0.023	0.005	0.050	–0.056	0.000	0.104
Zambia	1980	–0.047	0.000	0.117	0.099	0.030	0.040	0.185	0.160
	1981	0.042	0.000	0.068	0.069	0.059	–0.019	–0.129	0.085
	1982	0.117	0.000	0.063	0.261	–0.027	0.116	–0.186	0.165
	1983	–0.069	0.266	0.169	0.104	–0.022	–0.125	–0.078	0.069
	1984	–0.146	0.319	0.170	0.157	–0.007	0.106	–0.084	0.009
	1985	–0.095	0.404	0.345	0.210	0.016	0.047	–0.149	0.222

continued on page 348

Table 16.5 continued

Year	*rer*	*e*	*infl*	*money*	*gdp*	*rb/y*	*def/y*	*a/y*
1986	–0.723	1.135	0.598	0.659	0.009	0.015	0.000	0.122
1987	0.068	0.294	0.393	0.372	0.023	0.051	–0.137	0.056
1988	0.465	–0.038	0.455	NA	0.065	–0.024	–0.088	0.198

Notes:
rer = real devaluation
e = nominal devaluation
infl. = inflation
money = money growth
gdp = output growth
rb/y = resource balance
def/y = budget deficit
a/y = foreign aid–GDP ratio

1980, presents some interesting differences among country experiences. In Kenya, a substantial depreciation of the real exchange rate was not associated with a rekindling of inflation; indeed, it actually declined. At the other end of the spectrum are Malawi and Zambia, which have both resorted to frequent devaluations, without however provoking any enduring effect on the real exchange rate. The case of Zambia is quite revealing. The policy of pegging its nominal exchange rate to the SDR from 1980 to 1982 induced a significant real appreciation. With the support of a number of IMF programmes, the exchange rate steadily devalued and inflation moderately increased. In 1985, bowing to external pressure, the government introduced a foreign exchange auction. The exchange rate then collapsed, with the rate of devaluation reaching 211 per cent in 1986 and inflation shooting up from 18.5 per cent in 1984 to 82.9 per cent in 1986. In 1987, the government decided to discontinue the auction. One major factor underlying the rocketing inflation and the inflation-devaluation spiral was the budget deficit increase brought about by higher interest payments. What is quite surprising is that external assistance declined during this period from 2.2 per cent of GDP in 1985 to only 0.6 per cent in 1987. Clearly, more generous support from external donors would have provided the government an alternative source for budget financing, thereby lightening the burden of higher interest payments. It is difficult to deny that the behaviour of external creditors was quite myopic in this circumstance.

Ghana and Senegal present quite different experiences. In Senegal, the policy of pegging the exchange rate to the French Franc has been extremely successful in containing inflation, particularly since 1985, but has induced a significant real appreciation. Ghana, on the other hand, provides neat confirmation to the claim that, with widespread black markets, even a major devaluation (882.6 per cent in 1984) may have no effect on inflation. Indeed, official inflation declined after 1984. Interestingly, even further nominal devaluations have not been wiped out by a resurgence of inflation, but have been effective in inducing a real depreciation. A greater availability of external funds (no larger though than the average for sub-Saharan Africa) has undoubtedly played a role in this context. In more recent years, however, the link between devaluation and inflation has become less favourable, with inflation apparently responding more rapidly to devaluation.

IV CONCLUSION

Overall, devaluation can represent an important component in the adjustment process. A grossly overvalued exchange rate, as for instance in Ghana at the beginning of the 1980s, requires a currency realignment. The alternative of relying on a more or less automatic adjustment mechanism would have been much more costly, as the Senegalese experience indicates. Yet, devaluation may at times be excessive, which tends to spark inflation, despite the lack of widespread indexation systems. It is therefore essential that specific country conditions be carefully assessed to ensure that the proposed policy package, including devaluation, does not yield undesired effects. The results for our sample countries also suggest that a real depreciation is typically associated with an improvement in the balance of trade and increased output. But the quantitative effects, especially on output, are quite modest, which suggests that devaluation works to a significant extent by compressing demand. There is no need however to resurrect the old-standing controversy between pricism and structuralism in Africa. Existing empirical evidence suggests that both price and non-price factors play an important role in the context of the adjustment process (Binswanger, 1990; Faini, 1991). To rely on only one of these sets of factors would most likely gravely impair the quality of an adjustment programme and its chances of success.

NOTES

1. More generally, it could be assumed that total expenditure is a function of real income and of the excess supply of money balances:

$$Z = Y + y\ (M^s - M^d) \tag{2}$$

where M^s and M^d denote respectively supply and demand for money. If we then assume an accommodating monetary policy, we find that $M^s = M^d$ and $Y = Z$.
2. In the previous paragraph, it was assumed that the nominal price of non-traded goods was fixed.
3. We obviously abstract here from the factors which may make devaluation contractionary and focus only on the trade-off between its inflationary and expansionary effects.
4. Balassa's results could however be explained by an intrasectoral shift from illegal to legal trade following a devaluation. This effect is likely to be important at an individual country level (i.e. Ghana exports being smuggled through the Côte d'Ivoire), but not for Africa as a whole and cannot account therefore for the improved trade performance of the region. Similarly, the shift from food to export crops, with little aggregate supply response and possibly a negative import effect, may account for Balassa's findings. As a matter of fact, empirical evidence suggests that aggregate supply elasticities for agricultural production are not particularly high (Bond, 1983; Binswanger, 1990). Two caveats are in order: first, these studies do not consider the impact of relative price changes on quasi-fixed factors; second they do not allow for the fact that higher availability of consumer goods brought by larger export receipts has stimulating effects on the supply response in agriculture.
5. Paradoxically enough, the same prediction is made by the monetarist model.
6. The coefficient is somewhat smaller, but less precisely determined, for the instrumental variable estimates.

Annex

This annex presents a detailed derivation of the model discussed in Section II. The structure of the model can be described as follows. Production levels in both the traded and non-traded goods sectors are assumed to be a function of labour and capital, with capital fixed in the short run:

$$Q_i = F_i\ (L_i, K_i)$$
$$i = T, N \tag{A1–A2}$$

where Q_i, L_i, and K_i denote respectively output, labour and capital in sector i. The two subscripts, T and N, refer to the traded and the non-traded goods sectors respectively. Profit maximisation subject to equations (A1–A2) will determine labour demand:

$$L_i = L_i\ (w/p_i,\ K_i)$$
$$i = T,\ N \qquad \text{(A3–A4)}$$

where w denotes the (fixed) nominal wage and p_i is the price of good i. The price of traded goods is determined by the purchasing power parity condition:

$$p_T = eP^*_T \qquad \text{(A5)}$$

where p^*_T and e denote respectively the international price of traded goods and the nominal exchange rate. On the demand side, we assume that total expenditure (Z) is equal to income (Y), i.e.:

$$Z = Y = p_TQ_T + p_NQ_N \qquad \text{(A6)}$$

whereas demand for good i is equal to:

$$D_i = D_i\ (Z,\ p_T,\ p_N) \qquad \text{(A7–A8)}$$

Finally, equilibrium in the non-traded goods market requires that:

$$Q_N = D_N \qquad \text{(A9)}$$

As discussed in the text, under the assumption of a fixed nominal wage, the economy may settle at a less than full employment equilibrium. To investigate the effect of a devaluation, let us log-differentiate the system of equations (A1–A9). Consider first the supply block:

$$Q'_i = \alpha_i L'_i \qquad \text{(A1'–A2')}$$
$$L'_i - Q'_i = -\ \delta_i\ (w' - p'_i) \qquad \text{(A3'–A4')}$$

where a prime indicates a log-derivative, whereas α_i and δ_i are the labour shares and the elasticity of substitution in sector i. Solving for output:

$$Q'_i = \in_i\ (p'_i - w') \qquad \text{(A1''–A2'')}$$

where $\in_i$ denotes the price elasticity of supply and is equal to $\alpha_i\delta_i/(1 - \alpha_1)$. Given equation (A5), the rate of change of the price of traded goods is simply equal to the rate of nominal devaluation:

$$p'_T = e' \qquad \text{(A5')}$$

while income and expenditure evolve according to:

$$Z' = Y' = \gamma_T\ (p'_T + Q'_T) + \gamma_N\ (p'_N + Q'_N) \qquad \text{(A6')}$$

where $\gamma_i = p_i Q_i / Y$ is the income share of good i. Finally, the change in the demand for non-traded goods is equal to:

$$D'_N = \eta_N Y' + \tilde{\eta}_{NT} p'_T + \tilde{\eta}_{NN} p'_N \tag{A7'}$$

where η_N is the income elasticity of demand for good (N) and $\tilde{\eta}_{Nt}$ denotes the Marshallian price elasticity of demand. We use the Slutsky decomposition:

$$\tilde{\eta}_{Ni} = \eta_{Ni} - \eta_N d_i \tag{A8'}$$

where $d_i = p_i D_i / Y$ is the consumption share of good i and η_{Ni} is the Hicksian price elasticity of demand.

To derive equation (4) in the text, we need to substitute equations (A1"–A2") in equation (A6') (recalling that $w' = 0$) and substitute again the resulting expression as well as equation (A8') in equation (A7'). We get:

$$D'_N = \eta_N ((\gamma_T(1 + \epsilon_T) - d_T)p'_T$$
$$+ (\gamma_N(1 + \epsilon_N) - d_N)p'_N + \eta_{NT} p'_T + \eta_{NN} p'_N \tag{A9'}$$

Recalling that $d_i = \gamma_i$ (assuming initial internal and external balance), $\eta_{NT} = -\eta_{NN}$ (because of the singularity of the substitution matrix) and $D'_N = Q'_N = \epsilon_N p'_N$ (because of equations (A9) and (A1")), equation (4) in the text can be easily derived.

17 New Trade Issues: Traditional Versus Non-traditional Exports

Samuel Wangwe

I INTRODUCTION

Structural adjustment programmes have been under implementation now in sub-Saharan Africa for more than a decade. These adjustment programmes have consisted of demand management policies on the demand side and switching policies on the supply side. One expectation of the supply-side policies has been the reallocation of resources from non-traded goods sectors to the traded goods sectors. This is often assumed to be an essential component of trade reform. Within the context of the structural adjustment programmes, however, trade reform is usually silent about the allocation of resources within the traded sectors, presumably leaving this question up to the market. Indeed, in much of SSA, the market has continued to reinforce the production of traditional exports still in place from the colonial period. However, even if there were a shift in resources toward the production of existing traditional exports, there are indications that such a course of action may not be consistent with the long-term development objective of creating a viable and dynamic export sector in African economies (on this point, see Chapters 2, 5 and 16).

Africa's major exports have been primary agricultural and mineral products. Indeed, the structure of exports has hardly changed in much of sub-Saharan Africa over the past two to three decades. The share of primary commodities in total exports from sub-Saharan Africa declined marginally from 92 per cent in 1965 to 86 per cent in 1987 (World Bank, 1989a). For the low-income countries of the region, this share has even increased marginally, from 92 per cent in 1965 to 94 per cent in 1987 (World Bank, 1989a). The primary-dominated export structure is not presently undergoing change to any significant extent.

This unchanging export structure may suggest that the export pessimism associated with traditional primary commodities has not been taken seriously in the design and implementation of development policies (either before or after structural adjustment programmes). Export pessimism was first based either on declining terms of trade for primary products (Prebisch, 1984) or on the notion that the absorptive capacity of foreign markets was low (i.e. elasticity pessimism), as argued by Nurkse (1959). The future of most of the traditional commodity exports is rather bleak considering the low income elasticities of demand associated with these products. Markets for many of the traditional commodities are showing signs of saturation. For instance, studies on the cocoa world market, to which African exports contribute 55 per cent, have shown that over the 20 year period (1960–5 to 1980–5), cocoa consumption increased by only 40 per cent, with negligible increases in the major consumer markets such as the EEC (12 per cent) and USA (19 per cent) over the period (ITC, 1987).

The empirical evidence available on terms of trade in sub-Saharan Africa suggests that the export pessimism thesis continues to hold. A World Bank study, taking the year 1980 as the base, indicates that the index of terms of trade declined to 91 in 1985 and 84 in 1987 (World Bank, 1989a). In a recent and more general survey of empirical studies on the subject, Killick (1992) concludes that 'there is now wider acceptance than was formerly the case of the declining real commodity price thesis'.

The key question which this chapter seeks to respond to is whether this unchanged export structure can be consistent with the long-term development objective of making exports an engine of growth in at least two contexts: first, making exports the earners of the foreign exchange needed to import technology and other goods and services for development; second, making exporting a major source of technological learning.

As regards the first context, available evidence points to the suggestion that traditional exports are not performing the function of an engine of growth. One evaluation of the impact of SAPs in sub-Saharan Africa found that the volume of exports of nine major export commodities in the adjusting countries increased by 75 per cent for the period 1985–90 compared with the 1977–9 averages. Yet export earnings from these exports fell by 40 per cent over the same period as a result of deteriorating barter terms of trade (Husain, 1993). The evidence is less direct for the second context of technological learning. However, to the extent that production of most traditional exports is associated with relatively limited technological dynamism, further pessimism would appear to be warranted.

The importance of increasing responsiveness to changing world technological and market conditions cannot be overemphasised. However, as the small countries of Africa are not likely to exert a significant influence on these conditions, it would be in their best interests to adjust to the changing world economy. The bleak future for many traditional primary commodity exports is imminent. What is startling is the observation that many African countries experiencing long-term declining terms of trade do not seem to be responding by restructuring their export sectors.

This chapter aims to contribute to the discussion on whether an emphasis on both non-traditional exports[1] and greater regional trade could represent a viable external strategy for SSA over the next 10 to 20 years. It proceeds on the premise that diversification into non-traditional exports is a necessary but by no means sufficient condition for turning exports into an engine of growth.

The experience with exports of some categories of non-traditional products from sub-Saharan Africa suggests that much more needs to be done to acquire and maintain international competitiveness in such export markets. Non-traditional exports from the manufacturing sector, for instance, have not only been small and declining, but have also tended to be dominated by further processed goods destined for markets outside SSA (Riddell et al., 1990). After the 1960s, the trend in manufactured exports from Africa shows a decline in its share of world manufactured exports, dropping from 0.38 per cent in 1965 to 0.23 per cent in 1986. There was even a decline in its share of developing country manufactured exports, going from 4.6 per cent to 1.5 per cent over the same period. These trends are cause for concern as they could be pointing to the existence of lower industrial productivity growth and technological learning and innovations in Africa than in other developing regions. This rather gloomy picture indicates that the issue of diversification into non-traditional exports may not in itself be sufficient. It needs to be complemented with the accumulation of the necessary technological, organisational and marketing capabilities as necessary components for attaining and maintaining international competitiveness in the export markets.

The chapter is structured as follows. Section II examines relevant insights offered by trade theory on the question of restructuring exports. Some considerations on developing non-traditional exports are presented in Section III, and Section IV addresses some implications which thus arise for regional trade. Finally, Section V puts forward the conclusions.

II TRADE THEORY AND RELEVANT IMPLICATIONS FOR RESTRUCTURING THE EXPORT SECTOR

Classical theories of trade, notably of the Ricardian type, place emphasis on production, stressing international differences in technology and real wage levels. The view of the classical economists (Ricardo and Mill, for instance) on comparative advantage had its origins in the capacity to produce based on labour productivity and capital accumulation.

Developments of trade theories in the neo-classical framework shifted attention away from the analysis of differences in technology and reduced the basis of trade to the more static concept of factor endowments. The core of the conventional trade theory is the factor proportions theory of the Heckscher-Ohlin model and its extensions. This theory is based on general equilibrium models and the assumptions associated with it. As part of the general case for free markets, the case for free trade derives from the view that as a production process, international trade is likely to be carried out more efficiently if it is left to the market mechanism.

This conventional trade theory has been questioned on both methodological and empirical grounds. The explanatory and predictive power of the theory has increasingly come under attack from both inside and outside the neo-classical framework of analysis. These changing ideas on the efficacy of the conventional theory are in part a response to the changing character of international trade, the changing roles and relative competitive positions of countries in the world economy (for instance, the role of the US economy in world trade and competitiveness, especially in relation to Japan) and changing views in the field of economics, especially concerning the analysis of industrial structure and competition (such as a broadening of the kit of tools of economic analysis by borrowing from other fields).

Critics who have emphasised the methodological problems of the conventional model are mainly associated with non-neo-classical formulations (for instance, evolutionary theory), while those who have questioned the empirical validity of the model have come both from within and outside the neo-classical framework.

The approach adopted by critics from within the neo-classical framework has basically been one of analysing the outcomes and trade implications of the behaviour of firms operating in conditions falling short of the ideals of perfect competition (monopolistic competition, imperfect competition, presence of increasing returns to scale). Much of the literature in this category represents sympathetic attempts to relax the basic assumptions of the Heckscher-Ohlin model and test its robustness (Kierzkowski, 1989). Within this context, monopolistic competition and other forms of imperfect competition have come to be central to the literature on trade theory, largely reflecting the persistence of intra-industry trade in reality (Dixit and Norman, 1980; Krugman, 1979).

Critics from outside the neo-classical framework have largely followed the evolutionary theory of economic change. They have attempted to lay out a formal theory of economic activity driven by industrial innovation (consistent with the Schumpeterian view), seeking to understand technical change, its sources and its impacts at micro and macro levels (Nelson and Winter, 1982; Dosi et al., 1990). Evolutionary theory here consists of heterogeneous modelling efforts which emphasise various aspects of economic change, such as responses to market conditions by firms and industries, economic growth and competition through innovation. Many underlying ideas can be traced back to classical political economy (including Smith, Marx and Schumpeter) or to contributions adopted from other fields.

The theory of dynamic firm (or industry) capabilities presented in the context of the evolutionary theory of economic change focuses on three related features of a firm (Nelson and Winter, 1982; Nelson, 1991): first, the firm's strategy consisting of a set of broad commitments that define and rationalise its objectives and the ways in which it intends to pursue them; second, the structure of the firm or industry in terms of how it is organised and governed and how decisions are actually made and carried out, and; third, its core capabilities, including core organisational capabilities (which define how lower-order organisational skills are coordinated with higher-order decision procedures in order to make choices about what is to be done at lower levels) and R&D capabilities (particularly in relation to innovation and taking economic advantage of innovation on a continuous basis). Having dropped the neo-classical world of perfect foresight and static equilibrium, the presumed world of the followers of the evolutionary theory of economic change is so deeply complicated with uncertainties that firms will tend to choose somewhat different strategies, which will in turn lead to them having different structures and different core capabilities. The way these evolve over time will reflect their past experiences and histories.

At least two main contributions on the part of critics of the neoclassical trade theory can be identified in reference to the concern for restructuring the export sector. First, the recognition that economies of scale (and the associated market structures) have considerable influence on trade reinforces the justification for shifting attention away from small-scale import substitution industrialisation toward exploring ways of tapping the larger regional markets through integration or other forms of regional cooperation. The second contribution lies in the recognition that differences in technologies exert substantial influence on international competitiveness, leading to the vitally important message that such differences are a fundamental force in shaping comparative advantages. If this is so, the implication is that trade policy should be designed with explicit consideration of technological change. Furthermore, if, as put forward earlier, exports act as an engine of growth in at least two contexts – making exports the earners of the foreign exchange needed to import technology and other goods and services for development and making exporting a major source of technological learning – then one implication of this conception of technology is that the balance is tilted in favour of the second context.[2]

III TOWARDS THE DEVELOPMENT OF NON-TRADITIONAL EXPORTS

The changing world market conditions do not preclude the possibility that sub-Saharan Africa can carve out windows of opportunities in world trade. Differences in income levels, historical backgrounds and other environmental considerations suggest that there are bound to be inter-country and intra-country differences in demand structures. The diversity of demand structures between the South and the North and within both the North and the South make it possible for sub-Saharan Africa to dynamically exploit some areas of market opportunities. In order to exploit and maintain such market opportunities (whether in the markets of the industrialised economies of the North or in the less developed economies of the South) requirements for international competitiveness (not only in terms of price, but more importantly in terms of consistency in quality and timeliness of delivery) are likely to become more stringent rather than more relaxed. This makes it imperative that the restructuring of the export sectors in sub-Saharan Africa be interpreted in the context of the role of technological development and innovations, recognising the importance of being forward-looking in the assessment of trade potentials, emphasising the centrality of acquiring detailed knowledge of the structures and capabilities of exporting industries and firms as a basis for formulating export-promotion policies and policies to promote industries with dynamic comparative advantages.

If technology is so instrumental in influencing international competitiveness, then restructuring the export sector will need to be grounded in considerations of technological learning and the building up of technological capabilities. In this context, restructuring the export sector can be examined from at least three angles: first, exploring the possibilities of improving the efficiency of production of existing exports so as to release resources to non-traditional exports with minimum disruption to foreign exchange inflow; second, examining the possibilities of deepening the export base in the direction of further processing of existing exports in order to benefit from additional value added in terms of earnings and technological learning; third, investigating possibilities for widening the export base into new exports so as to tap advantages of more dynamic exports.

(A) Raising productivity levels of existing export production

In some export sectors, such as natural resources including minerals and tropical products, African countries may continue to have a competitive edge arising from natural conditions supplemented by technological change. Even in those sectors, however, the centrality of technological change and innovation in the analysis of trade and growth issues can be relevant in order to enhance comparative advantage based on natural resource endowments. It is in this context that the influence of technological capability on the realisation of potentials in natural resource endowments needs to be pursued (David, 1991). Technological capability and, in particular, the prudent adoption of relevant new technologies applied in exploration, exploitation and processing various natural resources can facilitate the realisation of the potentials of natural resource endowments.

As mentioned earlier, the sub-Saharan African export structure in the area of primary commodity production has not changed to any significant extent. The fact that SSA has been losing its share to other regions for several commodities suggests that productivity growth in

SSA may have lagged behind that of those regions. Increases in productivity are important in influencing levels of returns from factors used in the production of commodities. In this respect, technological capabilities in commodity production can have at least two influences. First, productivity increase can have a positive effect on the factorial terms of trade. Second, it can facilitate the release of some resources which can then be reallocated to the development of non-traditional exports.

An example from the Malaysian experience may help to demonstrate this point. Malaysia's diversification efforts into cocoa production have been technology-based, leading to productivity increases in production and marketing. Although Malaysia has higher labour costs than West Africa, it has been particularly successful in achieving very high yields from the new hybrid varieties developed by its crop-breeding programmes. In addition, the discovery that coconut can provide shade for cocoa has made the two crops natural complements and has reduced the costs of producing cocoa. For Malaysia, shifting into cocoa production came about as part of the diversification away from rubber (where rising labour costs are making it less profitable) and palm oil (where the market shows signs of saturation). Cocoa output in Malaysia increased from 2000 tons in the late 1960s to 100 000 tons (5 per cent of the world total) in 1984–5, compared with a decline in Ghana from 550 000 tons in 1964–5 to 175 000 tons in 1984–5. For Ghana, cocoa remains dominant in the unrestructured export sector, while in Malaysia it is a very small part of a diversified sector.

(B) Deepening the export base

Deepening the export base in the direction of further processing of existing primary exports is expected to contribute to value added in terms of earnings in foreign exchange as well as in terms of further technological learning. The latter is probably more challenging as it will require the accumulation of technological, organisational and marketing capabilities not only in primary sectors, but also in the secondary sectors with which they have linkages. Difficulties in attaining competitiveness in processing activities have often been associated with deficiencies in other sectors. For instance, cocoa-producing countries account for less than 5 per cent of world exports of chocolates and chocolate products. The main inhibiting factors have been identified as: refrigeration energy needs; investment costs and machine maintenance; packaging and labelling requirements; costs of certain raw materials such as sugar, milk and butter oil which are cheaper in the main manufacturing countries; competition from large companies with established markets, high degree of vertical integration, product differentiation and large advertising expenditures (ITC, 1987). This indicates that the problems of processing cocoa are linked to weaknesses in the industrial and services sectors in cocoa-producing countries.

If any headway is to be made on this front, market studies should provide a guide in taking decisions on whether, and to what extent, further processing is advisable. On the supply side, the challenge of technological capability building should generally extend to all supportive activities linked to the particular processing sector.

(C) Diversification into new exports and markets

New exports and markets can be identified in any sector of the economy (agriculture, industry or services). The identification of such dynamic markets, wherever they may be, will be a product of the careful study of market trends, technological developments and emerging potentials.

Building up non-traditional exports should be defined broadly to include the development of potentials in agriculture, industry and services. In agriculture, for instance, the possibility exists of developing non-traditional exports whose income elasticities are high, and market trends point to a reasonably bright future in this regard. Investment decisions in such new areas should carefully consider relevant factors. A continual upgrading of production and quality levels and the quality of export service is necessary if sub-Saharan Africa is to attain and maintain international competitiveness. The development of appropriate export marketing strategies based on the latest market intelligence and research will also be necessary. In this case, the relationship between buyers and sellers is important for the realisation of market requirements.

The fruit and vegetable juice market is one example of a dynamic non-traditional export, with world trade tripling in the past decade. Research has shown that per capita consumption is likely to rise further in the major consuming markets and in non-traditional markets such as Japan and Korea. This growth in consumption is favoured by several technological and demand factors: product development, including the introduction of new flavours and blends; innovation in packaging and retail organisations; aggressive marketing; increasing use of fruit juice in other food and beverage products; and greater health awareness among consumers. Trends in consumer behaviour indicate that freshness is increasingly appreciated, quality is valued even if it means paying more, and the scale and variety of consumption has been found to increase with the standard of living. In addition, regarding the total vegetables and fruit assortment, there is space for off-season products, especially in winter.

In the manufacturing sector, doubts have often been expressed as to whether the less industrialised countries can compete with the industrialised countries in frontier technologies. But even here it is likely that windows of opportunity exist. It is apparent that competition in various industries may result from the selective adoption of sophisticated frontier technologies which are competitive at very high wages or from less sophisticated semi-automated technologies which are competitive at relatively lower wage levels. In garments and textiles, for instance, Mody and Wheeler (1990) found that producers in the newly industrialising countries (NIC) are facing competition from the export operations of the newly invigorated economies of Asia (China, India and Indonesia, among others) based on low wages. Concurrently with this increase in wage-based competition, semi-automated technology is now viable in a number of operations at very low wages, making it possible to raise levels of productivity and real wages. As long as the wage levels in developing countries are relatively low, it would be possible to be competitive in technologies which are not necessarily at the frontier while striving to close the technology gap as productivity and wages rise. There are indications that market opportunities for the non-frontier technologies will continue to arise as a result of the changing world market conditions. For instance, the dominance of small firms in the apparel industry can be explained by the rapid variations in style and colour which require the production of small-sized lots and the ability to respond quickly to changing demand (Mody and Wheeler, 1990). Even within the framework of intra-industry trade, it has been found that such trade in the US is dominated by intermediate goods which are primarily of the made-to-order type produced by small firms (Ray, 1991). For instance, the US-Brazil intra-trade largely consists of made-to-order goods produced by small firms using labour-intensive production techniques.

In order to cope with the changing patterns of market opportunities, the process of growing competitiveness will need to be continuous and dynamic. The challenge seems to centre on working out how to promote selectivity in adopting new technologies in various processes in ways that are consistent with capabilities in the respective countries at present and over time.

The choice of strategies for restructuring exports will need to consider each of these three angles. Careful study will need to be undertaken of the structure of markets and their trends as well as the state of technological developments in the world economy so as to form a basis for the selection of non-traditional exports to develop. There is also a strong need to formulate studies on industrial organisation for each chosen industry, incorporating the following features: focus on the international competitive process and its welfare impacts; market characteristics of all the trading countries engaged in the chosen industry; identification of the underlying determinants of the structural characteristics of those markets; analysis of the principal forms of market conduct of leading enterprises in the industry; and elaboration of data over a sufficiently long period of time to enable a sound understanding of the competitive process in the industry (Lee, 1992).

IV SOME IMPLICATIONS FOR REGIONAL TRADE

The focus of new trade theories is primarily on North–North trade. However, some elements of the role of economies of scale, product diversity and explanations for intra-industry trade can be applied to sub-Saharan Africa. The treatment of these issues in the new trade theories can be adapted to considerations of intra-SSA trade or to broader South–South trade by tackling such questions as whether innovations could take place in more appropriate products and processes for the South as a basis for South–South trade (Stewart, 1991b), and according to which conditions South–South trade could be feasible and viable, drawing lessons from the emerging patterns of trade.

Trends in intra-regional trade in Africa indicate that the level of such trade has remained low, and has not manifested any clear evidence of increasing (see Chapter 18). However, there are at least two sources of optimism on the prospects of growth of regional cooperation in trade and investments: first, there are indications that a substantial volume of intra-regional trade is unrecorded; second, the degree of complementarity is often understated.

That the potential for regional trade is higher than trade figures suggest is indicated by results of demand and supply studies. For instance, the 'Promotion of Intra-regional Trade Through Supply and Demand Surveys' project was part of a more comprehensive programme of activities aimed at promoting trade between the member states of Preferential Trade Areas for Eastern and Southern African states (PTA).

The data show that many of the items imported into the PTA are also exported from the PTA, indicating that there is potential for intra-regional trade in a wide range of sectors. The most interesting finding of this supply and demand survey is that many products which are exported from the region are also imported into it. In spite of having the necessary raw materials, the region continues to be a net importer of various light manufactures. For instance, the region imports leather footwear ($15 million in 1985) and exports $1 million of leather footwear, it imported $3.3 million worth of cotton seed oil and $3.7 million of sunflower seed oil in 1985, while none was exported. The region even imported more railway sleepers ($2.8 million in 1982) and poles ($0.4 million in 1985) than it exported ($0.6 million of railway sleepers in 1982 and $0.1 million of poles in 1985).

Even within agriculture, a sector often cited as depicting competitive structures, the potential seems to be greater than that which official figures acknowledge. Differences in climatic and agronomic conditions in the region are a source of complementarity of production. For instance, in the case of Eastern and Southern Africa, Koester and Thomas (1992) assessed the agro-climatic suitability for growing food crops among Malawi, Tanzania, Zambia and Zimbabwe and found that the countries differ in their natural advantage for producing the main staples (maize, cassava, beans, sorghum and millet). Differences in rainfall variability were found to exist within each country and between adjacent subregions across countries. Similar results have been obtained in the case of West Africa, where it has been found that the difference across countries in the opportunities for international trade, in historical conditions and technological accumulation, and in consumer preferences suggest that there is good potential for specialisation (Badiane, 1992).

A further relevant direction of intra- and inter-regional cooperation could be represented by the analysis and shaping of patterns of trade and investment flows among developing countries (Lecraw, 1981; UNESCAP, 1990). Lecraw has addressed three issues relating to transnational corporations (TNC) from developing countries: types of technology developed, mechanisms of transfer of technology, and impacts on home and host countries. As regards types of technologies, it was found that TNCs from developing countries undertook various modifications in response to the characteristics of raw materials (type, quality and input mix), size (scaling down), product quality and product mix (degree of diversification), machinery (simplicity and capacity) and factor intensity. It was found that these TNCs tend to produce simpler, lower technology products; favour low-cost products requiring little marketing ability to sell in world markets; have a higher propensity to form joint ventures with local firms, use more local human resources and raw materials; and often down-scale imported technologies. It has been pointed out that the case study of an Indian joint venture in Thailand showed that developing country firms, being themselves in a learning stage, transfer not only the know-how but also the know-why (UNESCAP, 1990). To the extent that economies of scale are exerting greater influence on international competitiveness, regional cooperation in the area of investments is likely to assume greater significance.

VI CONCLUSION

The main conclusion of this chapter is therefore that an unchanged export structure in sub-Saharan Africa is not consistent with the long-term development objective of making exports an engine of growth in at least two contexts: exports as the earners of the foreign exchange needed to import technology and other goods and services for development, and exporting as a major source of technological learning.

Considering that exploiting and maintaining any market opportunities requires the attainment of international competitiveness, it is imperative that the restructuring of the export sectors in sub-Saharan Africa be interpreted within a framework of technological development and innovations, recognising the importance of being forward-looking in the assessment of trade potentials and emphasising the centrality of acquiring detailed knowledge of the structures and capabilities of exporting industries and firms as a basis of formulating export promotion policies and policies to promote industries with dynamic comparative advantages.

The strategy towards export development will need to be approached from three fronts: first, improving the efficiency of production of existing exports so as to release resources to non-traditional exports with minimum disruption to current foreign exchange inflow; second, deepening the export base in the direction of further processing of existing exports so as to benefit from additional value added in terms of earnings and technological learning; and finally, widening the export base into new exports in order to tap advantages of more dynamic exports.

NOTES

1. In general, non-traditional exports have not been defined in precise terms in the literature. For the purposes of this chapter, non-traditional exports will primarily refer to exports that have not been among the major exports from African countries in the past 15 years. Secondarily, in discussing possibilities of developing non-traditional exports, reference will be made to the diversification of markets to non-traditional markets.
2. It should be noted that the two contexts need not be viewed as competing objectives in the longer run. The success of technological learning through exporting would form a more robust basis for foreign exchange earning over time.

18 Long-term Development in Sub-Saharan Africa: Would Regional Integration Help?

T. Ademola Oyejide and Mufutau I. Raheem

I INTRODUCTION

The economic difficulties that have plagued sub-Saharan African countries are broadly manifested by the general decline or stagnation in their average GDP growth rates (both absolute and per capita) as well as by sharp declines in their export growth coupled with marked losses in the region's share of world trade, particularly during the 1980s (World Bank, 1989c). In terms of both policy and action, the predominant response to these difficulties has taken the form of the adoption, by the large majority of SSA countries, of structural adjustment programmes, with the encouragement and active support of the World Bank and the International Monetary Fund. In their basic orientation, these programmes have generally emphasised the development of outward-looking trade regimes to be brought about through unilateral trade liberalisation. In addition, the programmes have been designed for and have focused upon individual countries. Hence, they have generally ignored existing regional integration schemes among various sets of SSA countries, including the extent to which particular trade, exchange rate and other macroeconomic policies articulated for implementation in the context of specific country SAPs are consistent with (or contradict) regional integration obligations previously entered into by such countries.

This contrasts rather sharply with the continued and sustained concern among African leaders over the past three decades with the question of regional integration and economic cooperation and the crucial role that such integration can play in improving Africa's economic prospects in the 1990s and beyond. Thus, gatherings of African leaders, within the context of the Economic Commission for Africa (ECA) or under the umbrella of the Organization of African Unity (OAU), have continued to discuss and sometimes actually sign agreements and treaties meant to realise their 'grand design' of an African Economic Community (AEC) or Common Market (Oyejide, 1992). Starting with the Lagos Plan of Action (LPA) adopted by the OAU in 1980, the most recent manifestation of this trend was the signing in July 1991 of the treaty to establish the AEC.

It is obviously of great policy relevance to examine the issue of a regional integration scheme in sub-Saharan Africa: whether, and to what extent, such a scheme could play a significant role in helping SSA countries cope with and overcome their current economic difficulties, and what type of scheme would be appropriate. In doing so, it should be of more than passing interest to explore the observed sharp incongruity between the unanimous aggregate African support for regional integration in rhetorical terms and the equally (and apparently) strong concerted action in implementing SAPs at the individual country level, particularly when the latter generally ignore (and, in some respects, even negate) several important components of the former.

This chapter briefly reviews the objectives and design of SSA's regional integration schemes (Section II), as a prelude to examining the evidence on the 'failure' of these schemes in Africa and the factors that may be responsible (Section III). Section IV concludes the chapter with a forward-looking assessment of regional integration schemes in sub-Saharan African countries, focusing on such issues as the consistency between national policies and regional integration aspirations, the role of international agencies in the choice of development strategies, and appropriate major elements of a new regional integration approach.

II OBJECTIVES AND DESIGN OF AFRICAN REGIONAL INTEGRATION SCHEMES

In the numerous and small nation states of SSA emerging from colonial rule in the 1960s an urgent need was felt for collective economic self-reliance and security as an integral part of their overt political efforts at nation-building and in order to promote economic development and political stability generally. Early efforts to establish regional economic integration arrangements were motivated by the expectation that they could serve as one of the key vehicles for achieving the shared aspirations of these countries for rapid economic growth and development.

Given their small populations and low per capita income, the limits of import substitution industrialisation as a growth strategy within the confines of the national market clearly suggested regional economic integration as a means of ensuring a larger market which would allow the benefits of greater specialisation and external economies of scale to be realised. Import substitution on a regional basis could also be more efficient as the integration of national markets would generate greater competition within the region and thus promote increased overall levels of productivity.

Given the general political context in which the integrated schemes were articulated, a recurring principle among their objectives was that a regional economic integration arrangement could broaden the production base of the region through explicit public sector planning and coordination of investment and production programmes. In particular, these activities were expected to feature joint projects in infrastructures and those manufacturing industries likely to have significant economies of scale. To the extent that coordination of investments and projects was successful, this was expected to lead to a more rational division of labour in the region and a widening of scope for efficient private sector investments.

Another set of considerations motivating the establishment of regional economic integration arrangements in SSA viewed the region against the rest of the world. In effect, regional economic integration was expected to help SSA improve its terms of trade by pooling the exports of member countries, thereby influencing world market prices, increasing the region's bargaining power in the context of multilateral negotiations and decreasing its degree of external dependence.

In essence, therefore, three broad types of objectives have underlied regional economic integration arrangements in SSA. These include the promotion of growth of intra-regional trade by removing tariff and non-tariff barriers; the promotion of regional economic development through public sector planning, coordination and mobilisation of funds in order to execute regional infrastructural and large-scale manufacturing projects; and, simultaneously, the enhancement of intra-regional movement of labour, capital and entrepreneurs. Furthermore, a harmonisation of macroeconomic policies and investment codes would be achieved. Finally, the grand design would be completed, and the Common Market created, by the simple removal of all inter-regional barriers against the free movement of goods, services and factors of production.

In broad terms, the sequence adopted by the LPA as its unifying framework for regional economic integration in SSA is largely consistent with traditional gradations (in terms of 'closeness') of types of integration arrangements, although one may legitimately take issue with both the degree of closeness envisaged at each stage and the time schedule laid out for implementing the grand design. Even more surprising is that, in spite of the poor progress made in achieving the phased goals of the LPA (see Section III), the OAU actually proceeded to jump its own gun by signing the treaty for the African Economic Community (AEC) at its meeting in Abuja (Nigeria) in July 1991. This action would appear to be an abandonment of the evolutionary process and timetable set down in the LPA or, on the contrary, perhaps another 'great leap forward'.

What the LPA had designed as a series of 'separate but convergent' efforts toward integration was to be centred on three SSA subregions, i.e. West Africa, Eastern and Southern Africa, and Central Africa. Indeed, the global approach of the LPA was superimposed on several existing and autonomous regional economic integration arrangements (see Annex to this chapter for a list of major regional economic integration schemes). In West Africa, for example, these existing arrangements include the Economic Community of West African States (ECOWAS), which was established in 1975 and some of whose member countries are also in the francophone Economic Community of West Africa (CEAO) and the Mano River Union (MRU). In the Eastern and Southern African subregion, the main regional economic integration arrangement is the Preferential Trade Area (PTA) established in 1981, since the much older East African Community had been dissolved. A central regional body has not yet emerged in Central Africa, although the Economic Community of Central African States (CCEAC) has been under negotiation, on and off, for some time. But some arrangements do exist in this subregion. Among these are the francophone Customs and Economic Union of Central Africa (UDEAC) and the Economic Community of the Great Lakes Countries (CEPGL).

III THE FAILURE OF REGIONAL INTEGRATION SCHEMES

Several assessments of the regional economic integration arrangements in SSA have recently been carried out (see for instance World Bank, 1989c; Berg, 1991; Lipumba and Kasekende, 1991; de la Torre and Kelly, 1992; and Foroutan, 1992). The studies address different issues and do not necessarily focus on the same concerns or regional arrangements. But, taken together, they offer a broad evaluation of the most important of these arrangements. A selective summary of the major findings of these studies will follow.

To start with, de la Torre and Kelly (1992) note that SSA has the largest number of ineffective and/or dormant economic groupings compared with other regions of the world. In addition, several of the regional economic integration arrangements in SSA have considerable overlapping memberships. This feature has been an important source of friction and implementation problems, particularly in West Africa.

The available assessment studies have generally evaluated performance of the regional integration initiatives in terms of their degree of success in achieving their fundamental goal of significantly increasing trade within the integrated area and expanding the area's overall trade, as well as the extent to which they have succeeded in carrying out agreed obligations with respect to the elimination of barriers to the free movement of goods, services and factors of production. As Table 18.1 shows, intra-regional trade as a proportion of total trade is low in SSA's economic integration arrangements, and compares unfavourably with similar organisations in Asia and Latin America.

The star performer among economic groupings in SSA is the CEAO; its intra-regional trade as a proportion of the area's total trade almost doubled between 1970 (prior to being founded in 1972) and 1990. The next best performer is the PTA whose intra-regional trade averaged just over 8 per cent of total trade during the 1970–90 period. It should be noted, however, that this ratio actually declined from a high of 9.4 per cent in 1975 (prior to the establishment of the PTA in 1981) to 7 per cent in 1985. It may be noted also that the ECOWAS doubled its ratio of intra-regional trade to total trade (from 3 to 6 per cent) between 1970 and 1990; but in general, none of these regional groups appears to have succeeded in markedly boosting intra-regional trade in their integrated areas.

Judged against the extent to which regional economic integration arrangements in SSA succeeded in boosting the total exports of the integrated areas relative to total world exports, Table 18.2 shows that they uniformly failed. In every single case, this ratio stagnated or declined steadily between 1970 and 1990; the establishment of these integrated areas did not halt the downward trend that often preceded their birth.

A third indicator of the trade performance of SSA's integrated areas is the change in their trade to GDP ratios over time. Data presented in Table 18.3 show that, in spite of the establishment of the regional economic groupings, trade performance worsened significantly during

Table 18.1 Intra-regional exports as percentage of total exports, 1975–90

Regional groupings	*1970*	*1975*	*1980*	*1985*	*1990*
CEAO	6.3	11.6	9.4	8.2	11.3
CEPGL	0.4	0.3	0.1	0.8	0.6
ECOWAS	3.0	4.2	3.5	5.3	6.0
MRU	0.2	0.4	0.8	0.4	0.3
PTA	8.4	9.4	8.9	7.0	8.5
UDEAC	5.0	2.7	1.7	2.1	4.6

Source: Extracted from de la Torre and Kelly (1992).

Table 18.2 Total regional exports as percentage of world exports, 1970–90

Regional groupings	*1970*	*1975*	*1980*	*1985*	*1990*
CEAO	0.3	0.2	0.2	0.2	0.2
CEPGL	0.3	0.1	0.1	0.1	–
ECOWAS	1.0	1.4	1.7	1.1	0.6
MRU	0.1	0.1	–	–	–
PTA	1.1	0.6	0.4	0.3	0.2
UDEAC	0.2	0.2	0.2	0.2	0.1

Source: Extracted from de la Torre and Kelly (1992).

Table 18.3 Change in trade to GDP ratios (%)

		Regional	*External*	*Total*
CEAO	1970–80	7.4	2.0	9.5
	1980–90	−12.9	–	−12.9
CEPGL	1975–90	0.3	0.2	0.4
ECOWAS	1975–80	2.1	–	2.1
	1980–5	−12.3	0.1	−12.2
MRU	1970–80	12.8	0.2	13.1
	1980–90	−27.2	−0.2	−27.4
PTA	1980–5	−8.9	−0.9	−9.8
	1985–90	11.3	0.9	12.2
UDEAC	1965–75	−1.3	1.0	−0.3
	1975–90	12.6	−0.1	−12.7

Source: Extracted from de la Torre and Kelly (1992).

the 1980s. It is also clear that intra-regional trade bore the brunt of this sharp downturn in trade performance. Clearly, therefore, the establishment of integrated areas in sub-Saharan Africa did not succeed in arresting the region's general economic decline in the 1980s. After surveying the evidence, Berg (1991) concludes that:

> Africa integration efforts have been less successful than those in other parts of the world in several respects. First, despite the goal of collective self-reliance, members in the African trade organizations have become more dependent on external trade since the mid-1960s, which has not been the case in other regions. And secondly, trade between member countries of most of the African trade organizations expanded less than did member country trade with other African countries.

Various explanations have been offered for the apparent 'failure' of regional integration schemes in SSA. For analytical convenience, one may classify these explanations into three broad groups: these include political constraints, structural weaknesses, and policy failures. The behaviour of SSA's political leaders with regard to the question of regional integration over the past three decades amply demonstrates an apparent lack of political commitment to actually implementing measures agreed upon in the various high-level meetings and negotiations that have been held on the subject. Poor implementation of agreed obligations as and when due is reflected in the constant shifts of deadlines set for the removal of barriers against the movement of goods and services and factor mobility. These implementation problems also represent symptoms of an absence of automaticity in the execution of agreed changes, and a lack of effective and universally accepted central (regional) enforcement mechanisms. Embedded in these problems is, perhaps, the unwillingness of many SSA countries to accept the authority of supranational rules so soon after achieving sovereign status.

The argument of lack of political will pales into insignificance in comparison with those relating to the alleged structural weaknesses of SSA economies which render them unviable as regional integration partners. Basing its arguments on a study of these weaknesses, a recent survey (de Melo et al., 1992) concludes that 'regional integration among low-income developing countries is unlikely to yield major gains'. Central to this conclusion is the traditional assertion that SSA countries exhibit a high degree of similarity in resource endowment and production patterns and that they import similar products from the developed countries. These trends mean that they are not natural trading partners for each other and hence the potential for expanding intra-regional trade among such countries is substantially restricted. This implies that even if such countries were willing and able to dismantle all trade barriers between themselves, intra-regional trade would still be quite small and possible trade-related gains from regional integration would therefore be limited. In support of the position that regional integration efforts in SSA are largely ineffective, Foroutan (1992) offers evidence from a gravity-model analysis, which shows that the observed low levels of bilateral trade flows between SSA countries actually approximate the 'normal' level predicted by the model.

Badiane (1992) finds, however, that this argument does not necessarily hold, at least in the case of West Africa. In this region, the observed patterns of agricultural production show that countries have followed different paths of specialisation which reflect their geographical location. These differences constitute potential trade opportunities. In addition, the negatively correlated production fluctuations across these countries provide strong trade incentives, while the computed revealed comparative advantage indicators for many West African countries point strongly to divergences in their production structures. Taken together, these indicators suggest that the potential for intra-regional trade could be much higher than is reflected by actual or recorded trade flow data. A recent rough estimate (World Bank, 1989c) of the untapped intra-regional exports potential in SSA amounts to US$4–5 billion. If this potential were realised, the ratio of intra-regional trade to total trade in SSA would increase dramatically.

Two other elements of structural weakness characterising sub-Saharan African countries often come up for mention as part of the reason for the failure or ineffectiveness of the region's integration schemes. Firstly, the typical SSA country is heavily dependent on trade taxes as its major source of government revenue. Such countries are unlikely to be willing to eliminate trade barriers in the context of regional integration, given the implication in terms of revenue losses. Secondly, existing regional integration schemes in SSA have experienced large differences in the distribution of costs and benefits among them and have not succeeded in designing a workable and effective compensation mechanism, which has caused implementation delays.

The impact of past policy failures in inhibiting regional integration seems to be emerging as a major factor that can explain the failure of these schemes. In this respect, Badiane (1992) and Foroutan (1992) lay considerable emphasis on import substitution development strategies and policies that kept up trade restrictions, sustained overvalued exchange rates and thus produced strongly anti-export biased regimes in many SSA countries. These policy failures not only discouraged or penalised trade generally, they also created an environment in which each individual country's specific objectives and policies were incompatible with those required for promoting and sustaining regional integration and expanded intra-regional trade.

IV FUTURE PROSPECTS

The general conclusion that regional integration schemes have failed in SSA is probably not justified. It is more tenable to describe the schemes as having been ineffective, given that the conditions for their success (i.e., effective implementation of agreed obligations particularly in terms of trade barrier elimination, consistency between regional commitments and national policies, among others) have often not been met.

The existing regional integration arrangements among SSA countries seem to have been designed, by and large, as extensions of an import substitution strategy from the narrow national to the larger regional market. They are thus inherently inward-looking; even worse, country-specific policies have continued to reflect national concerns, which has meant that the potentials of the larger regional markets could not, in fact, be tapped. Current SAPs being implemented in the majority of SSA countries are pushing them *individually* in the general direction of an environment of outward-oriented development strategy and policies. In addition, the preferred route for the SAPs outward orientation appears to be through unilateral trade liberalisation. Thus, if SAP policies regarding the trade and exchange rate regime are faithfully and fully implemented across the SSA countries, the region will move from an inward-looking development strategy, which provided too much protection in many tiny markets, to an outward-oriented regime, which denies any protection to all the economic activities of a large market (if regionally integrated). Producers could then be expected to become reasonably competitive, in time, if they had the breathing space within which to learn and grow. It would seem, however, to be counterproductive to move from the bad extreme of overprotection caused by previous policy failures to the equally bad extreme of no protection in the guise of an ultra-outward-oriented SAP.

Regional integration in the general environment of outward-oriented policies could provide an important vehicle for autonomous and sustainable growth of both trade and output in SSA countries. Substantially reduced trade barriers within an integrated area could provide the efficiency-enhancing competitive pressures associated with outward orientation without entirely giving up, *ab initio*, the advantages derivable from moderate protection for local producers in the integrated area. Regional integration arrangements designed in the context of this basically outward-oriented environment would imply building strong regional dimensions into the articulation, negotiation and implementation of SAPs. In particular, this calls for greater coordination of trade and exchange rate policies and payment arrangements across countries within specific integrated areas. This is to ensure that national policies are consistent with and enhanced by corresponding regional integration obligations; and that both are, in turn, compatible with SAPs negotiated with the international agencies.

In addition to their role in facilitating coordination of national and regional policies in the context of SAP negotiations, the international agencies can also play a vital role in designing and giving financial assistance to appropriate compensation mechanisms without which the difficulties in implementing regional integration schemes in SSA are likely to remain.

Prevailing adjustment policies have aimed at producing outward-oriented trade regimes, which are thought to be more conducive to efficient development. But their focus is country-specific and they rely too heavily on unilateral trade liberalisation. To this extent, they neglect the important role that carefully designed and implemented regional integration arrangements can play in the development of SSA countries. Adding this missing regional component could improve the design and effectiveness of future SAPs by exploiting the potentials for a more autonomous and sustainable growth path for SSA countries. It could also contribute to the general acceptability of SAPs by incorporating what is apparently a deeply-felt need and aspiration for closer economic cooperation in the region. Development assistance directed at eliminating problems associated with compensation mechanisms could play a key role in the revival of regional integration in sub-Saharan African countries.

Annex

CEAO	Communaute Economique de l'Afrique de l'Ouest (7 members); founded: 1972; established: 1974. Benin, Burkina Faso, Côte d'Ivoire, Mali, Mauritania, Niger and Senegal.
CEPGL	Communaute Economique des Pays des Grands Lacs (3 members); founded: 1976. Burundi, Rwanda, Zaire.
ECOWAS	Economic Community of West African States (16 members – 15 initially, but Cape Verde split from Guinea-Bissau). (Also known as CEDEAO – Communaute Economique des Etats de l'Afrique de l'Ouest); founded: 1975. Benin, Burkina Faso, Cape Verde, Côte d'Ivoire, Gambia, Ghana, Guinea, Guinea-Bissau, Liberia, Mali, Mauritania, Niger, Nigeria, Senegal, Sierra Leone, Togo (integrates the CEAO members and MRU members and Cape Verde, Gambia, Ghana, Guinea-Bissau, Nigeria, Togo).
MRU	Mano River Union (also known as Union du Fleuve Mano) (3 members); founded: 1973; established 1974. Guinea, Liberia, Sierra Leone (Guinea joined in 1980).
PTA	Preferential Trade Area (15 members); established: 1981; ratified 1984 (1 July). Burundi, Comoros, Djibouti, Ethiopia, Kenya, Lesotho, Malawi, Mauritius, Rwanda, Somalia, Swaziland, Tanzania, Uganda, Zambia, Zimbabwe.
UDEAC	Union Douaniere et Economique de l'Afrique Centrale (4 members); founded 1964; established: 1966. Cameroon, Central African Republic, Congo, Gabon, Equatorial Guinea.

References

Abbate, F. and A. Tran-Nguyen (1991), 'Official Debt Reduction: A Comparative Analysis of The Toronto Options, The U.K. Proposal and The Netherlands Initiative', *African Development Review*, vol. 3, no. 2.

Adam, C., W. Cavendish and P. Mistry (1992), *Adjusting Privatisation: Case Studies for Developing Countries* (London: James Currey).

Africa International (1992), 'Code des Investissement: Le Tapis Rouge', *Africa International*, March/April.

African Business (1988), 'The Anatomy of a Privatisation Scheme: The Togo Example', February.

African Development Bank (1993), *African Development Report* (Abidjan: African Development Bank).

Alderman, H. (1990), 'Nutritional Status in Ghana and Its Determinants', *Cornell Food and Nutrition Policy Program Working Paper*, no. 1 (Ithaca, NY: Cornell University).

Alderman, H. (1991), 'Downtown and Economic Recovery in Ghana: Impacts on the Poor', *Cornell Food and Nutrition Policy Program Monograph* (Ithaca, New York: Cornell University).

Alderman, H., D.E. Sahn and J. Arulpragasam (1991), 'Food Subsidies in an Environment of Distorted Exchange Rates: Evidence from Mozambique', *Food Policy,* October.

Alesina, A. (1988), 'Macroeconomics and Politics', in S. Fischer (ed.), *NBER Macroeconomic Annual* (Cambridge, Mass.: MIT Press).

Alexandratos, N. (1991), 'World Agriculture in the Next Century: Challenges for Production and Distribution', paper presented to the XXI International Conference of Agricultural Economists, Tokyo, August (Rome: FAO).

Allan, W. (1965), *The African Husbandman* (Edinburgh: Oliver and Boyd).

Amadeo, E. and T. Banuri (1991), 'Policy, Governance and the Management of Conflict', in T. Banuri (ed.), *Economic Liberalisation: No Panacea* (Oxford: Clarendon Press).

Amsden, A. (1989), *Asia's Next Giant: South Korea and Late Industrialisation* (New York: Oxford University Press).

Anderson, D. and Farida Khambata (1985), 'The Merits and Limitations of "Commercial" Interest Rate Policies in Developing Countries', *Economic Development and Cultural Change*, vol. 35.

Anyang Nyongo, P. (ed.) (1987), *Popular Struggles for Democracy in Africa* (London: Zed Press).

Aoulou, Y. (1992), 'Privatisation: La Grande Braderie?', *Jean Afrique Economie*, no. 107.

Ariyo, A. and M.I. Raheem (1991), 'Enhancing Trade Flows within the ECOWAS: An Appraisal and Some Recommendations', in A. Chhibber and S. Fischer (eds), *Economic Reform in Sub-Saharan Africa* (Washington, DC: World Bank).

Arulpragasam, J. and D.E. Sahn (forthcoming), 'Economic Reform in Guinea:

Adjusting for the Past', *Cornell Food and Nutrition Policy Program Monograph* (New York: New York University Press).
Aschauer, D.A. (1989), 'Does Public Capital Crowd out Private Capital?', *Journal of Monetary Economics*, vol. 24, pp. 171–88.
Badiane, O. (1989), 'The Potential for an "Espace Regional Cerealier (ERC)" among West African Countries and its Possible Contribution to Food Security', paper presented at the Seminar on Regional Cereals Markets in West Africa (Lomé: CILSS/OECD/Club du Sahel).
Badiane, O. (1992), 'Macroeconomic Policies and Inter-country Trade in West Africa', *IFPRI*, September. (Also presented at the Second Biennial Conference on African Economic Issues, Abidjan, 13–15 October 1992.)
Bagachwa, M.D. and F. Stewart (1992), 'Rural Industries and Rural Linkages in Sub-Saharan Africa: A Survey', in F. Stewart, S. Lall and S. Wangwe (eds), *Alternative Development Strategies for Sub-Saharan Africa* (London: Macmillan).
Balassa, B. (1976), 'Reforming the System of Incentives in Developing Countries', *World Development*, vol. 3, no. 6.
Balassa, B. (1988), 'Public Finance and Economic Development', *PPR Working Paper*, no. 31 (Washington, DC: World Bank).
Balassa, B. (1989), 'Incentive Policies in Sub-Saharan Africa', in B. Balassa, *New Directions in the World Economy* (London: Macmillan).
Bangura, Y. (1991), 'Authoritarian Rule and Democracy in Africa', in P. Gibbon, Y. Bangura and A. Ofstad (eds), *Authoritarianism, Democracy and Adjustment* (Uppsala: SIAS).
Barba Navaretti, G. (1992), 'Joint Ventures and Autonomous Industrial Development: The Case of the Cote D'Ivoire', in F. Stewart, S. Lall and S. Wangwe (eds), *Alternative Development Strategies for Sub-Saharan Africa* (London: Macmillan).
Barrett, S. (1990), *Macroeconomic Policy Reforms and Third World Soil Conservation* (London: London Business School).
Barro, R. (1990), 'A Cross-Country Study of Growth, Saving and Government', *Working Paper*, no. 2855 (Cambridge, Mass.: National Bureau of Economic Research).
Barro, R. (1991), 'Economic Growth in a Cross-Section of Countries', *Quarterly Journal of Economics*, no. 2, May.
Barrows, R. and M. Roth (1989), 'Land Tenure and Investment in African Agriculture: Theory and Evidence', *Land Tenure Centre Paper*, no. 136 (Wisconsin, Madison: Land Tenure Center, University of Wisconsin).
Bates, R. (1981), *Markets and States in Tropical Africa: The Political Basis of Agricultural Policies* (Berkeley: University of California Press).
Beckman, B. (1991), 'Empowerment or Repression? The World Bank and the Politics of African Adjustment', *Africa Development*, vol. XVI, no. 1.
Befekadu, Degefe (1988), 'Traditional Adjustment Mechanism, the World Bank, the IMF and the Developing Economies; Survey of Theories and Issues', background paper for the African Alternative Framework to Structural Adjustment Programmes for Socio-economic Recovery and Transformation, UNECA, Addis Ababa, Ethiopia.
Bennell, P. (1990), 'British Industrial Investment in Sub-Saharan Africa: Corporate Responses to Economic Crisis in the 1980s', *Development Policy Review*, vol. 8, no. 2.

Berg, A. (1991), *Strategies for West African Integration: Issues and Approaches* (Paris: Club du Sahel, OECD).

Bernstein, B. and G.M. Boughton (1993), *Adjusting to Development*, Paper on Policy Analysis and Assessment of the International Monetary Fund (Washington, DC: International Monetary Fund).

Berry, R.A. and W.R. Cline (1979), *Agrarian Structure and Productivity in Developing Countries* (Baltimore, MD and London: Johns Hopkins University Press).

Berthélemy, J.C. and F. Bourguignon (1992), 'Growth and Crisis in Côte d'Ivoire', mimeo (Paris: Delta (Joint Research Unit. CNRS-ENS-EHESS)).

Besteman, C. (1990), 'Land Tenure in the Middle Jubba: Customary Tenure and the Effect of Land Registration', *Land Tenure Center Research Paper*, no. 104 (Wisconsin, Madison: Land Tenure Center, University of Wisconsin).

Bevan, D.L., P. Collier and J.W. Gunning (1987), 'Consequences of a Commodity Boom in a Controlled Economy: Accumulation and Redistribution in Kenya 1975–83', *The World Bank Economic Review*, vol. 1, no. 3.

Beynon, J.G. (1989), 'Pricism vs Structuralism in Sub-Saharan African Agriculture', *Journal of Agricultural Economics*, vol. 40, no. 3.

Bhagwati, J. (1982), 'Directly Unproductive Profit Seeking (DUP) Activities', *Journal of Political Economy*, vol. 90, no. 5.

Bienen, H. and J. Waterbury (1989), 'The Political Economy of Privatisation in Developing Countries', *World Development*, vol. 17, no. 5.

Binswanger, H. (1990), 'The Policy Response of Agriculture', in World Bank, *Proceedings of the World Bank Annual Conference on Development Economics* (Washington, DC: World Bank).

Binswanger, H., J. McIntire and C. Udry (1989), 'Production Relations in Semi-Arid African Agriculture', in P. Bardhan (ed.), *The Economic Theory of Agrarian Institutions* (New York: Oxford University Press).

Binswanger, H. and Prabhu Pingali (1989), 'Induced Technical and Institutional Change in African Agriculture', *Journal of International Development*, no. 1, January.

Binswanger, H. and D. Sillers (1983), 'Risk Aversion and Credit Constraints in Farmers' Decision-making: A Reinterpretation', *Journal of Development Studies*, vol. 19.

Blakey, G. (1993), 'Economic Integration in Sub-Saharan Africa: The Implications for Direct Investment', paper presented at the IDRC/ECOWAS Conference on West African Integration, Dakar, 11–15 January.

Blejer, M.I. and M.S. Khan (1984), 'Government Policy and Private Investment in Developing Countries', *IMF Staff Papers*, vol. 31, no. 2.

Bond, M. (1983), 'Agricultural Responses to Prices in Sub-Saharan Africa', *IMF Staff Papers*, vol. 30, no. 4.

Booth, A. (1990) 'Agricultural Growth in Indonesia and its Implications for other Developing Countries', *World Development*, vol. 17, no. 8.

Borenzstein, E. (1990), 'Debt Overhang, Credit Rationing and Investments', *Journal of Development Economics*, vol. 32, no. 2.

Borooah, V. and F. Schneider (eds) (1991), 'Politico-Economic Modelling', *European Journal of Political Economy*, special issue, vol. 7, no. 4.

Boserup, E. (1965), *The Conditions of Agricultural Growth: The Economics*

of Agrarian Change Under Population Pressure (London: Allen and Unwin).
Bourgi, A. and C. Casterna (1991), *Le printemps de l'Afrique* (Paris: Hachette).
Bourguignon, F. and C. Morrisson (1992), 'Adjustment and Equity in Developing Countries', *Development Centre Studies* (Paris: OECD Development Centre).
Bourguignon, F., J. de Melo and C. Morrisson (1991), 'Adjustment with Growth and Equity', *World Development*, special issue, vol. 19, no. 11.
Bratton, M. (1986), 'Financing Smallholder Production: A Comparison of Individual and Group Schemes in Zimbabwe', *Public Administration and Development*, vol. 6.
Bratton, M. and D. Rothchild (1991), 'The Institutional Bases of Governance in Africa', in G. Hyden and M. Bratton (eds), *Governance and Politics in Africa* (Boulder, Col.: Lynne Rienner).
Buchanan, J. (1981), 'Rent-Seeking and Profit-Seeking', in J. Buchanan, D. Tollison and G. Tullock (eds), *Toward a Theory of the Rent-Seeking Society* (College Station: Texas A&M University Press).
Buffie, E. (1984), 'The Macroeconomics of Trade Liberalization', *Journal of International Economics*, 17.
Buffie, E. (1986), 'Devaluation, Investment and Growth in LDCs', *Journal of Development Economics*, 16.
Buiter, W. (1988), 'Structural and Stabilization Aspects of Fiscal and Financial Policy in the Dependent Economy', *Oxford Economic Papers*, vol. 40, no. 2.
Cameron, R. (ed.) (1972), *Banking and Economic Development: Some Lessons of History* (Oxford and New York: Oxford University Press).
Campbell, B. and J. Loxley (1989), *Structural Adjustment in Africa* (London: Macmillan).
Carter, M.R., K. Wiebe and B. Blarel (1991), 'Tenure Security for Whom? Differential Impacts of Land Policy in Kenya', *Land Tenure Center Research Paper*, no. 106 (Wisconsin, Madison: Land Tenure Center, University of Wisconsin).
Caskey, J. (1992), 'Macroeconomic Implications of Financial Sector Reform Programs in Sub-Saharan Africa', mimeo.
CBI (1990), *Market Study: Fresh Fruits and Vegetables* (Rotterdam: Centrum tot Bevordering van de Import uit ontwikkelingslanden).
CGIAR (Consultative Group on International Agricultural Research) (1992), *Review of CGIAR Priorities and Strategies – Part I* (Washington, DC: TAC Secretariat, Food and Agriculture Organization).
Chazan, N. and D. Rothchild (eds) (1987), *The Precarious Balance: State and Society in Africa* (Boulder, Col.: Westview Press).
Chhibber, A. (1992), 'Exchange Reforms, Supply Response and Inflation in Africa', in I. Goldin and A. Winters (eds), *Open Economies: Structural Adjustment and Agriculture* (Cambridge: Cambridge University Press).
Chhibber, A. and N. Shafik (1990), 'Exchange Reform, Parallel Markets and Inflation in Africa: The Case of Ghana', *PRE Working Papers*, no. 427 (Washington, DC: World Bank).
Chhibber, A. and S. Fischer (eds) (1991), *Economic Reform in Sub-Saharan Africa* (Washington, DC: World Bank).
Chiejena, T. (1992), *African Economic Digest*, vol. 12, 8–14 January.

Chimedza, R. (1990), 'Zimbabwe's Informal Financial Sector: An Overview', *Working Paper* AEE 4/90 (Harare: University of Zimbabwe, Department of Agricultural Economics and Extension).

Chipeta, C. and M.L.C. Mkandawire (1992), 'The Informal Financial Sector in Malawi', *African Review of Money, Finance and Banking*, vol. 2.

Cleaver, K. (1985), 'The Impact of Price and Exchange Rate Policies on Agriculture in Sub-Saharan Africa', *World Bank Staff Working Papers*, no. 728 (Washington, DC: World Bank, 1985).

Cleaver, K. (1993), 'A Strategy to Develop Agriculture in Sub-Saharan Africa and a Focus for the World Bank', *World Bank Technical Paper*, no. 203, Africa Technical Department Series (Washington, DC: World Bank).

Cockcroft, L. (1992), 'The Past Record and Future Potential of Foreign Investment', in F. Stewart, S. Lall and S. Wangwe (eds), *Alternative Development Strategies for Sub-Saharan Africa* (London: Macmillan).

Colclough, C. and J. Manor (eds) (1991), *States or Markets: Neo-liberalism and the Development Policy Debate* (Oxford: Clarendon Press).

Collander, D.C. (1982), 'Introduction', in D.C. Collander (ed.), *Neoclassical Political Economy* (Cambridge: Balinger Publishing Company).

Collier, P. (1991), 'Gender Aspects of Labour Allocation During Structural Adjustment', mimeo (Oxford: Unit for the Study of Africa Economies, Oxford University).

Collier, P. (1992), 'Trade, Price and Financial Reforms in the Transition from African Socialism', mimeo (Cambridge, MA: Kennedy School of Government).

Collinson, M. (1989), 'Small Farmers and Technology in Eastern and Southern Africa', *Journal of International Development*, 1.

Commander, S. and Killick, T. (1988), 'Privatisation in Developing Countries: A Survey of the Issues', in P. Cook and C. Kirkpatrick, *Privatisation in Less Developed Countries* (London: Harvester Wheatsheaf).

Conroy, A. (1992), 'The Economics of Smallholder Maize Production in Malawi with Reference to the Market for Seed and Fertiliser', unpublished PhD thesis, IDPM, University of Manchester.

Corbo, V. and S. Fischer (1992), 'Adjustment Programs and Bank Support: Rationale and Main Results', in V. Corbo et al. (1992), *Adjustment Lending Revisited: Policies to Restore Growth*, A World Bank Symposium, Washington, DC.

Corbo, V. and P. Rojas (1992), 'World Bank-Supported Adjustment Programs: Country Performance and Effectiveness', in V. Corbo et al., *Adjustment Lending Revisited: Policies to Restore Growth*, A World Bank Symposium, Washington, DC.

Corbo, V., S. Fischer and S.B. Webb (eds) (1992), *Adjustment Lending Revisited: Policies to Restore Growth*, A World Bank Symposium, Washington, DC.

Corden, M. (1974), *Trade Policy and Economic Welfare* (Oxford: Clarendon Press).

Corden, M. (1990), 'Exchange Rate Policy in Developing Countries', *PRE Working Papers*, no. 412 (Washington, DC: World Bank).

Cornia, G.A. (1985), 'Farm Size, Land Yields and the Agricultural Production Function: An Analysis for Fifteen Developing Countries', *World Development*, vol. 13, no. 4.

Cornia, G.A. and R. Strickland (1990), 'Rural Differentiation, Poverty and Agricultural Crisis in Sub-Saharan Africa: Toward an Appropriate Policy Response', *Innocenti Occasional Papers*, Economic Policy Series, no. 4 (Florence: UNICEF International Child Development Centre).

Cornia, G.A. and F. Stewart (1993), 'Two errors of Targeting', *Journal of International Development*, vol. 5, no. 2.

Cornia, G.A., R. Jolly and F. Stewart (eds) (1987), *Adjustment with a Human Face*, vol. 1: *Protecting the Vulnerable and Promoting Growth* (Oxford: Clarendon Press).

Cornia, G.A., R. Jolly and F. Stewart (eds) (1988), *Adjustment with a Human Face*, vol. II:, *Ten Country Case Studies* (Oxford: Clarendon Press).

Cornia, G.A., R. Van der Hoeven and T. Mkandawire (eds) (1992), *Africa's Recovery in the 1990s: From Stagnation and Adjustment to Human Development* (London and New York: Macmillan and St Martin's).

Cournamel, A. (1989), 'L'Afrique et la Deregulation du Transport Aerien', *Africa Development*, vol. XIV, no. 2.

David, P. (1991), 'Technology, Resource Endowments, Property Rights and Trade: An Open Developing Country's Viewpoint', *CEPR Series*, no. 278, Center for Economic Policy Research, December.

de Janvry, A. and E. Sadoulet (1992), 'Structural Adjustment under Transactions Costs', paper prepared for the Conference of European Association of Agricultural Economists, Hohenheim (Germany), September.

de Janvry, A., M. Fafchamps and E. Sadoulet (1991), 'Peasant Household Behaviour with Missing Markets: Some Paradoxes Explained', *Economic Journal*, vol. 101.

de la Torre, A. and M.R. Kelly (1992), 'Regional Trade Arrangements', *Occasional Paper*, no. 93 (Washington, DC: International Monetary Fund).

de Melo, J., A. Panagariya and D. Rodrik (1992), 'The New Regionalism: A Country Perspective', World Bank Conference on Regionalism, Washington, 2–3 April 1992.

de Melo, J. and J. Typout (1986), 'The Effect of Financial Liberalization on Savings and Investment in Uruguay', *Economic Development and Cultural Change*, vol. 34, no. 6.

Dei, G.J.S. (1990), 'The Changing Land Use and Allocation Patterns of a West African Community', *Africa Development*, vol. 15, no. 1.

Demery, L. (1993), 'Fettered Adjustment: The Case of Côte d'Ivoire in the 1980s', mimeo, Africa Region, World Bank.

Demery, L. and T. Addison (1987), *The Alleviation of Poverty Under Structural Adjustment* (Washington, DC: World Bank).

Demery, L. and I. Husain (1993), 'External Finance and Economic Performance in Low-Income African Countries during the 1980s', mimeo, Africa Region, World Bank.

Demographic and Health Surveys (DHS) (1989), *Uganda: Demographic and Health Survey 1988/1989* (Columbia, MD: Institute for Resource Development/Westinghouse).

Desai, B.M. and J.W. Mellar (1993) *Institutional Finance for Agricultural Development* (Washington, DC: International Food Policy Research Institute).

Devarajan, S. and J. de Melo (1990), 'Membership in the CFA Zone: Odyssean Journey or Trojan Horse?', *PRE Working Paper*, no. 482 (Washington, DC: World Bank).

Devarajan, S., J.D. Lewis and S. Robinson (1993), 'External Shocks, Purchasing Power Parity, and the Equilibrium Real Exchange Rate', *The World Bank Economic Review*, vol. 7, no. 1.

Diamond, L. (1988), 'Nigeria Pluralism, Statism and the Struggle for Democracy', in L. Diamond et al., *Democracy in Developing Countries (Vol. 2): Africa* (Boulder, Col.: Lynne Rienner).

Diamond, L. (1989), 'Beyond Autocracy: Prospects for Democracy in Africa', paper presented at the Inaugural Seminar of the Governance in Africa Programme, Carter Centre, 17–18 February 1989.

Dickerman, C.W. and P. Bloch (1991), 'Land Tenure and Agricultural Productivity in Malawi', *Land Tenure Center Research Paper*, no. 142 (Wisconsin, Madison: Land Tenure Center, University of Wisconsin).

Dixit, A.K. and V. Norman (1980), *Theory of International Trade* (Cambridge: Cambridge University Press).

Dollar, D. (1992), 'Outward-Oriented Developing Economies Really Do Grow More Rapidly: Evidence from 95 LDCs, 1976–85', *Economic Development and Cultural Change*, vol. 40, no. 3.

Dornbusch, R. (1986), 'Special Exchange Rates for Capital Account Transactions', *The World Bank Economic Review*, 1 (Washington, DC: World Bank).

Dornbusch, R. and S. Edwards (1990), 'Macroeconomic Populism', *Journal of Development Economics*, vol. 32, no. 1.

Dorosh, P.A. and D.E. Sahn (1993), 'A General Equilibrium Analysis of the Effect of Macroeconomic Adjustment on Poverty in Africa', *Cornell Food and Nutrition Policy Program Working Paper*, no. 39 (Ithaca, NY: Cornell University).

Dorosh, P.A., R.E. Bernier and A.H. Sarris (1990), 'Macroeconomic Adjustment and the Poor: The Case of Madagascar', *Cornell Food and Nutrition Policy Program Monograph*, no. 9 (Ithaca, NY: Cornell University).

Dosi, G. (1991), 'Perspectives on Evolutionary Theory', *Science and Public Policy*, vol.18, no. 6.

Dosi, G., K. Pavitt and L. Soete (1990), *The Economics of Technical Change and International Trade* (London: Harvester Wheatsheaf).

Easterly, W. and K. Schmidt-Hebbel (1993), 'Fiscal Deficits and Macroeconomic Performance in Developing Countries', *The World Bank Research Observer*, vol. 8, no. 2.

ECA (1986), *Survey of Economic and Social Conditions in Africa 1983–84* (New York: United Nations).

ECA (1992), *Survey of Economic and Social Conditions in Africa 1980–90* (New York: United Nations).

Edwards, S. (1988), 'Exchange Rate Misalignment in Developing Countries', *Occasional Paper*, no. 2 (Washington, DC: World Bank).

Edwards, S. (1989), *Real Exchange Rates, Devaluation, and Adjustment: Exchange Rate Policy in Developing Countries* (Cambridge, Mass.: MIT Press).

Ega, L.A. (1984), 'Land Acquisition and Land Transfer in Zaria Villages in Nigeria', *Agricultural Administration*, 15.

Elbadawi, I.A. (1992), 'Have World Bank-Supported Adjustment Programs Improved Economic Performance in Sub-Saharan Africa?', *Policy Research, Working Papers*, Transition and Macro-Adjustment, WPS 1001 (Washington, DC: Country Economics Department, World Bank).

Elbadawi, I.A., D. Ghura and G. Uwujaren (1992), 'Why Structural Adjustment Has Not Succeeded in Sub-Saharan Africa', *Policy Research, Working Papers*, Transition and Macro-Adjustment, WPS 1000 (Washington, DC: Country Economics Department, World Bank).

Ellis, F. (1988), *Peasant Economics: Farm Households and Agrarian Development* (Cambridge: Cambridge University Press).

Elmekki, A. (1992), 'Reflections on the Politics of Famine and Agrarian Crisis in Sudan', paper presented at the Bellagio Conference on Reflections on Development, 21–26 September 1992.

Elson, D. (1991), 'Gender and Adjustment in the 1990s: An Update on Evidence and Strategies', mimeo (Manchester: Economics Department, University of Manchester).

Emmerij, L. (1993), 'A Critical Review of the World Bank's Approach to Social Sector Lending and Poverty Alleviation', paper prepared for the Group of Twenty-Four, mimeo.

Ephson, B. (1988), 'Ghana's Divestiture', *West Africa*, 27 June.

Faini, R. (1991), 'Infrastructure, Relative Prices and Agricultural Adjustment', in I. Goldin and A. Winters (eds), *International Dimensions to Structural Adjustment* (Cambridge: Cambridge University Press).

Faini, R. and J. de Melo (1990), 'Adjustment, Investment and the Real Exchange Rate in Developing Countries', *Economic Policy*, 11.

Faini, R., J. de Melo, A. Senhadji-Semlali and J. Stanton (1991), 'Macro Performance under Adjustment Lending', in V. Thomas, A. Chhibber, M. Dailami and J. de Melo (eds), *Restructuring Economics in Distress, Policy Reform and the World Bank* (Oxford: Oxford University Press for the World Bank).

Faini, R., L. Pritchett and F. Clavijo (1992), 'Import Demand in Developing Countries', in M. Dagenais and P. Muet (eds), *International Trade Modelling* (London: Chapman and Hall).

Fallows, J. (1990), 'The Great Japanese Misunderstanding', *New York Review of Books*, vol. xxxvii, no. 17.

FAO (1987), *FAO Production Yearbook 1986* (Rome: Food and Agriculture Organization).

FAO (1989), *The State of Food and Agriculture* (Rome: Food and Agriculture Organization).

FAO (1991), *FAO Production Yearbook 1990* (Rome: Food and Agriculture Organization).

FAO (1992a), *Quarterly Bulletin of Statistics*, vol. 5, no. 4 (Rome: Food and Agriculture Organization).

FAO (1992b), *FAO Production Yearbook 1991* (Rome: Food and Agriculture Organization).

Feder, G., R. Just and D. Zilberman (1985), 'Adoption of Agricultural Innovations in Developing Countries: A Survey', *Economic Development and Cultural Change*, vol. 33.

Felix, D. (1974), 'Technological Dualism in Later Industrialisers: On Theory,

History and Policy', *Journal of Economic History*, vol. XXXIV, no. 1.

Felix, D. (1992), 'Privatising and Rolling Back the Latin American State', *CEPAL Review*, no. 46.

Fischer, S. (ed.) (1988), *NBER Macroeconomic Annual* (Cambridge, Mass.: MIT Press).

Fischer, S. (1991), 'Growth Macroeconomics and Development', *NBER Working Paper*, no. 3702.

Foroutan, F. (1992), 'Regional Integration in Sub-Saharan Africa: Past Experience and Future Prospects', World Bank Conference on Regionalism, Washington, 2–3 April 1992.

Frey, B.S. and F. Schneider (1986), 'Competing Models of International Lending Activity', *Journal of Development Economics*, 20.

Frey, B.S. and R. Eichenberger (1992), 'The Political Economy of Stabilization Programmes in Developing Countries', *Technical Papers*, no. 59 (Paris: OECD Development Centre).

Friendland, J. (1986), 'The New Togolese Efforts Spur Hopes, Problems', *The Development Business: The Business Edition of the Development Forum*, 30 April.

Ghai, D. (1988), 'Participatory Development: Some Perspectives from Grassroots Experience', *UNRISD Discussion Paper*, no. 5 (Geneva: UNRISD).

Ghai, Y. (1985), 'The State and the Market in the Management of Public Enterprises in Africa: Ideology and False Comparisons', *Public Enterprise*, vol. 6.

Ghai, D. and S. Radwan (eds) (1983), *Agrarian Policies and Rural Poverty in Africa* (Geneva: International Labour Organisation).

Gibbon, D., H. Rees Jones and J.C.H. Morris (1980), *Kitale Agricultural Research Station, Kenya 1972–78: Evaluation Report* (London: Overseas Development Administration Evaluation Unit).

Gibbon, P. (1994), 'Toward a Political Economy of the World Bank', in T. Mkandawire and A. Olukushi (eds), *Between Liberalisation and Repression: The Politics of Adjustment in Africa* (Dakar: CODESRIA).

Giovannini, A. (1985), 'Saving and the Real Interest Rate in LDCs', *Journal of Development Economics*, vol. 18.

Glick, P., D.E. Sahn and C. del Ninno (1992), 'The Labor Markets and Time Allocation in Conakry', *Encomec Findings Bulletin*, no. 6.

Gold, J. (1979), 'Conditionality', *IMF Pamphlet Series*, no. 31 (Washington, DC: International Monetary Fund).

Government of Kenya (GOK) (1991), *Statistical Abstracts* (Nairobi: Government Printers).

Government of the Republic of Zimbabwe (GRZ) (1989), *Statistical Yearbook 1989* (Harare: Government Printer).

Government of the Republic of Zimbabwe (GRZ) (1992), *Second Annual Report of Farm Management Data for Communal Area Farm Units* (Harare: Ministry of Lands, Agriculture and Rural Resettlement, Farm Management Research Section).

Greene, J. and D. Villanueva (1991), 'Private Investment in Developing Countries: An Empirical Analysis', *IMF Staff Papers*, 38, no.1 (Washington, DC: International Monetary Fund).

Griffin, C.C. (1990), 'Pricing of Health Services and the Implications for the

Economic Consequences of Health Programs', paper from the Expert Meeting on the Economic Consequences of Health Programs, National Academy of Sciences, Committee on Population, 25–6 June 1990.

Griffin, K. and J. Knight (eds) (1989), 'Human Development in the 1980s and Beyond', *Journal of Development Planning*, special number, 19.

Grindle, M. (1991), 'The New Political Economy: Positive Economics and Negative Politics', in G. Meier (ed.), *Politics and Policy Making in Developing Countries: Perspectives on the New Political Economy* (San Francisco: ICS Press).

Grosh, B. (1988), 'Comparing Parastatal and Private Manufacturing Firms: Would Privatisation Improve Performance?', in P. Coughlin and G. Ikiara (eds), *Industrialisation in Kenya: In Search of a Strategy* (Nairobi: Heinemann Kenya).

Grosh, M.E. (1990), 'Social Spending in Latin America: The Story of the 1980s', *World Bank Discussion Paper*, no. 106 (Washington, DC: World Bank).

Guissinger, S.E. (1985), *Investment Incentives and Performance Requirements: Patterns of International Trade, Production and Investment* (New York: Praeger).

Gulhati, R., S. Bose and V. Atukorala (1985), 'Politiques de taux de change dans l'Afrique de l'est et du sud, 1965–1983', *World Bank Staff Working Papers*, no. 720 (Washington, DC: World Bank).

Gyimah-Boadi, E. (1991), 'State Enterprises Divestiture: Recent Ghanaian Experiences', in D. Rothchild, *Ghana: The Political Economy of Recovery* (Boulder, Col.: Lynne Rienner).

Haddad, L. (1992), 'Gender and Adjustment: Theory and Evidence to Date', paper presented at the workshop 'The Effects of Policies and Programs on Women', International Policy Research Institute, Washington, DC, 16 January 1992.

Haggblade S., C. Liedholm and D. Mead (1990), 'The Effect of Policy and Policy Reforms on Non-agricultural Enterprises and Employment in Developing Countries: A Review of Past Experiences', in F. Stewart, H. Thomas and T. de Wilde (eds), *The Other Policy* (London: Intermediate Technology Publications).

Hardy, C. (1992), 'The Prospects for Intra-regional Trade Growth in Africa', in F. Stewart, S. Lall and S. Wangwe (eds), *Alternative Development Strategies for Sub-Saharan Africa* (London: Macmillan).

Harrigan, J. (1991), 'Malawi', in P. Mosley, J. Harrigan and J. Toye, *Aid and Power*, 2 vols (London: Routledge).

Harrison, P. (1987), *The Greening of Africa: Breaking Through in the Battle for Land and Food* (London: Paladin).

Hayami, Y. and V.W. Ruttan (1985), *Agricultural Development: An International Perspective* (Baltimore: Johns Hopkins University Press).

Helleiner, G.K. (1987), 'Stabilization, Adjustment and the Poor', *World Development*, vol. 15, no. 12.

Helleiner, G.K. (1988), 'Growth-oriented Adjustment Lending: A Critical Appraisal of IMF/World Bank Approaches', paper for South Commission (Toronto: University of Toronto, Department of Economics).

Helleiner, G.K. (1992a), 'The IMF, the World Bank and Africa's Adjustment and External Debt Problems: an Unofficial View', *World Development*, vol. 20, no. 6.

Helleiner, G.K. (1992b), 'Trade Policy, Exchange Rates, and Relative Prices in sub-Saharan Africa: Interpreting the 1980s', paper prepared for a conference in Gothenburg, Sweden, 6–8 September 1992.

Helleiner, G.K. (1992c), 'Structural Adjustment and Long-term Development in Sub-Saharan Africa', in F. Stewart, S. Lall and S. Wangwe (eds), *Alternative Development Strategies for Sub-Saharan Africa* (London: Macmillan).

Helleiner, G.K. (1993), 'UNICEF Paper on Sub-Saharan African Debt Relief', mimeo (New York: UNICEF).

Helpman, E. and P.R. Krugman (1985), *Market Structure and Foreign Trade* (Cambridge, Mass.: MIT Press).

Heming, R. and A. Mansour (1988), 'Privatisation and Public Enterprises', *Occasional Paper 56* (Washington, DC: International Monetary Fund).

Herbst, J. (1990), 'The Structural Adjustment of Politics in Africa', *World Development*, vol. 18, no. 7.

Hewitt, D. (1993), 'Military Expenditures 1972–1990: The Reasons Behind the Post-1985 Fall in World Military Spending', *Working Papers* (Washington, DC: International Monetary Fund).

Heyer, J., J.K. Maitha, and W.M. Senga (eds) (1976), *Agricultural Development in Kenya. An Economic Assessment* (Oxford: Oxford University Press, metricated).

Hill, A. (1991), 'Infant and Child Mortality: Levels, Trends and Data Deficiencies', in R.G. Feachman and D.T. Jamison (eds), *Disease and Mortality in Sub-Saharan Africa* (New York: Oxford University Press, for the World Bank).

Hill, K. and A. Pebley (1989), 'Child Mortality in the Developing World: A Case for Guarded Optimism', *Population and Development Review*, vol. 15, no. 4.

Hirschman, A. (1958), *The Strategy of Economic Development* (New Haven: Yale University Press).

Hirschman, A. (1970), *Exit, Voice and Loyalty: Responses to Decline in Firms, Organisations and States* (Cambridge, Mass.: Harvard University Press).

Horsefield, J.K. (1969), *International Monetary Fund 1945–65. Vol. I Chronicle* (Washington, DC: International Monetary Fund).

Horton, B. (1990), 'Morocco: Analysis and Reform of Economic Policy', *EDI Development Policy Case Series 4* (Washington, DC: Economic Development Institute, World Bank).

Hulme, D. (1990), 'Can the Grameen Bank be Replicated? Recent Experiments in Malaysia, Malawi and Sri Lanka', *Development Policy Review*, vol. 8.

Husain, I. (1993), 'Structural Adjustment and the Long-Term Development of sub-Saharan Africa', paper presented at the DGIS/ISSAS Conference on Structural Adjustment and Beyond, The Hague, 1–3 June.

Husain, I. and J. Underwood (eds) (1991), *African External Finance in the 1990s* (Washington, DC: World Bank).

Hutchful, E. (1989), 'From "Revolution" to "Monetarism": The Economics and Politics of the Adjustment Programme in Ghana', in B. Campbell and

J. Loxley, *Structural Adjustment in Africa* (London: Macmillan).

Hyden, G. (1980), *Beyond Ujama in Tanzania: Underdevelopment and an Uncaptured Peasantry* (Berkeley: University of California Press).

Idachaba, F. (1991), 'Policy Options for African Agriculture', in J. Dreze and A. Sen (eds), *The Political Economy of Hunger*, vol. 3 (Oxford: Oxford University Press).

IMF (1986), 'Fund-Supported Programs, Fiscal Policy and Income Distribution', *Occasional Paper*, no. 45 (Washington, DC: International Monetary Fund).

IMF (1987), *Government Finance Statistics Yearbook* (Washington, DC: International Monetary Fund).

IMF (1988), 'The Implications of Fund-Supported Adjustment Programs for Poverty', *Occasional Paper*, no. 58 (Washington, DC: International Monetary Fund).

IMF (1990), *International Financial Statistics Yearbook 1990* (Washington, DC: International Monetary Fund).

IMF (1991a) *Government Finance Statistics Yearbook* (Washington, DC: International Monetary Fund).

IMF (1991b), *International Financial Statistics* (Washington, DC: International Monetary Fund).

IMF (various issues), *World Economic Outlook* (Washington, DC: International Monetary Fund).

Islam, N. and A. Subramanian (1989), 'Agricultural Exports of Developing Countries: Estimates of Income and Price Elasticities of Demand and Supply', *Journal of International Economics*, vol. 40, no. 2.

Islam, R. and D. Wetzel (1991), 'The Macroeconomics of the Public Sector Deficit. The Case of Ghana', paper presented at the conference on 'The Macroeconomics of the Public Sector Deficit', World Bank, Washington.

ITC (1987), *COCOA: Trader's Guide* (Geneva: International Trade Centre).

ITC (1991), *Market Study: Fruit Juices with Special Reference to Citrus and Tropical Fruit Juices. A Study of the World Market* (Geneva: International Trade Centre).

Jabara, C.L. (1990), 'Economic Reform and Poverty in The Gambia: A Survey of Pre- and Post-ERP Experience', *Cornell Food and Nutrition Policy Program Monograph*, no. 8 (Ithaca, NY: Cornell University).

Jabara, C.L. (1991), 'Structural Adjustment and Stabilization in Niger: Macroeconomic Consequences and Impacts on the Poor', *Cornell Food and Nutrition Policy Program Monograph*, no. 11 (Ithaca, NY: Cornell University).

Jabara, C., M. Tolvanen, M.K.A. Lundberg and R. Wadda (1991), 'Incomes, Nutrition, and Poverty in The Gambia: Results from the CFNPP Household Survey', mimeo (Ithaca, NY: Cornell Food and Nutrition Policy Program).

Jacquemot, P. (1988), 'La desetatisation en Afrique subsaharienne', *Revue Tiers Monde*, no. 114.

James, J. (1985), 'Bureaucratic, Engineering, and Economic Man: Decision Making for Technology in Tanzania's State-owned Industries', in S. Lall and F. Stewart (eds), *Theory and Reality in Development* (London: Macmillan).

Jaycox, E.V.K. (1993a), 'Capacity Building: The Missing Link in African Development', address to a conference sponsored by the African American Institute, mimeo, Reston, Virginia, 20 May.

Jaycox, E.V.K. (1993b), 'Africa: From Stagnation to Recovery', mimeo (Washington, DC: World Bank).

Jayne, T.S., M. Rukuni, M. Hajek, G. Sithole and G. Mudinu (1991), *Structural Adjustment and Food Security in Zimbabwe: Strategies to Maintain Access to Maize by Low-Income Groups During Maize Market Restructuring* (Harare: University of Zambia and Michigan State University).

Jazairy, I., M. Alamgir and T. Panuccio (1992), *The State of World Rural Poverty: An Inquiry into Its Consequences* (New York: International Fund for Agricultural Development by New York University Press).

Jespersen, E. (1992), 'External Shocks, Adjustment Policies and Economic and Social Performance', in G.A. Cornia, R. van der Hoeven and T. Mkandawire (eds), *Africa's Recovery in the 1990s: From Stagnation and Adjustment to Human Development* (London and New York: Macmillan and St. Martin's).

Jha, D. and B. Hojjati (1993), 'Fertilizer Use on Smallholder Farms in Eastern Province, Zambia', *Research Report*, no. 94 (Washington, DC: International Food Policy Research Institute).

Johnson, O.E.G. (1992), 'Managing Adjustment, Political Authority, and the Implementation of Adjustment Programs in Africa', *Working Papers*, DM/92/2 (Washington DC: International Monetary Fund).

Johnson, T.H., R.O. Slater and P. McGovan (1984), 'Explaining African Military Coups d'État, 1960–1982', *American Political Science Review*, vol. 78, no. 3.

Joint Bank/Fund Development Committee (1992), 'Development Issues', presentations to the 44th Meeting of the Development Committee, Washington DC, 21 September 1992.

Jolly, R. (1991), 'Adjustment with a Human Face: A UNICEF Record and Perspective on the 1980s', *World Development*, vol. 19, no. 12.

Jolly, R. and R. van der Hoeven (1989), 'Protecting the Poor and Vulnerable during Adjustment: The Case of Ghana', mimeo (New York: UNICEF).

Jorgenson, D.W. (1967), 'The Theory of Investment Behaviour', in R. Ferber (ed.), *Determinants of Investment Behavior* (New York: National Bureau of Economic Research).

Jorgenson, D.W. (1971), 'Econometric Study of Investment Behaviour: A Survey', *Journal of Economic Literature*, 9.

Juster, F.T. and F.P. Stafford (1991), 'The Allocation of Time: Empirical Findings, Behavioral Models, and Problems of Measurements', *Journal of Economic Literature*, XXIX, June.

Kamguem, M. (1992), 'L'intèrêt de Privatisations pour L'Afrique', *Jean Afrique Economie*, no. 157.

Karanja, D.D. (1990), *The Impact of Research on Maize Yields in Kenya 1955–1988* (Nairobi: Kenya Agricultural Research Institute).

Kennedy, E. and H. Bouis (1989), 'Traditional Cash Crop Schemes' Effects on Production, Consumption, and Nutrition: Sugarcane in the Philippines and Kenya', mimeo (Washington, DC: International Food Policy Research Institute).

Kennedy, P. (1988), *African Capitalism: The Struggle for Ascendancy* (Cambridge: Cambridge University Press).

Keynes, J.M. (1926), *The End of Laissez-Faire* (London: Macmillan).

Khan, A.R. (1992), Structural Adjustment and Income Distribution: A Review of Issues and Experiences', *International Employment Policies Working Paper*, no. 31 (Geneva: ILO World Employment Programme).

Khan, M.S. (1990), 'The Macroeconomic Effects of Fund-Supported Adjustment Programs', *IMF Staff Papers*, vol. 37, no. 2.

Khan, M. and M. Knight (1985), 'Fund-Supported Adjustment Programs and Economic Growth', *IMF Occasional Papers*, no. 41 (Washington, DC: International Monetary Fund).

Khan, M. and C. Reinhart (1990), 'Private Investment and Growth in Developing Countries', *World Development*, vol. 18, no. 1.

Kharas, H. and B. Pinto (1989), 'Exchange Rate Rules, Black Market Premia and Fiscal Deficits: The Bolivian Hyperinflation', *The Review of Economic Studies*, 56.

Kierzkowski, H., (ed.) (1989), *Monopolistic Competition and International Trade* (Oxford: Oxford University Press).

Killick, T. (1990), 'Structure, Development and Adaptation', *Special Paper*, no. 2 (Nairobi: African Economic Research Consortium).

Killick, T. (1991a), 'The Developmental Effectiveness of Aid to Africa', in I. Husain and J. Underwood (eds), *African External Finance in the 1990s* (Washington, DC: World Bank).

Killick, T. (1991b), 'Financial Management and Economic Development: Some Issues', *The South African Journal of Economics*, vol. 59, no. 3.

Killick, T. (1992), 'Explaining Africa's Post-independence Development Experiences', paper presented at the Second Biennial Conference on African Economic Issues, Abidjan, 13–15 October 1992.

King, R.G. and R. Levine (1992), 'Financial Indicators and Growth in a Cross Section of Countries', *PRE Working Paper* (Washington, DC: World Bank Policy Research Department).

Kirkpatrick, C. (1991), 'Some Background Observations on Privatisation', in V.V. Ramanadhan (ed.), *Privatisation in Developing Countries* (London: Routledge).

Knight, J.B. (1992), 'Public Enterprises and Industrialisation in Africa', in F. Stewart, S. Lall and S. Wangwe (eds), *Alternative Development Strategies for Sub-Saharan Africa* (London: Macmillan).

Koester, U. and M. Thomas (1992), 'Agricultural Trade Among Malawi, Tanzania, Zambia and Zimbabwe', *IFPRI*, February. (Also presented at the Second Biennial Conference on African Economic Issues, Abidjan, 13–15 October 1992.)

Krueger, A. (1974), 'The Political Economy of the Rent Seeking Society', *American Economic Review*, vol. 64, no. 3.

Krueger, A. and D. Orsmond (1990), 'Impact of Government on Growth and Trade', *Working Paper*, no. 3545 (National Bureau of Economic Research, Inc., December).

Krueger, A., Y. Schiff and A. Valdés (1991), *The Political Economy of Agricultural Pricing Policy: A World Bank Comparative Study* (Baltimore,

Maryland: Johns Hopkins University Press).
Krugman, P.R. (1979), 'A Model of Innovation, Technology Transfer and the World Distribution of Income', *Journal of Political Economy*, vol. 87.
Krugman, P. and L. Taylor (1978), 'Contractionary Effects of Devaluation', *Journal of International Economics*, 8.
Krumm, K. (1985), 'The External Debt of Sub-Saharan Africa. Origins, Magnitude and Implications for Action', *World Bank Staff Working Papers*, no. 741 (Washington, DC: World Bank).
Kydd, J. (1989), 'Maize Research in Malawi: Lessons from Failure', *Journal of International Development*, 1.
Lafay, J.D. (1981), 'Empirical Analysis of Politico-Economic Interaction in the East European Countries', *Soviet Studies*, vol. 33, no. 3.
Lafay, J.D. and J. Lecaillon (1993), *The Political Dimension of Adjustment* (Paris: OECD Development Centre).
Lal, D. (1983), *The Poverty of 'Development Economics'* (London: Institute of Economic Affairs).
Lall, S. (1987), *Long-term Perspectives on Sub-Saharan Africa* (Washington, DC: World Bank).
Lall, S. (1990), *Building Industrial Competitiveness in Developing Countries* (Paris: OECD).
Lall, S. (1992), 'Structural Problems of African Industry', in F. Stewart, S. Lall and S. Wangwe (eds), *Alternative Development Strategies for Sub-Saharan Africa* (London: Macmillan).
Lawry, S.W. and D.M. Stienbarger (1991), 'Tenure and Alley Farming in the Humid Zone of West Africa: Final Report of Research in Cameroon, Nigeria, and Togo', *Land Tenure Center Research Paper*, no. 105 (Wisconsin, Madison: Land Tenure Center, University of Wisconsin).
Lecraw, D. (1977), 'Direct Investment by Firms from Less Developed Countries', *Oxford Economic Papers*.
Lecraw, D. (1981), 'Technological Activities of LDC-based Multinationals', *Annals*, AAPSS.
Lee, N. (1992), 'Market Structure and Trade in Developing Countries', in G.K. Helleiner (ed.), *Trade Policy, Industrialization and Development* (Oxford: Clarendon Press).
Lele, U. and M. Agarwal (1989), *Smallholder and Large-Scale Agriculture: Are There Trade-Offs in Growth and Equity?* (Washington, DC: World Bank).
Lele, U. and A. Goldsmith (1989), 'The Development of National Research Capacity: India's Experience with the Rockefeller Foundation and its Significance for Africa', *Economic Development and Cultural Change*, vol. 37.
Lele, U. and R. Meyers (1989), 'Growth and Structural Change in East Africa: Domestic Policies, Agricultural Performance and World Bank Assistance, 1963–86', *World Bank MADIA Discussion Paper*, no. 3.
Lele, U., R. Christiansen and K. Kadiresan (1989), 'Fertiliser Policy in Africa: Lessons from Development Programmes and Adjustment Lending 1970–87', *World Bank MADIA Discussion Paper*, no. 5.
Lessler, B. (1991), 'When Government Fails, Will the Market Do Better? The Privatisation/Market Liberalisation Movement in Developing Coun-

tries', *Canadian Journal of Development Studies*, vol. XII, no. 1.

Lewis, W.A. (1954), 'Economic Development with Unlimited Supplies of Labor', *Manchester School of Economics and Social Studies*, vol. 22, no. 2.

Liedholm, C. and D. Mead (1987), 'Small-scale Industries in Developing Countries: Empirical Evidence and Policy Implications', *MSU International Development Paper*, no. 9 (Michigan: Michigan State University, Department of Agricultural Economics).

Lipton, M. (1988), 'The Place of Agricultural Research in the Development of Sub-Saharan Africa', *World Development*, vol. 16.

Lipton, M. (1990), 'Requiem for Adjustment Lending?', *Development Policy Review*, vol. 8.

Lipton, M. (1993), 'Land Reform as Commenced Business: The Evidence Against Stopping', *World Development*, vol. 21, no. 4.

Lipton, M., with R. Longhurst (1989), *New Seeds and Poor People* (London: Unwin Hyman).

Lipumba, N.H.I. and L. Kasekende (1991), 'The Record and Prospects of the Preferential Trade Area for Eastern and Southern African States', in A. Chhibber and S. Fischer (eds), *Economic Reform in Sub-Saharan Africa* (Washington, DC: World Bank).

Little, I., T. Scitovsky and M. Scott (1970), *Industry and Trade in Some Developing Countries* (London: Oxford University Press).

Lizondo, S. (1987), 'Exchange Rate Differentials and Balance of Payments under Dual Exchange Markets', *Journal of Development Economics*, 26.

Lizondo, S. (1991), 'Alternative Dual Exchange Market Regimes', *IMF Staff Papers*, no. 38.

Loxley, J. (1986), 'Alternative Approaches to Stabilization in Africa', in G.K. Helleiner (ed.), *Africa and the International Monetary Fund* (Washington, DC: International Monetary Fund).

Lucas, R.E. (1988), 'On the Mechanism of Economic Growth', *Journal of Monetary Economics*, vol. 22.

MacBean, A. (1966), *Export Instability and Economic Development* (Cambridge, Mass.: Harvard University Press).

MacNamara, R. (1969), *Sécurité américaine et paix mondiale* (Paris: Fayard).

Maizels, A. (1986), *The Terms of Trade and the External Financing Problems of Commodity Exporting Developing Countries* (Helsinki: WIDER, United Nations University).

Malloy, J. (1991), 'Democracy, Economic Crisis and the Problem of Governance: The Case of Bolivia', *Studies in Comparative International Development*, vol. 26, no. 2.

Mamdani, M., T. Mkandawire, and Wamba Dia wamba (1988), 'Social Movements, Social Transformation and Democratisation in Africa', *CODESRIA Working Papers*, no. 1.

Marcel, M.B. (1991), 'Restructuration et Evolution de l'Employé dans le Secteur Public et Para-Public en Côte d'Ivoire', *Africa Development*, vol. XVI.

Marchés Tropicaux, Weekly Issues from 1980 to 1990.

Maren, M.P. (1987), 'Togo's Privatisation', *The Development Business: The Business Edition of the Development Forum*, 16 April.

Marquez, J. (1985), 'Foreign Exchange Constraints and Growth Possibilities

in the LDCs', *Journal of Development Economics*, 19.
Matlon, P.J. (1990), 'Improving Productivity in Sorghum and Pearl Millet in Semi-arid Africa', *Food Research Institute Studies*, vol. 22, no. 1.
May, D. (1987), 'Moribund Mills in Togo: Profit from Privatisation', *The Washington Times*, 30 March.
MayaTech (1991), *Gender and Adjustment*, Series TR 91–1026–02 (Silver Spring, MD: The MayaTech Corporation).
Mazzucato V., P.G. Pardey and S. Ly (1993), 'Investing Sustainable Agricultural Research Systems: The Case of INRAN, Niger', mimeo (The Hague: International Service for National Agricultural Research).
Mbembe, A. (1989), 'Economic Liberalisation and the Post-Colonial African State', paper presented at the Inaugural Seminar of the Governance in Africa Programme, Carter Centre, 17–18 February 1989.
McKinnon, D. (1988), 'Financial Liberalisation in Retrospect: Interest Rates in LDCs', in G. Ranis and T. Paul Schultz, *The State of Development Economics* (Cambridge: Blackwell).
McKinnon, R.I. (1973), *Money and Capital in Economic Development* (Washington, DC: The Brookings Institution).
Meier, G. (ed.) (1991), *Politics and Policy Making in Developing Countries: Perspectives on the New Political Economy* (San Francisco: ICS Press).
Mellor, J., C. Delgado and M.J. Blackie (eds) (1987), *Accelerating Food Production in Sub-Saharan Africa* (Baltimore and London: Johns Hopkins University Press).
Merhav, M. (1969), *Technological Dependence, Monopoly and Growth* (Franklin: Franklin Book Company).
Migot-Adholla, S., P. Hazell, B. Blarel, and F. Place (1991), 'Indigenous Land Rights Systems in Sub-Saharan Africa: A Constraint on Productivity?', *The World Bank Economic Review*, vol. 5, no. 1.
Millward, R. (1988), 'Measured Sources of Inefficiency in the Performance of Private and Public Enterprises in LDCs', in P. Cook and C. Kirkpatrick, *Privatisation in Less Developed Countries* (London: Harvester Wheatsheaf).
Mkandawire, T. (1990), 'Growth Exercises on Zambia', paper prepared for the WIDER Project on Medium-term Adjustment Strategies, Helsinki.
Mkandawire, T. and A. Olukushi (eds) (1994), *Between Liberalisation and Repression: The Politics of Adjustment in Africa* (Dakar: CODESRIA).
Mody, A. and D. Wheeler (1990), *Automation and World Competition: New Technologies, Industrial Location and Trade* (Basingstoke and London: Macmillan).
Moran, C. (1989), 'Imports under a Foreign Exchange Constraint', *The World Bank Economic Review*, 3.
Morisset, J. (1993), 'Does Financial Liberalisation Really Improve Private Investment in Developing Countries?', *Journal of Development Economics*, vol. 40, no.1.
Mosley, P. (1983), *The Settler Economies: Studies in the Economic History of Kenya and Southern Rhodesia 1900–1963* (Cambridge: Cambridge University Press).
Mosley, P. (1986), 'Agricultural Performance in Kenya since 1970: Has the World Bank Got it Right?', *Development and Change*, vol. 17.
Mosley, P. (1987), 'Conditionality as Bargaining Process: Structural Adjust-

ment Lending, 1980–86', *Princeton Paper in International Finance*, no. 168 (Princeton, NJ: Princeton University Press).

Mosley P. (1988), 'Privatisation, Policy-based Lending and World Bank Behaviour', in P. Cook and C. Kirkpatrick, *Privatisation in Less Developed Countries* (London: Harvester Wheatsheaf).

Mosley, P. (1992), 'Comment', in Corbo et al., *Adjustment Lending Revisited: Policies to Restore Growth*, A World Bank Symposium, Washington, DC.

Mosley, P. (1993a), 'Decomposing the Effects of Structural Adjustment: The Case of Sub-Saharan Africa', paper presented to the International Seminar on Structural Adjustment and Long-term Development in Sub-Saharan Africa, The Hague, 1–3 June 1993.

Mosley, P. (1993b), 'Policy and Capital Market Constraints to the African Green Revolution: A Study of Maize and Sorghum Yields in Kenya, Malawi and Zimbabwe', *Innocenti Occasional Papers*, Economic Policy Series, no. 38 (Florence: UNICEF International Child Development Centre).

Mosley, P. and R.P. Dahal (1987), 'Credit for the Rural Poor: A Comparison of Policy Experiments in Nepal and Bangladesh', *Manchester Papers on Development*, 3.

Mosley, P. and J. Weeks (1993), 'Has Recovery Begun? Africa's Adjustment in the 1980s Revisited', *World Development*, vol. 21, no. 10.

Mosley, P., J. Harrigan and J. Toye (1991), *Aid and Power: The World Bank and Policy-based Lending*, vol. 1: *Analysis and Policy Proposals* (London: Routledge).

Mueller, D.C. (1989), *Public Choice II* (Cambridge: Cambridge University Press).

Mwape, F. (1989), 'Traditional Cropping Systems in Northern Province, Zambia', in *NORAGRIC Development and Environment*, no. 4, *Proceedings of the Symposium on the Sustainability of Agricultural Production Systems in Sub-Saharan Africa*, Aas, Norway, 4–7 September 1989.

Mytelka, L. (1989), 'The Unfulfilled Promise of African Industrialisation', *African Studies Review*, vol. 32.

Mytelka, L. (1992), 'Ivorian Industry at the Cross-roads', in F. Stewart, S. Lall and S. Wangwe (eds), *Alternative Development Strategies for Sub-Saharan Africa* (London: Macmillan).

Nadar, H.M. and W.A. Faught (1984), 'Maize Yield Response to Different Levels of Nitrogen and Phosphorous Fertiliser Application', *East African Agriculture and Forestry Journal*, vol. 44.

Nannenstadt, P. and M. Paldam (1992), 'The VP-Function. A Survey of the Literature on Vote and Popularity Functions', mimeo (Aarhus: Institute of Economics, Aarhus University).

Nashashibi, K. (1993), 'Fiscal Performance in Sub Saharan Africa in the 1980s under Alternative Strategies: Fixed and Variable Exchange Rates', *Working Paper* (Washington, DC: International Monetary Fund).

Ncube, P.D., M. Sakala and M. Ndulo (1987), 'The International Monetary Fund and the Zambian Economy', in K.J. Havenik (ed.), *The IMF and the World Bank in Africa* (Uppsala: Scandinavian Institute of African Studies).

N'daki, G. (1991), 'Africa Centrale Transparence Petrolière', *Africa*, December.

Ndlela, D.B. (1990), 'Macro-policies for Appropriate Technology in Zimbabwean Industry', in F. Stewart, H. Thomas and T. de Wilde (eds), *The Other Policy* (London: Intermediate Technology Publications).

Ndulu, B. (1990a), 'Growth and Adjustment in Sub-Saharan Africa', paper presented at the World Bank Conference on African Economic Issues, Nairobi, 4–7 June 1990.

Ndulu, B. (1990b), 'Macroeconomic Constraints on Growth: an Empirical Model for Tanzania', paper prepared for the WIDER Project on Medium-term Adjustment Strategies, Helsinki, 1990.

Ndulu, B. (1991), 'Growth and Adjustment in Sub-Saharan Africa', in A. Chhibber and S. Fischer (eds), *Economic Reform in Sub-Saharan Africa* (Washington, DC: World Bank).

Ndulu, B. (1992), 'Enhancing Income Distribution and Rationalising Consumption Patterns', in G.A Cornia, R. van der Hoeven and T. Mkandawire (eds), *Africa's Recovery in the 1990s: From Stagnation and Adjustment to Human Development* (London and New York: Macmillan and St. Martin's).

Nellis, J. and S. Kikeri (1989), 'Public Enterprise Reform: Privatisation and the World', *World Development*, vol. 17, no. 5.

Nelson, R.R. (1991), 'The Role of Firm Differences in an Evolutionary Theory of Technical Advance', *Science and Public Policy*, vol. 18, no. 6.

Nelson, R.R. and S. Winter (1982), *An Evolutionary Theory of Economic Change* (Cambridge, Mass.: Harvard University Press).

Norman, D., H. Sigwele and D. Baker (1987), 'Reflections on Two Decades of Research on Sorghum-based Farming Systems in Northern Nigeria and Botswana', paper presented at the Conference on Food Security Research in Southern Africa, Harare, 1987.

Norpoth, H., M.A. Lewis-Beck and J.D. Lafay (eds) (1991), *Economics and Politics: The Calculus of Support* (Ann Arbor: University of Michigan Press).

Nunnekamp, P. (1986), 'State Enterprises in Developing Countries', *Intereconomics*, July/August.

Nurkse, R. (1959), *Patterns of Trade and Development*, Wicksell Lectures, Stockholm.

OAU (1981), *Lagos Plan of Action for Economic Development of Africa 1980–2000* (Addis Ababa: Organisation for African Unity).

OECD (1991), *Development Co-operation Efforts and Policies of the Members of the Development Assistance Committee* (Paris: OECD).

OECD (1992), Development Assistance Committee, *DAC Principles for Effective Aid* (Paris: OECD).

Ohiorhenuan, J.E. and I.D. Paloamina (1992), 'Building Indigenous Technical Capacity in African Industry: The Nigerian Case', in F. Stewart, S. Lall and S. Wangwe (eds), *Alternative Development Strategies for Sub-Saharan Africa* (London: Macmillan).

O'Kane, R.H.T. (1981), 'A Probabilistic Approach to the Causes of Coups d'État', *British Journal of Political Science*, vol. 11, no. 3.

Onimode, B. (ed.) (1989), *The IMF, the World Bank and the African Debt* (London: Zed Press).

Oshikoya, T.W. (1992), 'Macroeconomic Adjustment, Uncertainty and Domestic Private Investment in Selected African Countries', *African Devel-*

opment Bank Economic Research Paper (Abidjan: African Development Bank).

Osmanzai, M. (1991), 'Cereals Agronomy Research 1989/90', in *Proceedings of the Seventh Regional Workshop on Sorghum and Millets for Southern Africa* (Bulawayo: SADCC/ICRISAT).

Ottichilo, W.K. and R.K. Sinange (1990), *Long Range Maize and Wheat Production Trends in Kenya for 1985–89* (Kenyan Government: Department of Resource Surveys and Remote Sensing).

Oyejide, T. (1992), 'Regional Economic Integration in Sub-Saharan Africa', CEPR Workshop on Market Integration, Regionalism and the Global Economy, La Coruna, Spain, 20–24 July 1992.

Oyejide, T. and M. Reheem (1990), 'Macroeconomic Constraints and Growth Programming. Empirical Evidence from Nigeria', paper prepared for the WIDER Project on Medium-term Adjustment Strategies, Helsinki, 1990.

Pagan, A. (1984), 'Econometric Issues in the Analysis of Regressions with Generated Regressors', *International Economic Review*, 25.

Page, J.M. and W.F. Steel (1984), 'Small Enterprise Development: Economic Issues from African Experience', *Technical Paper*, no. 26 (Washington, DC: World Bank).

Paldam, M. (1987), 'Inflation and Political Instability in Eight Latin American Countries 1946–83', *Public Choice*, vol. 52, no. 2.

Paldam, M. (1993), 'The Socio-Political Reactions to Balance-of-Payments Adjustments in LDCs', mimeo (Aarhus: University of Aarhus).

Pardey, P.G., J. Roseboom and J.R. Anderson (eds) (1991), *Agricultural Research Policy: International Quantitative Perspectives* (Cambridge: Cambridge University Press).

Patel, I.G. (ed.) (1992), *Policies for African Development, From the 1980s to the 1990s* (Washington, DC: International Monetary Fund).

Pearce, R. (1990), 'Food Consumption and Adjustment in Zambia', *Working Papers*, no. 2 (Oxford: Food Studies Group, International Development Centre, Queen Elizabeth House).

Pfeffermann, G.P. and A. Madarassy (1989), 'Trends in Private Investment in Developing Countries', *Discussion Paper*, no. 14 (Washington, DC: International Finance Corporation, World Bank).

Pimentel, D., B. Floyd, W. Tell and J. Bourn (1991), 'Deforestation, Biomass Depletion and Land Degradation Linkages to Policy Reform in Sub-Saharan Africa', in J. Lassoie and S. Kyle, *Cornell Natural Resources Research and Extension Series*, no. 34 (Ithaca, NY: Cornell University).

Pindyck, R. (1991), 'Irreversibility, Uncertainty and Investment', *Journal of Economic Literature*, vol. 29, no. 3.

Pinstrup-Andersen, P. (1982), *Agricultural Research and Technology in Economic Development* (London and New York: Longman).

Pinto, B. (1991), 'Black Markets for Foreign Exchange, Real Exchange Rates and Inflation', *Journal of International Economics*, 30.

Place, F. and P. Hazell (1993), 'Productivity Effects of Indigenous Land Tenure Systems in Sub-Saharan Africa', *American Journal of Agricultural Economics*, 75, February.

Platteau, J. (1992), 'Land Reform and Structural Adjustment in Sub-Saharan

Africa: Controversies and Guidelines', a report to FAO Economic and Social Policy Department (Rome: Food and Agriculture Organization).
Polak, J.J. (1989), 'Strengthening the Role of the IMF in the International Monetary System', in C. Gwin and R. Feinberg et al., *Pulling Together: The International Monetary Fund in a Multipolar World* (New Brunswick, NJ and Oxford: Transaction Books).
Polak, J.J. (1991), 'The Changing Nature of IMF Confidentiality', *Technical Papers*, no. 41 (Paris: OECD Development Centre).
Popov, G. (1990), 'Dangers of Democracy', *New York Review of Books*, 16 August.
Prebisch, R. (1959), 'Commercial in the Underdeveloped Countries', *American Economic Review*, Papers and Proceedings.
Prebisch, R. (1964), *Towards a new Trade Policy for Development: Report by the Secretary General UNCTAD* (New York: UNCTAD).
Prebisch, R. (1984), 'Five Stages in my Thinking about Development', in P. Bauer, G. Meier and D. Seers (eds), *Pioneers in Development* (New York: Oxford University Press).
Pritchett, L. (1991), 'The Real Exchange Rate and the Trade Surplus: An Empirical Analysis for Non-oil Exporting LDCs', mimeo (Washington, DC: Trade Policy Division, World Bank).
Ramadhan, V.V. (1989), 'Privatisation: The U.K. Experience and Developing Countries', in V.V. Ramadhan, *Privatisation in Developing Countries* (London: Routledge).
Ranis, G. and J. Fei (1988), 'Development Economics: What Next?', in G. Ranis and T.P. Schultz (eds), *The State of Development Economics* (Oxford: Blackwell).
Ranis, G., G. Stewart and E. Angeles-Reyes (1990), *Linkages in Developing Economies* (San Francisco: International Center for Economic Growth).
Rattso, J. and R. Davies (1990), 'Growth Programming for Zimbabwe', paper prepared for the WIDER Project on Medium-term Adjustment Strategies, Helsinki, 1990.
Ray, E.J. (1991), 'US Protection and Intra-industry Trade: The Message for Developing Countries', *Economic Development and Cultural Change*, vol. 40, no. 1.
Reed, D. (1992), *Structural Adjustment and the Environment* (Boulder, Col.: Westview Press).
Reserve Bank of India (1954), *All-India Rural Credit Survey*, vol. 1: *The Survey Report*, vol. 2: *The General Report*, vol. 3: *The Technical Report* (Bombay: Reserve Bank of India).
Reusse, E. (1987), 'Liberalisation and Agricultural Marketing: Recent Causes and Effects in Third World Economies', *Food Policy*, vol. 12, no. 4.
Riddell, R. and Associates (1990), *Manufacturing Africa: Performance and Prospects of Seven Countries in Sub-Saharan Africa* (London: James Currey).
Rodrik, D. (1990), 'How Should Structural Adjustment Programmes be Designed?', *World Development*, vol. 18, no. 7.
Rodrik, D. (1991), 'Policy Uncertainty and Private Investment in Developing Countries', *Journal of Development Economics*, vol. 36.
Romer, P.M. (1986), 'Increasing Returns and Long-Run Growth', *Journal of Political Economy*, vol. 94.
Rothchild, D. and R. Curry (1978), *Scarcity, Choice and Public Policy in*

Middle Africa (Berkeley: University of California Press).

Ruttan, V. (1991), 'What Happened to Political Development?', *Economic Development and Cultural Change*, vol. 39, no. 2.

Ruttan, V. and C. Thirtle (1989), 'Induced Technical and Institutional Change in African Agriculture', *Journal of International Development*, 1.

Sahn, D.E. (1987), 'Changes in the Living Standards of the Poor in Sri Lanka During a Period of Macroeconomic Restructuring', *World Development*, vol. 15, no. 6.

Sahn, D.E. (1990), 'The Impact of Export Crop Production on Nutritional Status in Côte d'Ivoire', *World Development*, vol. 18. no. 12.

Sahn, D.E. (1992), 'Public Expenditures in Sub-Saharan Africa during a Period of Economic Reforms', *World Development*, vol. 20, no. 5.

Sahn, D.E. (1993), 'The Nutritional Effects of Structural Adjustment in Sub-Saharan Africa', in M. Biswas and M. Gabr (eds), *Nutrition in the Nineties* (Oxford: Oxford University Press).

Sahn, D.E. and H. Alderman (1987), 'The Role of the Foreign Exchange and Commodity Auctions in Trade, Agriculture, and Consumption in Somalia', mimeo (Washington, DC: International Food Policy Research Institute).

Sahn, D.E. and R. Bernier (1993), 'Evidence from Africa on the Intrasectoral Allocation of Social Sector Expenditures', *Cornell Food and Nutrition Policy Program Working Paper*, no. 45 (Ithaca, NY: Cornell University).

Sahn, D.E. and L. Haddad (1992), 'The Gender Impacts of Structural Adjustment Programs in Africa: Discussion', *American Journal of Agricultural Economics*, December.

Sahn, D.E. and A.H. Sarris (1991), 'Structural Adjustment and Rural Smallholder Welfare: A Comparative Analysis', *World Bank Economic Review*, June.

Sahn, D.E., Y. Van Frausum and G. Shively (forthcoming), 'The Adverse Effects of Taxing Export Crops on Nutrition', *Economic Development and Cultural Change*.

Sandbrook, R. (1988), 'Patrimonialism and the Failing of Parastatals: Africa in Comparative Perspective', in C. Kirkpatrick and P. Cook (eds), *Privatisation in Less Developed Countries* (London: Harvester Wheatsheaf).

Sarris, A.H. and R. van den Brink (1993), *Economic Policy and Household Welfare During Crisis and Adjustment in Tanzania* (New York: New York University Press).

Schadler, S.M. (1986), 'Effect of a Slowdown in Industrial Economies on Selected Asian Countries', *IMF Staff Papers*, vol. 33, no. 2 (Washington, DC: International Monetary Fund).

Schadler, S., F. Rozwadowski, S. Tiwari and D. Robinson (1993) 'Economic Adjustment in Low-Income Countries, Experience Under the Enhanced Structural Adjustment Facility', *Occasional Paper*, no. 106 (Washington, DC: International Monetary Fund).

Schneider, F. and B.S. Frey (1988), 'Politico-Economic Models of Macroeconomic Policy: A Review of the Empirical Evidence', in T.D. Willett (ed.), *Political Business Cycles: The Political Economy of Money, Inflation, and Unemployment* (Durham: Duke University Press).

Sen, A.K. (1966), 'Peasants and Dualism With or Without Surplus Labour',

Journal of Political Economics, vol. 74, no. 5.

Serageldin, I.A., E. Elmendorf and El-El-Tigani (1992), 'Structural Adjustment and Health in Africa in the 1980s', unpublished paper.

Serven, L. and A. Solimano (1991), 'Adjustment Policies and Investment Performance in Developing Countries: Theory, Country Experiences and Policy Implications', *Working Papers*, series 606 (Washington, DC: World Bank).

Serven, L. and A. Solimano (1992a), 'Private Investment and Macroeconomic Adjustment: A Survey', *The World Bank Research Observer*, vol. 7, no. 1.

Serven, L. and A. Solimano (1992b), 'Economic Adjustment and Investment Performance in Developing Countries: The Experience of the 1980s', in V. Corbo et al., *Adjustment Lending Revisited: Policies to Restore Growth* (Washington: World Bank).

Seshamani, V. (1992), 'The Economic Policies of Zambia in the 1980s: Towards Structural Transformation with a Human Focus?', in G.A. Cornia, R. van der Hoeven and T. Mkandawire, *Africa's Recovery in the 1990s: From Stagnation and Adjustment to Human Development* (London: Macmillan).

Shaw, E. (1973), *Financial Deepening in Economic Development* (New York: Oxford University Press).

Sidell, S.R. (1988), *The IMF and Third-World Political Instability. Is There a Connection?* (London: Macmillan).

Singer, H.W. (1989), 'Lessons of Postwar Development Experience', *African Development Review*, vol. 1, no. 2.

Singer, P. (1985), 'Capital and the Nation State: A Historical Interpretation', in J. Walton (ed.), *Capital and Labour in the Urbanised World* (London: Sage Publications).

Singh, I. (1990), *The Great Ascent: The Rural Poor in South Asia* (Baltimore: Johns Hopkins University Press).

Sklar, R. (1989), 'Perestroika without Glasnost', paper presented at the Inaugural Seminar of the Governance in Africa Programme, Carter Centre, 17–18 February 1989.

Smale, M. et al. (1991), 'Chimanga cha Makolo, Hybrids and Composites: An Analysis of Farmers' Adoption of Maize Technology in Malawi 1989–91', *CIMMYT Economics Working Paper*, 91/04 (Mexico, DF:CIMMYT).

Sobhan, R. (1979), 'Public Enterprises and the Nature of the State', *Development and Change*, vol. 10, no. 1.

Solow, R.M. (1970), *Growth Theory: An Exposition* (Oxford: Clarendon Press).

Sorensen, G. (1991), *Democracy, Dictatorship and Development* (London: Macmillan).

Srinivasan, T.N. (1993), 'Adjustment Lending: Some Analytical and Policy Issues', mimeo (Washington, DC: World Bank, January).

Stallings, B. and R. Kaufman (eds) (1989), *Debt and Democracy in Latin America* (Boulder, Col.: Westview Press).

Stewart, F. (ed.) (1987), *Macro-Policies for Appropriate Technology* (Boulder, Col.: Westview Press).

Stewart, F. (1989), 'Recent Theories of International Trade: Some Implications for the South', in H. Kierzkowski (ed.), *Monopolistic Competition*

and International Trade (Oxford: Oxford University Press).
Stewart, F. (1991a), 'The Many Faces of Adjustment', *World Development*, vol. 19, no. 12.
Stewart, F. (1991b), 'A Note on "Strategic" Trade Theory and the South', *Journal of International Development*, vol. 3, no. 5.
Stewart, F. and G. Ranis (1990), 'Macro-Policies for Appropriate Technology: A Synthesis of Findings', in F. Stewart, H. Thomas and T. de Wilde (eds), *The Other Policy* (London: Intermediate Technology Publications).
Stewart, F., H. Thomas and T. de Wilde (eds) (1981), *The Other Policy* (London: Intermediate Technology Publications).
Stewart, F., S. Lall and S. Wangwe (eds) (1992), *Alternative Development Strategies in Sub-Saharan Africa* (London: Macmillan).
Stiglitz, J., and A. Weiss (1981), 'Credit Rationing in Markets with Imperfect Information', *American Economic Review*, vol. 71.
Stimson J.A. (1985), 'Regression in Space and Time: A Statistical Essay', *American Journal of Political Science*, vol. 29, no. 4.
Stoneman, P. (1987), *The Economic Analysis of Technology Policy* (Oxford: Clarendon Press).
Strauss, J. (1986), 'Does Better Nutrition Raise Farm Productivity?', *Journal of Political Economy*, 94, 2.
Strivisan, T.N. (1985), 'Neoclassical Political Economy, the State and Economic Development', *Asian Development Review*, vol. 3, no. 2.
Sylos-Labini, P. (1969), *Oligopoly and Technical Progress* (Cambridge, Mass.: Harvard University Press).
Tangri, R. (1991), 'The Politics of State Divestiture in Ghana', *African Affairs*, vol. 90, no. 361.
Tanzi, V. (1987), 'Fiscal Policy, Growth and Design of Stabilisation Programs', in A.M. Martirena-Mantel (ed.), *External Debt, Savings and Growth in Latin America* (Washington, DC: International Monetary Fund). Republished in Tanzi, V., *Public Finance in Developing Countries* (Aldershot, England: Edward Elgar Publishing Limited, 1991).
Tanzi, V. (1989), 'The Impact of Macroeconomic Policies on the Level of Taxation and the Fiscal Balance in Developing Countries', *Staff Papers*, vol. 36, no. 3 (Washington, DC: International Monetary Fund).
Tanzi, V. (1990), 'The IMF and Tax Reform', *IMF Working Paper* (Washington, DC: International Monetary Fund, April).
Tanzi, V. (1992), 'Structural Factors and Tax Revenue in Developing Countries: A Decade of Evidence', in I. Goldin and L. A. Winters (eds), *Open Economies: Structural Adjustments and Agriculture* (Cambridge: Cambridge University Press).
Taylor, L. (1988), *Varieties of Stabilisation Experience: Towards Sensible Macroeconomics in the Third World* (Oxford: Clarendon Press).
Thirtle, C. et al. (1993), 'Agricultural Productivity in Zimbabwe 1970–1990', *Economic Journal*, vol. 103.
Timothy, D.H., P.H. Harvey and C.R. Dowswell (1988), *Development and Spread of Improved Maize Varieties and Hybrids in Developing Countries* (Washington: USAID Bureau for Science and Technology).
Todaro, M.P. (1989), *Economic Development in the Third World* (New York: Longman, 4th ed.).

Toye, J. (1991), 'Is there a New Political Economy of Development?', in C. Colclough and J. Manor (eds), *States or Markets? Neo-Liberalism and the Development Policy Debate* (Oxford: Clarendon Press).

Toye, J. (1993), 'Structural Adjustment: Context, Assumptions, Origin and Diversity', paper presented at the DGIS/ISSAS Conference on Structural Adjustment and Beyond, The Hague, 1–3 June 1993.

Tun Wai, U. and C. Wong (1982), 'Determinants of Private Investment in Developing Countries', *Journal of Development Studies*, 19.

UNCTAD (1989), *Handbook of International Trade and Development Statistics, 1988* (New York: United Nations).

UNCTAD (1991), *Commodity Yearbook 1991* (New York: United Nations).

UNCTAD (1993), *Handbook of International Trade and Development Statistics 1992* (New York, United Nations).

UNDP (1990), *Human Development Report 1990* (New York: United Nations Development Programme).

UNDP (1991), *Human Development Report 1991* (New York: United Nations Development Programme).

UNDP (1993a), *Rethinking Technical Cooperation, Reforms for Capacity Building in Africa* (New York: United Nations Development Programme).

UNDP (1993b), *Human Development Report 1993* (New York: United Nations Development Programme).

UNDP and World Bank (1989), *African Economic and Financial Data* (New York and Washington, DC: United Nations Development Programme and World Bank).

UNDP and World Bank (1992), *African Development Indicators* (New York and Washington, DC: United Nations Development Programme and World Bank).

UN/ECA (1989), *African Alternative Framework to Structural Adjustment Programmes for Socio-Economic Recovery and Transformation*, E/ECA/CM. 15/6/Rev. 3, Addis Ababa.

UNESCAP (1990), *Technology Flows in Asia – Strategies for Enhancing the Flow of Technologies among Regional Developing Countries*, prepared by Prasada Reddy (Bangkok: UNESCAP).

UNICEF (1990), *Una propuesta de clasificación de las comunas del país* (Santiago de Chile: UNICEF).

United Nations (1990), *Africa's Commodity Problems, Towards a Solution* (Fraser Report).

United Nations (1991), 'The Triad in Foreign Direct Investment', *UN World Investment Report* (New York: United Nations).

United Nations (1992), *World Investment Report: Transnationals as Engines of Growth* (New York: United Nations).

Vaitsos, C. (1974), *Intercountry Income Distribution and Transnational Enterprises* (Oxford: Clarendon Press).

van der Hoeven, R. (1991), 'Adjustment with a Human Face: Still Relevant or Overtaken by Events?', *World Development*, vol. 19, no. 12.

van de Walle, N. (1991), 'The Decline of the Franc Zone: Monetary Politics in Francophone Africa', *African Affairs*, vol. 90.

van Wijnbergen, S. (1986), 'Exchange Rate Management and Stabilisation Policies in Developing Countries', *Journal of Development Economics*, 23.

Vaubel, R. (1991), 'The Political Economy of the International Monetary Fund: A Public Choice Analysis', in R. Vaubel and T.D. Willett (eds), *The Political Economy of International Organisations: A Public Choice Approach* (Boulder, Col.: Westview Press).

Vaubel, R. and T. D. Willett (eds) (1991), *The Political Economy of International Organizations: A Public Choice Approach* (Boulder, Col.: Westview Press).

Vernon, R. (1966), 'International Investment and International Trade in the Product Cycle', *Quarterly Journal of Economics*, May.

Vernon-Wortzel, H. and L. Wortzel (1989), 'Privatisation: Not the Only Answer', *World Development*, vol. 17, no. 5.

Vickers, J. and G. Yarrow (1991), 'Economic Perspectives on Privatisation', *Journal of Economic Perspectives*, vol. 5, no. 2.

Vogel, R.J. (1988), 'Cost Recovery in the Health Care Sector: Selected Country Studies in West Africa', *World Bank Technical Paper*, no. 82 (Washington, DC: World Bank).

von Braun, J. and E. Kennedy (1986), *Commercialization of Subsistence Agriculture: Income and Nutritional Effects in Developing Countries* (Washington, DC: International Food Policy Research Institute).

von Braun, J. and R. Pandya-Lorch (eds) (1991), 'Income Sources of Malnourished People in Rural Areas: Microlevel Information and Policy Implications', *Working Paper on Commercialization of Agriculture and Nutrition*, no. 5 (Washington, DC: International Food Policy Research Institute).

von Braun, J., D. Puetz and P. Webb (1989), 'Technological Change in Rice and Commercialization of Agriculture in a West African Setting: Effects on Production, Consumption, and Nutrition', *Research Report*, no. 75 (Washington, DC: International Food Policy Research Institute).

Wade, R. (1990), *Governing the Market: Economic Theory and the Role of Governments in East Asian Industrialization* (Princeton, NJ: Princeton University Press).

Wagao, J.H. (1992), 'Adjustment Policies in Tanzania, 1981–9: The Impact on Growth, Structure and Human Welfare', in G.A. Cornia, R. van der Hoeven and T. Mkandawire, *Africa's Recovery in the 1990s: From Stagnation and Adjustment to Human Development* (London: Macmillan).

Wangwe, S. and M. Bagachwa (1990), 'Impact of Economic Policies on Technological Choice in Tanzanian Industry', in F. Stewart, H. Thomas and T. de Wilde (eds), *The Other Policy* (London: Intermediate Technology Publications).

Weber, M. et al. (1988), 'Informing Food Security Decisions in Africa: Empirical Analysis and Policy Dialogue', *Staff Paper 88–50* (East Lansing: Michigan State University).

Willett, T.D. (ed.) (1988), *Political Business Cycles: The Political Economy of Money, Inflation, and Unemployment* (Durham: Duke University Press).

Williams, D.C. (1992), 'Measuring the Impact of Land Reform Policy in Nigeria', *Journal of Modern African Studies*, vol. 30, no. 4.

Williamson, J. (1990), *The Progress of Policy Reform in Latin America* (Washington DC: Institute for International Economics).

Wilson, E. (1986), 'The Public–Private Debate', *Africa Report*, July–August.

World Bank (1981), *Accelerated Development in Sub-Saharan Africa: An Agenda for Action* (Washington, DC: World Bank).

World Bank (1984), *World Development Report 1984* (Washington, DC: World Bank).

World Bank (1989a), *Sub-Saharan Africa, From Crisis to Sustainable Growth, A Long-Term Perspective Study* (Washington, DC: World Bank).

World Bank (1989b), *Long-Term Projection for Low and Middle-income Countries* (Washington, DC: World Bank).

World Bank (1989c), *Intra-Regional Trade in Sub-Saharan Africa*, Report no. 7685 (Washington, DC: World Bank).

World Bank (1989d), *World Development Report 1989* (Washington, DC: World Bank).

World Bank (1989e), *Africa's Adjustment and Growth in the 1980s* (Washington, DC: World Bank).

World Bank (1990a), 'Adjustment Lending Policies for Sustainable Growth', *Policy and Research Series*, no. 14 (Washington, DC: Country Economics Department, World Bank).

World Bank (1990b), *World Debt Tables 1990–91* (Washington, DC: World Bank).

World Bank (1990c), *World Development Report 1990* (Washington, DC: World Bank).

World Bank (1990d), *Report on Adjustment Lending II* (Washington, DC: World Bank).

World Bank (1991a), *Special Program of Assistance Growth, Aid and Debt* (Washington, DC: World Bank).

World Bank (1991b), *Annual Report* (Washington, DC: World Bank).

World Bank (1991c), *World Development Report 1991* (Washington, DC: World Bank).

World Bank (1992a), *World Development Report 1992* (Washington, DC: World Bank).

World Bank (1992b), 'Adjustment Lending and Mobilization of Private and Public Resources for Growth', *Policy and Research Series*, no. 22 (Washington, DC: Country Economics Department, World Bank).

World Bank (1993a), *World Development Report 1993* (Washington, DC: World Bank).

World Bank (1993b), *World Debt Tables 1992–3* (Washington, DC: World Bank).

World Bank (1994), *Adjustment in Africa: Refoms, Results and the Road Ahead* (Washington, DC: World Bank).

World Bank and UNDP (1989), *Africa's Adjustment and Growth in the 1980s* (Washington, DC: World Bank).

Yaron, J. (1991), 'Successful Rural Finance Institutions', unpublished reports, 2 vols (Washington, DC: Agricultural Policies Division).

Yoder, R., P. Borkholder and B. Friesen (1991), 'Privatisation and Development: The Empirical Evidence', *The Journal of Development Areas*, vol. 25.

Yotopolous, P.A. (1989), 'The (Rip)Tide of Privatisation: Lessons from Chile', *World Development*, vol. 17, no. 5.

Index